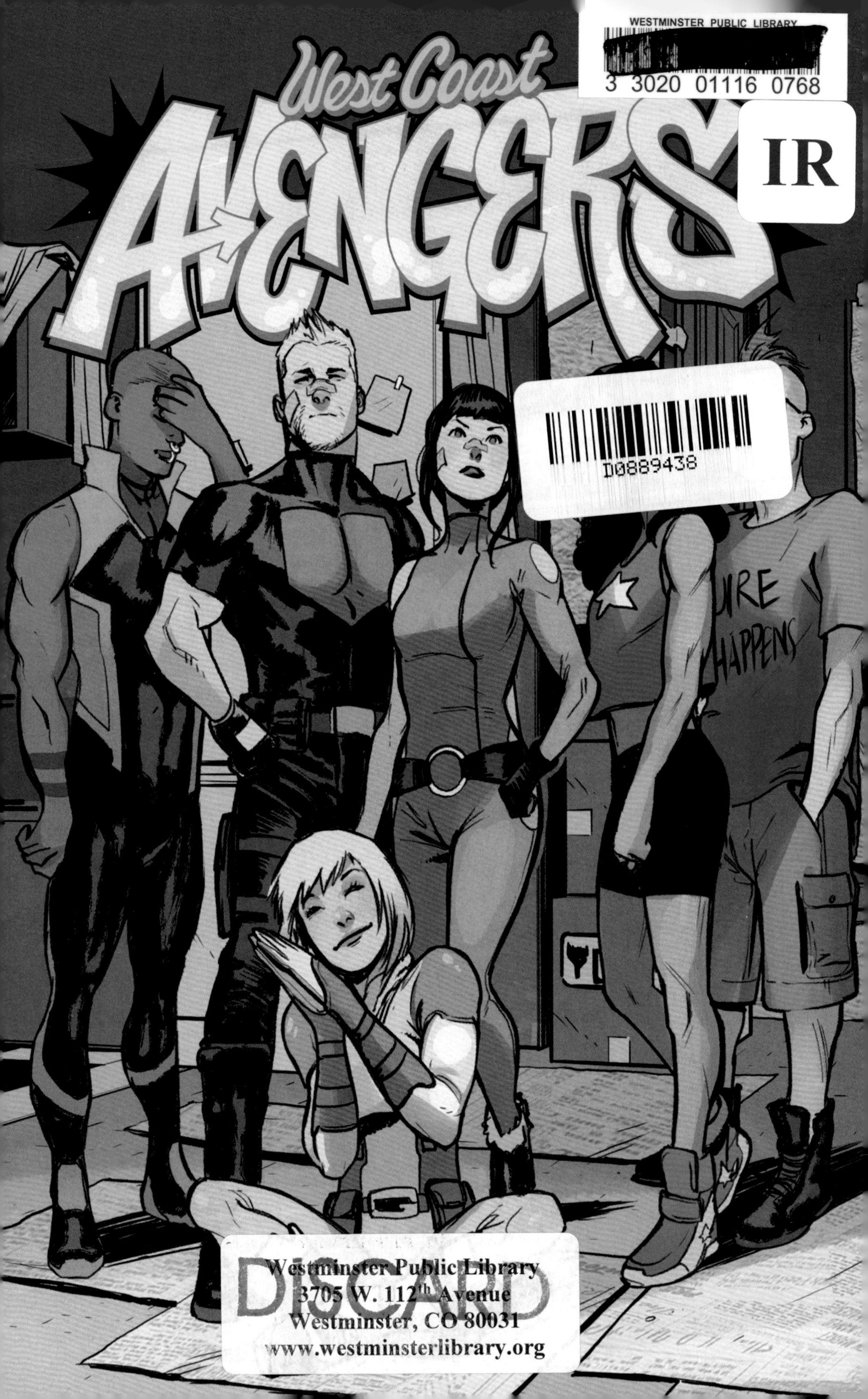
West Coast
AVENGERS

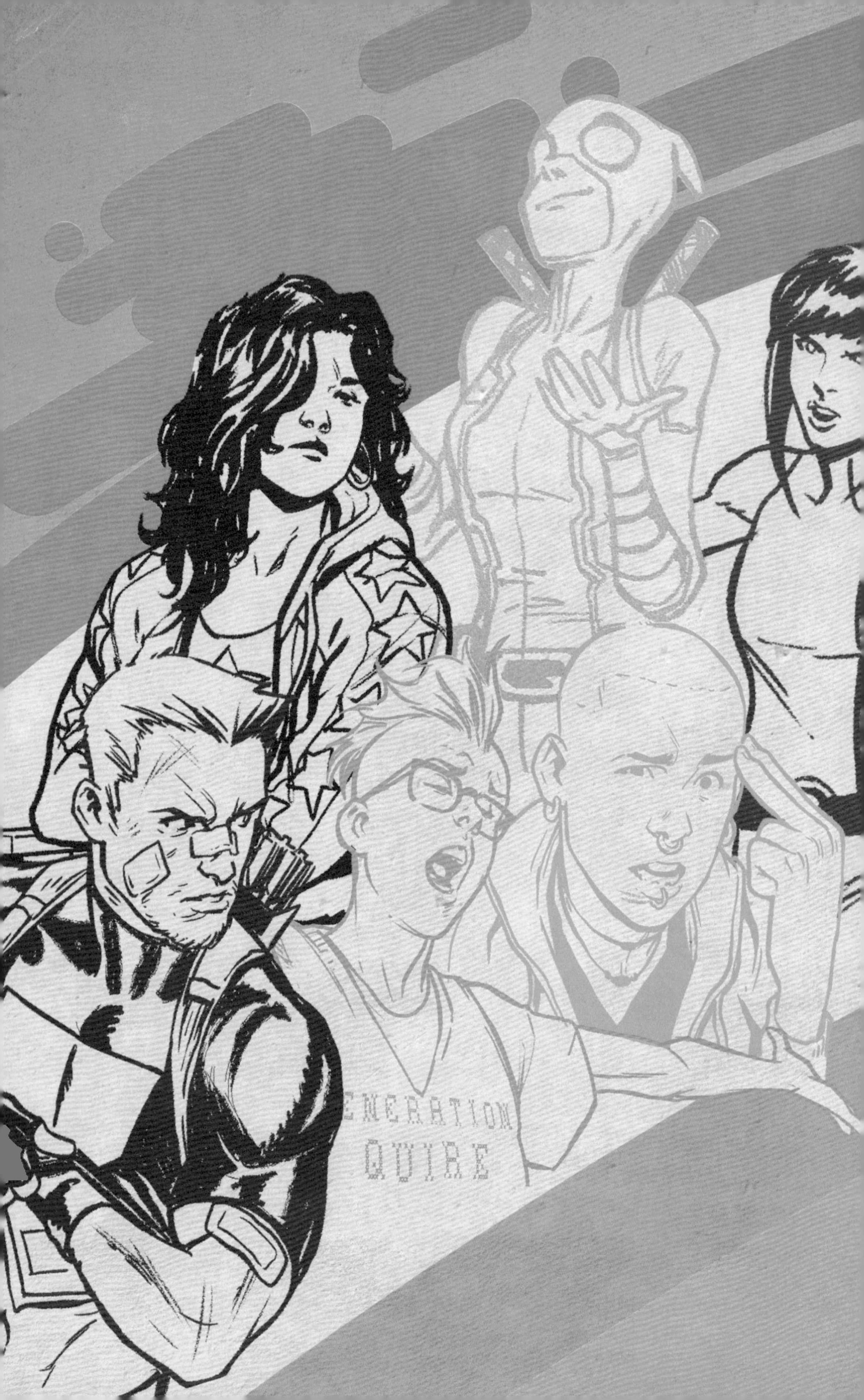
ENERATION
QUIRE

KATE BISHOP, A.K.A. HAWKEYE, RECENTLY MOVED OUT TO CALIFORNIA
TO START A NEW LIFE AS A PRIVATE INVESTIGATOR.
SO FAR, SHE'S BEEN ABLE TO HANDLE EVERYTHING THE WEST COAST HAS THROWN AT HER.
BUT IT'S BEEN THROWING A LOT HARDER LATELY...

West Coast AVENGERS
BEST COAST

KELLY THOMPSON
WRITER

STEFANO CASELLI
ARTIST

TRÍONA FARRELL
COLOR ARTIST

VC'S JOE CARAMAGNA
LETTERER

STEFANO CASELLI & NOLAN WOODARD
COVER ART

ALANNA SMITH
EDITOR

TOM BREVOORT
EXECUTIVE EDITOR

AVENGERS CREATED BY STAN LEE & JACK KIRBY

COLLECTION EDITOR *JENNIFER GRÜNWALD* · ASSISTANT EDITOR *CAITLIN O'CONNELL*
ASSOCIATE MANAGING EDITOR *KATERI WOODY* · EDITOR, SPECIAL PROJECTS *MARK D. BEAZLEY*
VP PRODUCTION & SPECIAL PROJECTS *JEFF YOUNGQUIST* · SVP PRINT, SALES & MARKETING *DAVID GABRIEL*
BOOK DESIGNER *JAY BOWEN*

EDITOR IN CHIEF *C.B. CEBULSKI* · CHIEF CREATIVE OFFICER *JOE QUESADA*
PRESIDENT *DAN BUCKLEY* · EXECUTIVE PRODUCER *ALAN FINE*

WEST COAST AVENGERS VOL. 1: BEST COAST. Contains material originally published in magazine form as WEST COAST AVENGERS #1-4, THE UNBELIEVABLE GWENPOOL #1, YOUNG AVENGERS PRESENTS #6. First printing 2018. ISBN 978-1-302-91345-8. Published by MARVEL WORLDWIDE, INC., a subsidiary of MARVEL ENTERTAINMENT, LLC. OFFICE OF PUBLICATION: 135 West 50th Street, New York, NY 10020. **Printed in Canada.** DAN BUCKLEY, President, Marvel Entertainment; JOHN NEE, Publisher; JOE QUESADA, Chief Creative Officer; TOM BREVOORT, SVP of Publishing; DAVID BOGART, SVP of Business Affairs & Operations, Publishing & Partnership; DAVID GABRIEL, SVP of Sales & Marketing, Publishing; JEFF YOUNGQUIST, VP of Production & Special Projects; DAN CARR, Executive Director of Publishing Technology; ALEX MORALES, Director of Publishing Operations; DAN EDINGTON, Managing Editor; SUSAN CRESPI, Production Manager; STAN LEE, Chairman Emeritus. For information regarding advertising in Marvel Comics or on Marvel.com, please contact Vit DeBellis, Custom Solutions & Integrated Advertising Manager, at vdebellis@marvel.com. For Marvel subscription inquiries, please call 888-511-5480. **Manufactured between 12/14/2018 and 1/28/2019 by SOLISCO PRINTERS, SCOTT, QC, CANADA.**

10 9 8 7 6 5 4 3 2 1

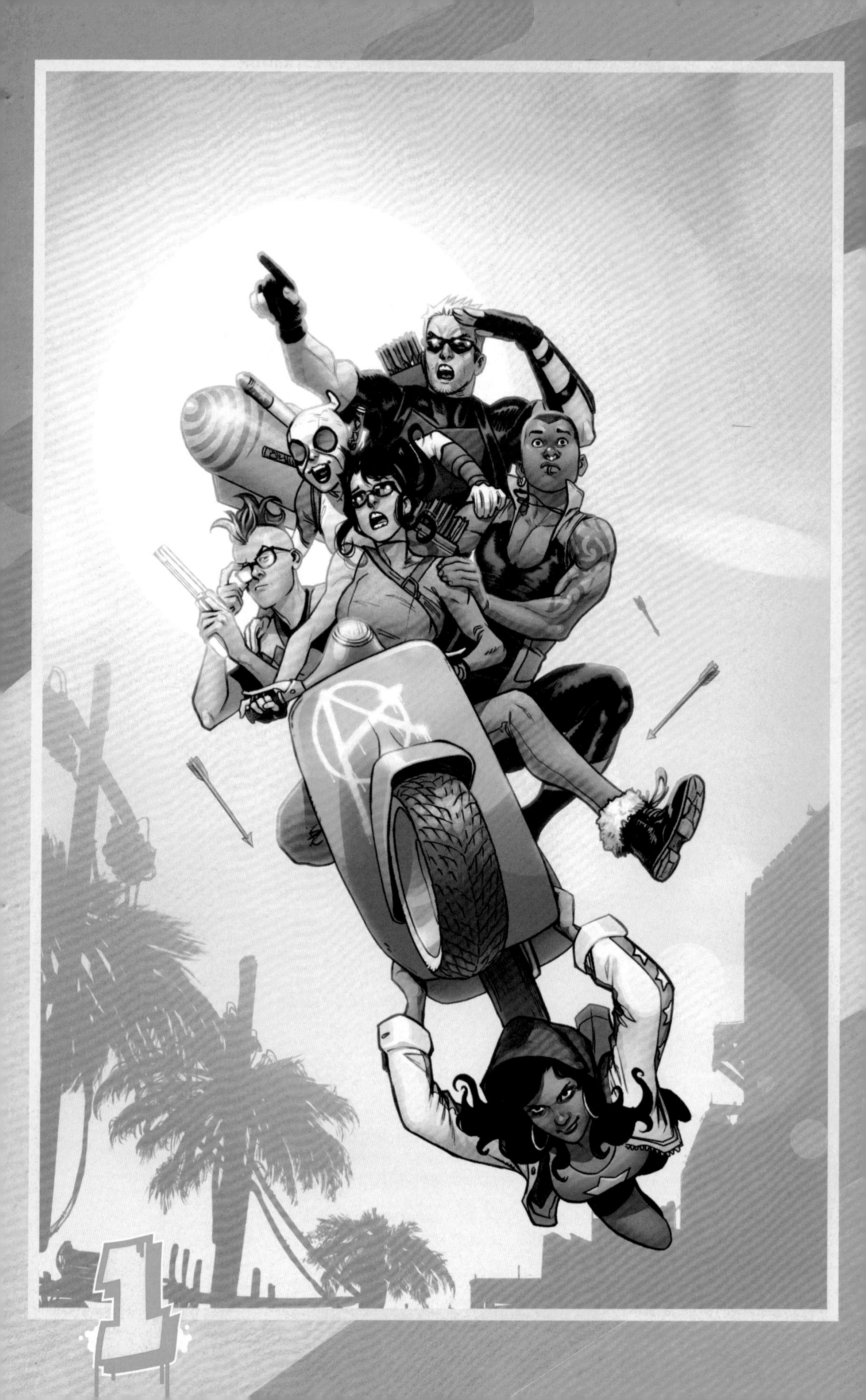
1

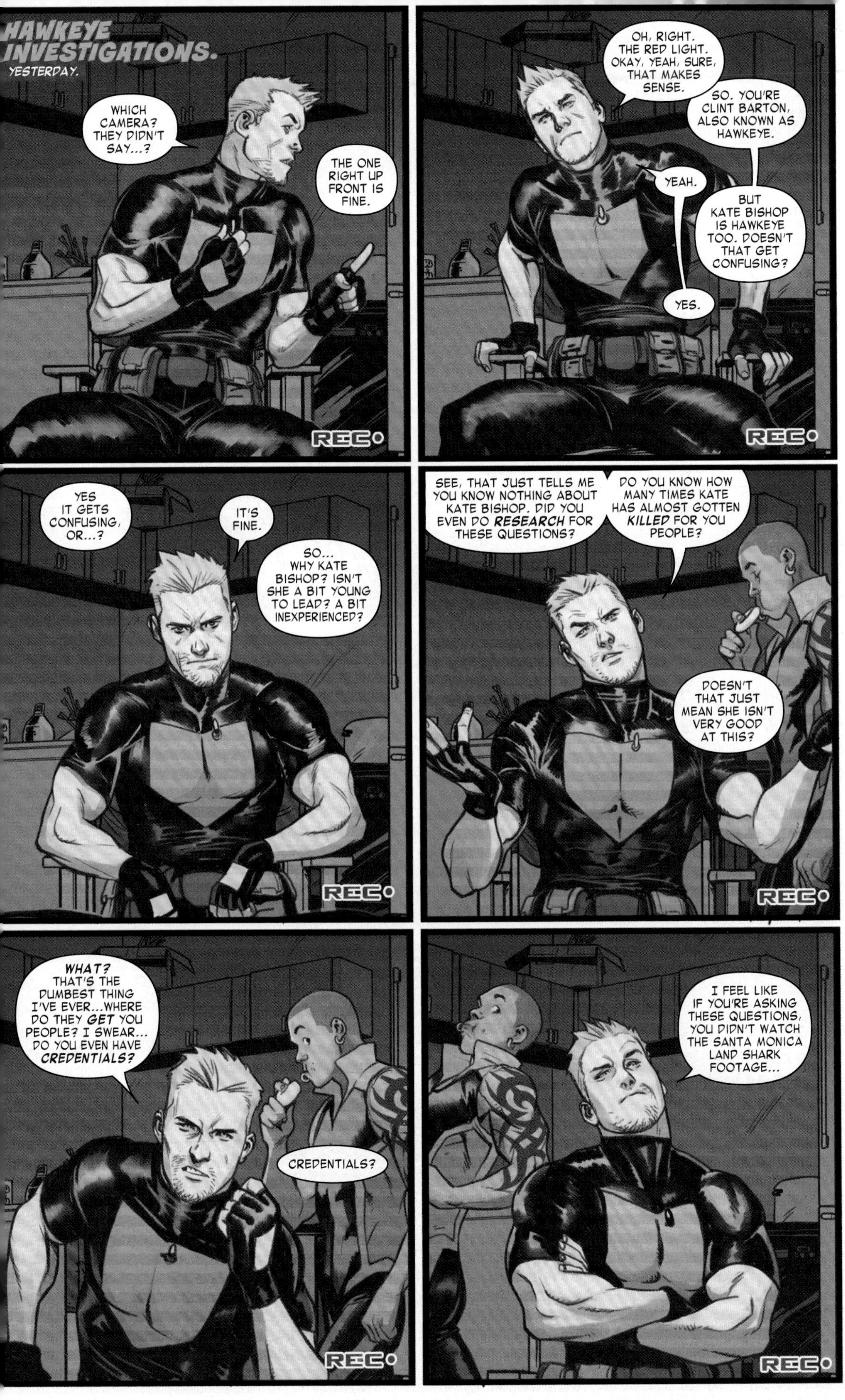
HAWKEYE INVESTIGATIONS.
YESTERDAY.
WHICH CAMERA? THEY DIDN'T SAY...?
THE ONE RIGHT UP FRONT IS FINE.
REC
OH, RIGHT. THE RED LIGHT. OKAY, YEAH, SURE, THAT MAKES SENSE.
SO. YOU'RE CLINT BARTON, ALSO KNOWN AS HAWKEYE.
YEAH.
BUT KATE BISHOP IS HAWKEYE TOO. DOESN'T THAT GET CONFUSING?
YES.
REC
YES IT GETS CONFUSING, OR...?
IT'S FINE.
SO... WHY KATE BISHOP? ISN'T SHE A BIT YOUNG TO LEAD? A BIT INEXPERIENCED?
REC
SEE, THAT JUST TELLS ME YOU KNOW NOTHING ABOUT KATE BISHOP. DID YOU EVEN DO RESEARCH FOR THESE QUESTIONS?
DO YOU KNOW HOW MANY TIMES KATE HAS ALMOST GOTTEN KILLED FOR YOU PEOPLE?
DOESN'T THAT JUST MEAN SHE ISN'T VERY GOOD AT THIS?
REC
WHAT? THAT'S THE DUMBEST THING I'VE EVER...WHERE DO THEY GET YOU PEOPLE? I SWEAR... DO YOU EVEN HAVE CREDENTIALS?
CREDENTIALS?
REC
I FEEL LIKE IF YOU'RE ASKING THESE QUESTIONS, YOU DIDN'T WATCH THE SANTA MONICA LAND SHARK FOOTAGE...
REC

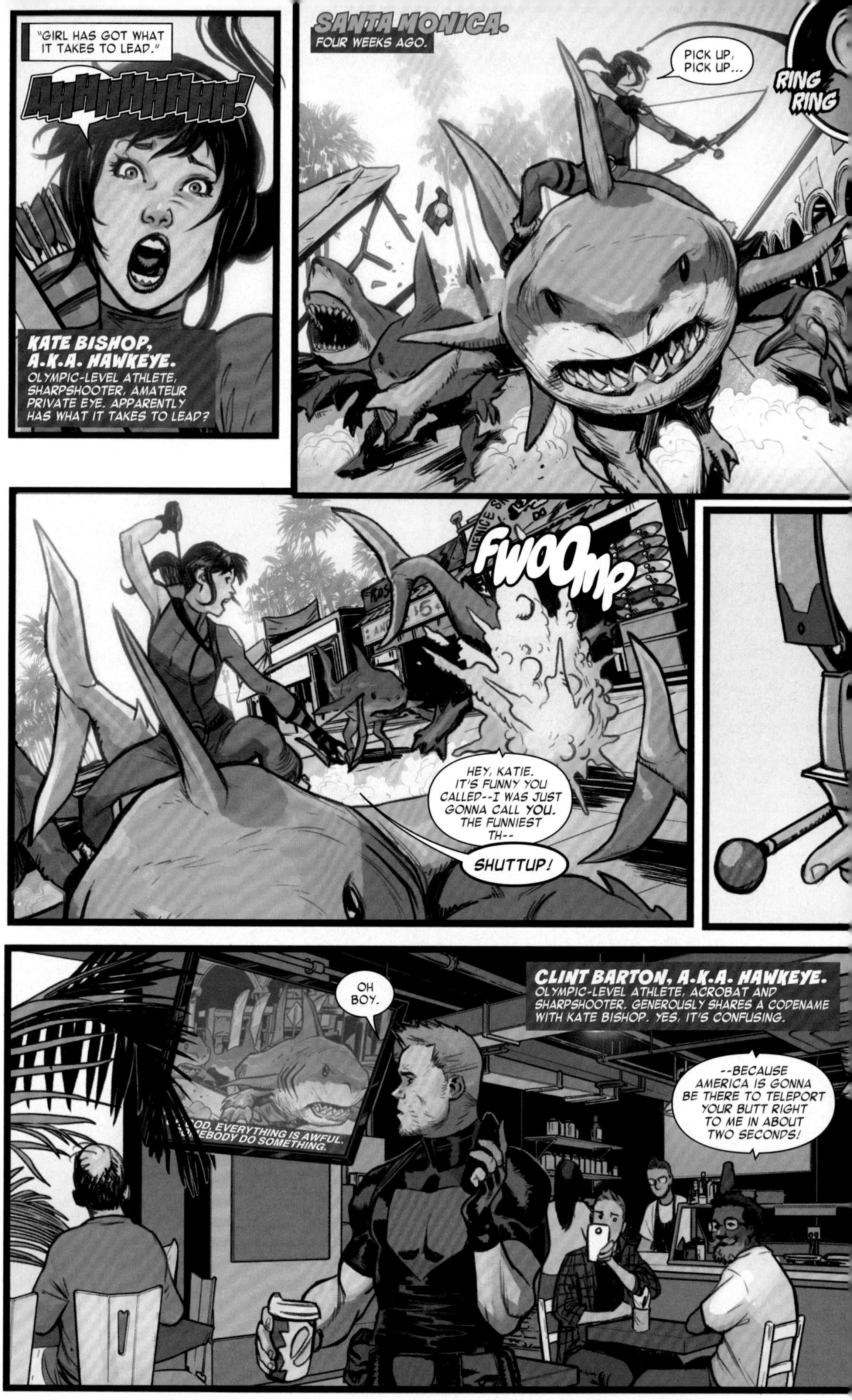

"GIRL HAS GOT WHAT IT TAKES TO LEAD."
AHHHHHHHH!
KATE BISHOP, A.K.A. HAWKEYE.
OLYMPIC-LEVEL ATHLETE, SHARPSHOOTER, AMATEUR PRIVATE EYE. APPARENTLY HAS WHAT IT TAKES TO LEAD?
SANTA MONICA.
FOUR WEEKS AGO.
PICK UP, PICK UP...
RING RING
FWOOMP
HEY, KATIE. IT'S FUNNY YOU CALLED--I WAS JUST GONNA CALL YOU. THE FUNNIEST TH--
SHUTTUP!
OH BOY.
GOD, EVERYTHING IS AWFUL.
EBODY DO SOMETHING.
CLINT BARTON, A.K.A. HAWKEYE.
OLYMPIC-LEVEL ATHLETE, ACROBAT AND SHARPSHOOTER. GENEROUSLY SHARES A CODENAME WITH KATE BISHOP. YES, IT'S CONFUSING.
--BECAUSE AMERICA IS GONNA BE THERE TO TELEPORT YOUR BUTT RIGHT TO ME IN ABOUT TWO SECONDS!

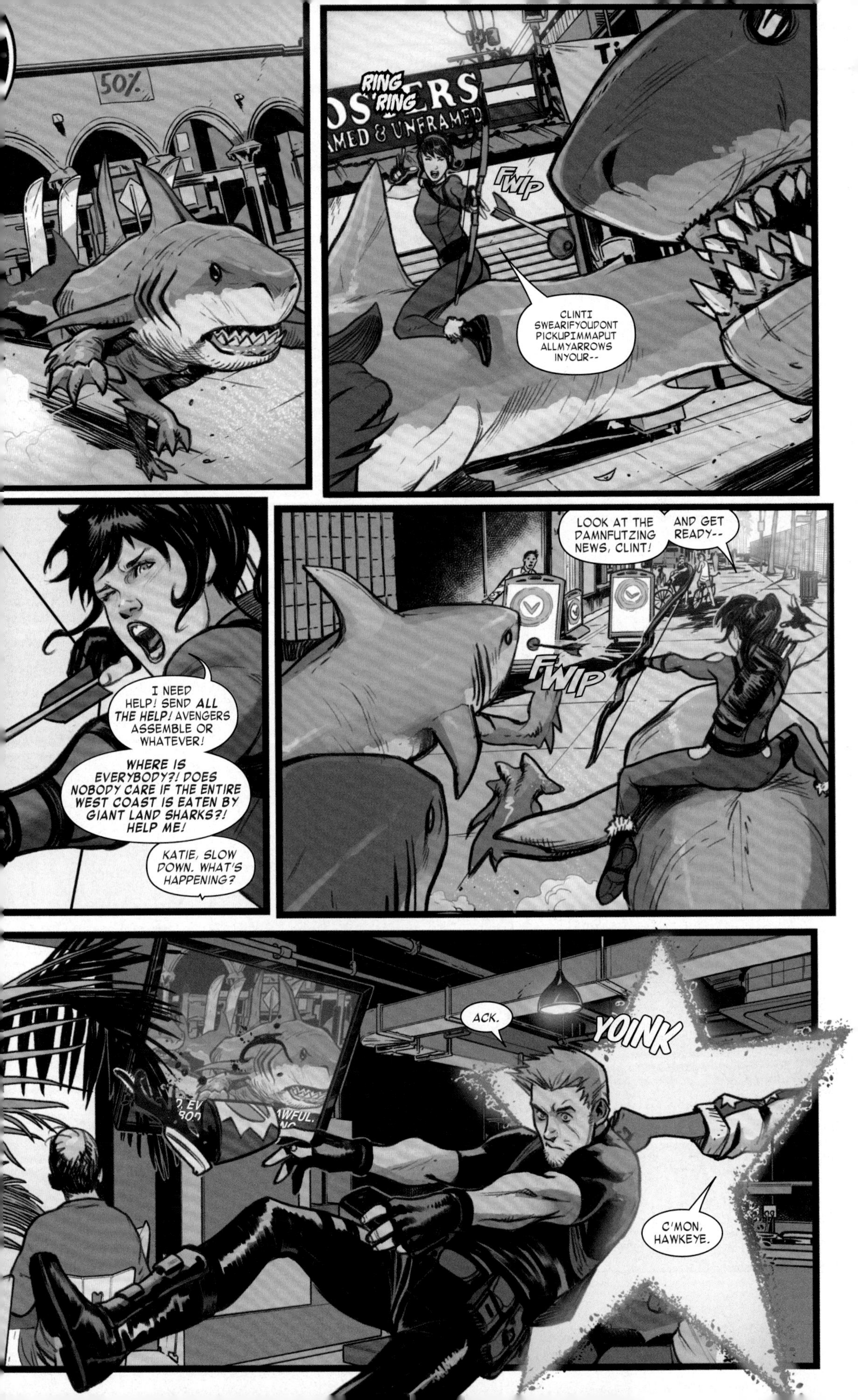

50%
RING RING
OSTERS
AMED & UNFRAMED
FWIP
CLINTI SWEARIFYOUDONT PICKUPIMMAPUT ALLMYARROWS INYOUR--
I NEED HELP! SEND ALL THE HELP! AVENGERS ASSEMBLE OR WHATEVER!
WHERE IS EVERYBODY?! DOES NOBODY CARE IF THE ENTIRE WEST COAST IS EATEN BY GIANT LAND SHARKS?! HELP ME!
KATIE, SLOW DOWN. WHAT'S HAPPENING?
LOOK AT THE DAMNFUTZING NEWS, CLINT!
AND GET READY--
FWIP
ACK.
YOINK
C'MON, HAWKEYE.

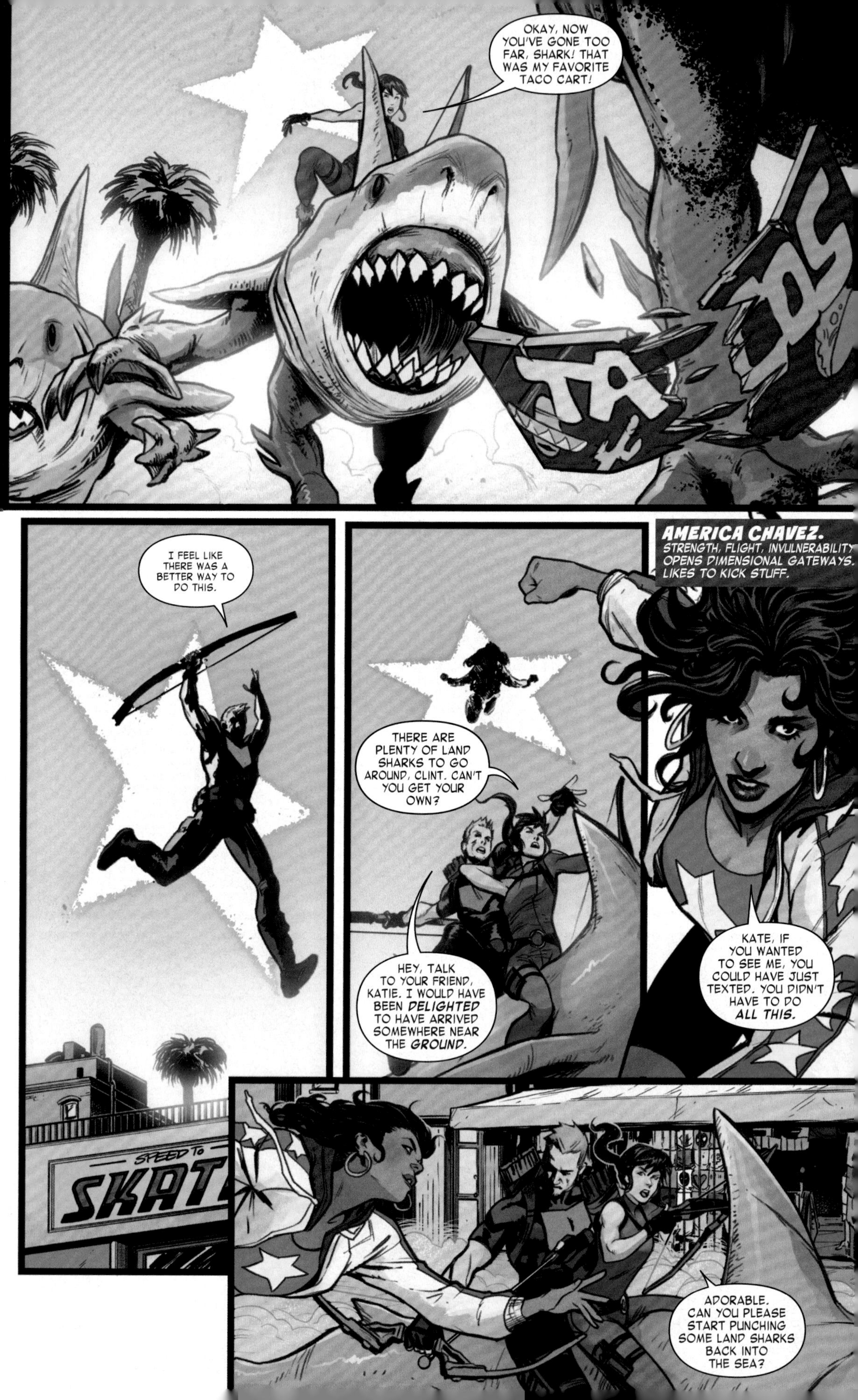
OKAY, NOW YOU'VE GONE TOO FAR, SHARK! THAT WAS MY FAVORITE TACO CART!
I FEEL LIKE THERE WAS A BETTER WAY TO DO THIS.
THERE ARE PLENTY OF LAND SHARKS TO GO AROUND, CLINT. CAN'T YOU GET YOUR OWN?
HEY, TALK TO YOUR FRIEND, KATIE. I WOULD HAVE BEEN DELIGHTED TO HAVE ARRIVED SOMEWHERE NEAR THE GROUND.
AMERICA CHAVEZ.
STRENGTH, FLIGHT, INVULNERABILITY. OPENS DIMENSIONAL GATEWAYS. LIKES TO KICK STUFF.
KATE, IF YOU WANTED TO SEE ME, YOU COULD HAVE JUST TEXTED. YOU DIDN'T HAVE TO DO ALL THIS.
SPEED TO
SKAT
ADORABLE. CAN YOU PLEASE START PUNCHING SOME LAND SHARKS BACK INTO THE SEA?

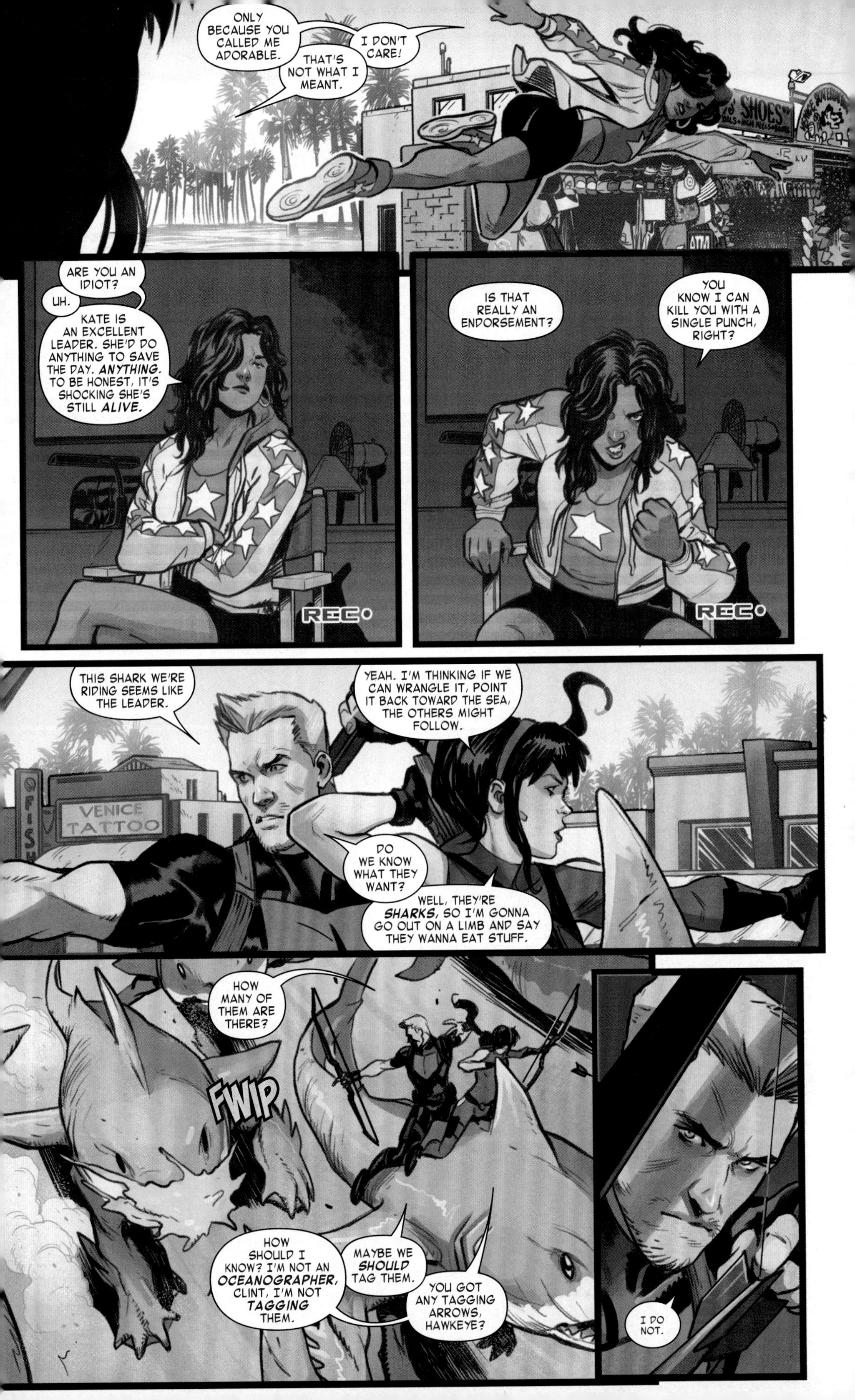
ONLY BECAUSE YOU CALLED ME ADORABLE.
I DON'T CARE!
THAT'S NOT WHAT I MEANT.
ARE YOU AN IDIOT?
UH.
KATE IS AN EXCELLENT LEADER. SHE'D DO ANYTHING TO SAVE THE DAY. ANYTHING. TO BE HONEST, IT'S SHOCKING SHE'S STILL ALIVE.
REC
IS THAT REALLY AN ENDORSEMENT?
YOU KNOW I CAN KILL YOU WITH A SINGLE PUNCH, RIGHT?
REC
THIS SHARK WE'RE RIDING SEEMS LIKE THE LEADER.
YEAH. I'M THINKING IF WE CAN WRANGLE IT, POINT IT BACK TOWARD THE SEA, THE OTHERS MIGHT FOLLOW.
VENICE TATTOO
DO WE KNOW WHAT THEY WANT?
WELL, THEY'RE SHARKS, SO I'M GONNA GO OUT ON A LIMB AND SAY THEY WANNA EAT STUFF.
HOW MANY OF THEM ARE THERE?
FWIP
HOW SHOULD I KNOW? I'M NOT AN OCEANOGRAPHER, CLINT, I'M NOT TAGGING THEM.
MAYBE WE SHOULD TAG THEM.
YOU GOT ANY TAGGING ARROWS, HAWKEYE?
I DO NOT.

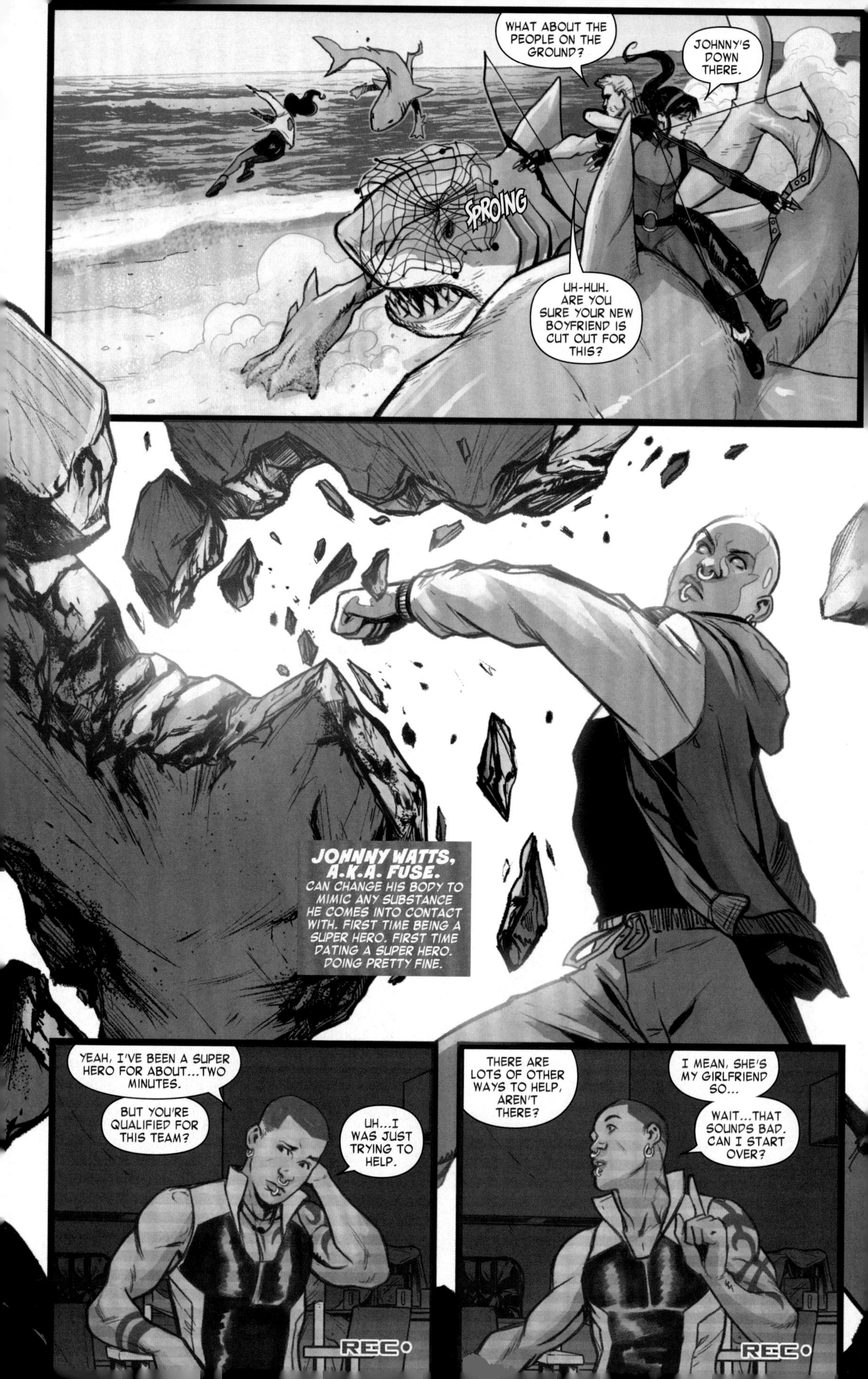
WHAT ABOUT THE PEOPLE ON THE GROUND?
JOHNNY'S DOWN THERE.
SPROING
UH-HUH. ARE YOU SURE YOUR NEW BOYFRIEND IS CUT OUT FOR THIS?
JOHNNY WATTS, A.K.A. FUSE.
CAN CHANGE HIS BODY TO MIMIC ANY SUBSTANCE HE COMES INTO CONTACT WITH. FIRST TIME BEING A SUPER HERO. FIRST TIME DATING A SUPER HERO. DOING PRETTY FINE.
YEAH, I'VE BEEN A SUPER HERO FOR ABOUT...TWO MINUTES.
BUT YOU'RE QUALIFIED FOR THIS TEAM?
UH...I WAS JUST TRYING TO HELP.
REC
THERE ARE LOTS OF OTHER WAYS TO HELP, AREN'T THERE?
I MEAN, SHE'S MY GIRLFRIEND SO...
WAIT...THAT SOUNDS BAD. CAN I START OVER?
REC

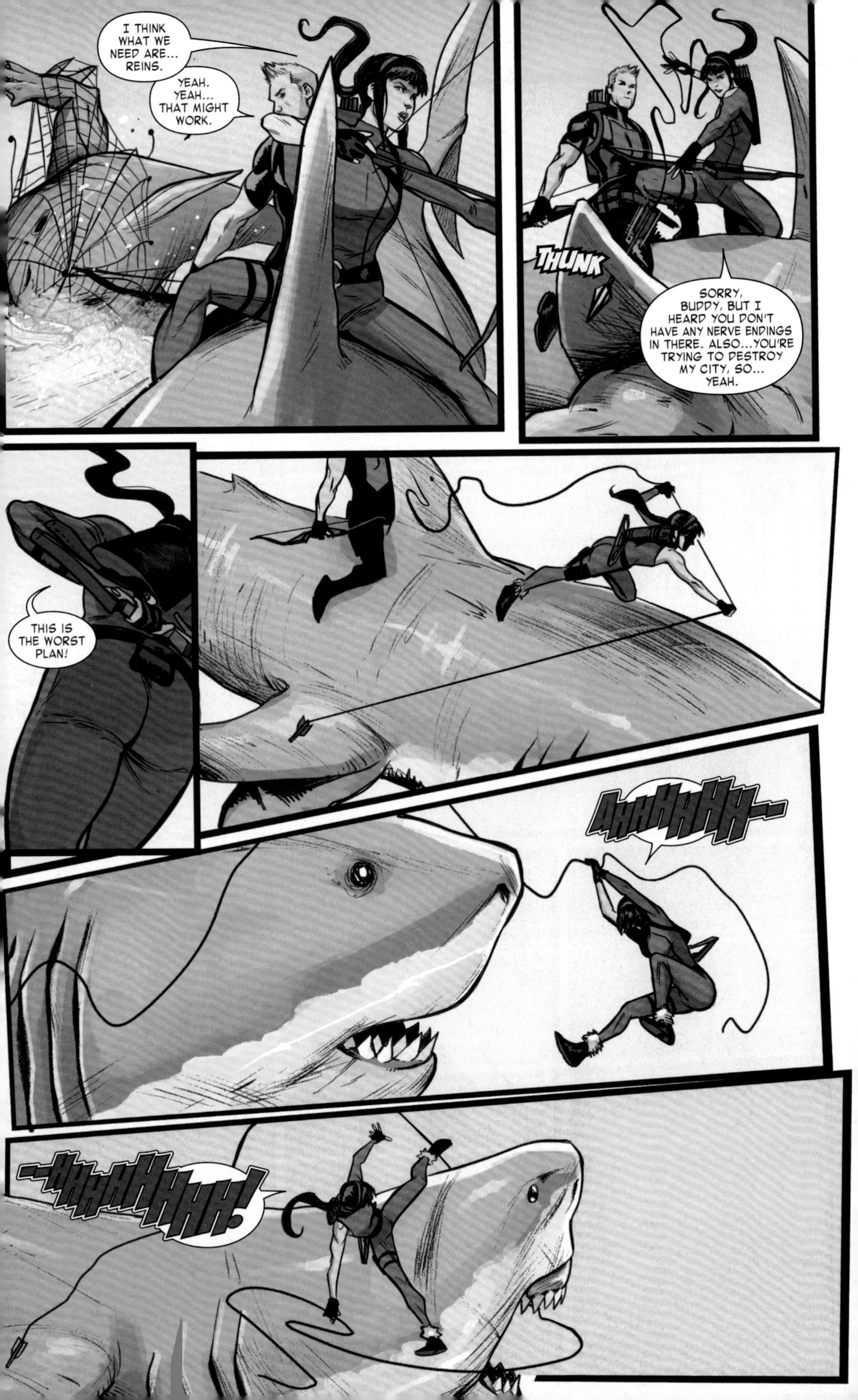
I THINK WHAT WE NEED ARE... REINS.
YEAH. YEAH... THAT MIGHT WORK.
THUNK
SORRY, BUDDY, BUT I HEARD YOU DON'T HAVE ANY NERVE ENDINGS IN THERE. ALSO...YOU'RE TRYING TO DESTROY MY CITY, SO... YEAH.
THIS IS THE WORST PLAN!
AHHHHHH--
--HHHHHHHH!

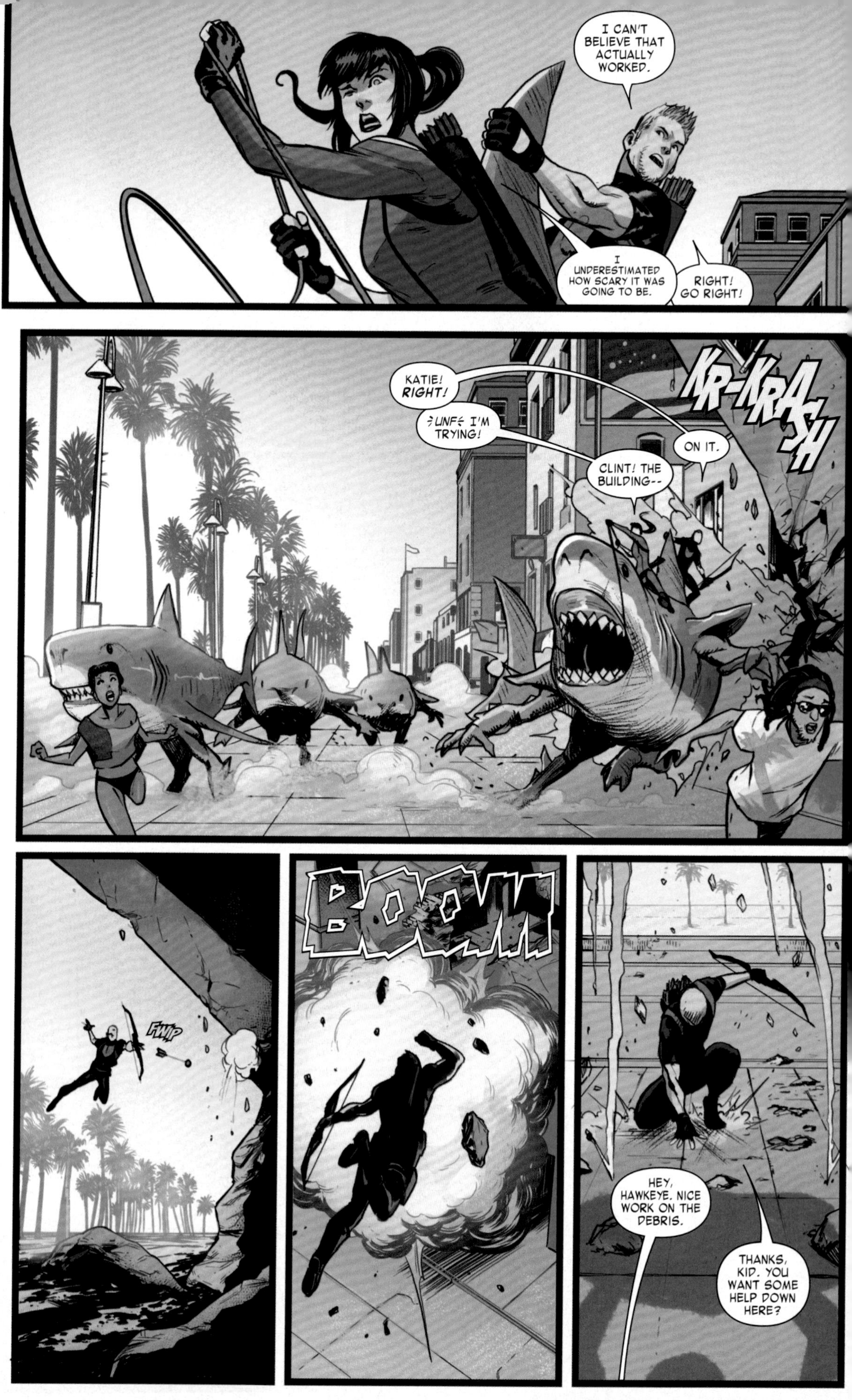
I CAN'T BELIEVE THAT ACTUALLY WORKED.
I UNDERESTIMATED HOW SCARY IT WAS GOING TO BE.
RIGHT! GO RIGHT!
KATIE! RIGHT!
UNF I'M TRYING!
ON IT.
CLINT! THE BUILDING--
KR-KRASH
FWIP
BOOM
HEY, HAWKEYE. NICE WORK ON THE DEBRIS.
THANKS, KID. YOU WANT SOME HELP DOWN HERE?

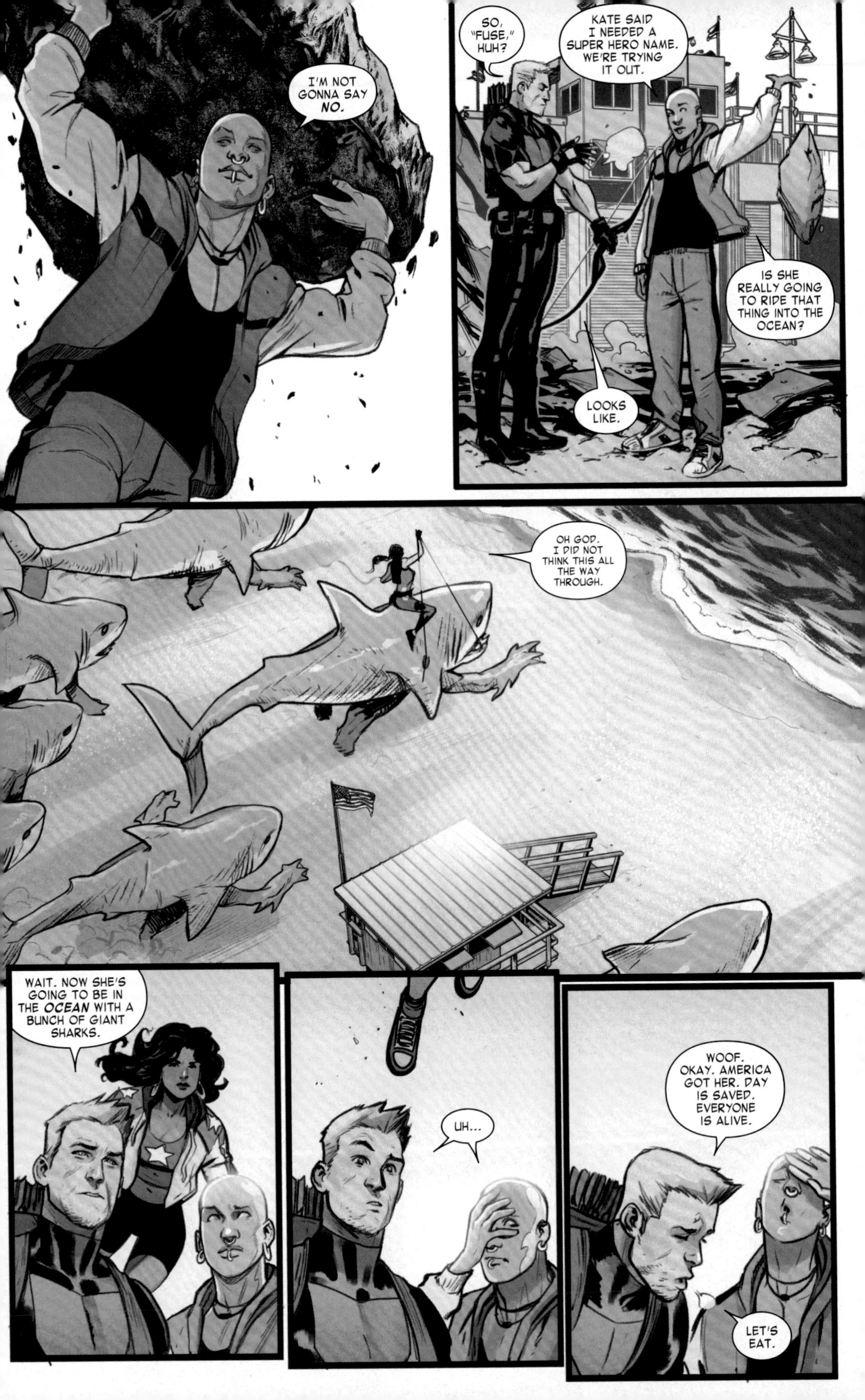
I'M NOT GONNA SAY NO.
SO, "FUSE," HUH?
KATE SAID I NEEDED A SUPER HERO NAME. WE'RE TRYING IT OUT.
IS SHE REALLY GOING TO RIDE THAT THING INTO THE OCEAN?
LOOKS LIKE.
OH GOD. I DID NOT THINK THIS ALL THE WAY THROUGH.
WAIT. NOW SHE'S GOING TO BE IN THE OCEAN WITH A BUNCH OF GIANT SHARKS.
UH...
WOOF. OKAY. AMERICA GOT HER. DAY IS SAVED. EVERYONE IS ALIVE.
LET'S EAT.

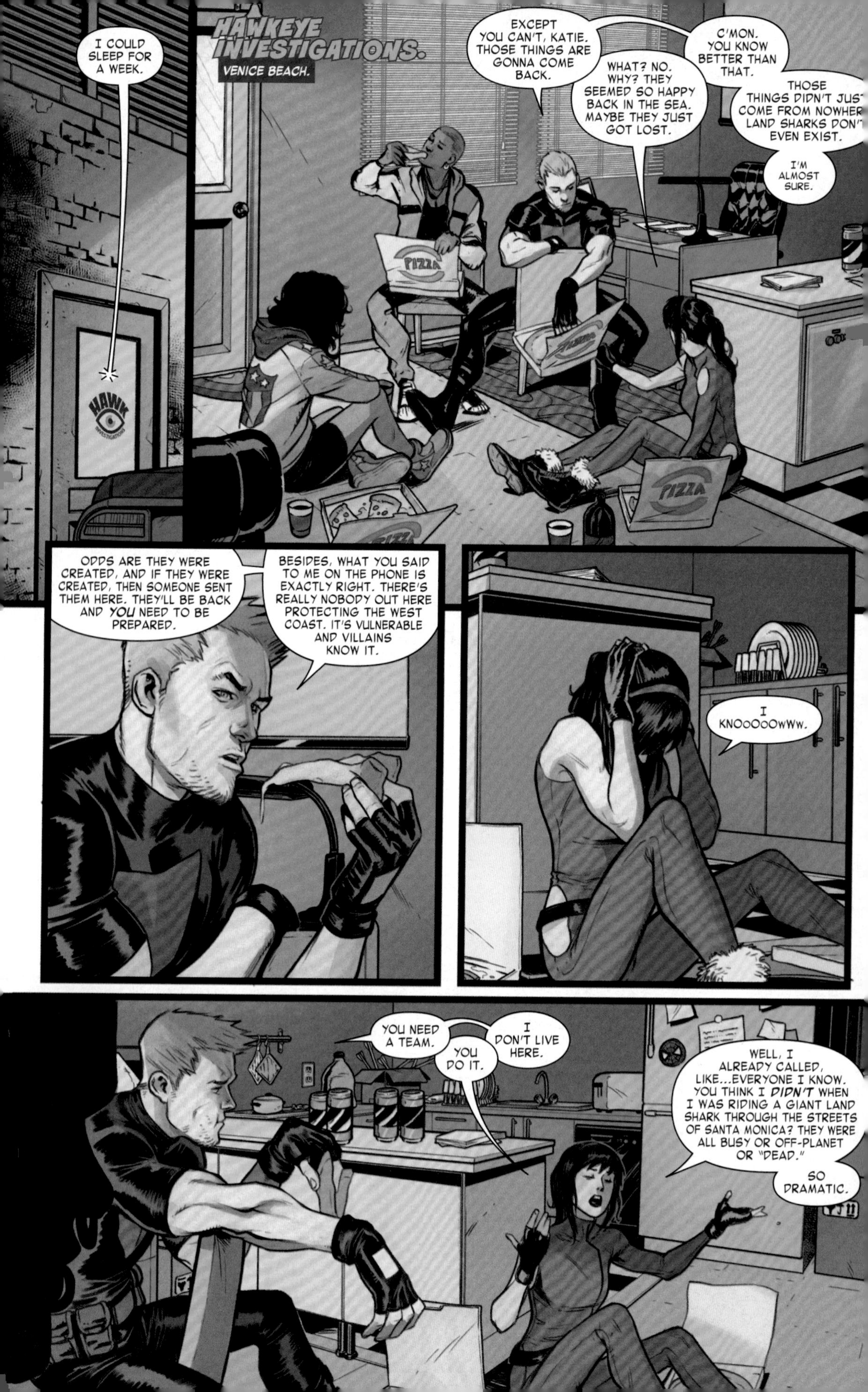
HAWKEYE INVESTIGATIONS.
VENICE BEACH.
I COULD SLEEP FOR A WEEK.
EXCEPT YOU CAN'T, KATIE. THOSE THINGS ARE GONNA COME BACK.
WHAT? NO. WHY? THEY SEEMED SO HAPPY BACK IN THE SEA. MAYBE THEY JUST GOT LOST.
C'MON. YOU KNOW BETTER THAN THAT.
THOSE THINGS DIDN'T JUST COME FROM NOWHER LAND SHARKS DON' EVEN EXIST.
I'M ALMOST SURE.
HAWK INVESTIGATIONS
PIZZA
ODDS ARE THEY WERE CREATED, AND IF THEY WERE CREATED, THEN SOMEONE SENT THEM HERE. THEY'LL BE BACK AND *YOU* NEED TO BE PREPARED.
BESIDES, WHAT YOU SAID TO ME ON THE PHONE IS EXACTLY RIGHT. THERE'S REALLY NOBODY OUT HERE PROTECTING THE WEST COAST. IT'S VULNERABLE AND VILLAINS KNOW IT.
I KNOoOOOwWw.
YOU NEED A TEAM.
YOU DO IT.
I DON'T LIVE HERE.
WELL, I ALREADY CALLED, LIKE...EVERYONE I KNOW. YOU THINK I *DIDN'T* WHEN I WAS RIDING A GIANT LAND SHARK THROUGH THE STREETS OF SANTA MONICA? THEY WERE ALL BUSY OR OFF-PLANET OR "DEAD."
SO DRAMATIC.

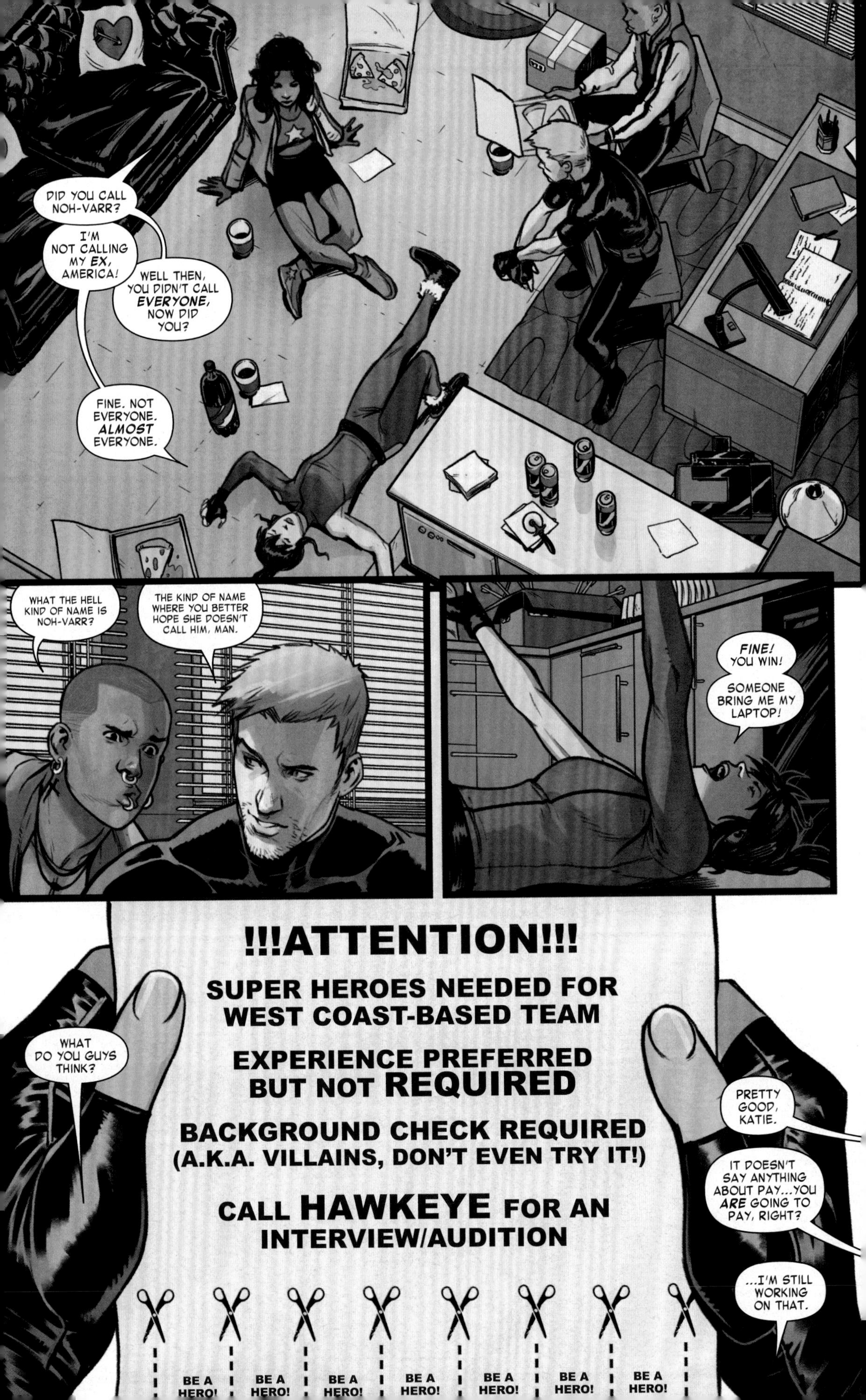

DID YOU CALL NOH-VARR?
I'M NOT CALLING MY EX, AMERICA!
WELL THEN, YOU DIDN'T CALL EVERYONE, NOW DID YOU?
FINE. NOT EVERYONE. ALMOST EVERYONE.
WHAT THE HELL KIND OF NAME IS NOH-VARR?
THE KIND OF NAME WHERE YOU BETTER HOPE SHE DOESN'T CALL HIM, MAN.
FINE! YOU WIN!
SOMEONE BRING ME MY LAPTOP!
!!!ATTENTION!!!
SUPER HEROES NEEDED FOR WEST COAST-BASED TEAM
EXPERIENCE PREFERRED BUT NOT REQUIRED
BACKGROUND CHECK REQUIRED (A.K.A. VILLAINS, DON'T EVEN TRY IT!)
CALL HAWKEYE FOR AN INTERVIEW/AUDITION
BE A HERO!
BE A HERO!
BE A HERO!
BE A HERO!
BE A HERO!
BE A HERO!
BE A HERO!
WHAT DO YOU GUYS THINK?
PRETTY GOOD, KATIE.
IT DOESN'T SAY ANYTHING ABOUT PAY...YOU ARE GOING TO PAY, RIGHT?
...I'M STILL WORKING ON THAT.

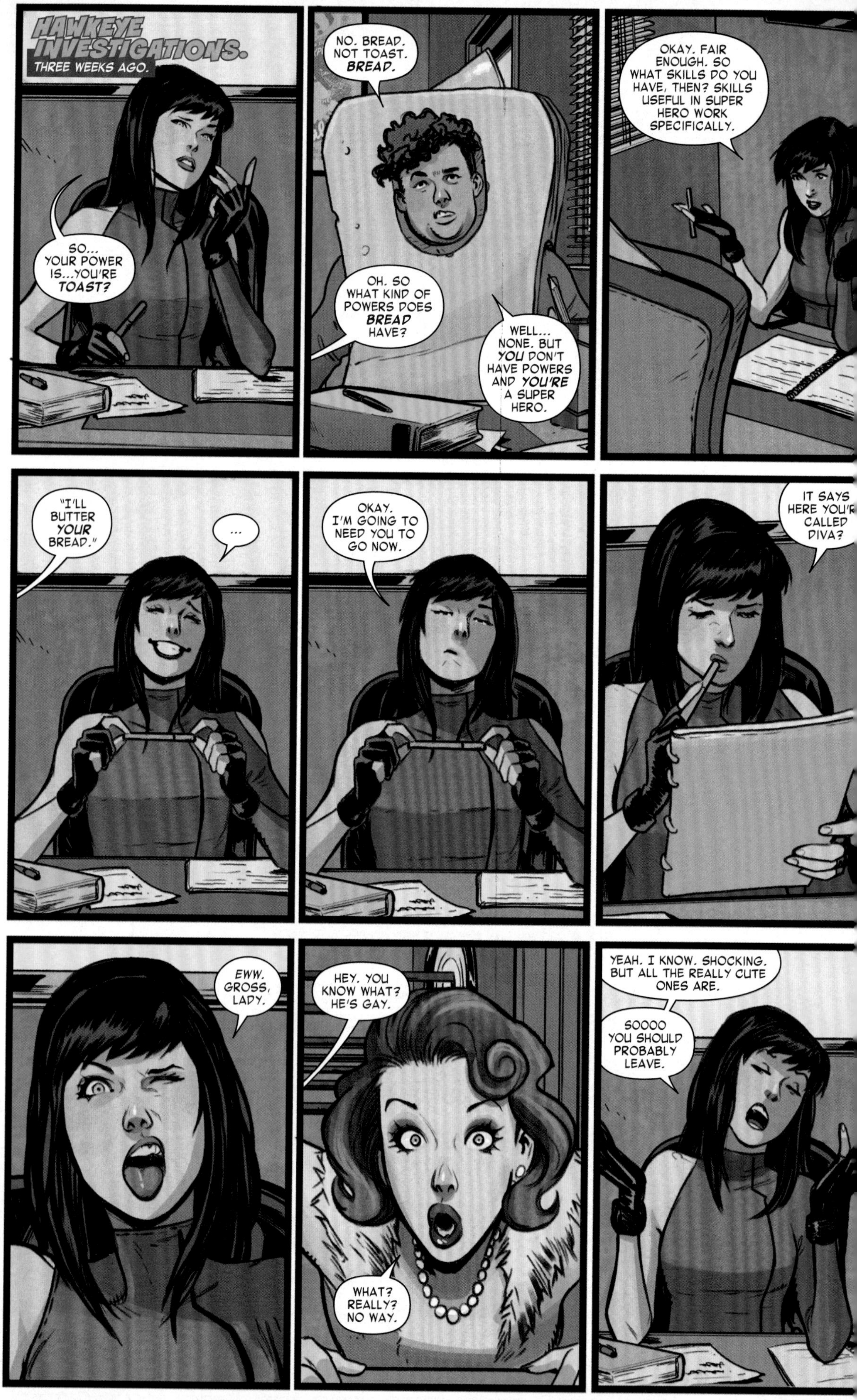
HAWKEYE INVESTIGATIONS.
THREE WEEKS AGO.
SO... YOUR POWER IS...YOU'RE TOAST?
NO. BREAD. NOT TOAST. BREAD.
OH. SO WHAT KIND OF POWERS DOES BREAD HAVE?
WELL... NONE. BUT YOU DON'T HAVE POWERS AND YOU'RE A SUPER HERO.
OKAY. FAIR ENOUGH. SO WHAT SKILLS DO YOU HAVE, THEN? SKILLS USEFUL IN SUPER HERO WORK SPECIFICALLY.
"I'LL BUTTER YOUR BREAD."
...
OKAY. I'M GOING TO NEED YOU TO GO NOW.
IT SAYS HERE YOU'R CALLED DIVA?
EWW. GROSS, LADY.
HEY. YOU KNOW WHAT? HE'S GAY.
WHAT? REALLY? NO WAY.
YEAH. I KNOW. SHOCKING. BUT ALL THE REALLY CUTE ONES ARE.
SOOOO YOU SHOULD PROBABLY LEAVE.

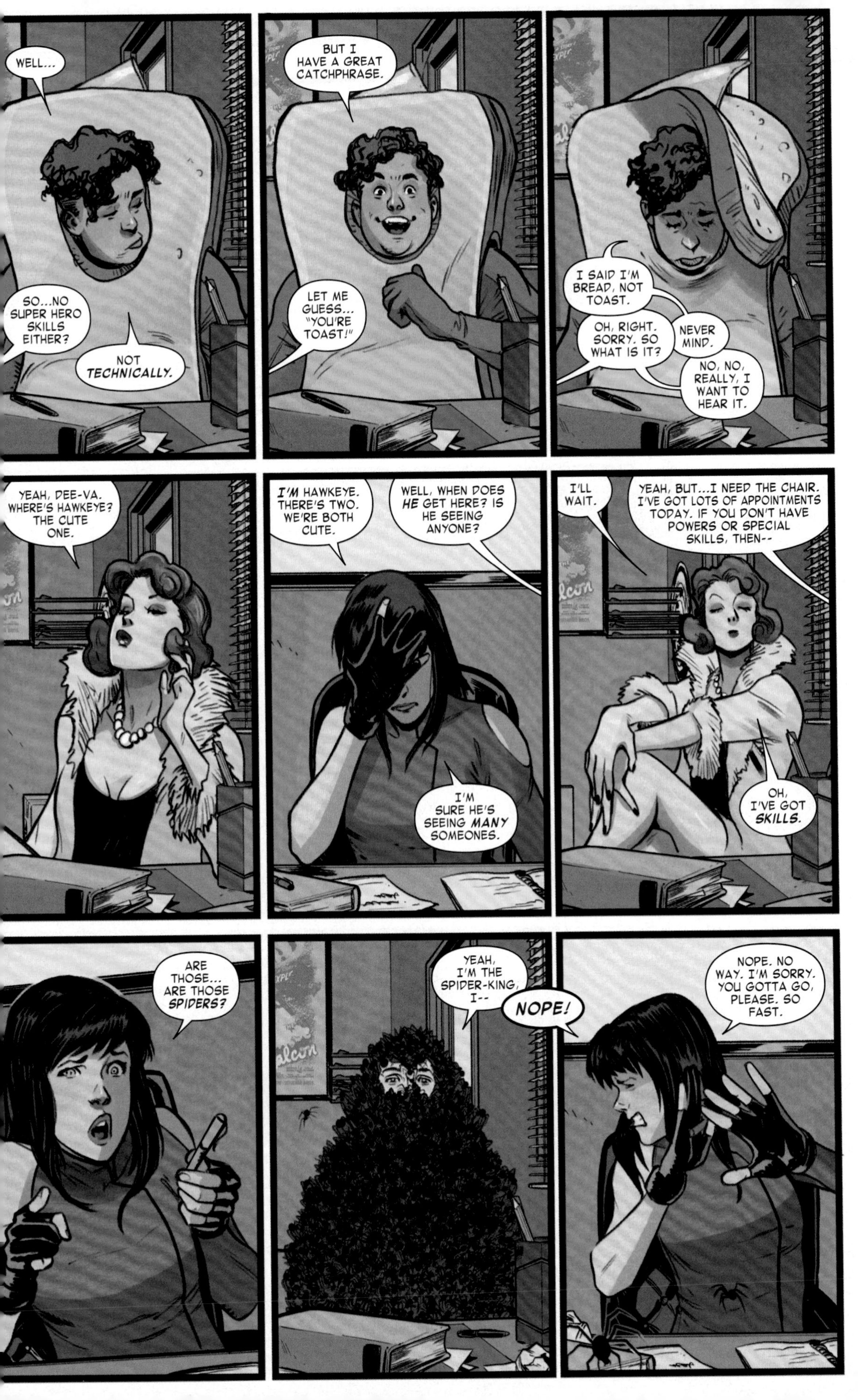

WELL...
SO...NO SUPER HERO SKILLS EITHER?
NOT *TECHNICALLY.*
BUT I HAVE A GREAT CATCHPHRASE.
LET ME GUESS... "YOU'RE TOAST!"
I SAID I'M BREAD, NOT TOAST.
OH, RIGHT. SORRY. SO WHAT IS IT?
NEVER MIND.
NO, NO, REALLY, I WANT TO HEAR IT.
YEAH, DEE-VA. WHERE'S HAWKEYE? THE CUTE ONE.
I'M HAWKEYE. THERE'S TWO. WE'RE BOTH CUTE.
WELL, WHEN DOES *HE* GET HERE? IS HE SEEING ANYONE?
I'M SURE HE'S SEEING *MANY* SOMEONES.
I'LL WAIT.
YEAH, BUT...I NEED THE CHAIR. I'VE GOT LOTS OF APPOINTMENTS TODAY. IF YOU DON'T HAVE POWERS OR SPECIAL SKILLS, THEN--
OH, I'VE GOT *SKILLS.*
ARE THOSE... ARE THOSE *SPIDERS?*
YEAH, I'M THE SPIDER-KING, I--
NOPE!
NOPE. NO WAY. I'M SORRY. YOU GOTTA GO, PLEASE. SO FAST.

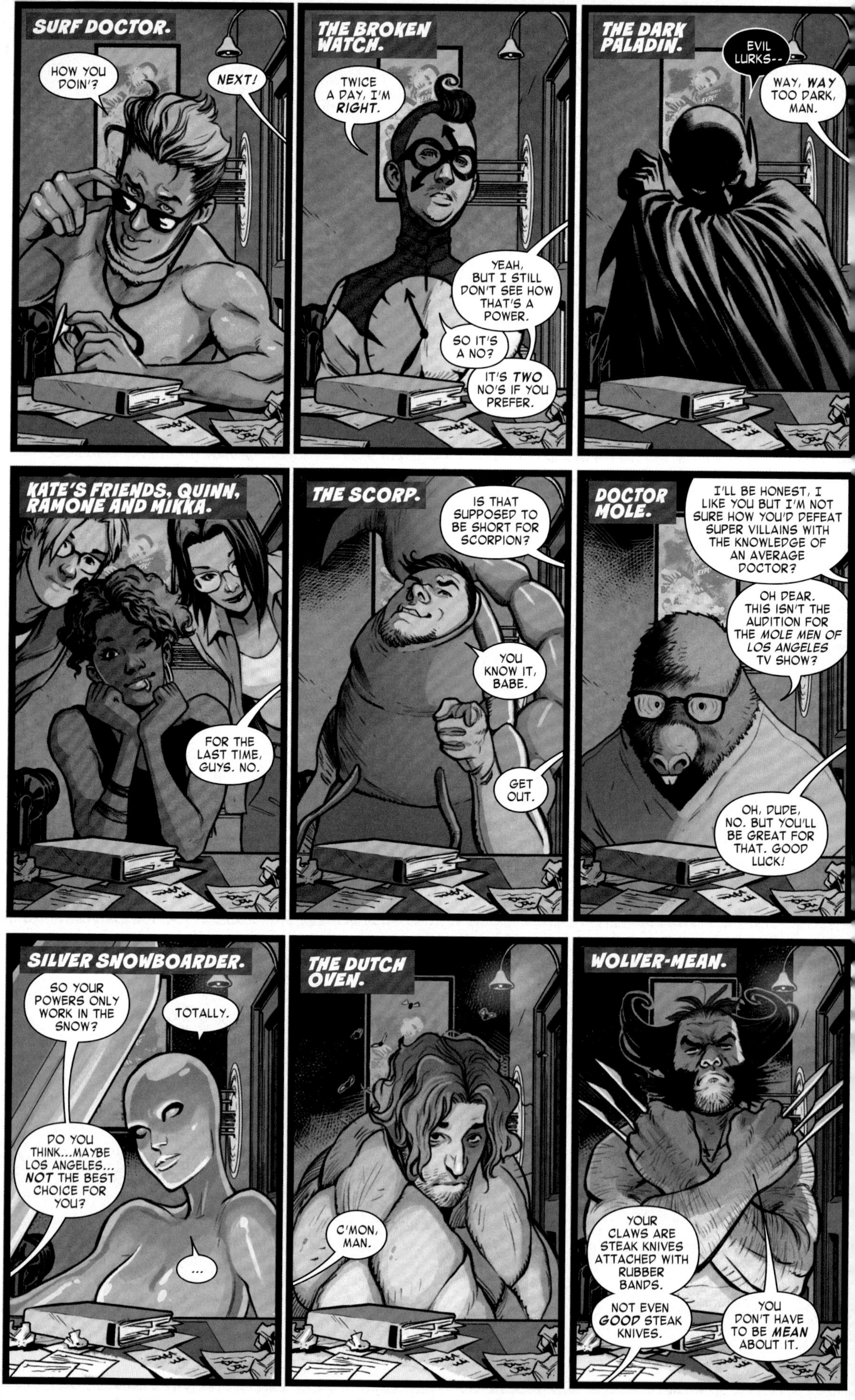
SURF DOCTOR.
HOW YOU DOIN'?
NEXT!
THE BROKEN WATCH.
TWICE A DAY, I'M RIGHT.
YEAH, BUT I STILL DON'T SEE HOW THAT'S A POWER.
SO IT'S A NO?
IT'S TWO NO'S IF YOU PREFER.
THE DARK PALADIN.
EVIL LURKS--
WAY, WAY TOO DARK, MAN.
KATE'S FRIENDS, QUINN, RAMONE AND MIKKA.
FOR THE LAST TIME, GUYS. NO.
THE SCORP.
IS THAT SUPPOSED TO BE SHORT FOR SCORPION?
YOU KNOW IT, BABE.
GET OUT.
DOCTOR MOLE.
I'LL BE HONEST, I LIKE YOU BUT I'M NOT SURE HOW YOU'D DEFEAT SUPER VILLAINS WITH THE KNOWLEDGE OF AN AVERAGE DOCTOR?
OH DEAR. THIS ISN'T THE AUDITION FOR THE MOLE MEN OF LOS ANGELES TV SHOW?
OH, DUDE, NO. BUT YOU'LL BE GREAT FOR THAT. GOOD LUCK!
SILVER SNOWBOARDER.
SO YOUR POWERS ONLY WORK IN THE SNOW?
TOTALLY.
DO YOU THINK...MAYBE LOS ANGELES... NOT THE BEST CHOICE FOR YOU?
...
THE DUTCH OVEN.
C'MON, MAN.
WOLVER-MEAN.
YOUR CLAWS ARE STEAK KNIVES ATTACHED WITH RUBBER BANDS.
NOT EVEN GOOD STEAK KNIVES.
YOU DON'T HAVE TO BE MEAN ABOUT IT.

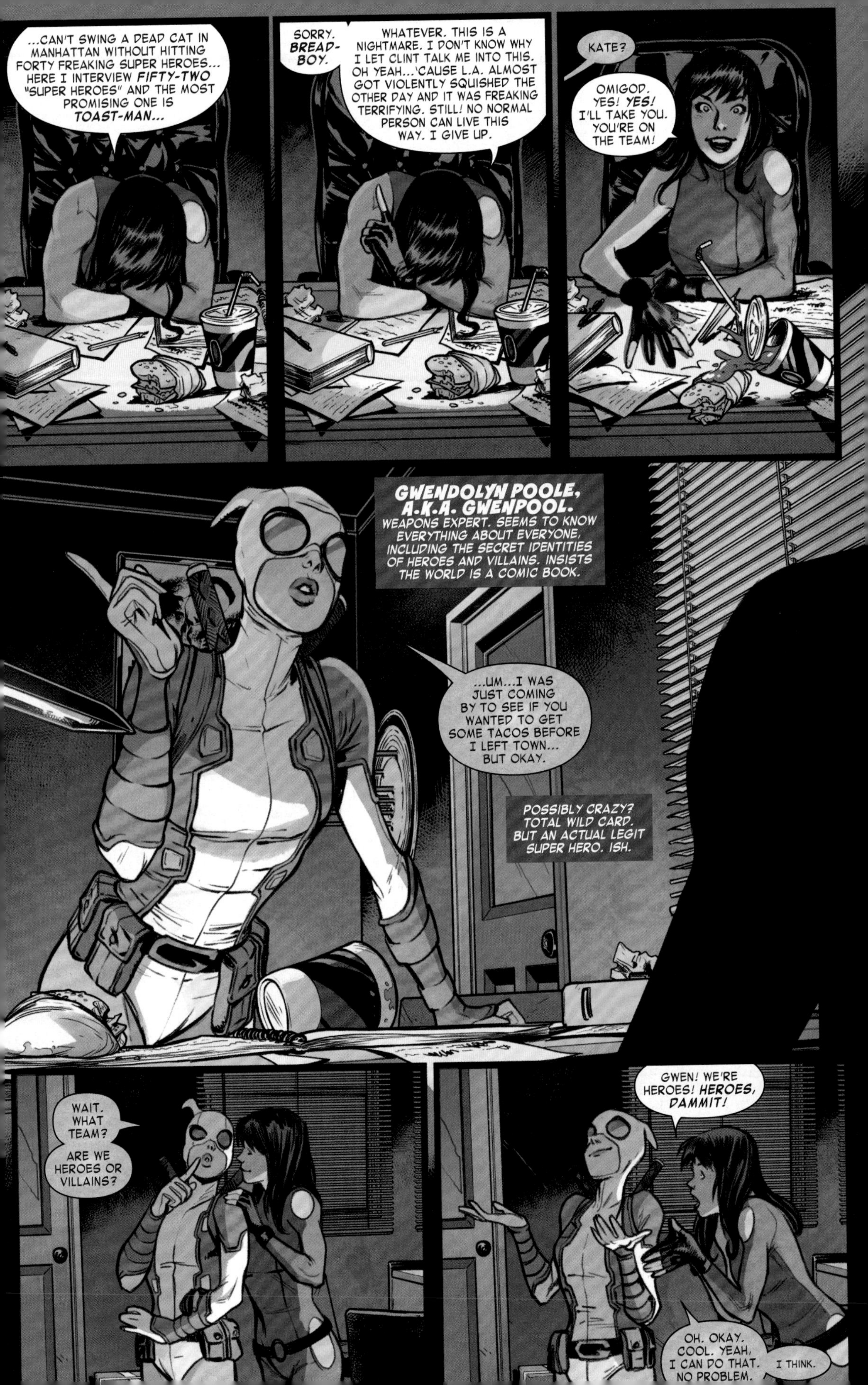
...CAN'T SWING A DEAD CAT IN MANHATTAN WITHOUT HITTING FORTY FREAKING SUPER HEROES... HERE I INTERVIEW FIFTY-TWO "SUPER HEROES" AND THE MOST PROMISING ONE IS TOAST-MAN...
SORRY. BREAD-BOY.
WHATEVER. THIS IS A NIGHTMARE. I DON'T KNOW WHY I LET CLINT TALK ME INTO THIS. OH YEAH...'CAUSE L.A. ALMOST GOT VIOLENTLY SQUISHED THE OTHER DAY AND IT WAS FREAKING TERRIFYING. STILL! NO NORMAL PERSON CAN LIVE THIS WAY. I GIVE UP.
KATE?
OMIGOD. YES! YES! I'LL TAKE YOU. YOU'RE ON THE TEAM!
GWENDOLYN POOLE, A.K.A. GWENPOOL.
WEAPONS EXPERT. SEEMS TO KNOW EVERYTHING ABOUT EVERYONE, INCLUDING THE SECRET IDENTITIES OF HEROES AND VILLAINS. INSISTS THE WORLD IS A COMIC BOOK.
...UM...I WAS JUST COMING BY TO SEE IF YOU WANTED TO GET SOME TACOS BEFORE I LEFT TOWN... BUT OKAY.
POSSIBLY CRAZY? TOTAL WILD CARD. BUT AN ACTUAL LEGIT SUPER HERO. ISH.
WAIT. WHAT TEAM?
ARE WE HEROES OR VILLAINS?
GWEN! WE'RE HEROES! HEROES, DAMMIT!
OH. OKAY. COOL. YEAH, I CAN DO THAT. NO PROBLEM.
I THINK.

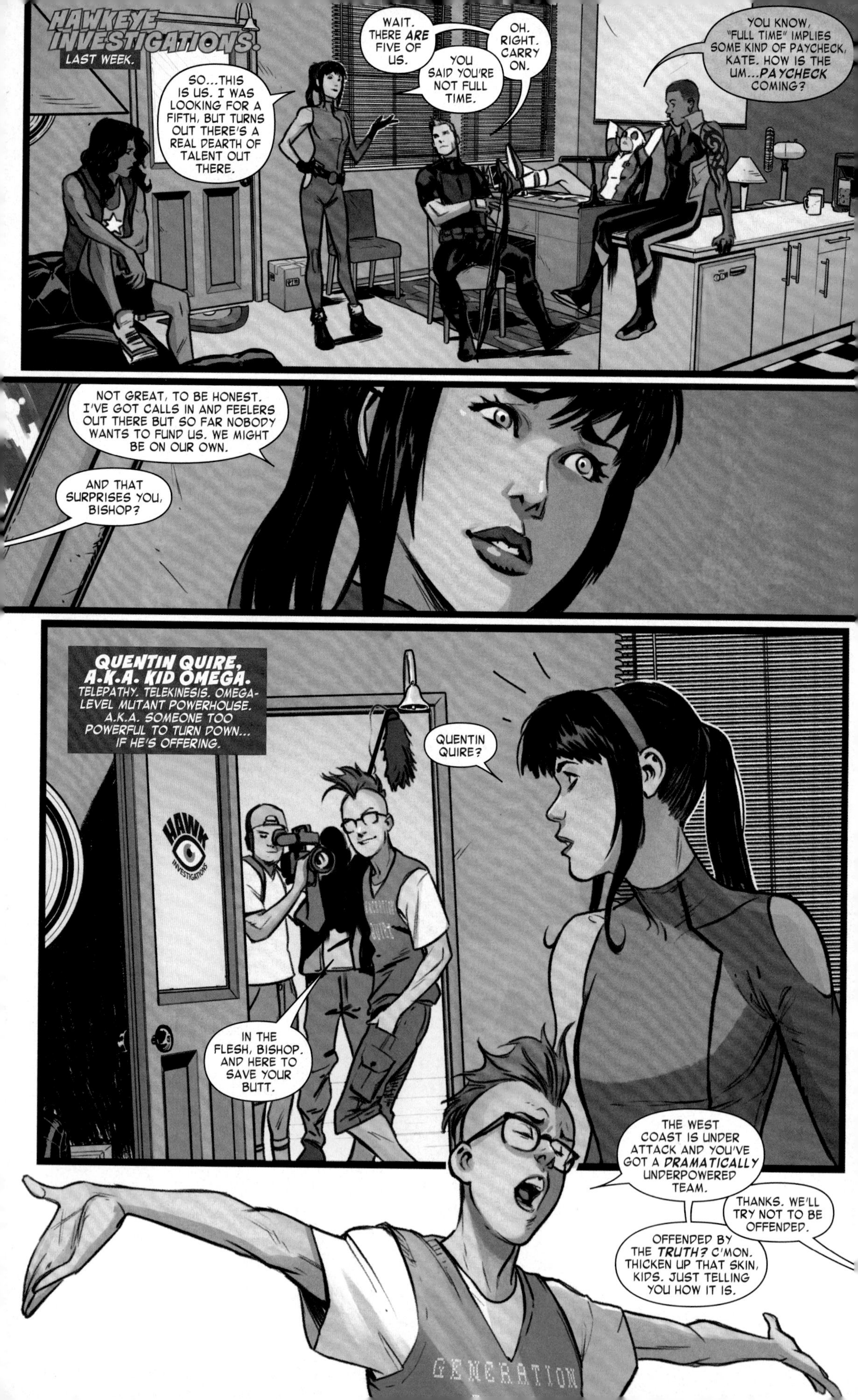
HAWKEYE INVESTIGATIONS.
LAST WEEK.
SO...THIS IS US. I WAS LOOKING FOR A FIFTH, BUT TURNS OUT THERE'S A REAL DEARTH OF TALENT OUT THERE.
WAIT. THERE ARE FIVE OF US.
YOU SAID YOU'RE NOT FULL TIME.
OH. RIGHT. CARRY ON.
YOU KNOW, "FULL TIME" IMPLIES SOME KIND OF PAYCHECK, KATE. HOW IS THE UM...PAYCHECK COMING?
NOT GREAT, TO BE HONEST. I'VE GOT CALLS IN AND FEELERS OUT THERE BUT SO FAR NOBODY WANTS TO FUND US. WE MIGHT BE ON OUR OWN.
AND THAT SURPRISES YOU, BISHOP?
QUENTIN QUIRE, A.K.A. KID OMEGA.
TELEPATHY. TELEKINESIS. OMEGA-LEVEL MUTANT POWERHOUSE. A.K.A. SOMEONE TOO POWERFUL TO TURN DOWN... IF HE'S OFFERING.
QUENTIN QUIRE?
IN THE FLESH, BISHOP. AND HERE TO SAVE YOUR BUTT.
THE WEST COAST IS UNDER ATTACK AND YOU'VE GOT A DRAMATICALLY UNDERPOWERED TEAM.
THANKS. WE'LL TRY NOT TO BE OFFENDED.
OFFENDED BY THE TRUTH? C'MON. THICKEN UP THAT SKIN, KIDS. JUST TELLING YOU HOW IT IS.
GENERATION

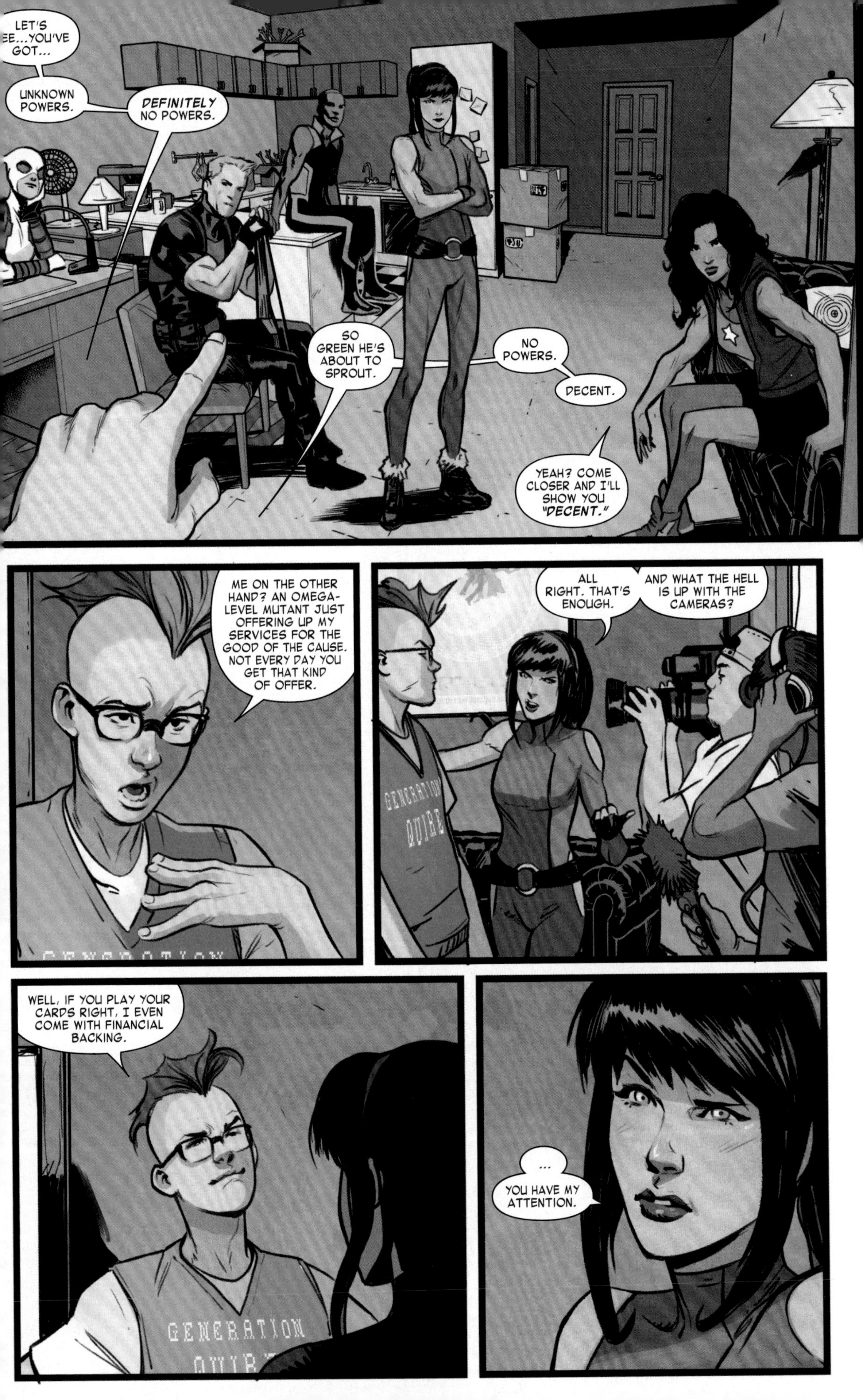
LET'S EE...YOU'VE GOT...
UNKNOWN POWERS.
DEFINITELY NO POWERS.
SO GREEN HE'S ABOUT TO SPROUT.
NO POWERS.
DECENT.
YEAH? COME CLOSER AND I'LL SHOW YOU *"DECENT."*
ME ON THE OTHER HAND? AN OMEGA-LEVEL MUTANT JUST OFFERING UP MY SERVICES FOR THE GOOD OF THE CAUSE. NOT EVERY DAY YOU GET THAT KIND OF OFFER.
GENERATION QUIRE
ALL RIGHT. THAT'S ENOUGH.
AND WHAT THE HELL IS UP WITH THE CAMERAS?
WELL, IF YOU PLAY YOUR CARDS RIGHT, I EVEN COME WITH FINANCIAL BACKING.
GENERATION
...
YOU HAVE MY ATTENTION.

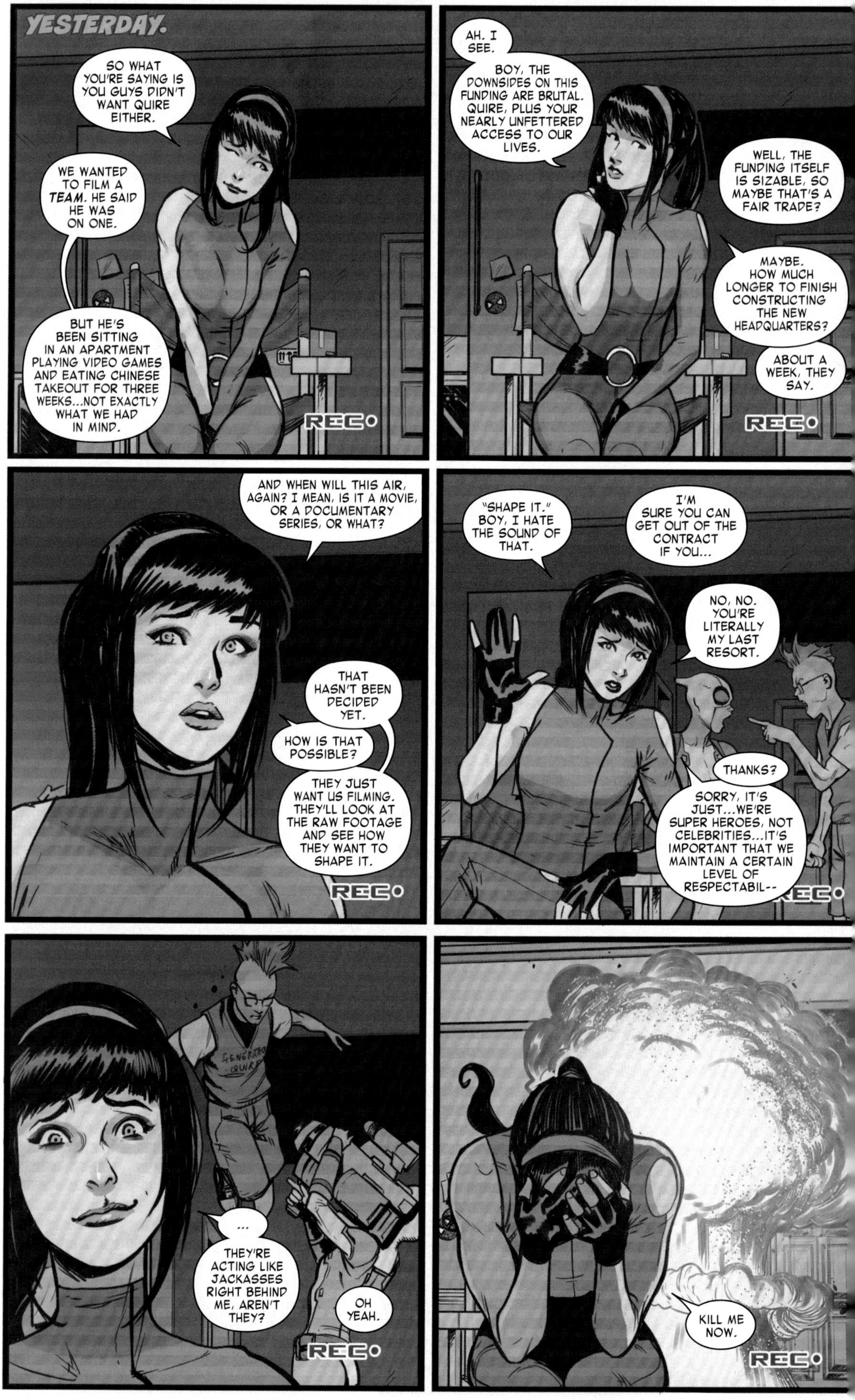
YESTERDAY.
SO WHAT YOU'RE SAYING IS YOU GUYS DIDN'T WANT QUIRE EITHER.
WE WANTED TO FILM A TEAM. HE SAID HE WAS ON ONE.
BUT HE'S BEEN SITTING IN AN APARTMENT PLAYING VIDEO GAMES AND EATING CHINESE TAKEOUT FOR THREE WEEKS...NOT EXACTLY WHAT WE HAD IN MIND.
REC
AH. I SEE.
BOY, THE DOWNSIDES ON THIS FUNDING ARE BRUTAL. QUIRE, PLUS YOUR NEARLY UNFETTERED ACCESS TO OUR LIVES.
WELL, THE FUNDING ITSELF IS SIZABLE, SO MAYBE THAT'S A FAIR TRADE?
MAYBE. HOW MUCH LONGER TO FINISH CONSTRUCTING THE NEW HEADQUARTERS?
ABOUT A WEEK, THEY SAY.
REC
AND WHEN WILL THIS AIR, AGAIN? I MEAN, IS IT A MOVIE, OR A DOCUMENTARY SERIES, OR WHAT?
THAT HASN'T BEEN DECIDED YET.
HOW IS THAT POSSIBLE?
THEY JUST WANT US FILMING. THEY'LL LOOK AT THE RAW FOOTAGE AND SEE HOW THEY WANT TO SHAPE IT.
REC
"SHAPE IT." BOY, I HATE THE SOUND OF THAT.
I'M SURE YOU CAN GET OUT OF THE CONTRACT IF YOU...
NO, NO. YOU'RE LITERALLY MY LAST RESORT.
THANKS?
SORRY, IT'S JUST...WE'RE SUPER HEROES, NOT CELEBRITIES...IT'S IMPORTANT THAT WE MAINTAIN A CERTAIN LEVEL OF RESPECTABIL--
REC
GENERATION QUIRE
...
THEY'RE ACTING LIKE JACKASSES RIGHT BEHIND ME, AREN'T THEY?
OH YEAH.
REC
KILL ME NOW.
REC

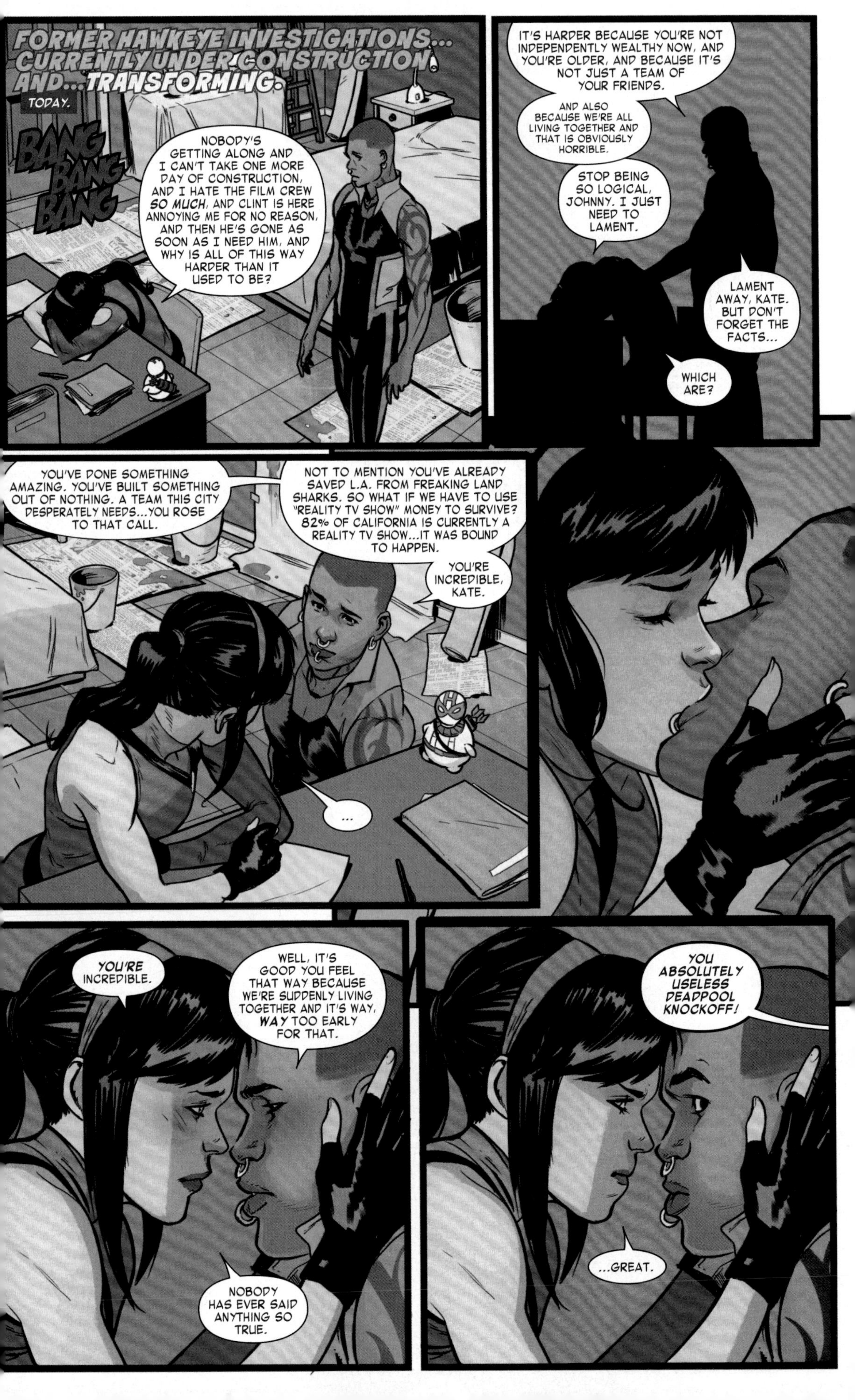
FORMER HAWKEYE INVESTIGATIONS... CURRENTLY UNDER CONSTRUCTION AND... TRANSFORMING.
TODAY.
BANG BANG BANG
NOBODY'S GETTING ALONG AND I CAN'T TAKE ONE MORE DAY OF CONSTRUCTION, AND I HATE THE FILM CREW SO MUCH, AND CLINT IS HERE ANNOYING ME FOR NO REASON, AND THEN HE'S GONE AS SOON AS I NEED HIM, AND WHY IS ALL OF THIS WAY HARDER THAN IT USED TO BE?
IT'S HARDER BECAUSE YOU'RE NOT INDEPENDENTLY WEALTHY NOW, AND YOU'RE OLDER, AND BECAUSE IT'S NOT JUST A TEAM OF YOUR FRIENDS.
AND ALSO BECAUSE WE'RE ALL LIVING TOGETHER AND THAT IS OBVIOUSLY HORRIBLE.
STOP BEING SO LOGICAL, JOHNNY. I JUST NEED TO LAMENT.
LAMENT AWAY, KATE. BUT DON'T FORGET THE FACTS...
WHICH ARE?
YOU'VE DONE SOMETHING AMAZING. YOU'VE BUILT SOMETHING OUT OF NOTHING. A TEAM THIS CITY DESPERATELY NEEDS...YOU ROSE TO THAT CALL.
NOT TO MENTION YOU'VE ALREADY SAVED L.A. FROM FREAKING LAND SHARKS. SO WHAT IF WE HAVE TO USE "REALITY TV SHOW" MONEY TO SURVIVE? 82% OF CALIFORNIA IS CURRENTLY A REALITY TV SHOW...IT WAS BOUND TO HAPPEN.
YOU'RE INCREDIBLE, KATE.
...
YOU'RE INCREDIBLE.
WELL, IT'S GOOD YOU FEEL THAT WAY BECAUSE WE'RE SUDDENLY LIVING TOGETHER AND IT'S WAY, WAY TOO EARLY FOR THAT.
NOBODY HAS EVER SAID ANYTHING SO TRUE.
YOU ABSOLUTELY USELESS DEADPOOL KNOCKOFF!
...GREAT.

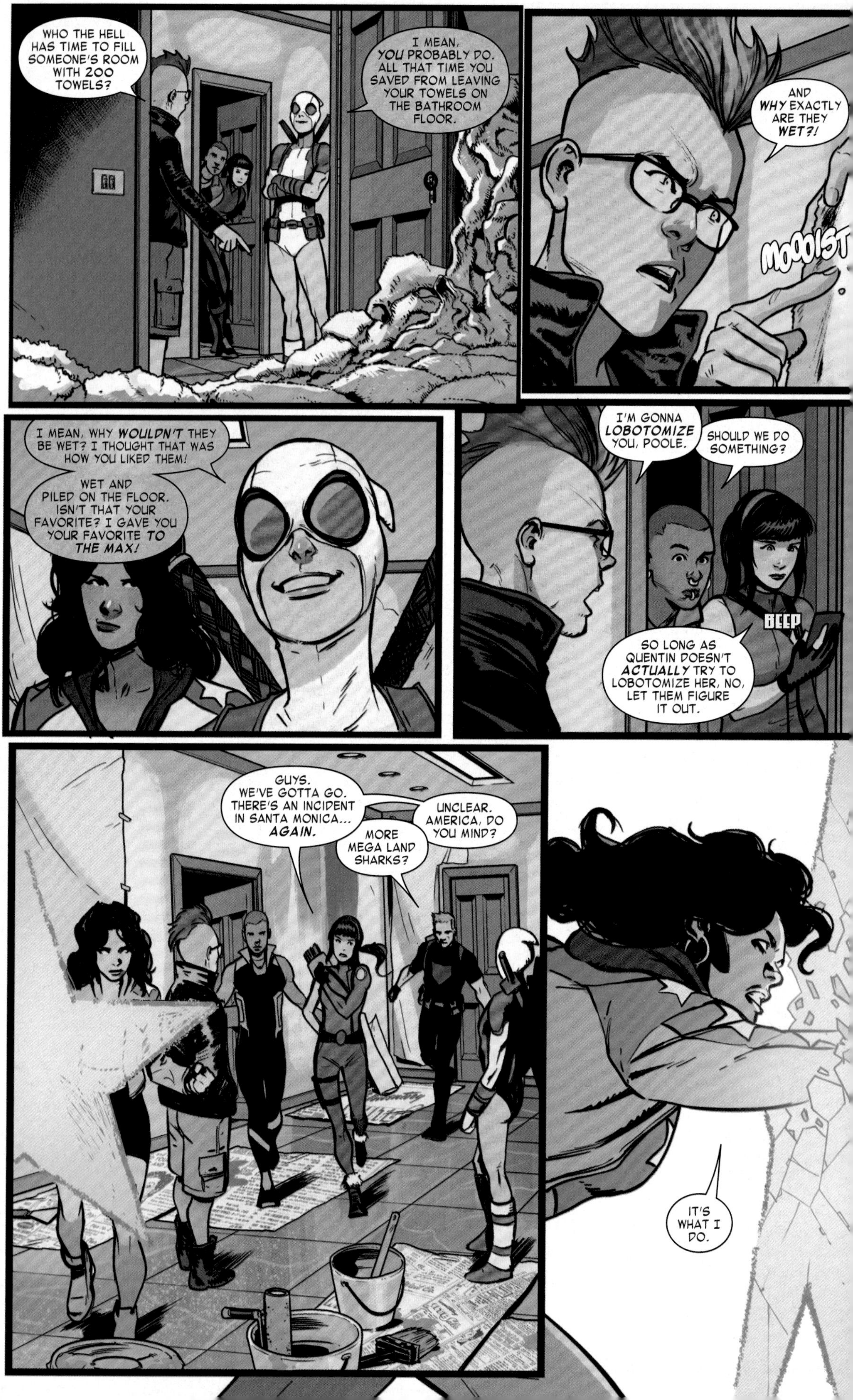
WHO THE HELL HAS TIME TO FILL SOMEONE'S ROOM WITH 200 TOWELS?
I MEAN, YOU PROBABLY DO. ALL THAT TIME YOU SAVED FROM LEAVING YOUR TOWELS ON THE BATHROOM FLOOR.
AND WHY EXACTLY ARE THEY WET?!
MOOOIST
I MEAN, WHY WOULDN'T THEY BE WET? I THOUGHT THAT WAS HOW YOU LIKED THEM!
WET AND PILED ON THE FLOOR. ISN'T THAT YOUR FAVORITE? I GAVE YOU YOUR FAVORITE TO THE MAX!
I'M GONNA LOBOTOMIZE YOU, POOLE.
SHOULD WE DO SOMETHING?
BEEP
SO LONG AS QUENTIN DOESN'T ACTUALLY TRY TO LOBOTOMIZE HER, NO, LET THEM FIGURE IT OUT.
GUYS. WE'VE GOTTA GO. THERE'S AN INCIDENT IN SANTA MONICA... AGAIN.
MORE MEGA LAND SHARKS?
UNCLEAR. AMERICA, DO YOU MIND?
IT'S WHAT I DO.

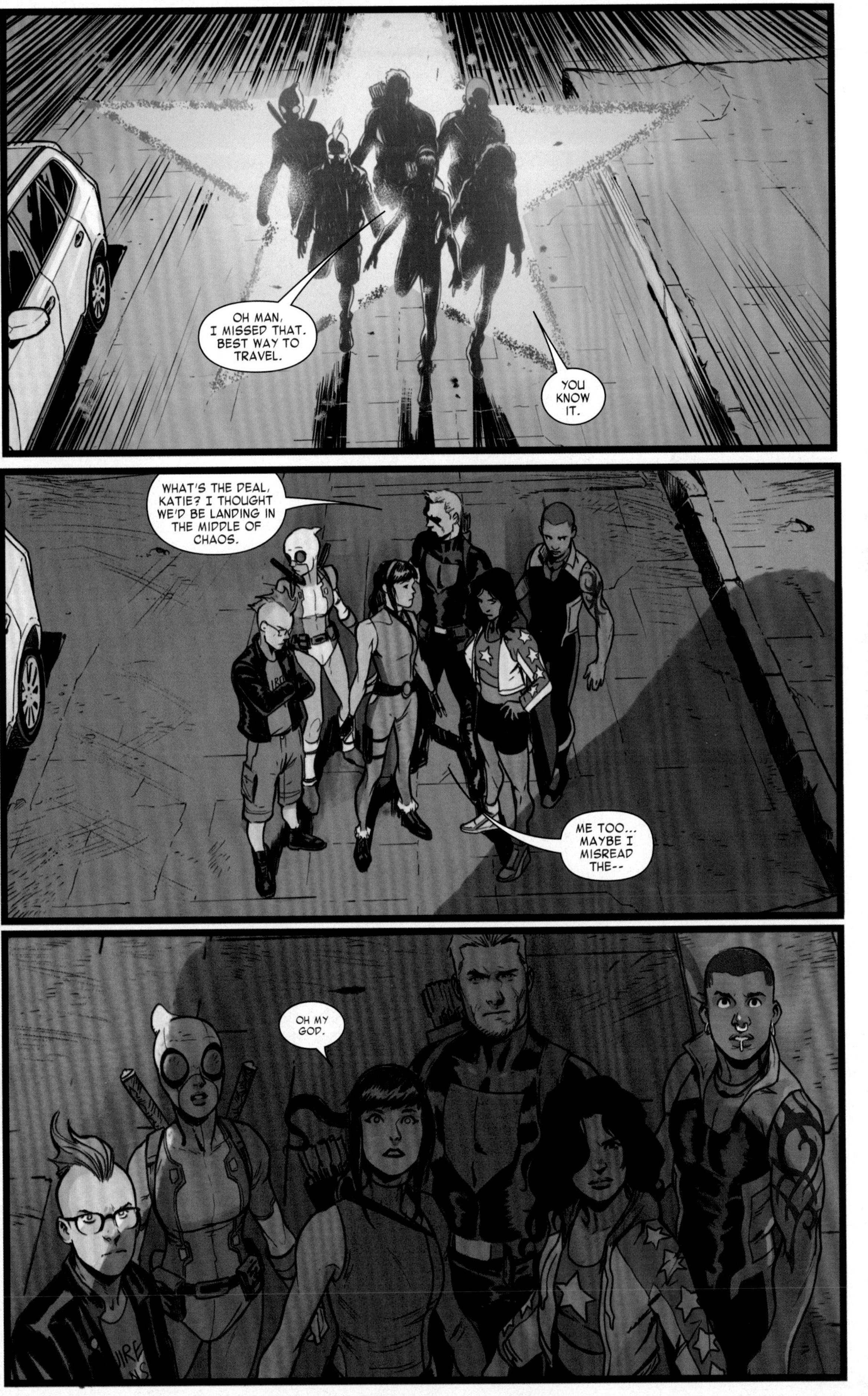
OH MAN, I MISSED THAT. BEST WAY TO TRAVEL.
YOU KNOW IT.
WHAT'S THE DEAL, KATIE? I THOUGHT WE'D BE LANDING IN THE MIDDLE OF CHAOS.
ME TOO... MAYBE I MISREAD THE--
OH MY GOD.

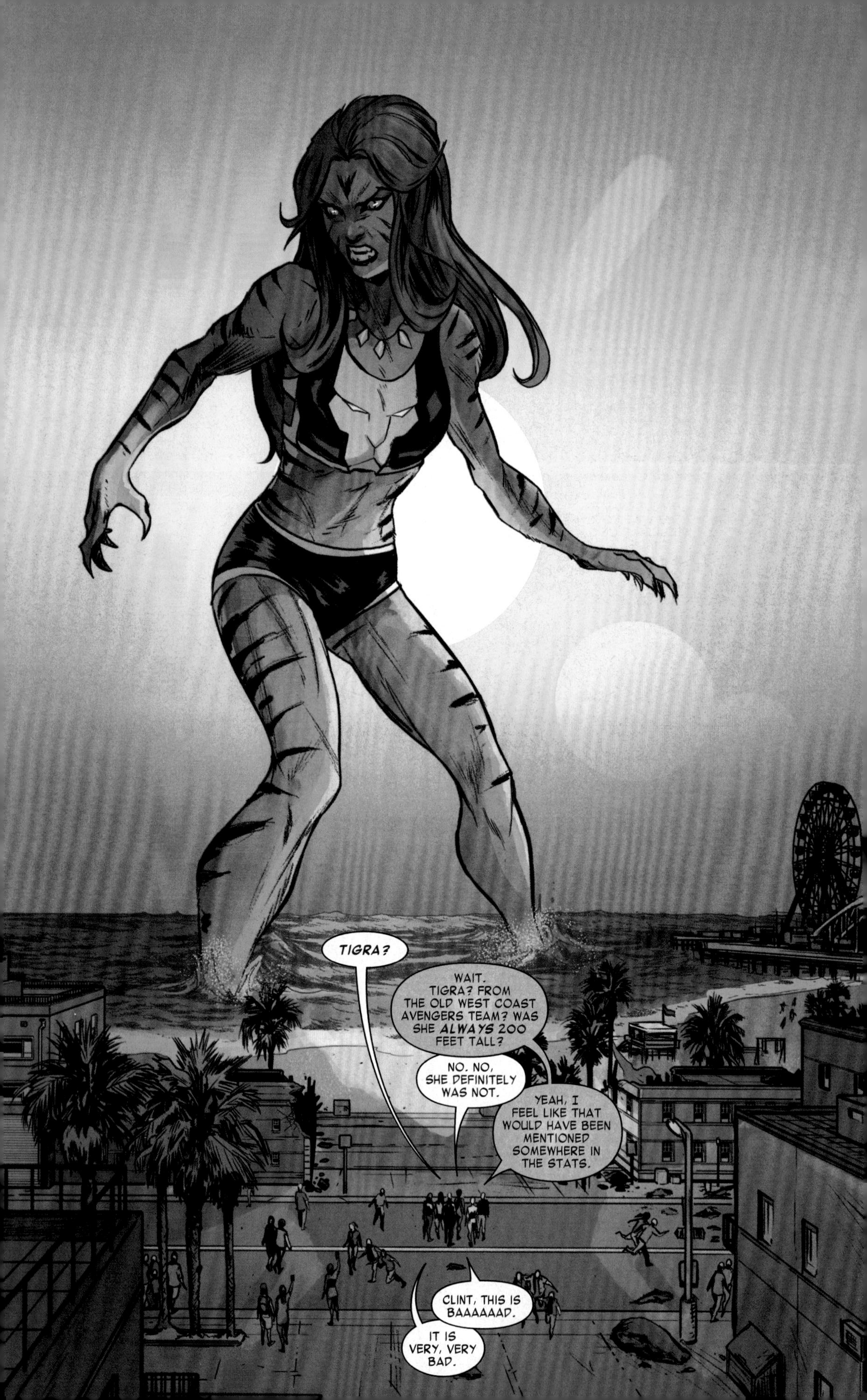
TIGRA?
WAIT. TIGRA? FROM THE OLD WEST COAST AVENGERS TEAM? WAS SHE *ALWAYS* 200 FEET TALL?
NO. NO, SHE DEFINITELY WAS NOT.
YEAH, I FEEL LIKE THAT WOULD HAVE BEEN MENTIONED SOMEWHERE IN THE STATS.
CLINT, THIS IS BAAAAAAD.
IT IS VERY, VERY BAD.

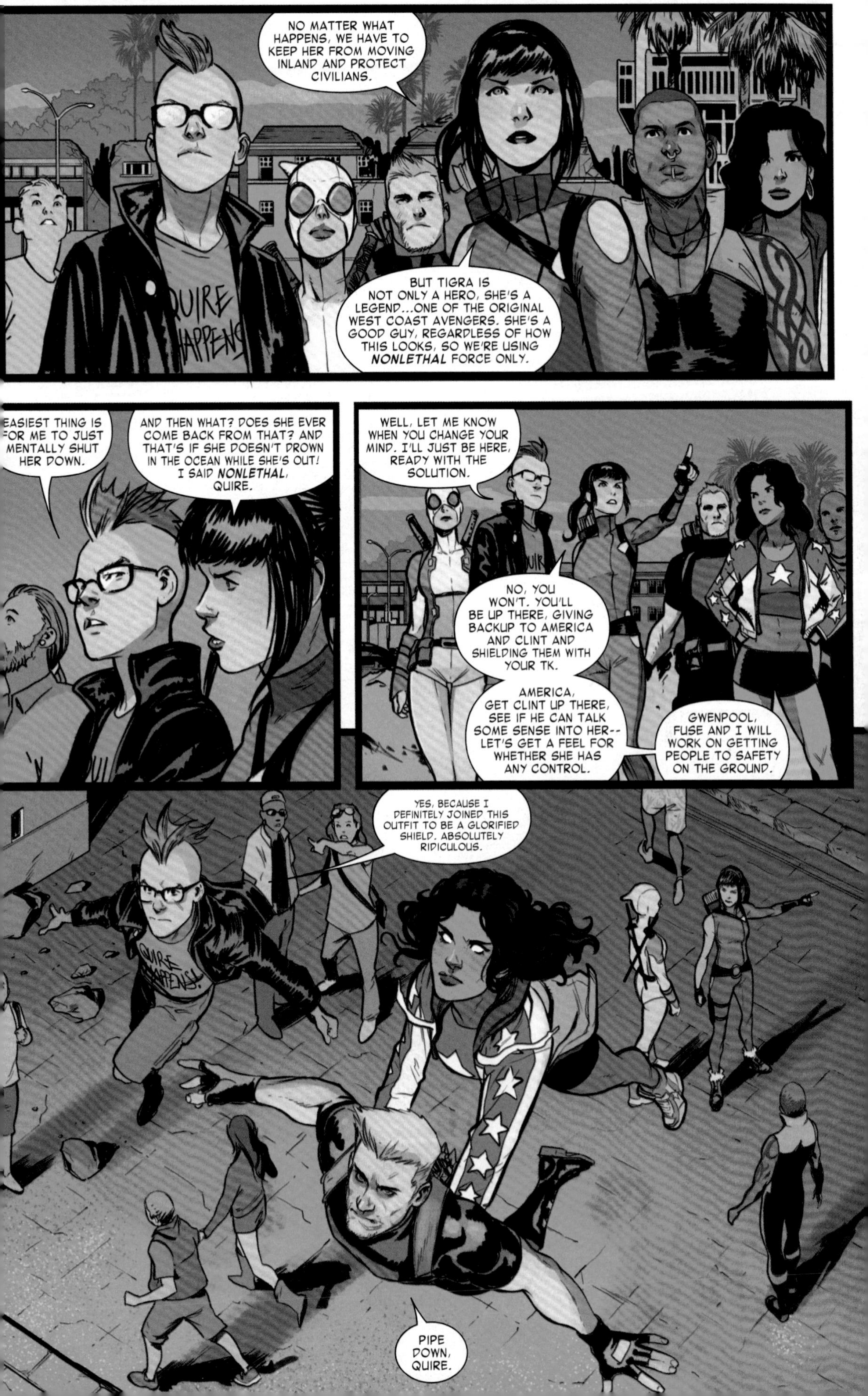
NO MATTER WHAT HAPPENS, WE HAVE TO KEEP HER FROM MOVING INLAND AND PROTECT CIVILIANS.
QUIRE HAPPENS
BUT TIGRA IS NOT ONLY A HERO, SHE'S A LEGEND...ONE OF THE ORIGINAL WEST COAST AVENGERS. SHE'S A GOOD GUY, REGARDLESS OF HOW THIS LOOKS, SO WE'RE USING NONLETHAL FORCE ONLY.
EASIEST THING IS FOR ME TO JUST MENTALLY SHUT HER DOWN.
AND THEN WHAT? DOES SHE EVER COME BACK FROM THAT? AND THAT'S IF SHE DOESN'T DROWN IN THE OCEAN WHILE SHE'S OUT! I SAID NONLETHAL, QUIRE.
WELL, LET ME KNOW WHEN YOU CHANGE YOUR MIND. I'LL JUST BE HERE, READY WITH THE SOLUTION.
NO, YOU WON'T. YOU'LL BE UP THERE, GIVING BACKUP TO AMERICA AND CLINT AND SHIELDING THEM WITH YOUR TK.
AMERICA, GET CLINT UP THERE, SEE IF HE CAN TALK SOME SENSE INTO HER--LET'S GET A FEEL FOR WHETHER SHE HAS ANY CONTROL.
GWENPOOL, FUSE AND I WILL WORK ON GETTING PEOPLE TO SAFETY ON THE GROUND.
YES, BECAUSE I DEFINITELY JOINED THIS OUTFIT TO BE A GLORIFIED SHIELD. ABSOLUTELY RIDICULOUS.
QUIRE HAPPENS!
PIPE DOWN, QUIRE.

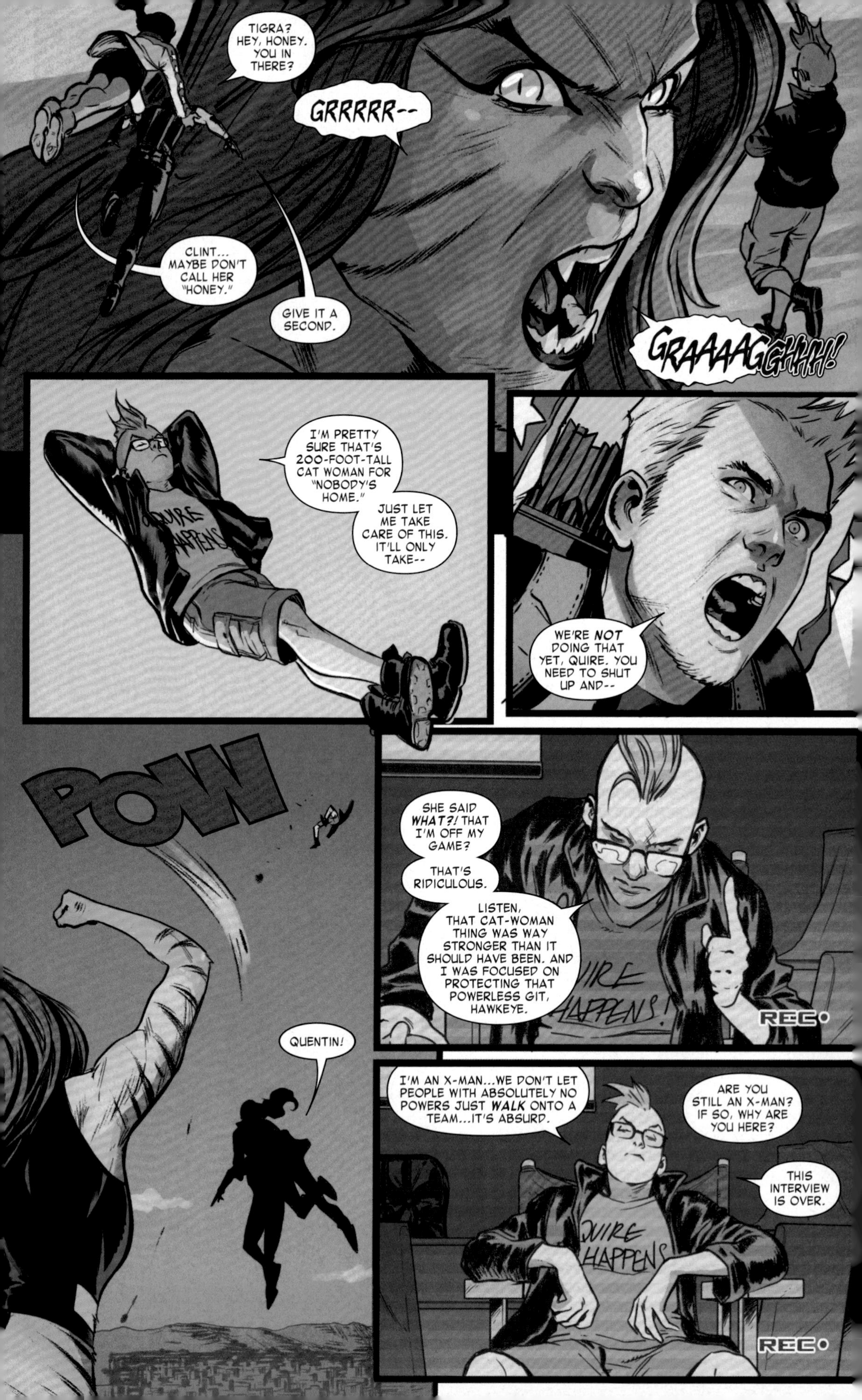
TIGRA? HEY, HONEY. YOU IN THERE?
GRRRRR--
CLINT... MAYBE DON'T CALL HER "HONEY."
GIVE IT A SECOND.
GRAAAAGGHHH!
I'M PRETTY SURE THAT'S 200-FOOT-TALL CAT WOMAN FOR "NOBODY'S HOME."
JUST LET ME TAKE CARE OF THIS. IT'LL ONLY TAKE--
WE'RE NOT DOING THAT YET, QUIRE. YOU NEED TO SHUT UP AND--
POW
QUENTIN!
SHE SAID WHAT?! THAT I'M OFF MY GAME?
THAT'S RIDICULOUS.
LISTEN, THAT CAT-WOMAN THING WAS WAY STRONGER THAN IT SHOULD HAVE BEEN. AND I WAS FOCUSED ON PROTECTING THAT POWERLESS GIT, HAWKEYE.
REC
I'M AN X-MAN...WE DON'T LET PEOPLE WITH ABSOLUTELY NO POWERS JUST WALK ONTO A TEAM...IT'S ABSURD.
ARE YOU STILL AN X-MAN? IF SO, WHY ARE YOU HERE?
THIS INTERVIEW IS OVER.
REC

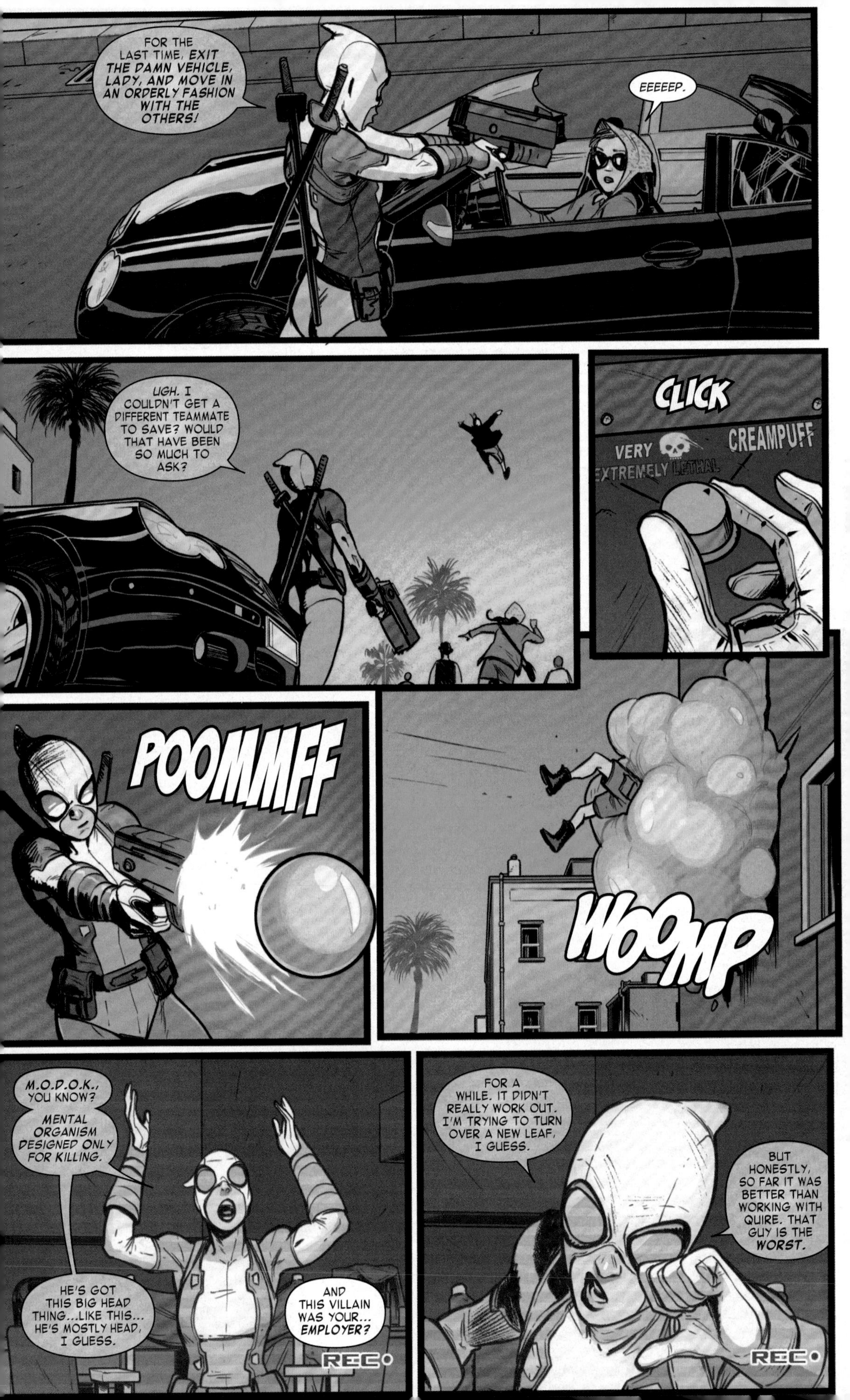
FOR THE LAST TIME, EXIT THE DAMN VEHICLE, LADY, AND MOVE IN AN ORDERLY FASHION WITH THE OTHERS!
EEEEEP.
UGH. I COULDN'T GET A DIFFERENT TEAMMATE TO SAVE? WOULD THAT HAVE BEEN SO MUCH TO ASK?
CLICK
VERY
EXTREMELY LETHAL
CREAMPUFF
POOMMFF
WOOMP
M.O.D.O.K., YOU KNOW?
MENTAL ORGANISM DESIGNED ONLY FOR KILLING.
HE'S GOT THIS BIG HEAD THING...LIKE THIS... HE'S MOSTLY HEAD, I GUESS.
AND THIS VILLAIN WAS YOUR... EMPLOYER?
REC
FOR A WHILE. IT DIDN'T REALLY WORK OUT. I'M TRYING TO TURN OVER A NEW LEAF, I GUESS.
BUT HONESTLY, SO FAR IT WAS BETTER THAN WORKING WITH QUIRE. THAT GUY IS THE WORST.
REC

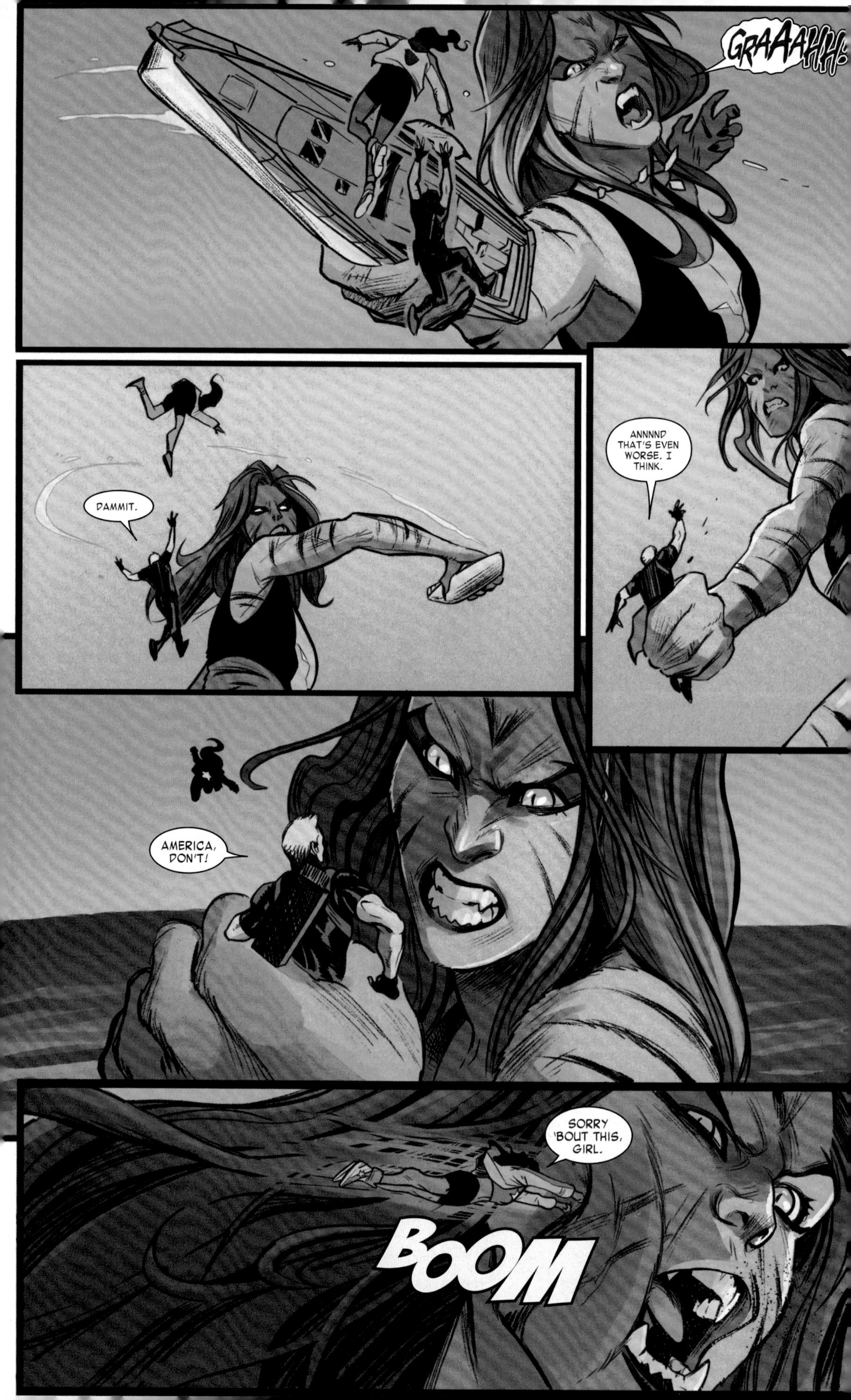
GRAAAHH!
DAMMIT.
ANNNND THAT'S EVEN WORSE. I THINK.
AMERICA, DON'T!
SORRY 'BOUT THIS, GIRL.
BOOM

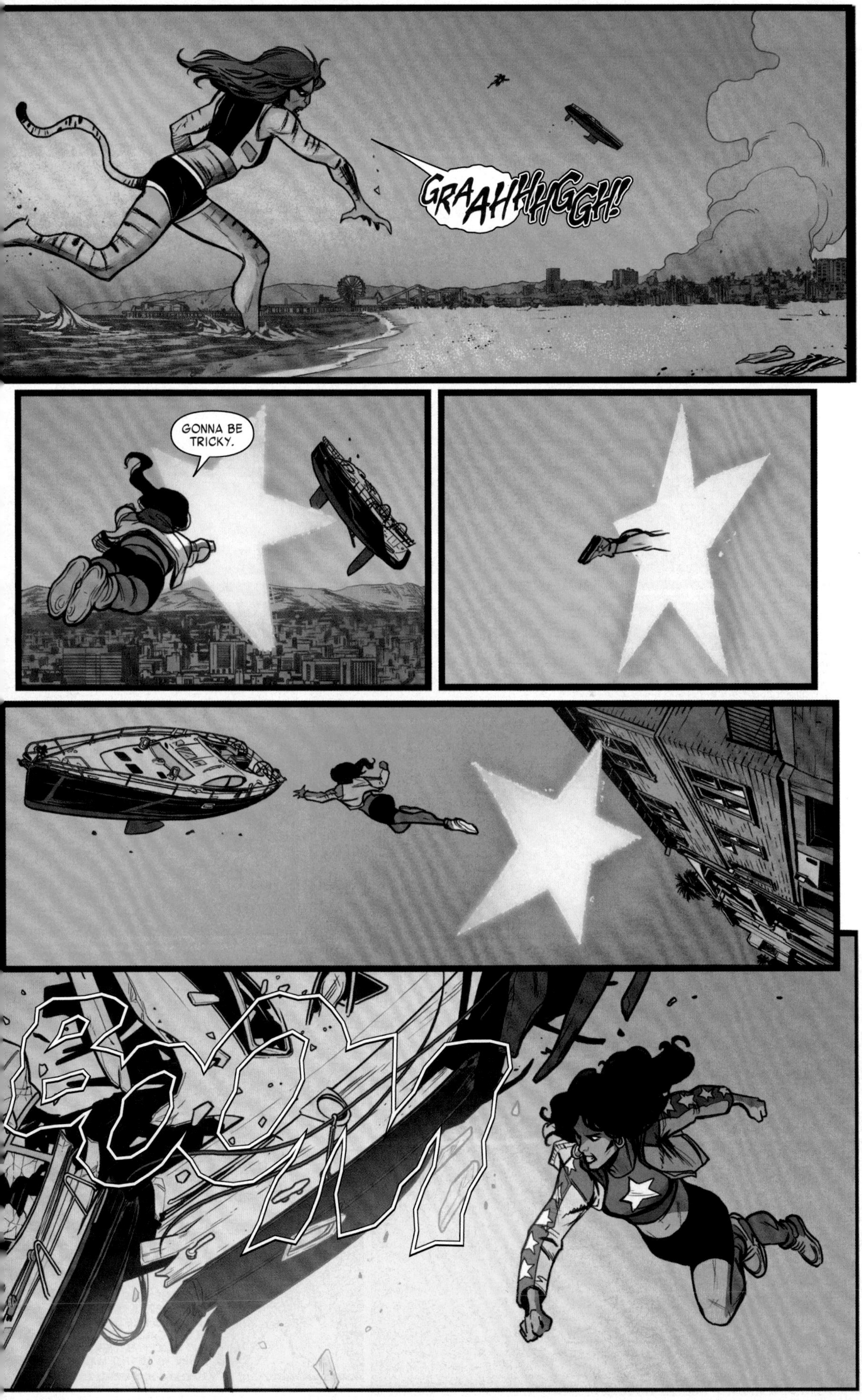
GRAAHHHGGH!
GONNA BE TRICKY.
BOOM

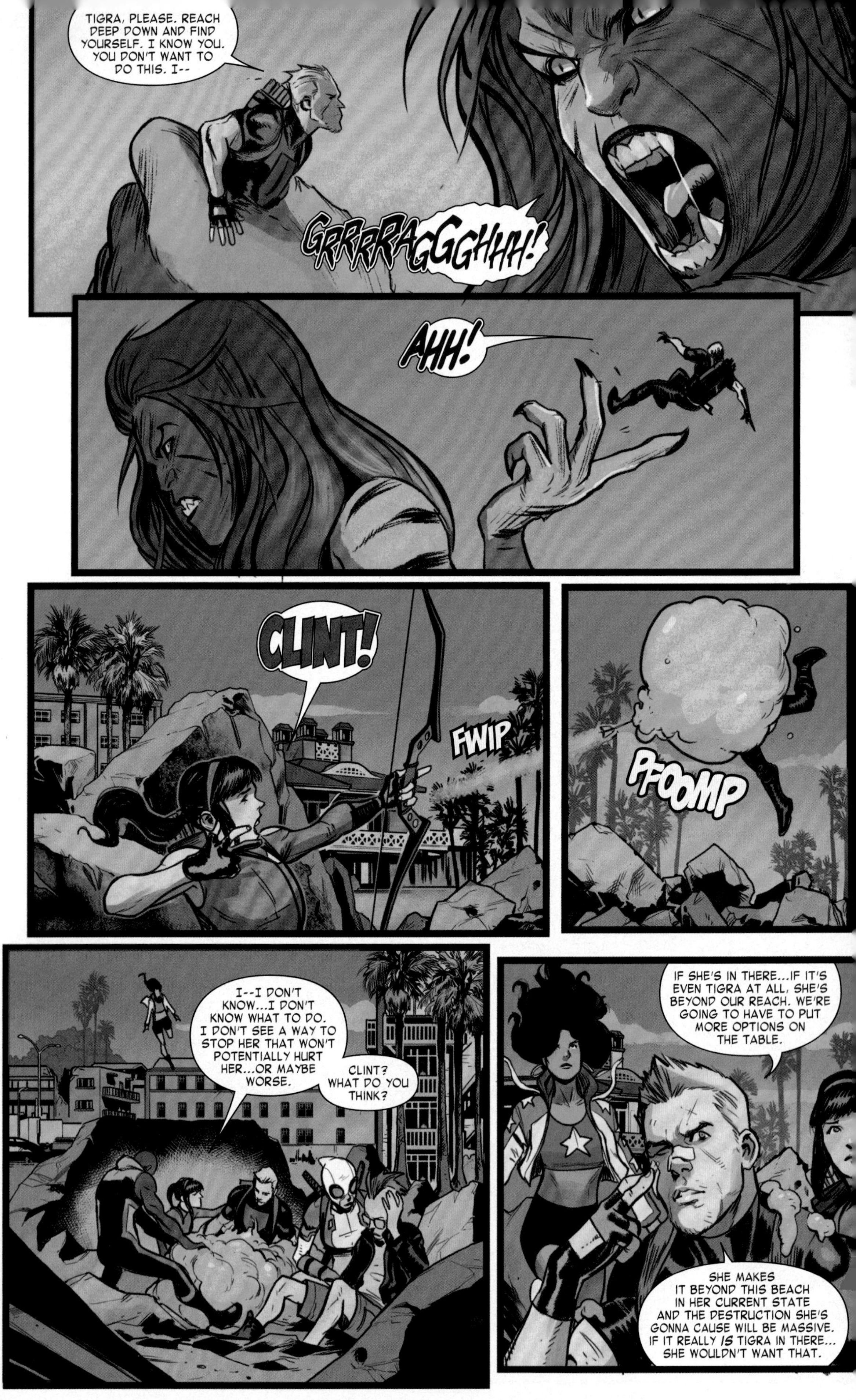
TIGRA, PLEASE. REACH DEEP DOWN AND FIND YOURSELF. I KNOW YOU. YOU DON'T WANT TO DO THIS. I--
GRRRRAGGGHHH!
AHH!
CLINT!
FWIP
PFOOMP
I--I DON'T KNOW...I DON'T KNOW WHAT TO DO. I DON'T SEE A WAY TO STOP HER THAT WON'T POTENTIALLY HURT HER...OR MAYBE WORSE.
CLINT? WHAT DO YOU THINK?
IF SHE'S IN THERE...IF IT'S EVEN TIGRA AT ALL, SHE'S BEYOND OUR REACH. WE'RE GOING TO HAVE TO PUT MORE OPTIONS ON THE TABLE.
SHE MAKES IT BEYOND THIS BEACH IN HER CURRENT STATE AND THE DESTRUCTION SHE'S GONNA CAUSE WILL BE MASSIVE. IF IT REALLY IS TIGRA IN THERE... SHE WOULDN'T WANT THAT.

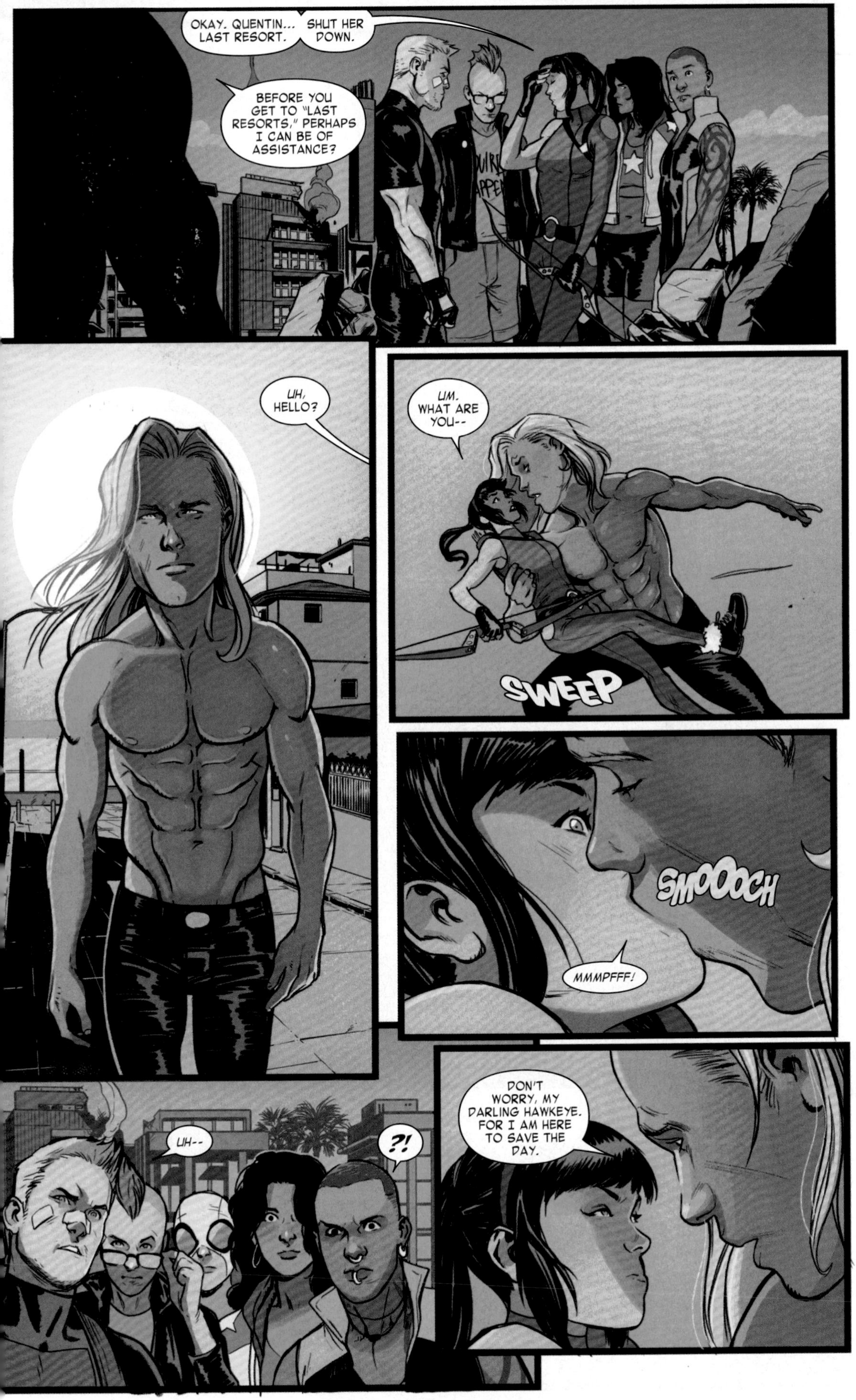
OKAY. QUENTIN... LAST RESORT.
SHUT HER DOWN.
BEFORE YOU GET TO "LAST RESORTS," PERHAPS I CAN BE OF ASSISTANCE?
UH, HELLO?
UM. WHAT ARE YOU--
SWEEP
SMOOOCH
MMMPFFF!
UH--
?!
DON'T WORRY, MY DARLING HAWKEYE. FOR I AM HERE TO SAVE THE DAY.

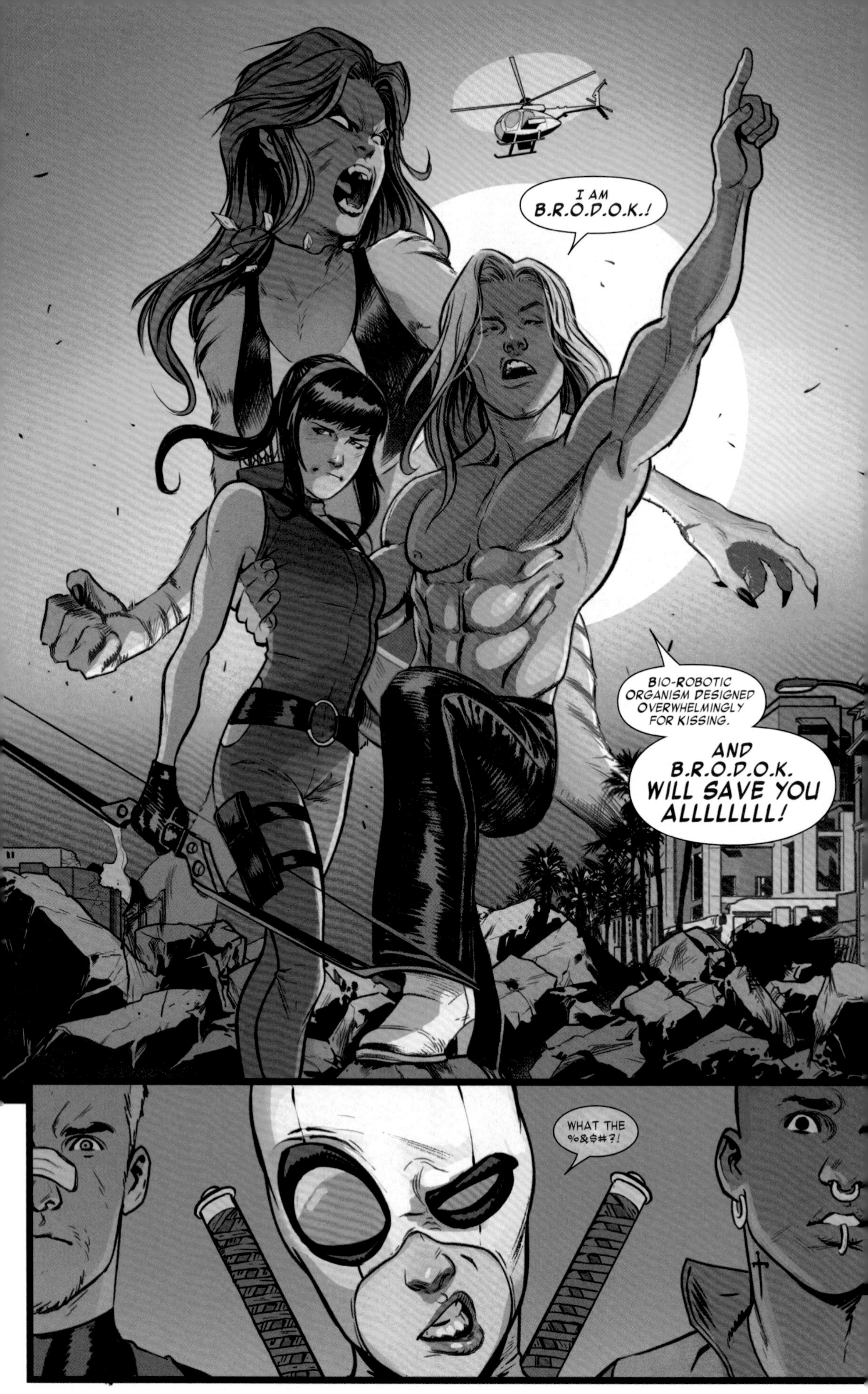
I AM B.R.O.D.O.K.!
BIO-ROBOTIC ORGANISM DESIGNED OVERWHELMINGLY FOR KISSING.
AND B.R.O.D.O.K. WILL SAVE YOU ALLLLLLLL!
WHAT THE %&$#?!

FROM THE KATE BISHOP FILES

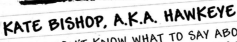

KATE BISHOP, A.K.A. HAWKEYE

WELL, I DON'T KNOW WHAT TO SAY ABOUT MYSELF. I'M ME. I'M AN AWESOME ARCHER AND A MOSTLY AWESOME SEMI-LICENSED PRIVATE EYE. HELLA SCRAPPY IN A FIGHT, EVEN AGAINST GIANT SHARKS WITH LEGS. I CAME FROM MONEY AND PROCEEDED TO CUT ALL TIES TO THAT MONEY...WHICH I MIGHT BE REGRETTING A LITTLE BIT NOW.

SUPPLEMENTAL NOTES:

I SAID I WAS AWESOME ALREADY, RIGHT?

ROLE:

TEAM LEADER, ARROWS, INVESTIGATE-Y STUFF

CLINT BARTON, A.K.A. HAWKEYE

THE OTHER HAWKEYE. OR IS THAT ME? OLYMPIC-LEVEL ATHLETE/ACROBAT WITH EXTENSIVE TRAINING IN HAND-TO-HAND COMBAT AND WEAPONS. ALSO HAPPENS TO BE THE BEST ARCHER ON EARTH. OR ONE OF TWO, AT LEAST. CLINT IS ALSO THE FOUNDER OF THE ORIGINAL WEST COAST AVENGERS, MY MENTOR AND--ALL RIGHT, FINE--MY FAMILY.

SUPPLEMENTAL NOTES:

I'M HOPING CLINT CAN GUIDE ME THROUGH THIS PROCESS AND MINIMIZE MY SCREWUPS.

ROLE:

CO-LEADER, SHOOTS ARROWS REAL GOOD

GWENDOLYN POOLE, A.K.A. GWENPOOL

GWEN IS STILL KIND OF A MYSTERY TO ME. I'M NOT REALLY SURE WHAT HER POWERS ARE...IF ANY. SHE'S GOT GOOD INSTINCTS AND SEEMS TO KNOW EVERYTHING ABOUT WEAPONS AND OTHER SUPER HEROES...BUT SHE MIGHT BE CRAZY? TBD?

SUPPLEMENTAL NOTES:

I THINK SHE'S DESPERATELY LOOKING FOR REDEMPTION, OR MAYBE A PLACE TO FIT IN? BUT THAT'S OKAY BY ME--LOTS OF PEOPLE COME TO L.A. SEARCHING FOR SOMETHING, WHY NOT HER?

ROLE:

TOTAL WILD CARD

QUENTIN QUIRE, A.K.A. KID OMEGA

I HAVE NO IDEA WHY HE LEFT THE X-MEN...OR THE X-WHATEVER-IT-WAS. HE'S KEEPING THAT INFORMATION PRETTY CLOSE TO THE VEST. BUT HE'S GOT SOME OMEGA-LEVEL PSYCHIC POWERS THAT, AS A LEADER OF A TEAM, ARE HARD TO TURN DOWN. I'M ALSO NOT SURE HE'D GO AWAY IF I TOLD HIM TO SO I'M JUST GONNA ROLL WITH IT AND HOPE IT DOESN'T GO BAD.

SUPPLEMENTAL NOTES:

SO FAR HE'S THE ONLY PERSON THAT'S ACTUALLY EXCITED ABOUT THE TV CAMERAS, WHICH IS... WORRYING.

ROLE:

TELEPATHIC DRAMA QUEEN

AMERICA CHAVEZ

WHEN YOU'RE FORMING A RAD NEW SUPER HERO TEAM, YOUR FIRST CALL IS OBVIOUSLY YOUR BFF. DOESN'T HURT WHEN YOUR BEST FRIEND IS INVULNERABLE, FLIES, PUNCHES PEOPLE INTO LITERAL STARDUST AND CAN KICK OPEN DIMENSIONAL PORTALS. ALTHOUGH, BEING YOUR BEST FRIEND'S BOSS CAN MAKE THINGS SUPER AWKWARD AT BRUNCH.

SUPPLEMENTAL NOTES:

IT'S NICE TO HAVE A BEST FRIEND WHO CAN KICK PEOPLE INTO THE SUN. I'M NEVER GONNA GET OVER HOW COOL THAT IS.

ROLE:

BFF AND FLYING MUSCLE WHO TELEPORTS

JOHNNY WATTS, A.K.A. FUSE

JOHNNY IS AS GREEN AS CAN BE, BUT HE'S GOOD AND KIND AND I TRUST HIM. PLUS HE CAN TURN INTO ANY MATERIAL HE TOUCHES AND GET THE POWER/STRENGTH/DURABILITY OF SAID MATERIAL. IT'S KINDA LIKE HE'S THAT SWORD IN *HARRY POTTER* THAT ONLY TAKES IN THAT WHICH MAKES IT STRONGER. WE SHOULD HAVE JUST NAMED HIM GRYFFINDOR. ALTHOUGH HUFFLEPUFF IS FUNNIER.

SUPPLEMENTAL NOTES:

NEW OFFICIAL NICKNAME: HUFFLEPUFF

ROLE:

INVULNERABLE MUSCLE WHO'S ALSO AN ADORABLE HUFFLEPUFF

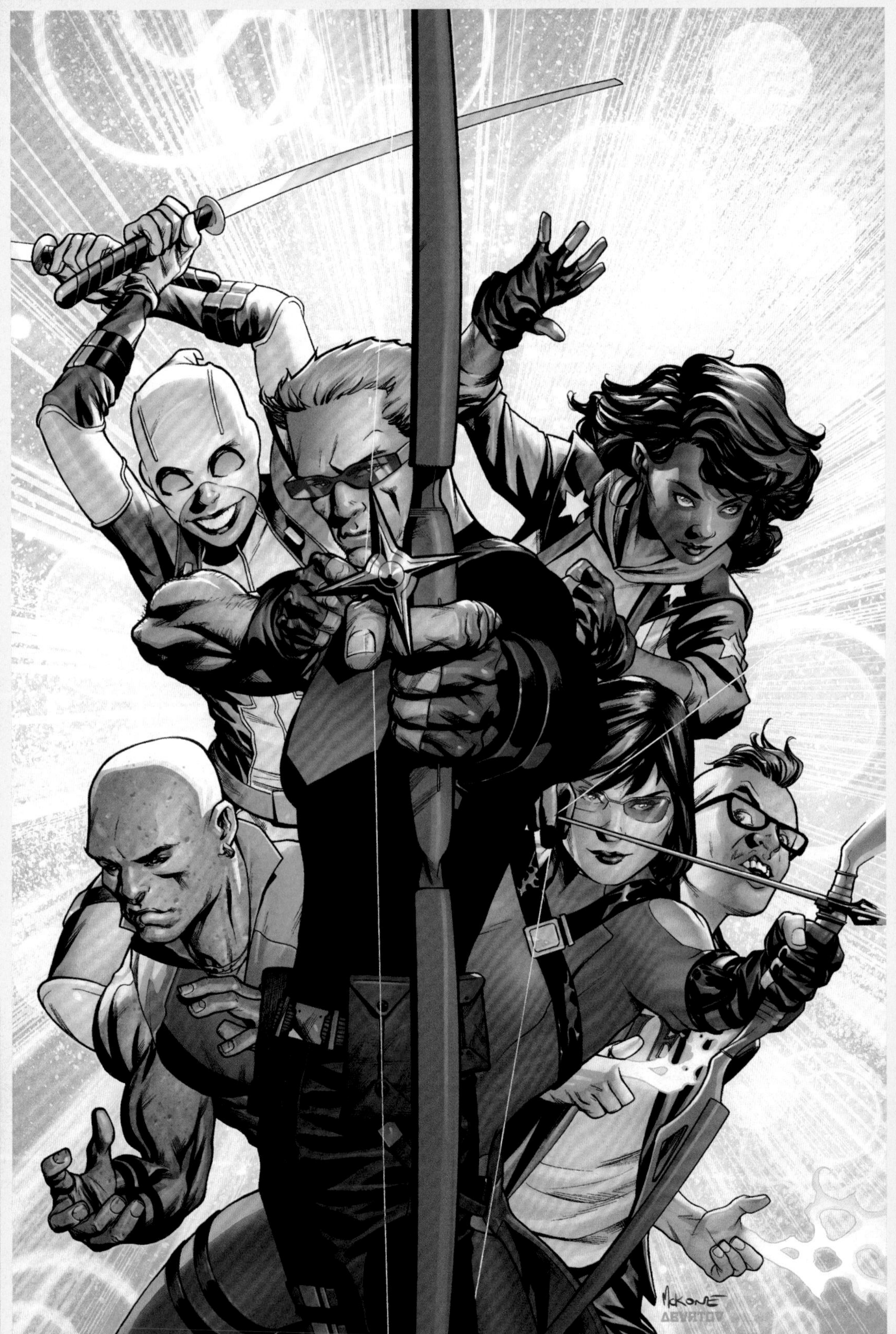

#1 VARIANT BY MIKE McKONE & JESUS ABURTOV

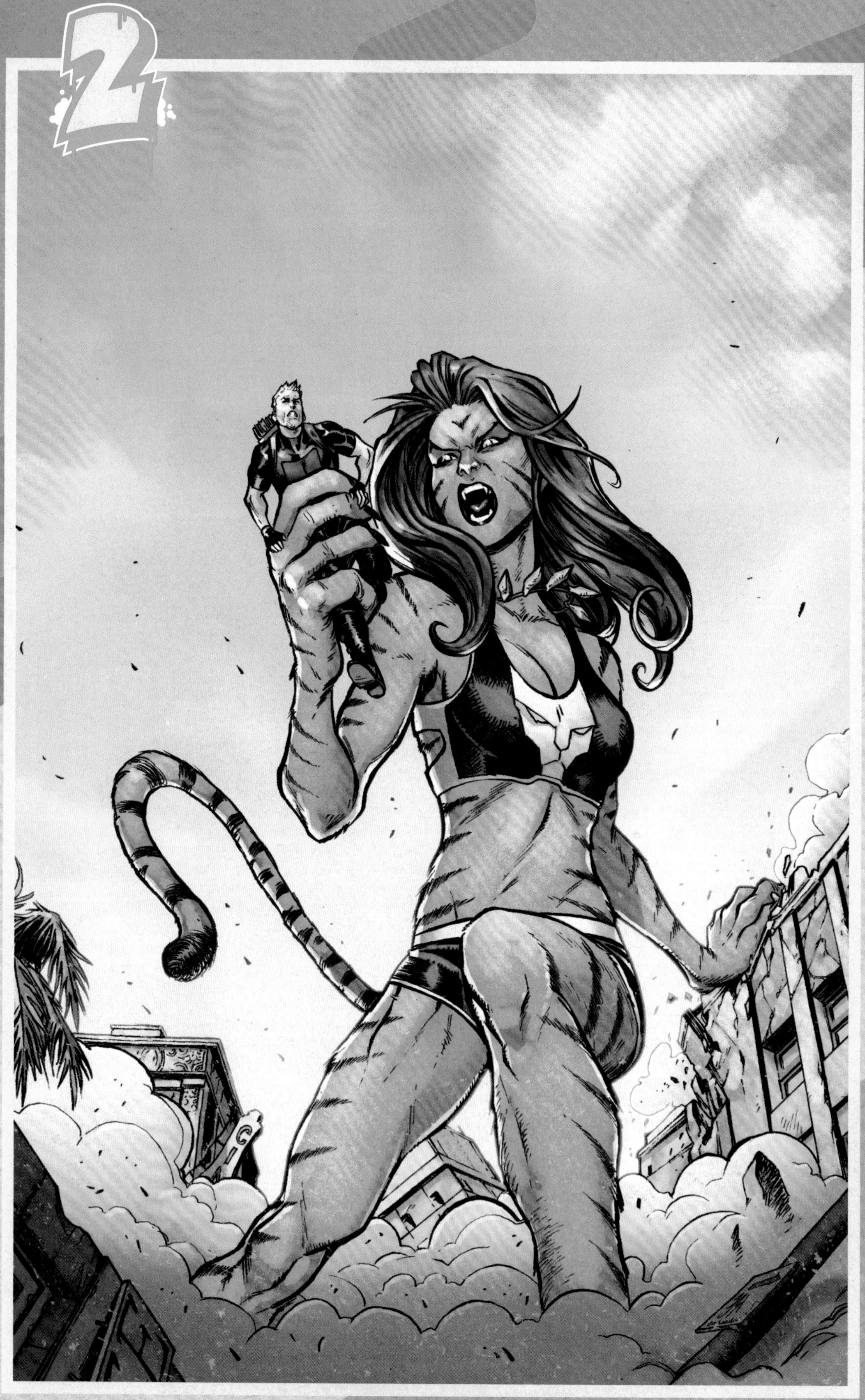
2

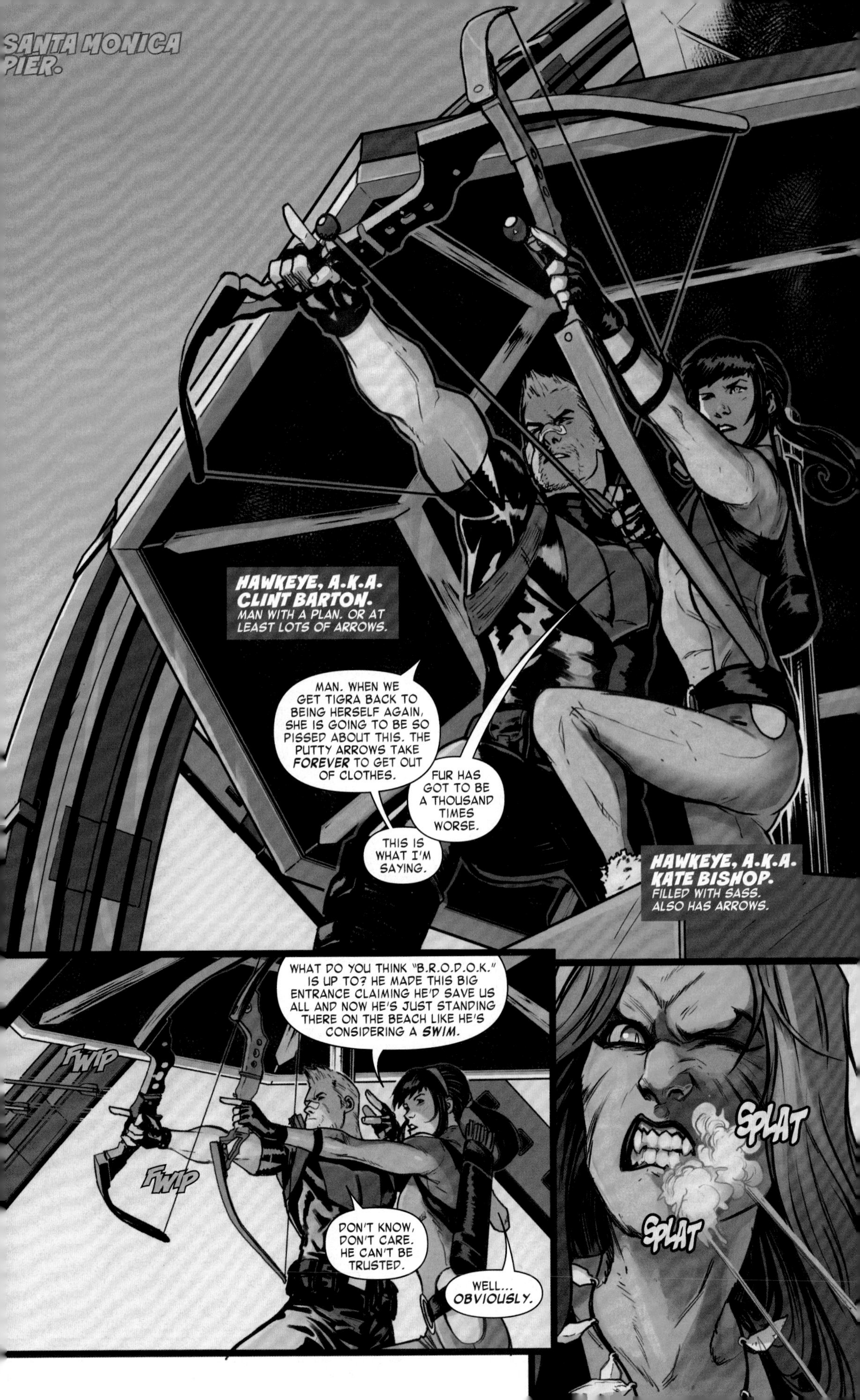
SANTA MONICA PIER.
HAWKEYE, A.K.A. CLINT BARTON. MAN WITH A PLAN. OR AT LEAST LOTS OF ARROWS.
MAN. WHEN WE GET TIGRA BACK TO BEING HERSELF AGAIN, SHE IS GOING TO BE SO PISSED ABOUT THIS. THE PUTTY ARROWS TAKE FOREVER TO GET OUT OF CLOTHES.
FUR HAS GOT TO BE A THOUSAND TIMES WORSE.
THIS IS WHAT I'M SAYING.
HAWKEYE, A.K.A. KATE BISHOP. FILLED WITH SASS. ALSO HAS ARROWS.
WHAT DO YOU THINK "B.R.O.D.O.K." IS UP TO? HE MADE THIS BIG ENTRANCE CLAIMING HE'D SAVE US ALL AND NOW HE'S JUST STANDING THERE ON THE BEACH LIKE HE'S CONSIDERING A SWIM.
FWIP
FWIP
DON'T KNOW, DON'T CARE. HE CAN'T BE TRUSTED.
WELL... OBVIOUSLY.
SPLAT
SPLAT

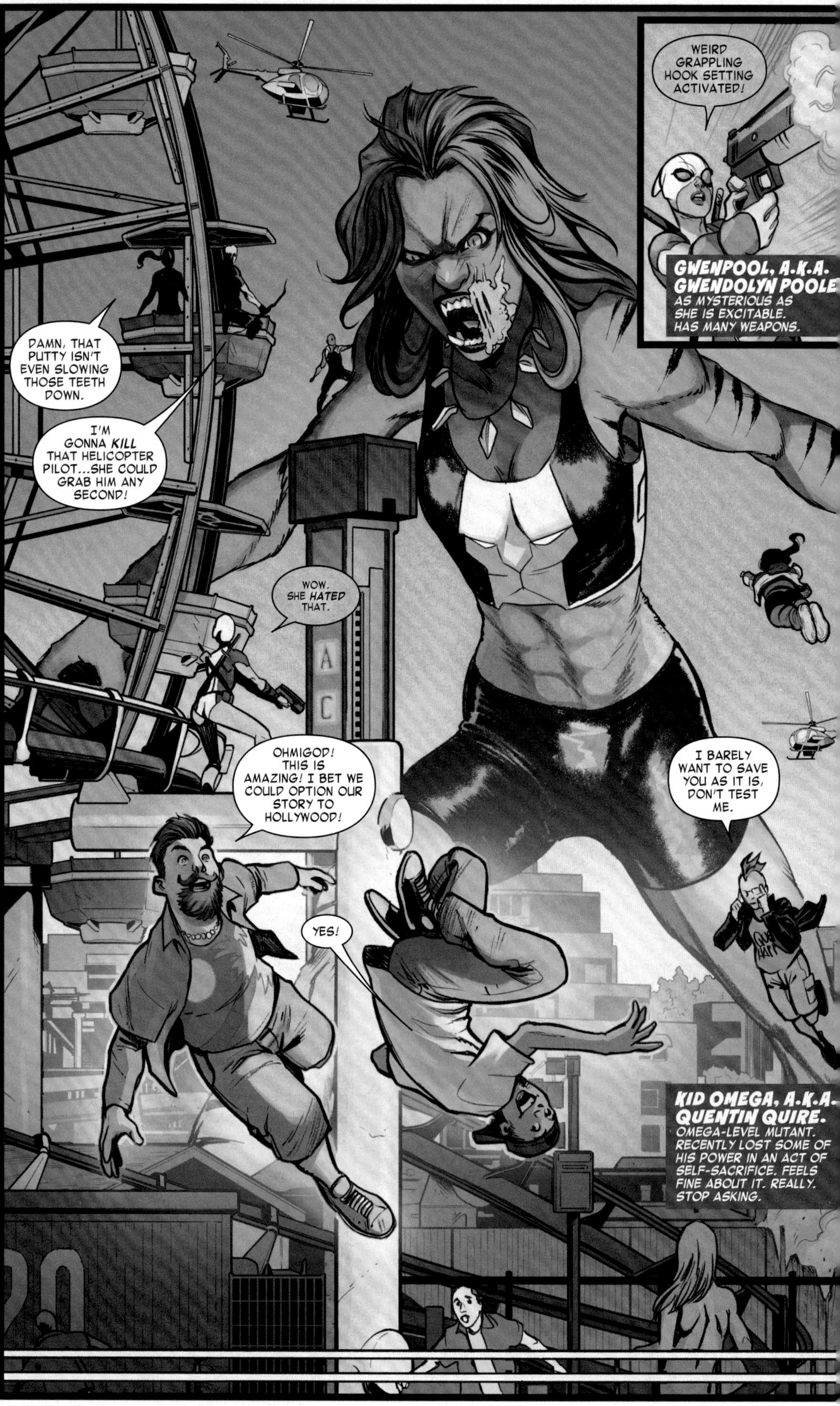
WEIRD GRAPPLING HOOK SETTING ACTIVATED!
GWENPOOL, A.K.A. GWENDOLYN POOLE
AS MYSTERIOUS AS SHE IS EXCITABLE. HAS MANY WEAPONS.
DAMN, THAT PUTTY ISN'T EVEN SLOWING THOSE TEETH DOWN.
I'M GONNA KILL THAT HELICOPTER PILOT...SHE COULD GRAB HIM ANY SECOND!
WOW. SHE HATED THAT.
OHMIGOD! THIS IS AMAZING! I BET WE COULD OPTION OUR STORY TO HOLLYWOOD!
I BARELY WANT TO SAVE YOU AS IT IS, DON'T TEST ME.
YES!
KID OMEGA, A.K.A. QUENTIN QUIRE.
OMEGA-LEVEL MUTANT. RECENTLY LOST SOME OF HIS POWER IN AN ACT OF SELF-SACRIFICE. FEELS FINE ABOUT IT. REALLY. STOP ASKING.

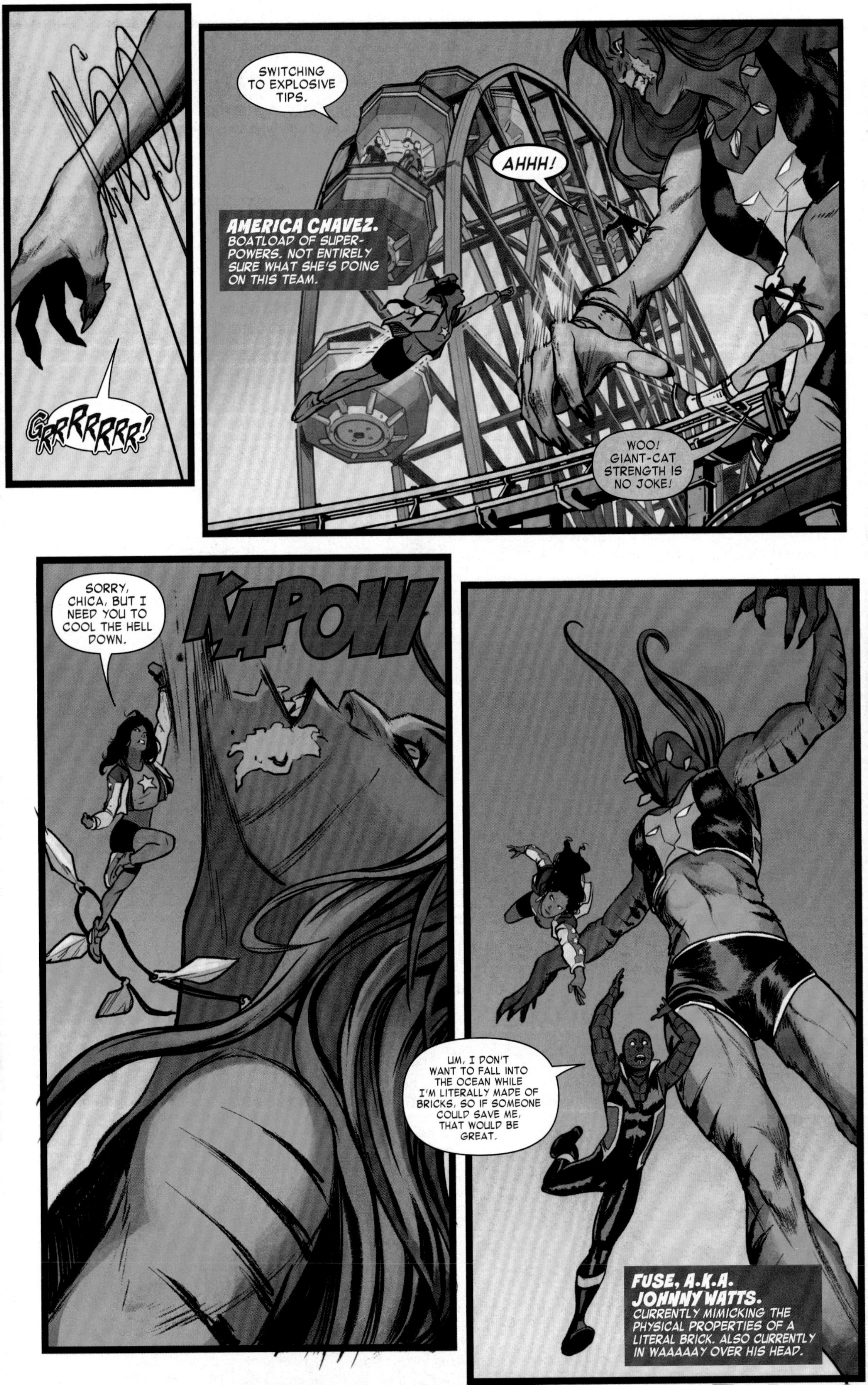
GRRRRRRR!
SWITCHING TO EXPLOSIVE TIPS.
AMERICA CHAVEZ.
BOATLOAD OF SUPER-POWERS. NOT ENTIRELY SURE WHAT SHE'S DOING ON THIS TEAM.
AHHH!
WOO! GIANT-CAT STRENGTH IS NO JOKE!
SORRY, CHICA, BUT I NEED YOU TO COOL THE HELL DOWN.
KAPOW
UM, I DON'T WANT TO FALL INTO THE OCEAN WHILE I'M LITERALLY MADE OF BRICKS, SO IF SOMEONE COULD SAVE ME, THAT WOULD BE GREAT.
FUSE, A.K.A. JOHNNY WATTS.
CURRENTLY MIMICKING THE PHYSICAL PROPERTIES OF A LITERAL BRICK. ALSO CURRENTLY IN WAAAAAY OVER HIS HEAD.

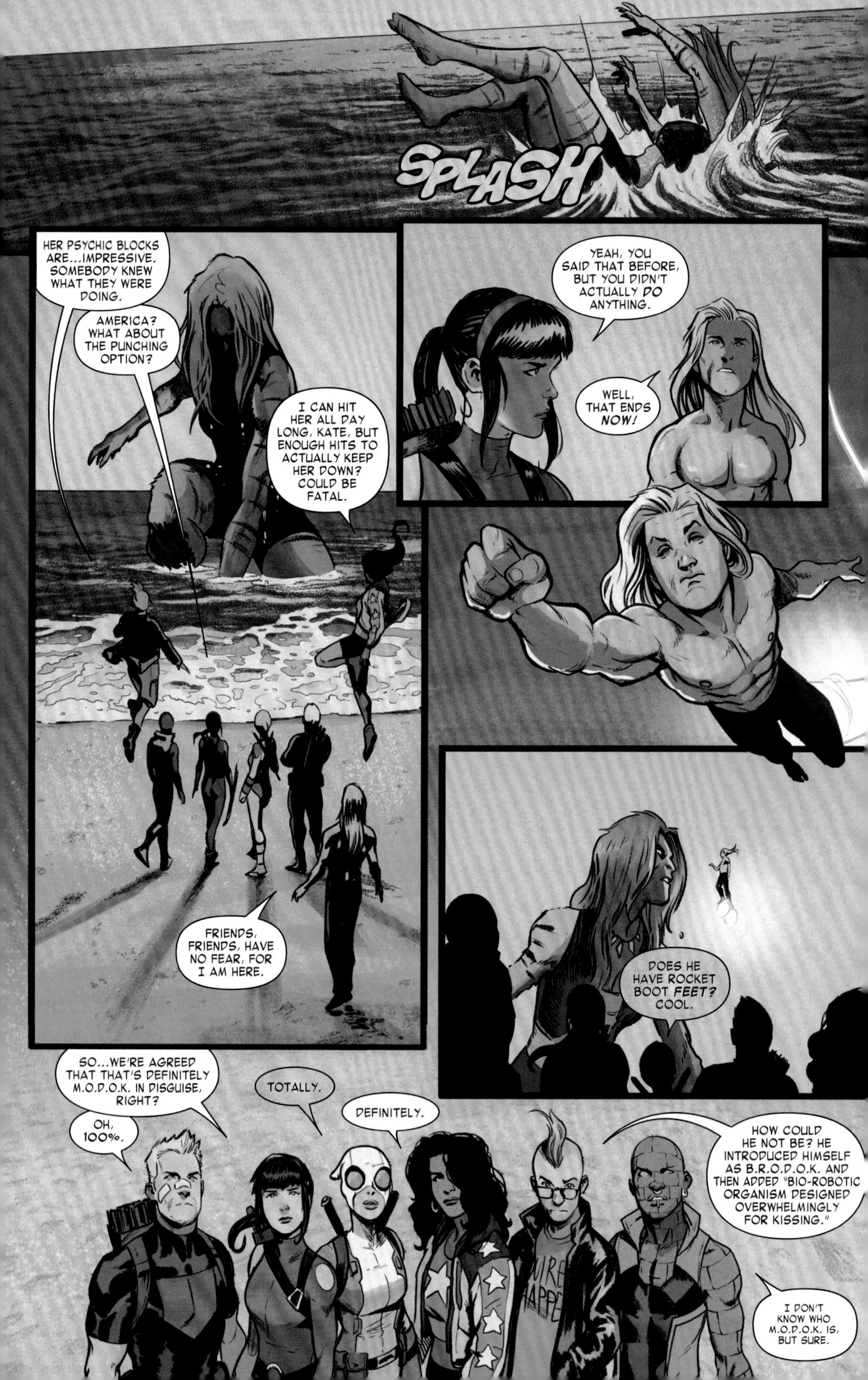
SPLASH
HER PSYCHIC BLOCKS ARE...IMPRESSIVE. SOMEBODY KNEW WHAT THEY WERE DOING.
AMERICA? WHAT ABOUT THE PUNCHING OPTION?
I CAN HIT HER ALL DAY LONG, KATE, BUT ENOUGH HITS TO ACTUALLY KEEP HER DOWN? COULD BE FATAL.
FRIENDS, FRIENDS, HAVE NO FEAR, FOR I AM HERE.
YEAH, YOU SAID THAT BEFORE, BUT YOU DIDN'T ACTUALLY DO ANYTHING.
WELL, THAT ENDS NOW!
DOES HE HAVE ROCKET BOOT FEET? COOL.
SO...WE'RE AGREED THAT THAT'S DEFINITELY M.O.D.O.K. IN DISGUISE, RIGHT?
OH, 100%.
TOTALLY.
DEFINITELY.
HOW COULD HE NOT BE? HE INTRODUCED HIMSELF AS B.R.O.D.O.K. AND THEN ADDED "BIO-ROBOTIC ORGANISM DESIGNED OVERWHELMINGLY FOR KISSING."
I DON'T KNOW WHO M.O.D.O.K. IS, BUT SURE.

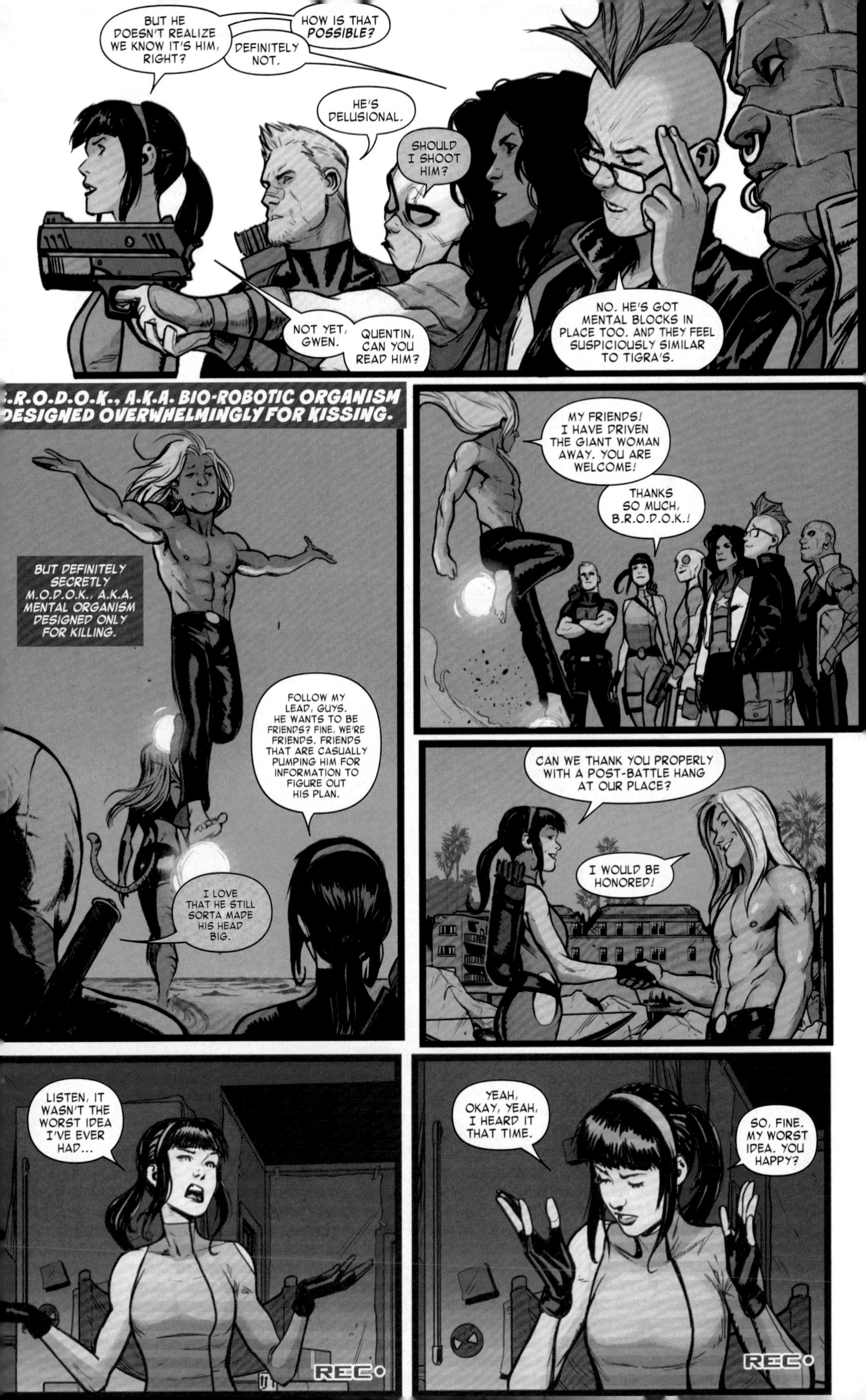

BUT HE DOESN'T REALIZE WE KNOW IT'S HIM, RIGHT?
HOW IS THAT POSSIBLE?
DEFINITELY NOT.
HE'S DELUSIONAL.
SHOULD I SHOOT HIM?
NOT YET, GWEN.
QUENTIN, CAN YOU READ HIM?
NO. HE'S GOT MENTAL BLOCKS IN PLACE TOO. AND THEY FEEL SUSPICIOUSLY SIMILAR TO TIGRA'S.
.R.O.D.O.K., A.K.A. BIO-ROBOTIC ORGANISM DESIGNED OVERWHELMINGLY FOR KISSING.
BUT DEFINITELY SECRETLY M.O.D.O.K., A.K.A. MENTAL ORGANISM DESIGNED ONLY FOR KILLING.
FOLLOW MY LEAD, GUYS. HE WANTS TO BE FRIENDS? FINE, WE'RE FRIENDS. FRIENDS THAT ARE CASUALLY PUMPING HIM FOR INFORMATION TO FIGURE OUT HIS PLAN.
I LOVE THAT HE STILL SORTA MADE HIS HEAD BIG.
MY FRIENDS! I HAVE DRIVEN THE GIANT WOMAN AWAY. YOU ARE WELCOME!
THANKS SO MUCH, B.R.O.D.O.K.!
CAN WE THANK YOU PROPERLY WITH A POST-BATTLE HANG AT OUR PLACE?
I WOULD BE HONORED!
LISTEN, IT WASN'T THE WORST IDEA I'VE EVER HAD...
REC
YEAH, OKAY, YEAH, I HEARD IT THAT TIME.
SO, FINE. MY WORST IDEA. YOU HAPPY?
REC

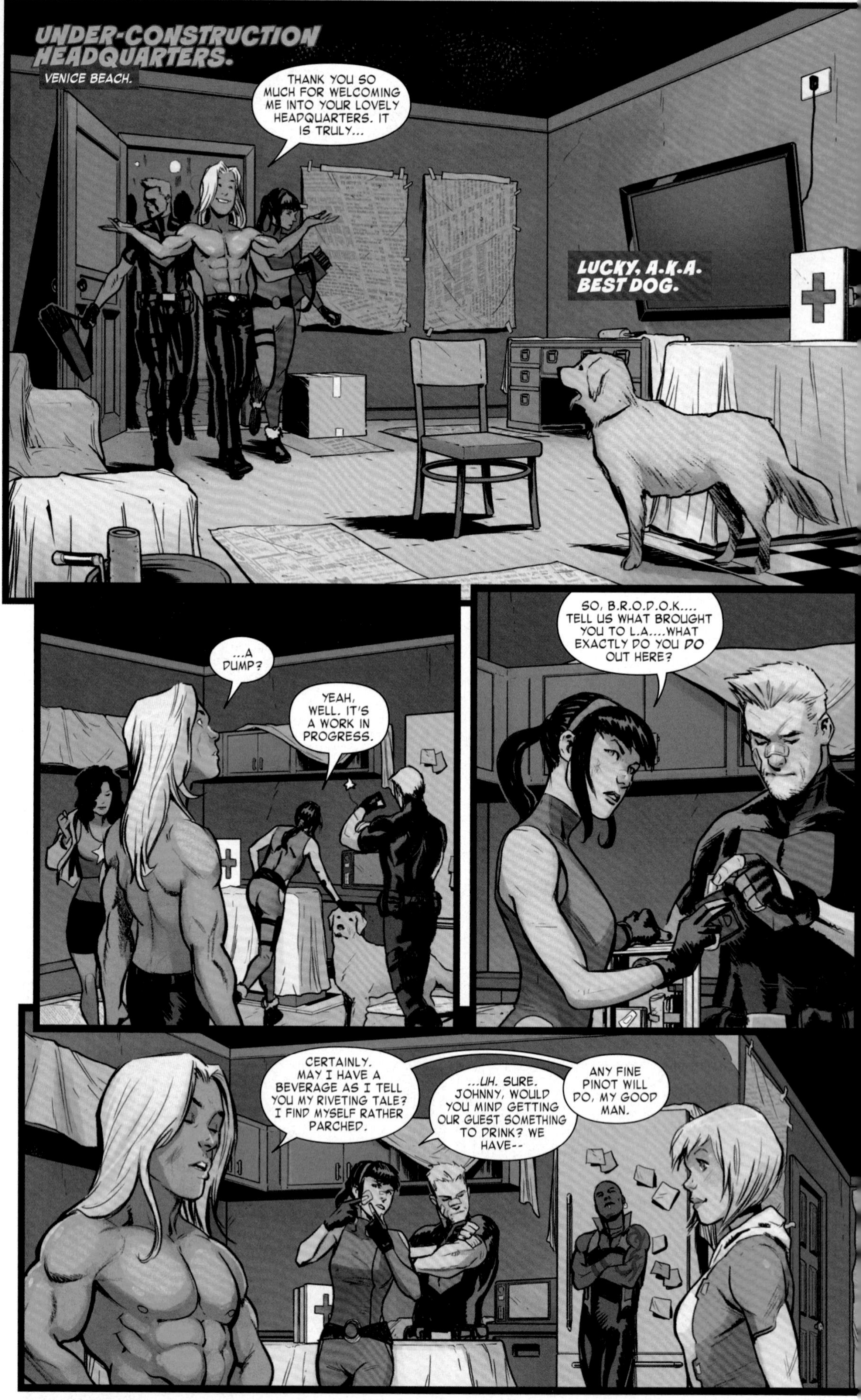
UNDER-CONSTRUCTION HEADQUARTERS.
VENICE BEACH.
THANK YOU SO MUCH FOR WELCOMING ME INTO YOUR LOVELY HEADQUARTERS. IT IS TRULY...
LUCKY, A.K.A. BEST DOG.
...A DUMP?
YEAH, WELL. IT'S A WORK IN PROGRESS.
SO, B.R.O.D.O.K.... TELL US WHAT BROUGHT YOU TO L.A.... WHAT EXACTLY DO YOU DO OUT HERE?
CERTAINLY. MAY I HAVE A BEVERAGE AS I TELL YOU MY RIVETING TALE? I FIND MYSELF RATHER PARCHED.
...UH. SURE. JOHNNY, WOULD YOU MIND GETTING OUR GUEST SOMETHING TO DRINK? WE HAVE--
ANY FINE PINOT WILL DO, MY GOOD MAN.

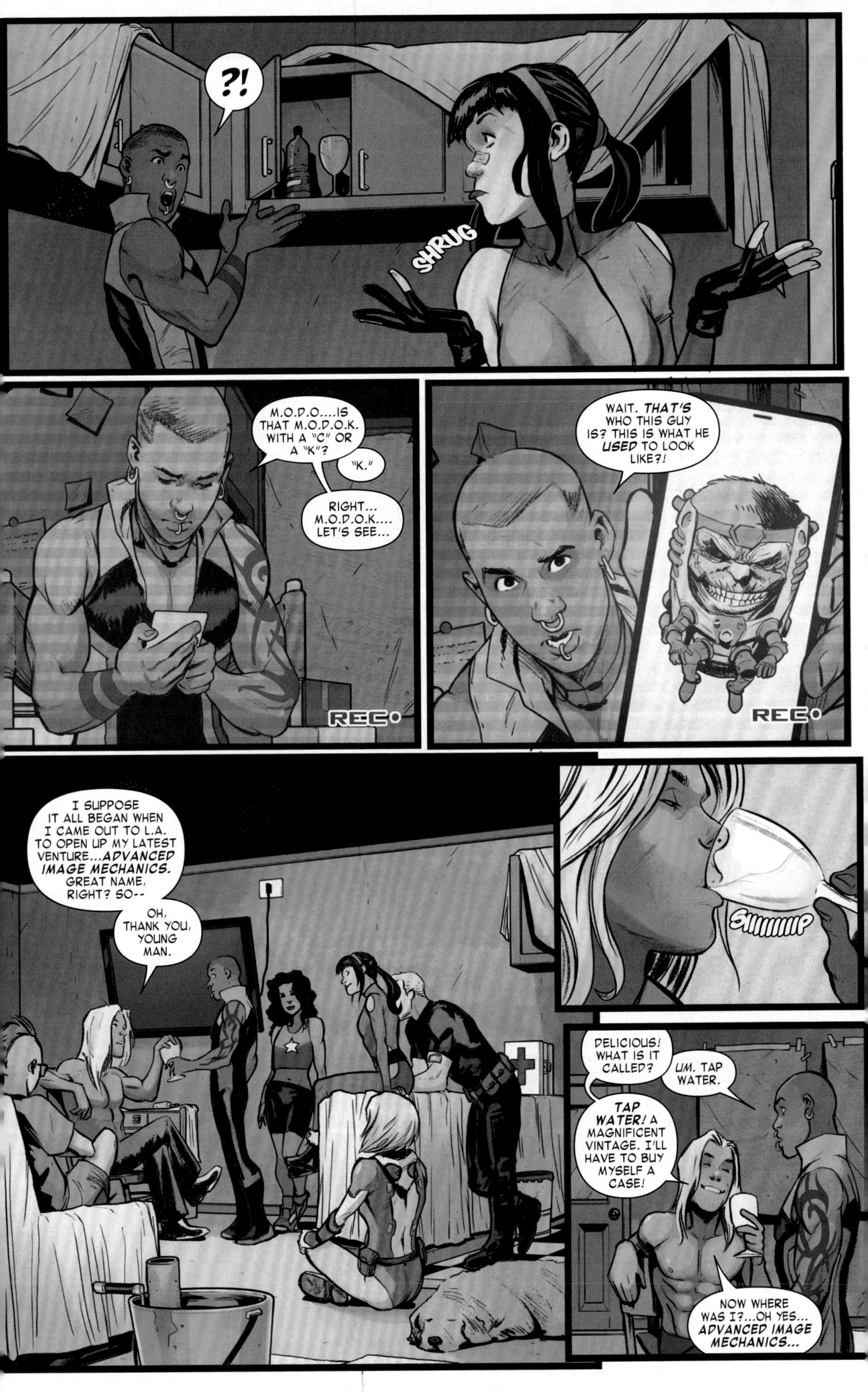

?!
SHRUG
M.O.D.O....IS THAT M.O.D.O.K. WITH A "C" OR A "K"?
"K."
RIGHT... M.O.D.O.K.... LET'S SEE...
REC
WAIT. *THAT'S* WHO THIS GUY IS? THIS IS WHAT HE *USED* TO LOOK LIKE?!
REC
I SUPPOSE IT ALL BEGAN WHEN I CAME OUT TO L.A. TO OPEN UP MY LATEST VENTURE...*ADVANCED IMAGE MECHANICS.* GREAT NAME, RIGHT? SO--
OH, THANK YOU, YOUNG MAN.
SHIIIIIIIP
DELICIOUS! WHAT IS IT CALLED?
UM. TAP WATER.
TAP WATER! A MAGNIFICENT VINTAGE. I'LL HAVE TO BUY MYSELF A CASE!
NOW WHERE WAS I?...OH YES... *ADVANCED IMAGE MECHANICS...*

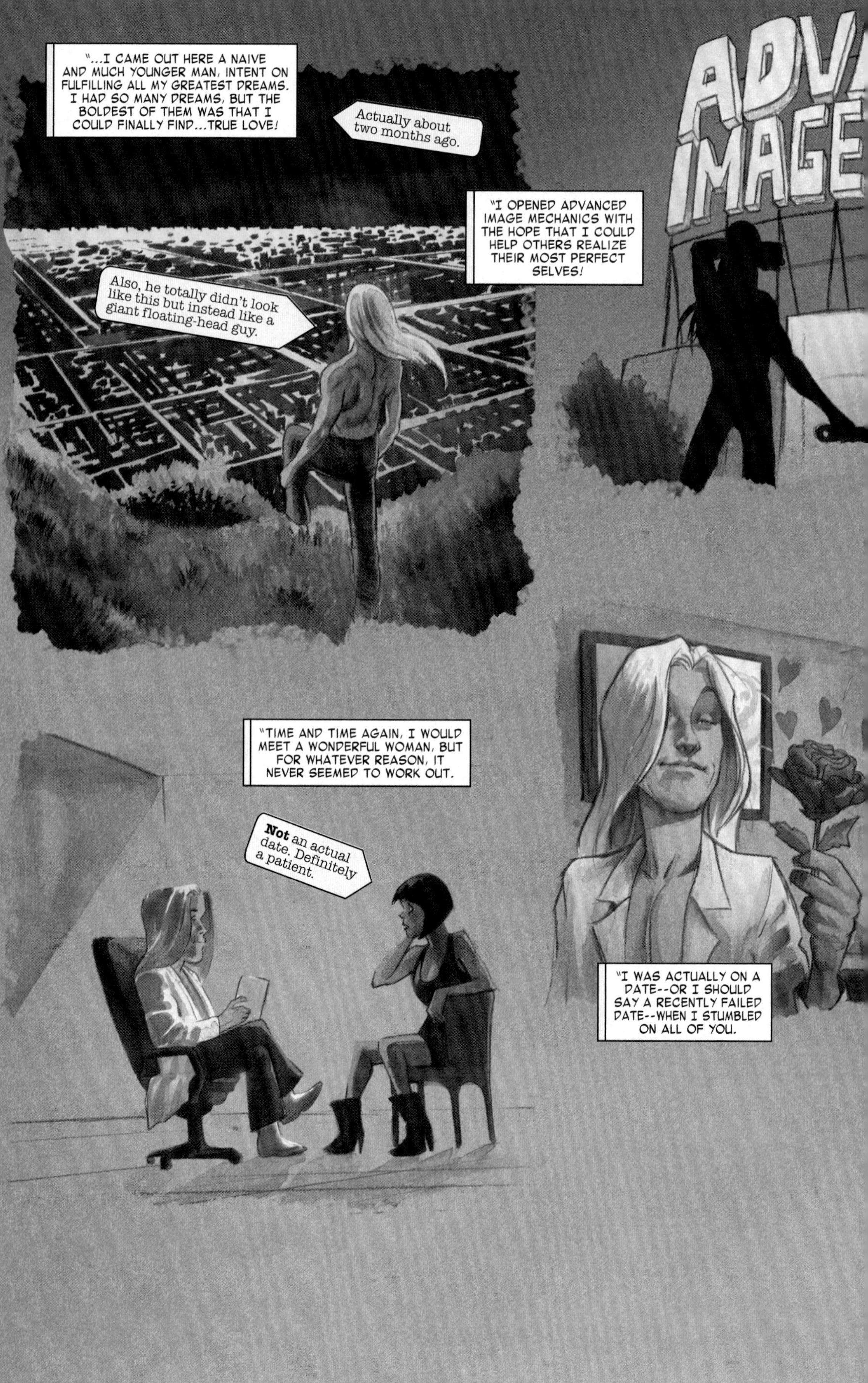
"...I CAME OUT HERE A NAIVE AND MUCH YOUNGER MAN, INTENT ON FULFILLING ALL MY GREATEST DREAMS. I HAD SO MANY DREAMS, BUT THE BOLDEST OF THEM WAS THAT I COULD FINALLY FIND...TRUE LOVE!
Actually about two months ago.
Also, he totally didn't look like this but instead like a giant floating-head guy.
"I OPENED ADVANCED IMAGE MECHANICS WITH THE HOPE THAT I COULD HELP OTHERS REALIZE THEIR MOST PERFECT SELVES!
ADV
IMAGE
"TIME AND TIME AGAIN, I WOULD MEET A WONDERFUL WOMAN, BUT FOR WHATEVER REASON, IT NEVER SEEMED TO WORK OUT.
Not an actual date. Definitely a patient.
"I WAS ACTUALLY ON A DATE--OR I SHOULD SAY A RECENTLY FAILED DATE--WHEN I STUMBLED ON ALL OF YOU.

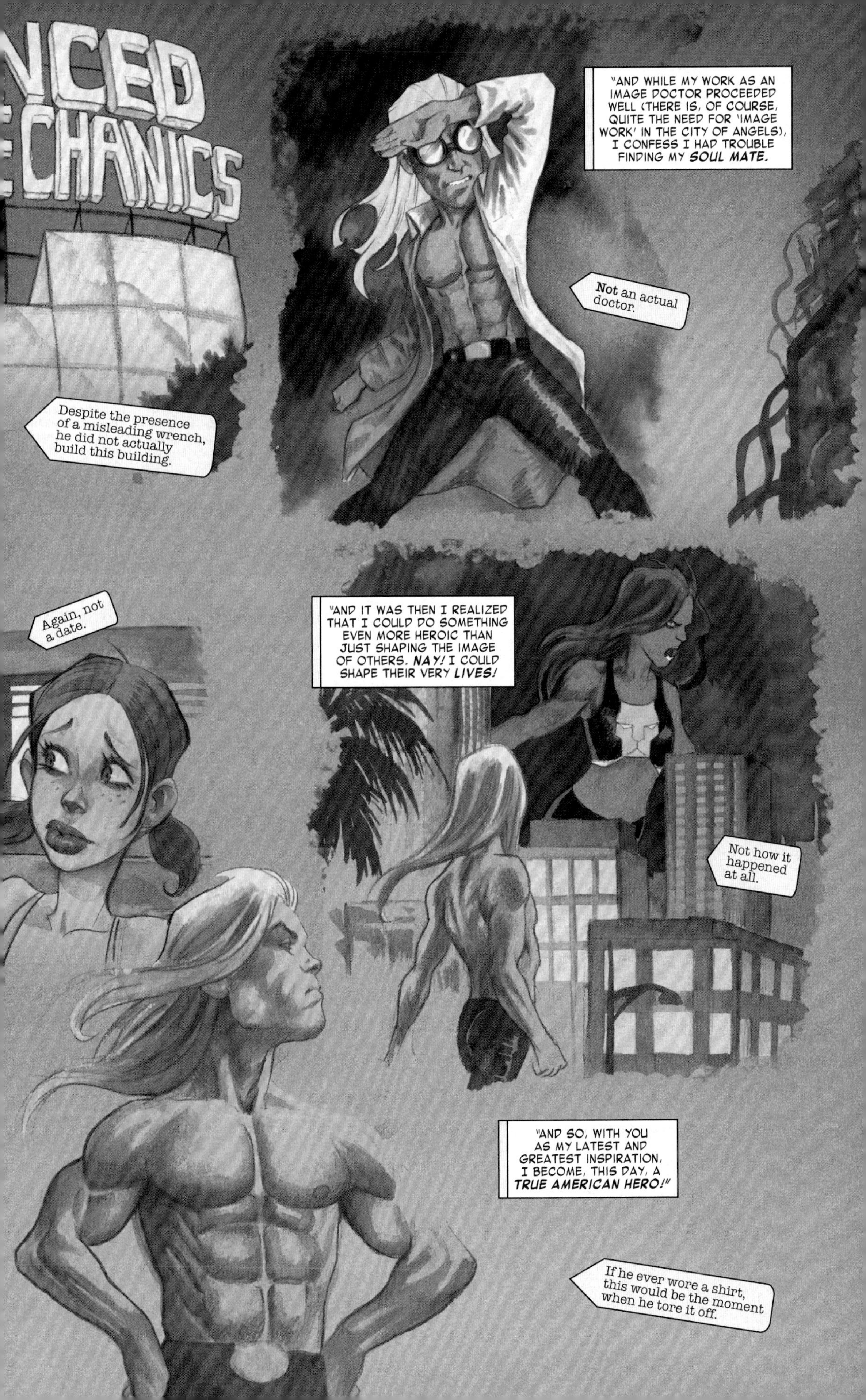
NCED
ECHANICS
Despite the presence of a misleading wrench, he did not actually build this building.
"AND WHILE MY WORK AS AN IMAGE DOCTOR PROCEEDED WELL (THERE IS, OF COURSE, QUITE THE NEED FOR 'IMAGE WORK' IN THE CITY OF ANGELS), I CONFESS I HAD TROUBLE FINDING MY SOUL MATE.
Not an actual doctor.
Again, not a date.
"AND IT WAS THEN I REALIZED THAT I COULD DO SOMETHING EVEN MORE HEROIC THAN JUST SHAPING THE IMAGE OF OTHERS. NAY! I COULD SHAPE THEIR VERY LIVES!
Not how it happened at all.
"AND SO, WITH YOU AS MY LATEST AND GREATEST INSPIRATION, I BECOME, THIS DAY, A TRUE AMERICAN HERO!"
If he ever wore a shirt, this would be the moment when he tore it off.

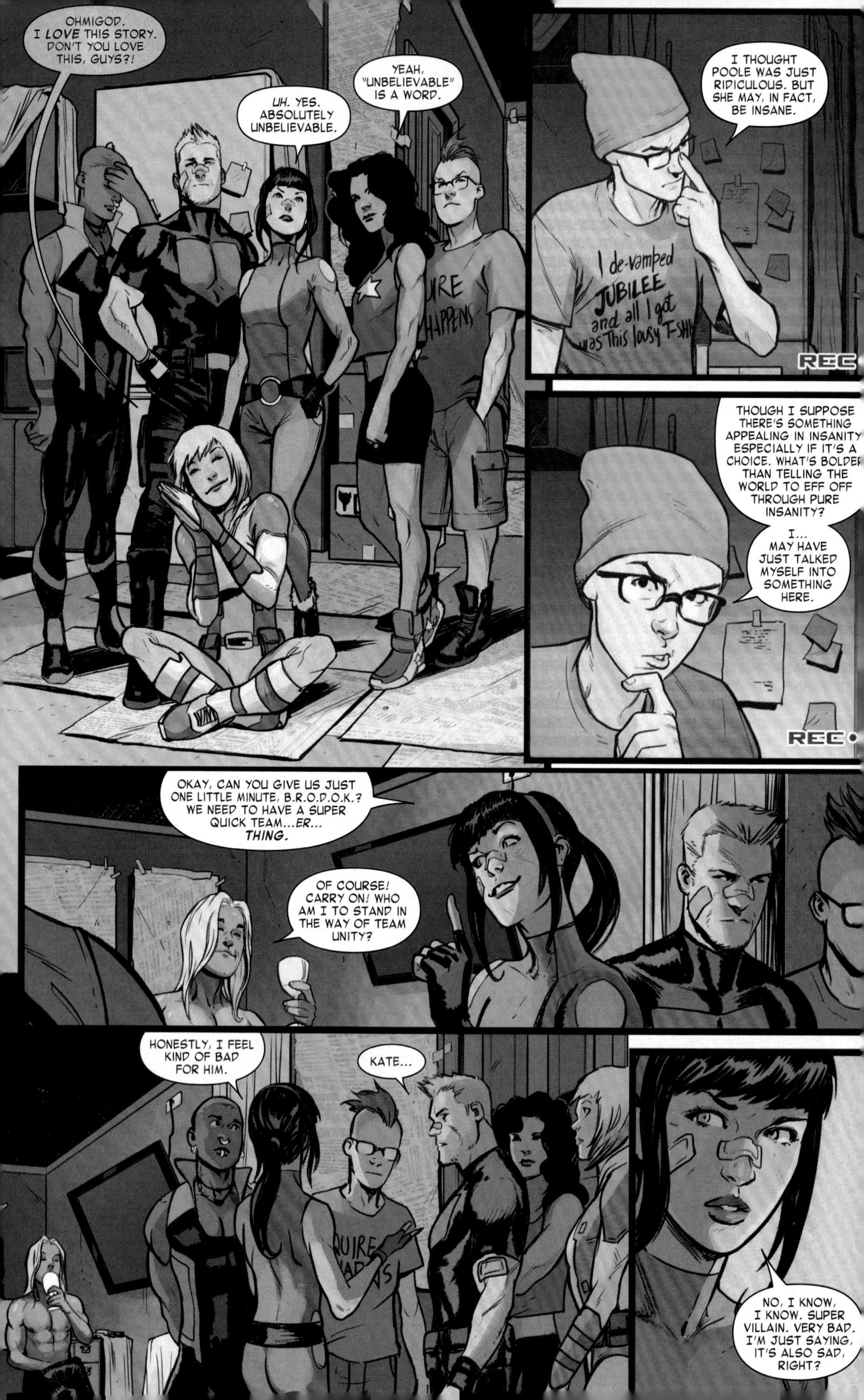
OHMIGOD. I LOVE THIS STORY. DON'T YOU LOVE THIS, GUYS?!
UH. YES. ABSOLUTELY UNBELIEVABLE.
YEAH, "UNBELIEVABLE" IS A WORD.
I THOUGHT POOLE WAS JUST RIDICULOUS. BUT SHE MAY, IN FACT, BE INSANE.
I de-vamped JUBILEE and all I got was This lousy T-SH
REC
THOUGH I SUPPOSE THERE'S SOMETHING APPEALING IN INSANITY. ESPECIALLY IF IT'S A CHOICE. WHAT'S BOLDER THAN TELLING THE WORLD TO EFF OFF THROUGH PURE INSANITY?
I... MAY HAVE JUST TALKED MYSELF INTO SOMETHING HERE.
REC
OKAY, CAN YOU GIVE US JUST ONE LITTLE MINUTE, B.R.O.D.O.K.? WE NEED TO HAVE A SUPER QUICK TEAM...ER... THING.
OF COURSE! CARRY ON! WHO AM I TO STAND IN THE WAY OF TEAM UNITY?
HONESTLY, I FEEL KIND OF BAD FOR HIM.
KATE...
NO, I KNOW, I KNOW. SUPER VILLAIN. VERY BAD. I'M JUST SAYING, IT'S ALSO SAD, RIGHT?

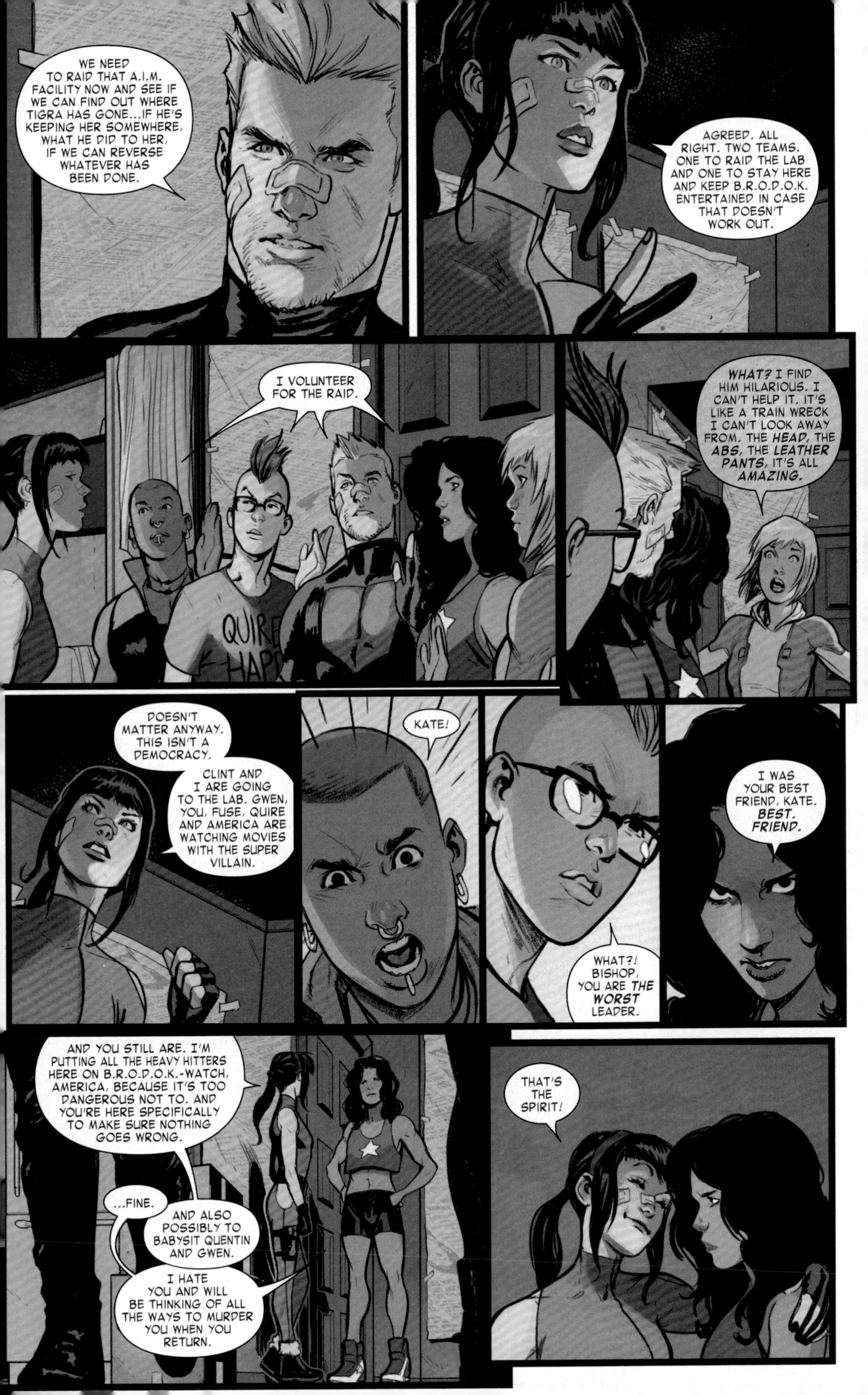
WE NEED TO RAID THAT A.I.M. FACILITY NOW AND SEE IF WE CAN FIND OUT WHERE TIGRA HAS GONE...IF HE'S KEEPING HER SOMEWHERE, WHAT HE DID TO HER, IF WE CAN REVERSE WHATEVER HAS BEEN DONE.
AGREED. ALL RIGHT. TWO TEAMS. ONE TO RAID THE LAB AND ONE TO STAY HERE AND KEEP B.R.O.D.O.K. ENTERTAINED IN CASE THAT DOESN'T WORK OUT.
I VOLUNTEER FOR THE RAID.
QUIRE HAPP
WHAT? I FIND HIM HILARIOUS. I CAN'T HELP IT. IT'S LIKE A TRAIN WRECK I CAN'T LOOK AWAY FROM. THE *HEAD,* THE *ABS,* THE *LEATHER PANTS,* IT'S ALL *AMAZING.*
DOESN'T MATTER ANYWAY. THIS ISN'T A DEMOCRACY.
CLINT AND I ARE GOING TO THE LAB. GWEN, YOU, FUSE, QUIRE AND AMERICA ARE WATCHING MOVIES WITH THE SUPER VILLAIN.
KATE!
WHAT?! BISHOP, YOU ARE *THE WORST* LEADER.
I WAS YOUR BEST FRIEND, KATE. *BEST. FRIEND.*
AND YOU STILL ARE. I'M PUTTING ALL THE HEAVY HITTERS HERE ON B.R.O.D.O.K.-WATCH, AMERICA, BECAUSE IT'S TOO DANGEROUS NOT TO. AND YOU'RE HERE SPECIFICALLY TO MAKE SURE NOTHING GOES WRONG.
...FINE.
AND ALSO POSSIBLY TO BABYSIT QUENTIN AND GWEN.
I HATE YOU AND WILL BE THINKING OF ALL THE WAYS TO MURDER YOU WHEN YOU RETURN.
THAT'S THE SPIRIT!

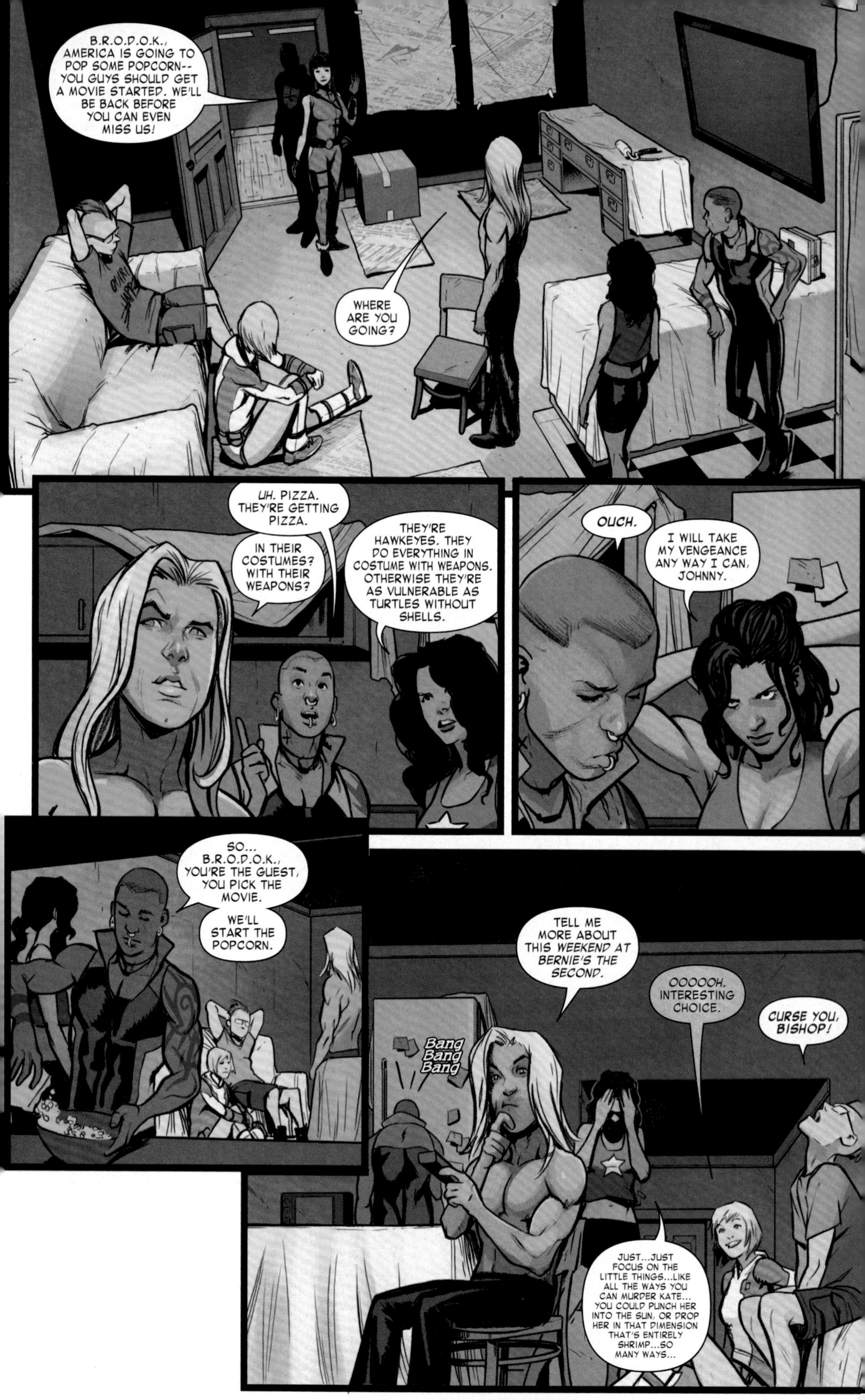
B.R.O.D.O.K., AMERICA IS GOING TO POP SOME POPCORN-- YOU GUYS SHOULD GET A MOVIE STARTED. WE'LL BE BACK BEFORE YOU CAN EVEN MISS US!
WHERE ARE YOU GOING?
UH. PIZZA. THEY'RE GETTING PIZZA.
IN THEIR COSTUMES? WITH THEIR WEAPONS?
THEY'RE HAWKEYES. THEY DO EVERYTHING IN COSTUME WITH WEAPONS. OTHERWISE THEY'RE AS VULNERABLE AS TURTLES WITHOUT SHELLS.
OUCH.
I WILL TAKE MY VENGEANCE ANY WAY I CAN, JOHNNY.
SO... B.R.O.D.O.K., YOU'RE THE GUEST, YOU PICK THE MOVIE.
WE'LL START THE POPCORN.
TELL ME MORE ABOUT THIS WEEKEND AT BERNIE'S THE SECOND.
OOOOOH. INTERESTING CHOICE.
CURSE YOU, BISHOP!
Bang Bang Bang
JUST...JUST FOCUS ON THE LITTLE THINGS...LIKE ALL THE WAYS YOU CAN MURDER KATE... YOU COULD PUNCH HER INTO THE SUN, OR DROP HER IN THAT DIMENSION THAT'S ENTIRELY SHRIMP...SO MANY WAYS...

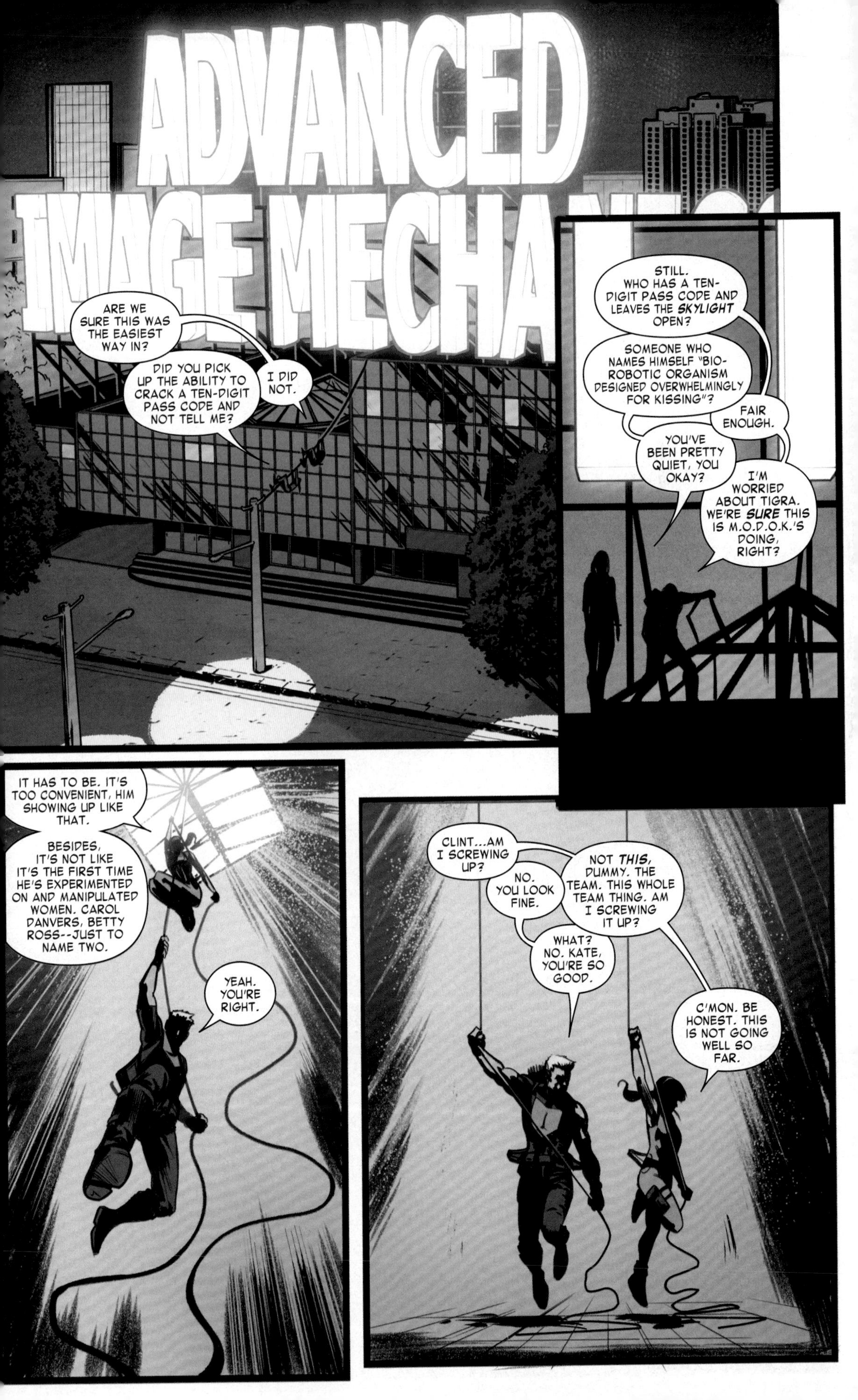
ADVANCED IMAGE MECHA
ARE WE SURE THIS WAS THE EASIEST WAY IN?
DID YOU PICK UP THE ABILITY TO CRACK A TEN-DIGIT PASS CODE AND NOT TELL ME?
I DID NOT.
STILL. WHO HAS A TEN-DIGIT PASS CODE AND LEAVES THE SKYLIGHT OPEN?
SOMEONE WHO NAMES HIMSELF "BIO-ROBOTIC ORGANISM DESIGNED OVERWHELMINGLY FOR KISSING"?
FAIR ENOUGH.
YOU'VE BEEN PRETTY QUIET, YOU OKAY?
I'M WORRIED ABOUT TIGRA. WE'RE SURE THIS IS M.O.D.O.K.'S DOING, RIGHT?
IT HAS TO BE. IT'S TOO CONVENIENT, HIM SHOWING UP LIKE THAT.
BESIDES, IT'S NOT LIKE IT'S THE FIRST TIME HE'S EXPERIMENTED ON AND MANIPULATED WOMEN. CAROL DANVERS, BETTY ROSS--JUST TO NAME TWO.
YEAH. YOU'RE RIGHT.
CLINT...AM I SCREWING UP?
NO. YOU LOOK FINE.
NOT THIS, DUMMY. THE TEAM. THIS WHOLE TEAM THING. AM I SCREWING IT UP?
WHAT? NO. KATE, YOU'RE SO GOOD.
C'MON. BE HONEST. THIS IS NOT GOING WELL SO FAR.

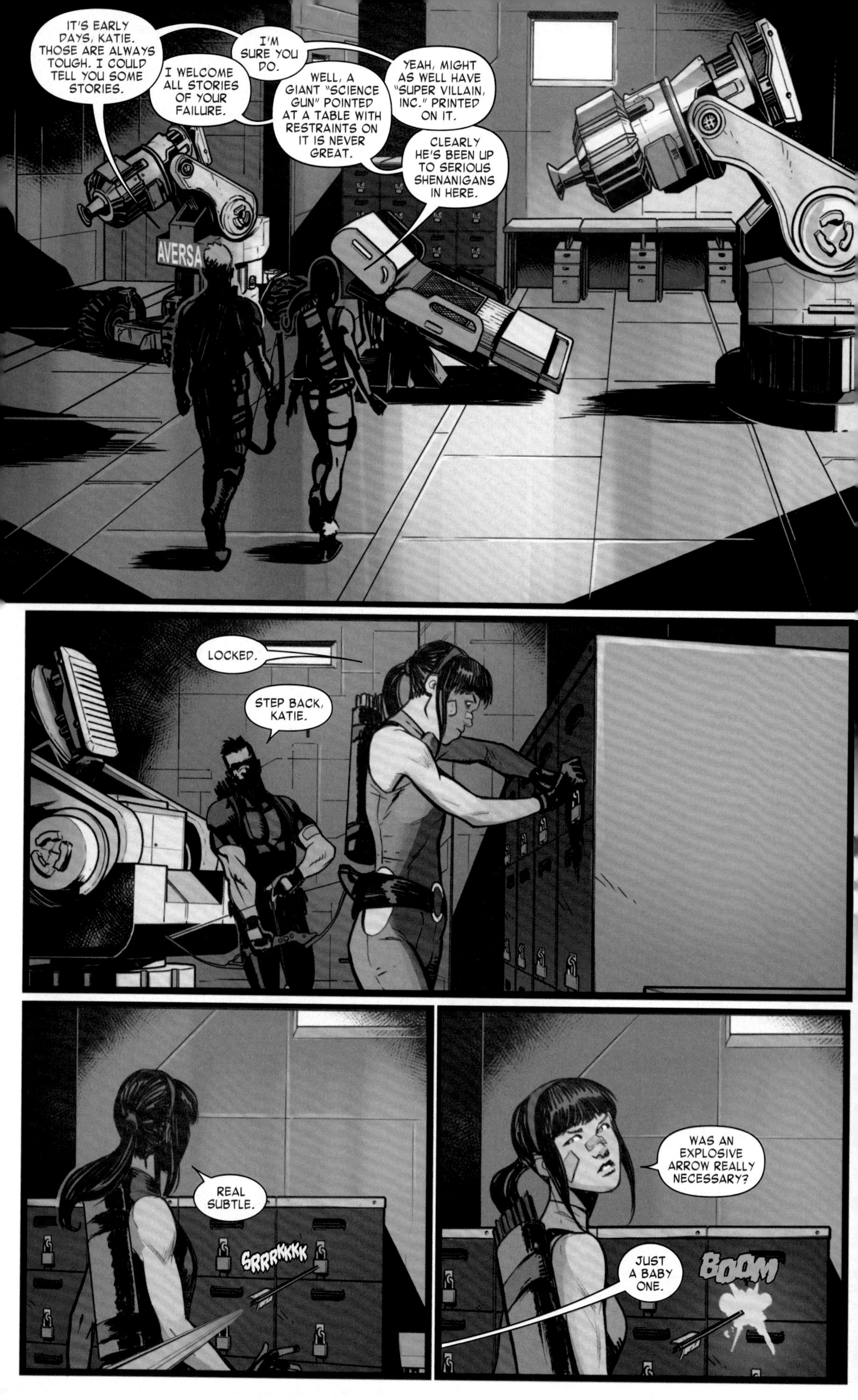
IT'S EARLY DAYS, KATIE. THOSE ARE ALWAYS TOUGH. I COULD TELL YOU SOME STORIES.
I'M SURE YOU DO.
I WELCOME ALL STORIES OF YOUR FAILURE.
WELL, A GIANT "SCIENCE GUN" POINTED AT A TABLE WITH RESTRAINTS ON IT IS NEVER GREAT.
YEAH, MIGHT AS WELL HAVE "SUPER VILLAIN, INC." PRINTED ON IT.
CLEARLY HE'S BEEN UP TO SERIOUS SHENANIGANS IN HERE.
AVERSA
LOCKED.
STEP BACK, KATIE.
REAL SUBTLE.
SRRRKKKK
WAS AN EXPLOSIVE ARROW REALLY NECESSARY?
JUST A BABY ONE.
BOOM

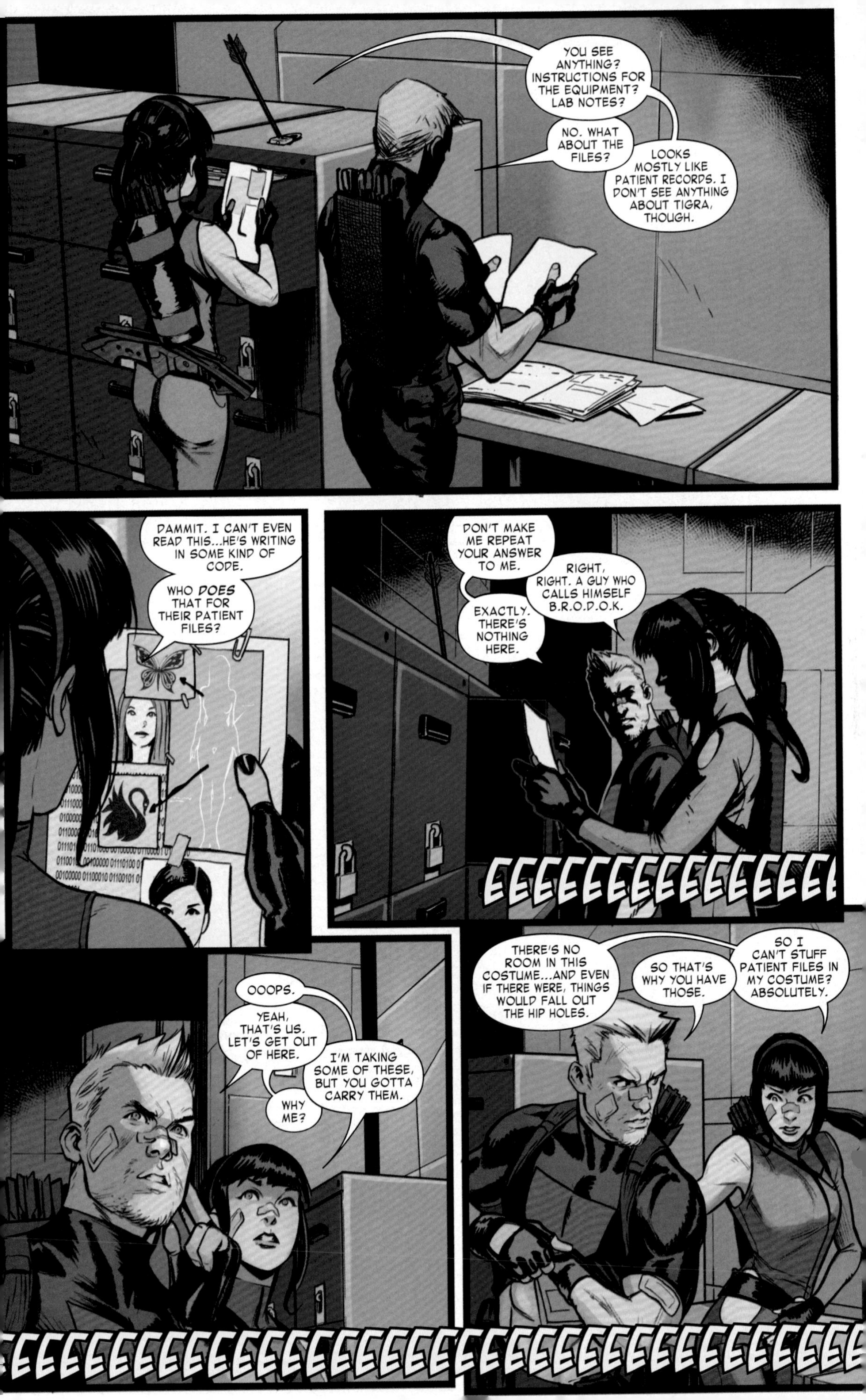
YOU SEE ANYTHING? INSTRUCTIONS FOR THE EQUIPMENT? LAB NOTES?
NO. WHAT ABOUT THE FILES?
LOOKS MOSTLY LIKE PATIENT RECORDS. I DON'T SEE ANYTHING ABOUT TIGRA, THOUGH.
DAMMIT. I CAN'T EVEN READ THIS...HE'S WRITING IN SOME KIND OF CODE.
WHO *DOES* THAT FOR THEIR PATIENT FILES?
DON'T MAKE ME REPEAT YOUR ANSWER TO ME.
RIGHT, RIGHT. A GUY WHO CALLS HIMSELF B.R.O.D.O.K.
EXACTLY. THERE'S NOTHING HERE.
EEEEEEEEEEEEEEEEE
OOOPS.
YEAH, THAT'S US. LET'S GET OUT OF HERE.
I'M TAKING SOME OF THESE, BUT YOU GOTTA CARRY THEM.
WHY ME?
SO I CAN'T STUFF PATIENT FILES IN MY COSTUME? ABSOLUTELY.
THERE'S NO ROOM IN THIS COSTUME...AND EVEN IF THERE WERE, THINGS WOULD FALL OUT THE HIP HOLES.
SO THAT'S WHY YOU HAVE THOSE.
EEEEEEEEEEEEEEEEEEEEEEEEEEEEEEEEEEEE

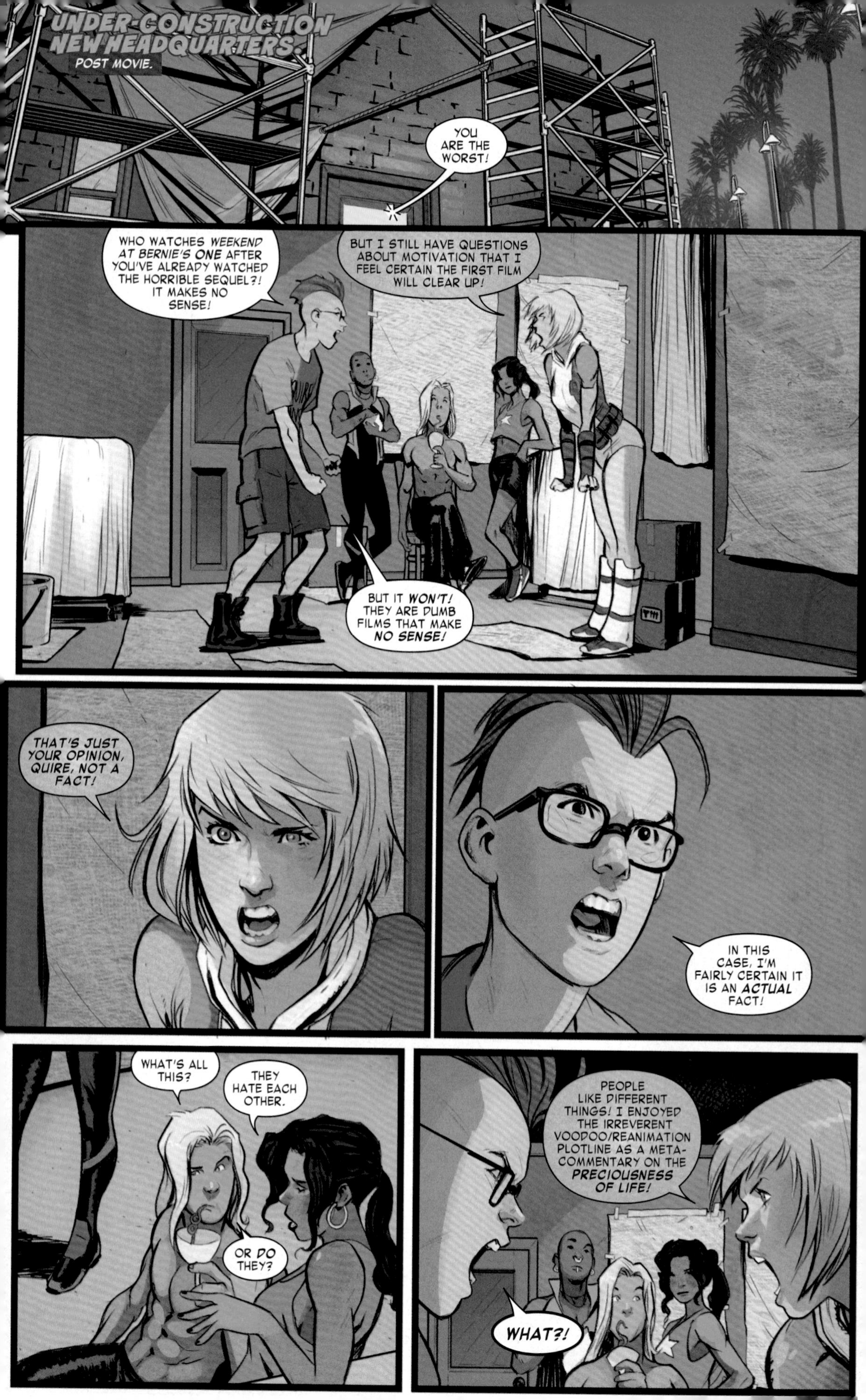
UNDER-CONSTRUCTION NEW HEADQUARTERS.
POST MOVIE.
YOU ARE THE WORST!
WHO WATCHES WEEKEND AT BERNIE'S ONE AFTER YOU'VE ALREADY WATCHED THE HORRIBLE SEQUEL?! IT MAKES NO SENSE!
BUT I STILL HAVE QUESTIONS ABOUT MOTIVATION THAT I FEEL CERTAIN THE FIRST FILM WILL CLEAR UP!
BUT IT WON'T! THEY ARE DUMB FILMS THAT MAKE NO SENSE!
THAT'S JUST YOUR OPINION, QUIRE, NOT A FACT!
IN THIS CASE, I'M FAIRLY CERTAIN IT IS AN ACTUAL FACT!
WHAT'S ALL THIS?
THEY HATE EACH OTHER.
OR DO THEY?
PEOPLE LIKE DIFFERENT THINGS! I ENJOYED THE IRREVERENT VOODOO/REANIMATION PLOTLINE AS A META-COMMENTARY ON THE PRECIOUSNESS OF LIFE!
WHAT?!

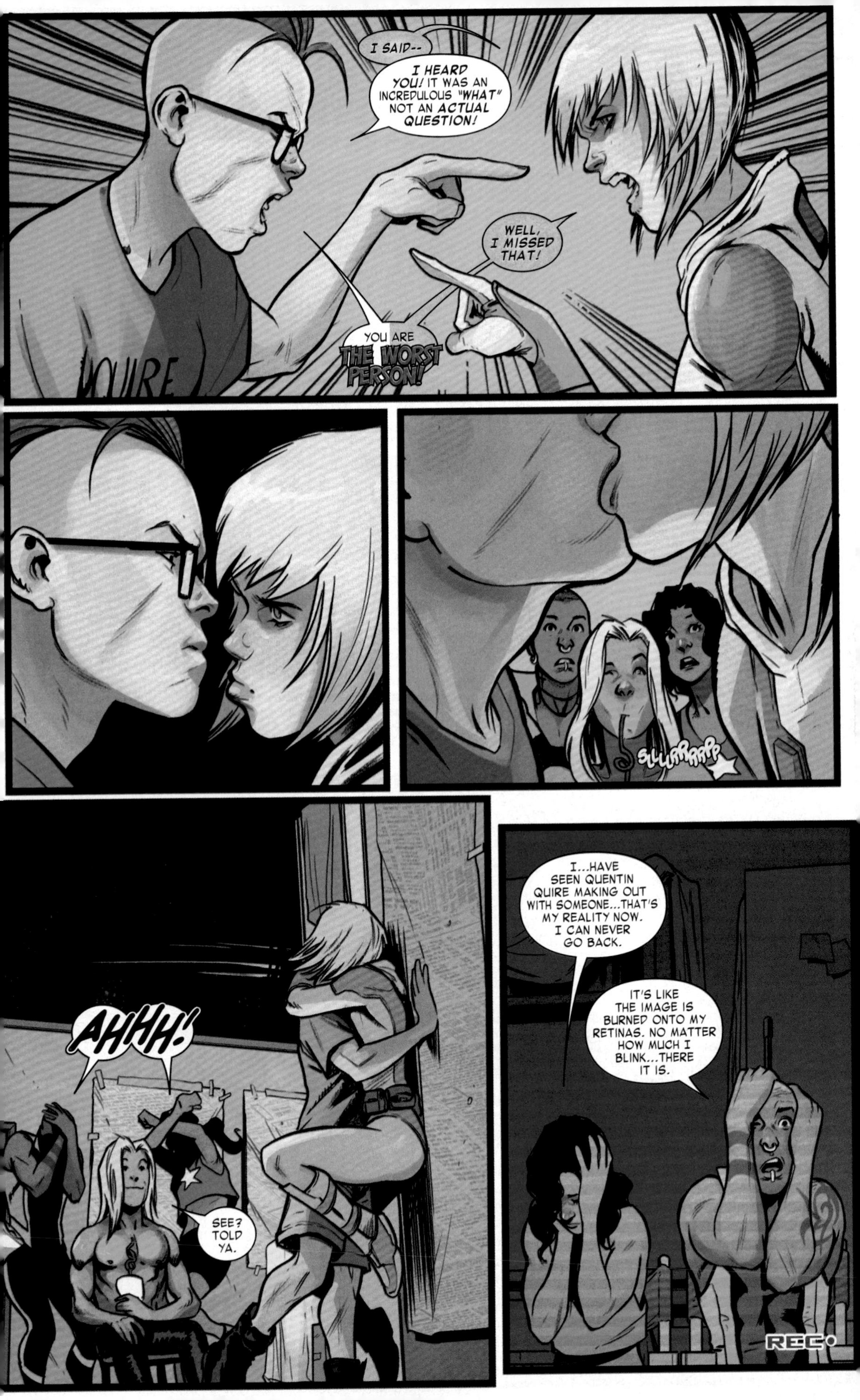

I SAID--
I HEARD YOU! IT WAS AN INCREDULOUS "WHAT" NOT AN ACTUAL QUESTION!
WELL, I MISSED THAT!
YOU ARE THE WORST PERSON!
SLLURRRRPP
AHHH!
SEE? TOLD YA.
I...HAVE SEEN QUENTIN QUIRE MAKING OUT WITH SOMEONE...THAT'S MY REALITY NOW. I CAN NEVER GO BACK.
IT'S LIKE THE IMAGE IS BURNED ONTO MY RETINAS. NO MATTER HOW MUCH I BLINK...THERE IT IS.
REC

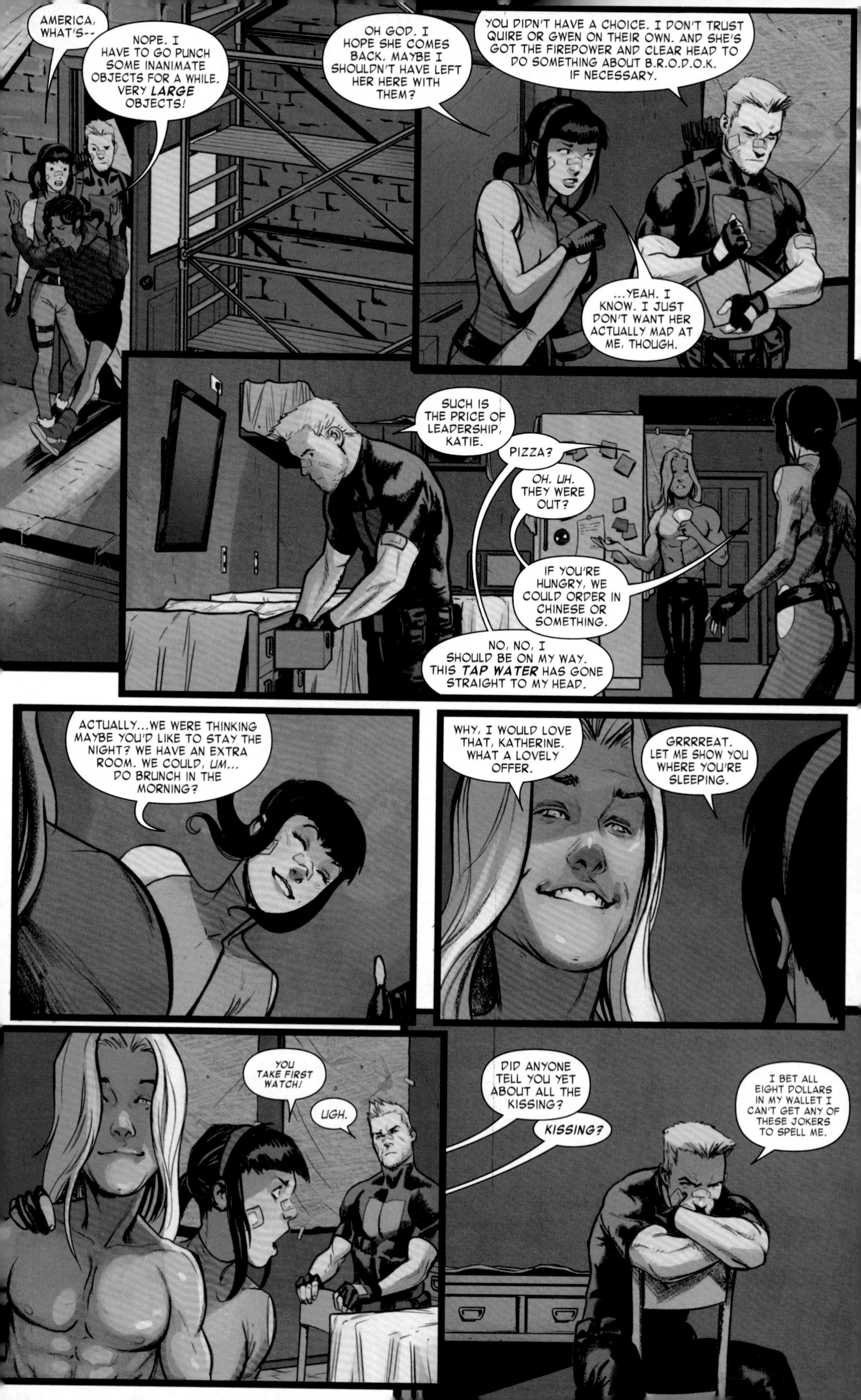
AMERICA, WHAT'S--
NOPE. I HAVE TO GO PUNCH SOME INANIMATE OBJECTS FOR A WHILE. VERY LARGE OBJECTS!
OH GOD. I HOPE SHE COMES BACK. MAYBE I SHOULDN'T HAVE LEFT HER HERE WITH THEM?
YOU DIDN'T HAVE A CHOICE. I DON'T TRUST QUIRE OR GWEN ON THEIR OWN. AND SHE'S GOT THE FIREPOWER AND CLEAR HEAD TO DO SOMETHING ABOUT B.R.O.D.O.K. IF NECESSARY.
...YEAH. I KNOW. I JUST DON'T WANT HER ACTUALLY MAD AT ME, THOUGH.
SUCH IS THE PRICE OF LEADERSHIP, KATIE.
PIZZA?
OH. UH. THEY WERE OUT?
IF YOU'RE HUNGRY, WE COULD ORDER IN CHINESE OR SOMETHING.
NO, NO, I SHOULD BE ON MY WAY. THIS TAP WATER HAS GONE STRAIGHT TO MY HEAD.
ACTUALLY...WE WERE THINKING MAYBE YOU'D LIKE TO STAY THE NIGHT? WE HAVE AN EXTRA ROOM. WE COULD, UM... DO BRUNCH IN THE MORNING?
WHY, I WOULD LOVE THAT, KATHERINE. WHAT A LOVELY OFFER.
GRRRREAT. LET ME SHOW YOU WHERE YOU'RE SLEEPING.
YOU TAKE FIRST WATCH!
UGH.
DID ANYONE TELL YOU YET ABOUT ALL THE KISSING?
KISSING?
I BET ALL EIGHT DOLLARS IN MY WALLET I CAN'T GET ANY OF THESE JOKERS TO SPELL ME.

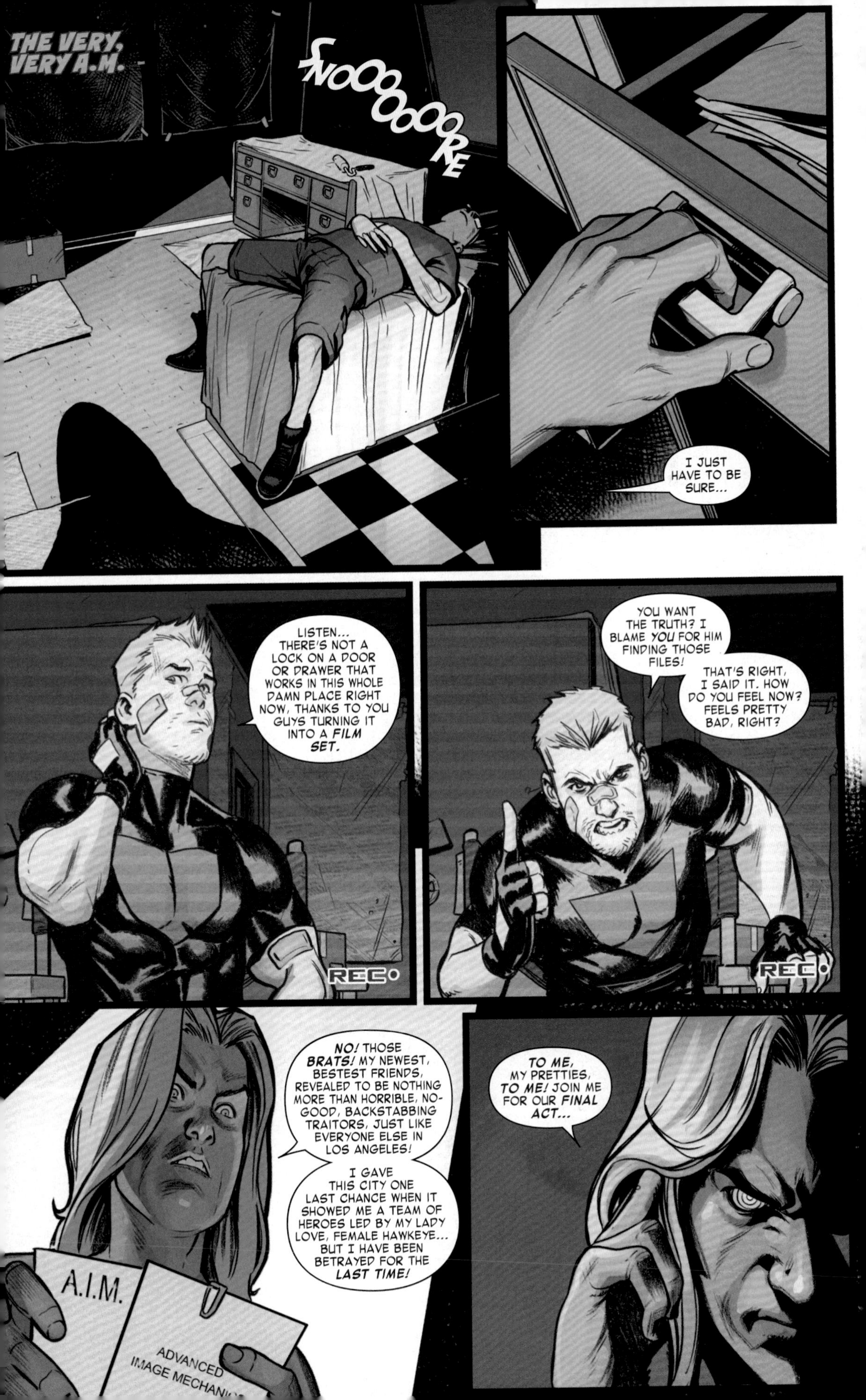

THE VERY, VERY A.M.
SNOOOOOOORE
I JUST HAVE TO BE SURE...
LISTEN... THERE'S NOT A LOCK ON A DOOR OR DRAWER THAT WORKS IN THIS WHOLE DAMN PLACE RIGHT NOW, THANKS TO YOU GUYS TURNING IT INTO A FILM SET.
REC
YOU WANT THE TRUTH? I BLAME YOU FOR HIM FINDING THOSE FILES!
THAT'S RIGHT, I SAID IT. HOW DO YOU FEEL NOW? FEELS PRETTY BAD, RIGHT?
REC
NO! THOSE BRATS! MY NEWEST, BESTEST FRIENDS, REVEALED TO BE NOTHING MORE THAN HORRIBLE, NO-GOOD, BACKSTABBING TRAITORS, JUST LIKE EVERYONE ELSE IN LOS ANGELES!
I GAVE THIS CITY ONE LAST CHANCE WHEN IT SHOWED ME A TEAM OF HEROES LED BY MY LADY LOVE, FEMALE HAWKEYE... BUT I HAVE BEEN BETRAYED FOR THE LAST TIME!
A.I.M.
ADVANCED IMAGE MECHANI
TO ME, MY PRETTIES, TO ME! JOIN ME FOR OUR FINAL ACT...

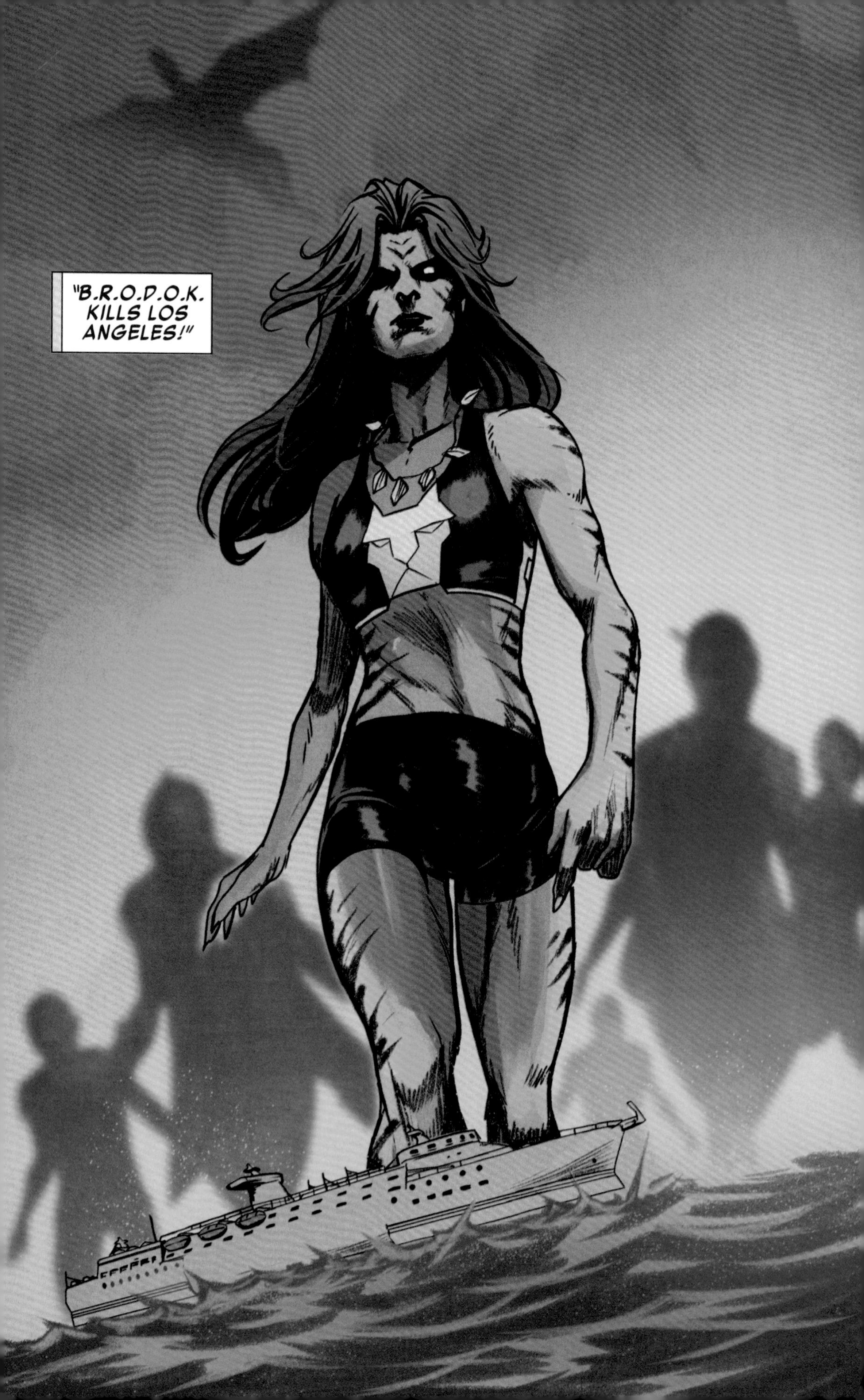
"B.R.O.D.O.K. KILLS LOS ANGELES!"

#1 VARIANT BY PAUL RENAUD

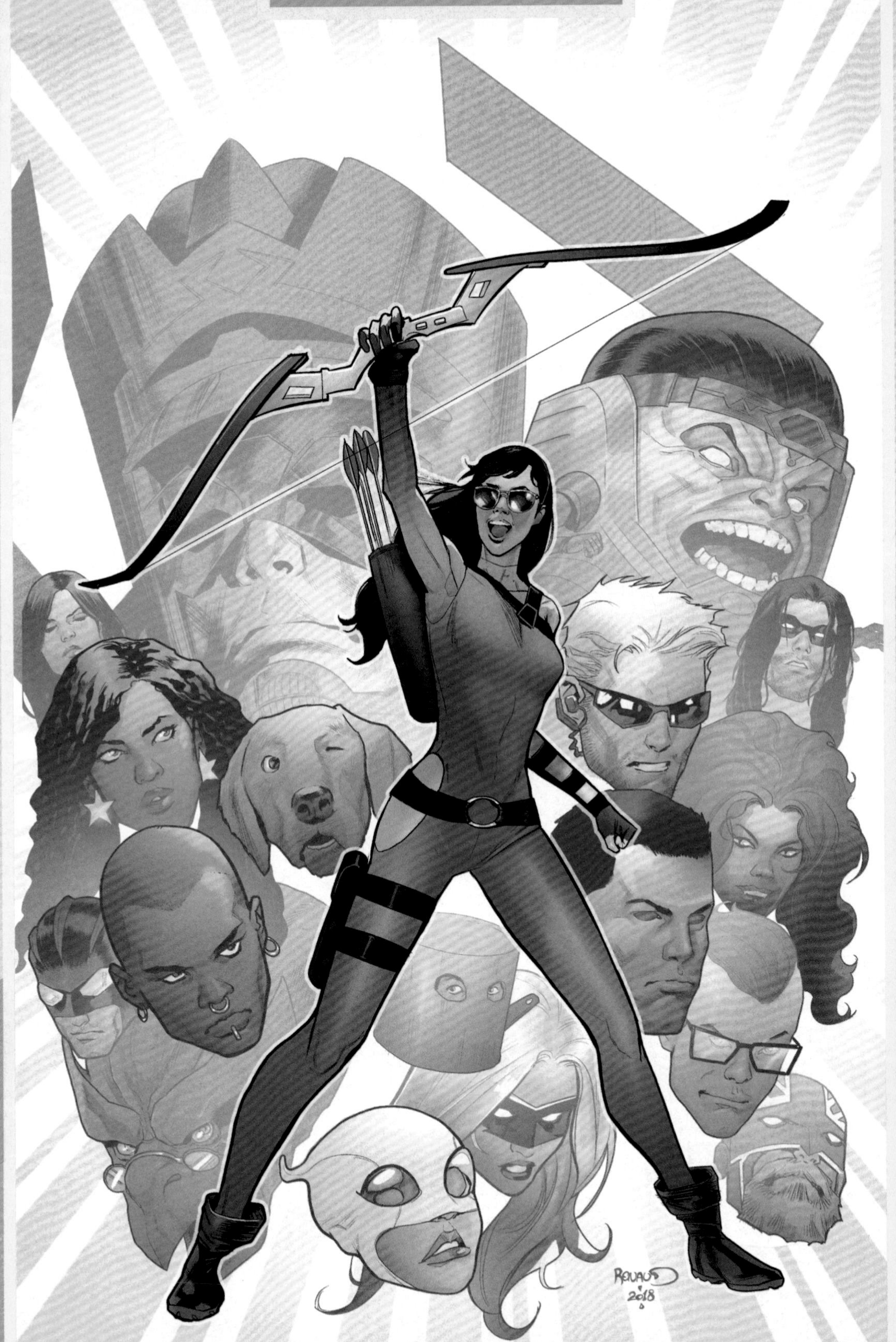
RENAUD
2018

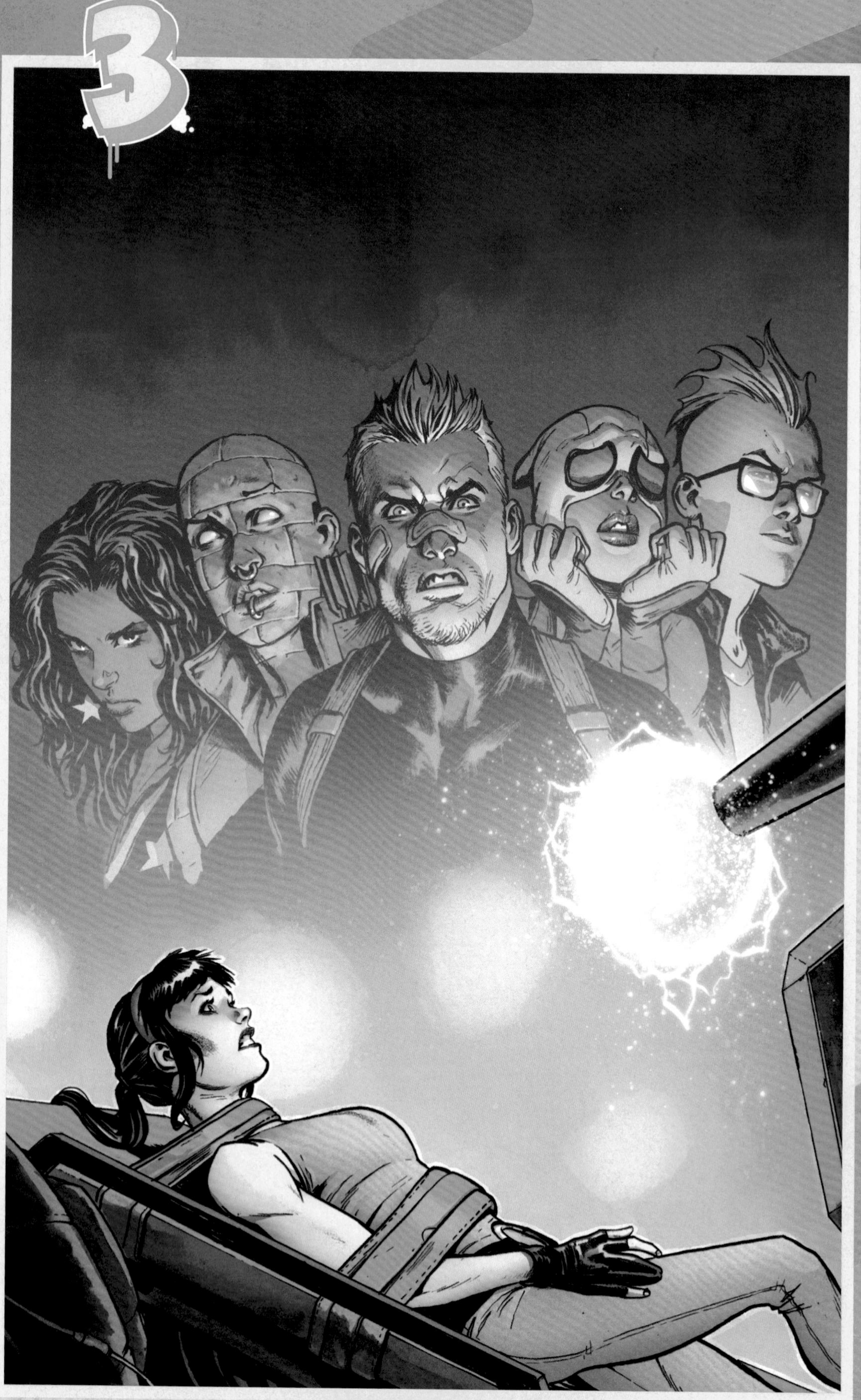
3

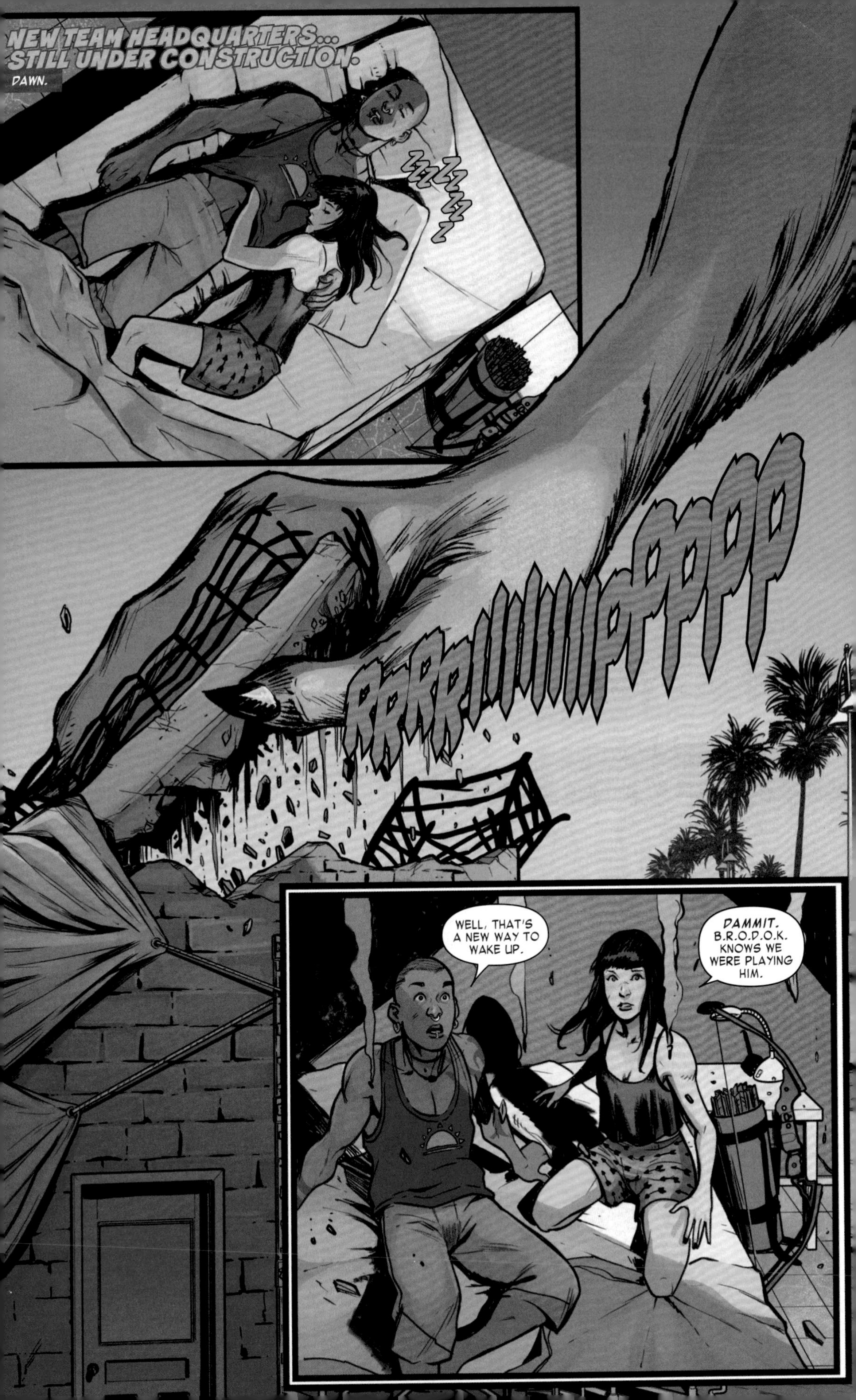
NEW TEAM HEADQUARTERS... STILL UNDER CONSTRUCTION.
DAWN.
ZZZZZZZZ
RRRIIIIIIIIIPPPPP
WELL, THAT'S A NEW WAY TO WAKE UP.
DAMMIT. B.R.O.D.O.K. KNOWS WE WERE PLAYING HIM.

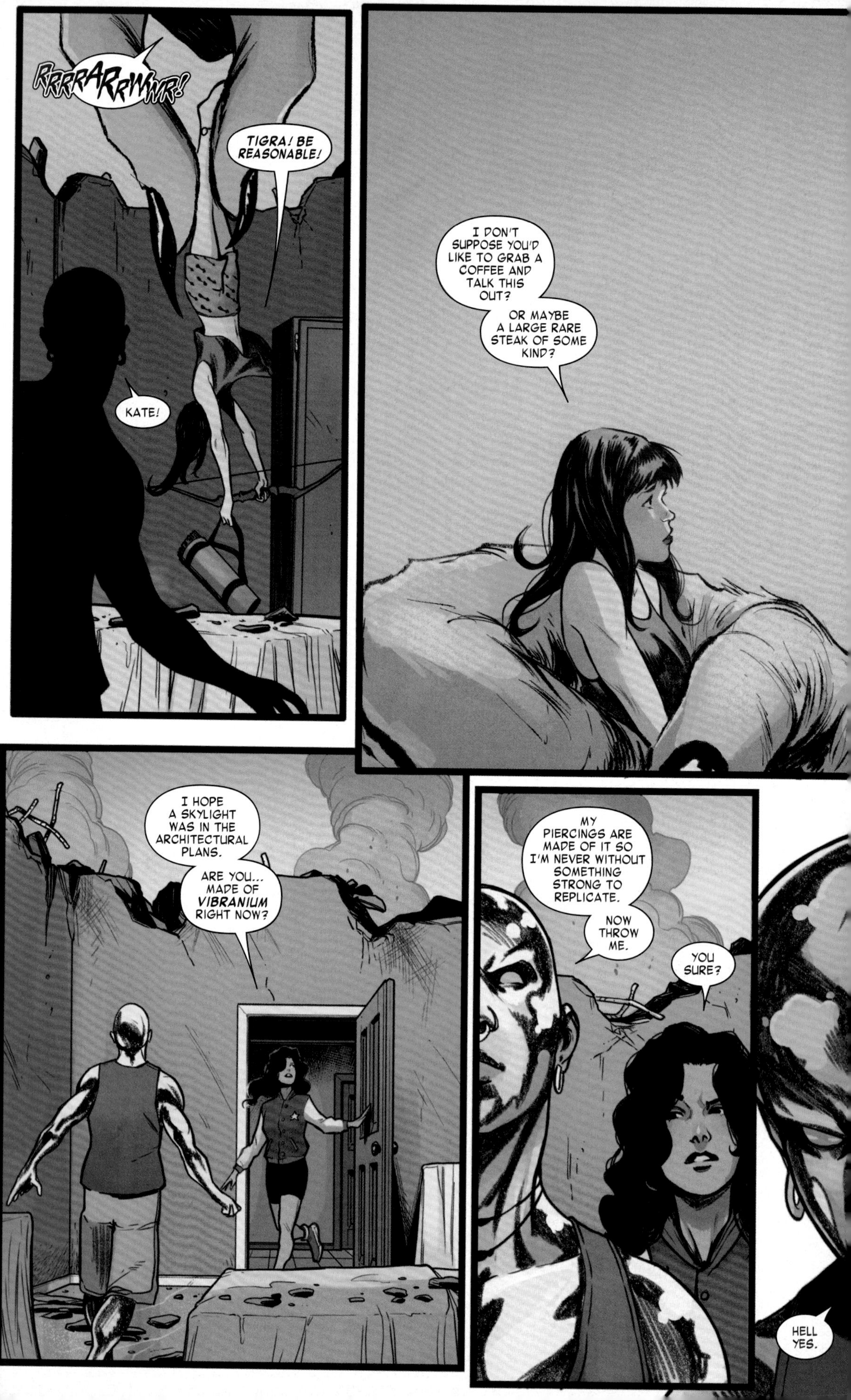
RRRRARRWWR!
TIGRA! BE REASONABLE!
KATE!
I DON'T SUPPOSE YOU'D LIKE TO GRAB A COFFEE AND TALK THIS OUT?
OR MAYBE A LARGE RARE STEAK OF SOME KIND?
I HOPE A SKYLIGHT WAS IN THE ARCHITECTURAL PLANS.
ARE YOU... MADE OF VIBRANIUM RIGHT NOW?
MY PIERCINGS ARE MADE OF IT SO I'M NEVER WITHOUT SOMETHING STRONG TO REPLICATE.
NOW THROW ME.
YOU SURE?
HELL YES.

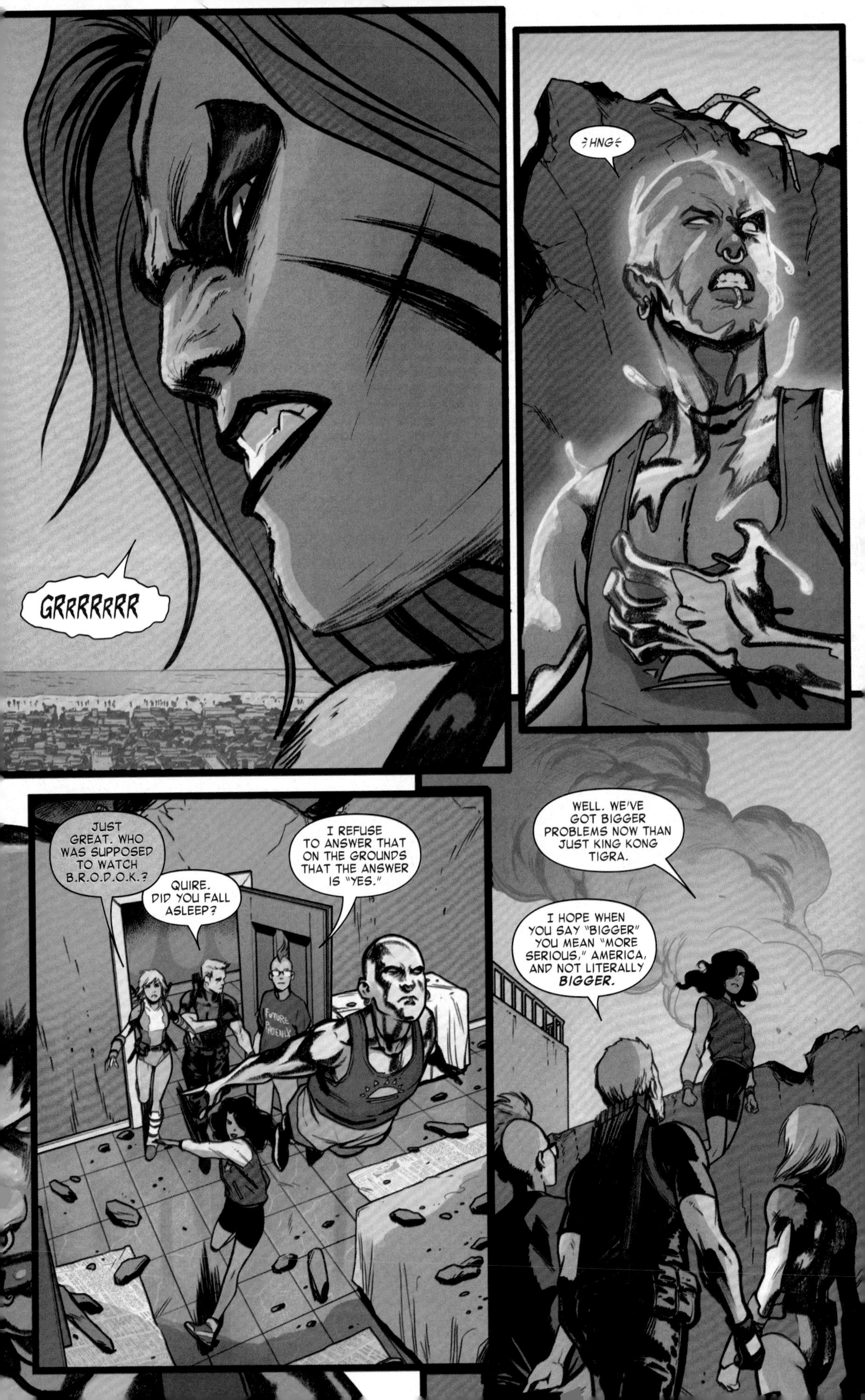
GRRRRRRR
HNG
JUST GREAT. WHO WAS SUPPOSED TO WATCH B.R.O.D.O.K.?
QUIRE. DID YOU FALL ASLEEP?
I REFUSE TO ANSWER THAT ON THE GROUNDS THAT THE ANSWER IS "YES."
WELL. WE'VE GOT BIGGER PROBLEMS NOW THAN JUST KING KONG TIGRA.
I HOPE WHEN YOU SAY "BIGGER" YOU MEAN "MORE SERIOUS," AMERICA, AND NOT LITERALLY BIGGER.
FUTURE PHOENIX

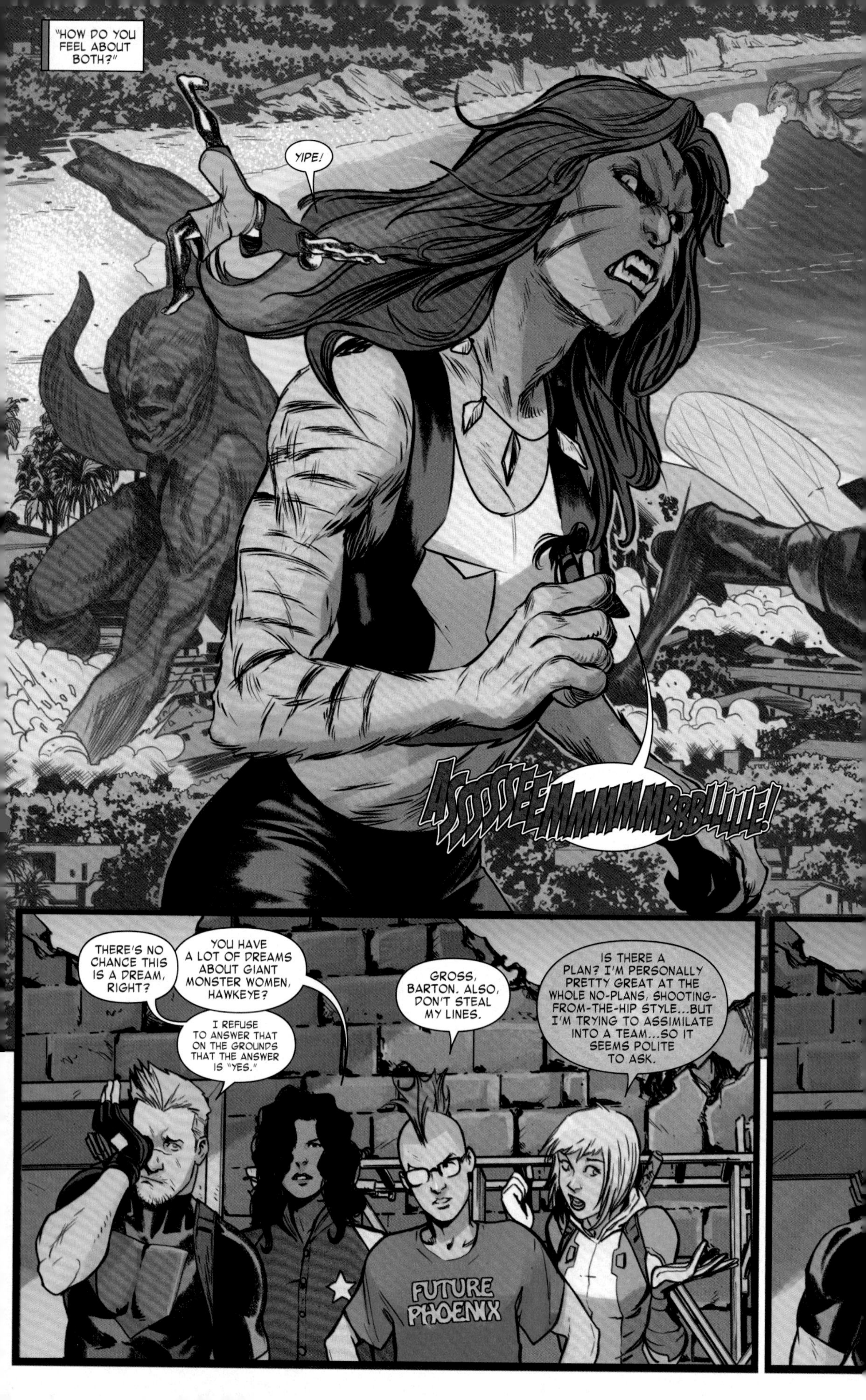

"HOW DO YOU FEEL ABOUT BOTH?"
YIPE!
ASSSSSEEMMMMMBBBLLLLE!
THERE'S NO CHANCE THIS IS A DREAM, RIGHT?
YOU HAVE A LOT OF DREAMS ABOUT GIANT MONSTER WOMEN, HAWKEYE?
I REFUSE TO ANSWER THAT ON THE GROUNDS THAT THE ANSWER IS "YES."
GROSS, BARTON. ALSO, DON'T STEAL MY LINES.
IS THERE A PLAN? I'M PERSONALLY PRETTY GREAT AT THE WHOLE NO-PLANS, SHOOTING-FROM-THE-HIP STYLE...BUT I'M TRYING TO ASSIMILATE INTO A TEAM...SO IT SEEMS POLITE TO ASK.
FUTURE PHOENIX

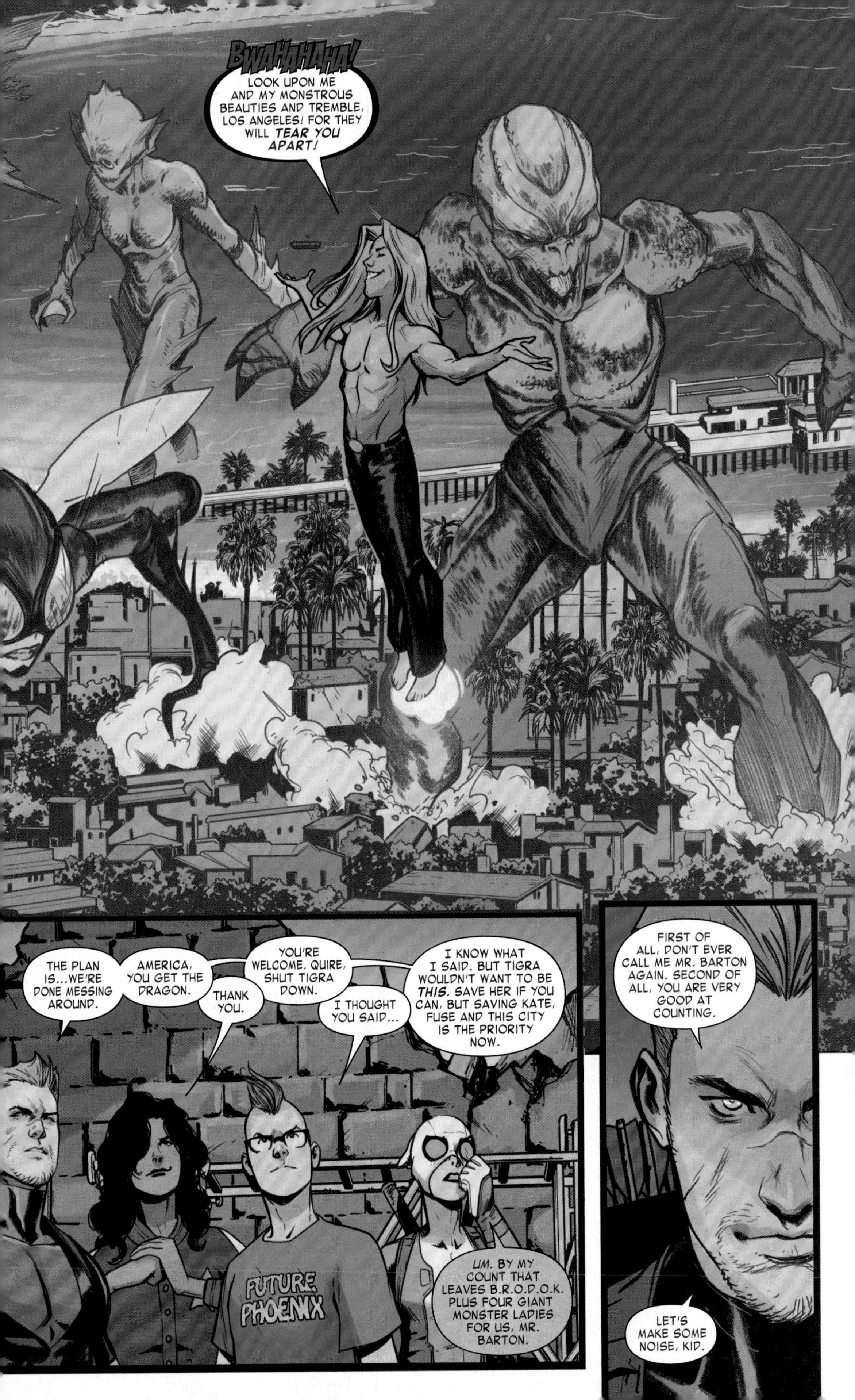
BWAHAHAHA!
LOOK UPON ME AND MY MONSTROUS BEAUTIES AND TREMBLE, LOS ANGELES! FOR THEY WILL TEAR YOU APART!
THE PLAN IS...WE'RE DONE MESSING AROUND.
AMERICA, YOU GET THE DRAGON.
THANK YOU.
YOU'RE WELCOME. QUIRE, SHUT TIGRA DOWN.
I THOUGHT YOU SAID...
I KNOW WHAT I SAID. BUT TIGRA WOULDN'T WANT TO BE THIS. SAVE HER IF YOU CAN, BUT SAVING KATE, FUSE AND THIS CITY IS THE PRIORITY NOW.
FUTURE PHOENIX
UM. BY MY COUNT THAT LEAVES B.R.O.D.O.K. PLUS FOUR GIANT MONSTER LADIES FOR US, MR. BARTON.
FIRST OF ALL, DON'T EVER CALL ME MR. BARTON AGAIN. SECOND OF ALL, YOU ARE VERY GOOD AT COUNTING.
LET'S MAKE SOME NOISE, KID.

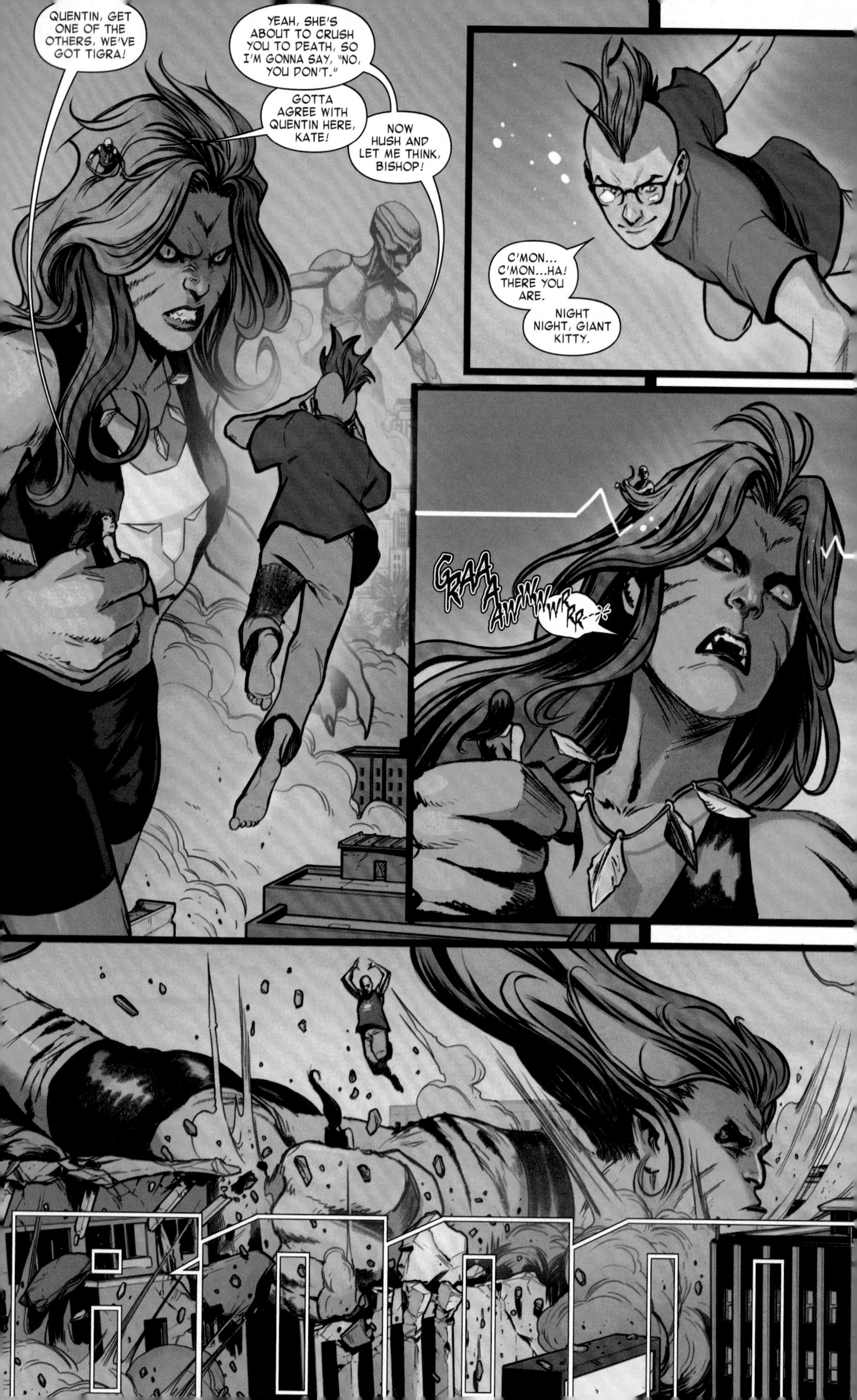
QUENTIN, GET ONE OF THE OTHERS, WE'VE GOT TIGRA!
YEAH, SHE'S ABOUT TO CRUSH YOU TO DEATH, SO I'M GONNA SAY, "NO, YOU DON'T."
GOTTA AGREE WITH QUENTIN HERE, KATE!
NOW HUSH AND LET ME THINK, BISHOP!
C'MON... C'MON...HA! THERE YOU ARE.
NIGHT NIGHT, GIANT KITTY.
GRAAAAWWWWWRRR--!

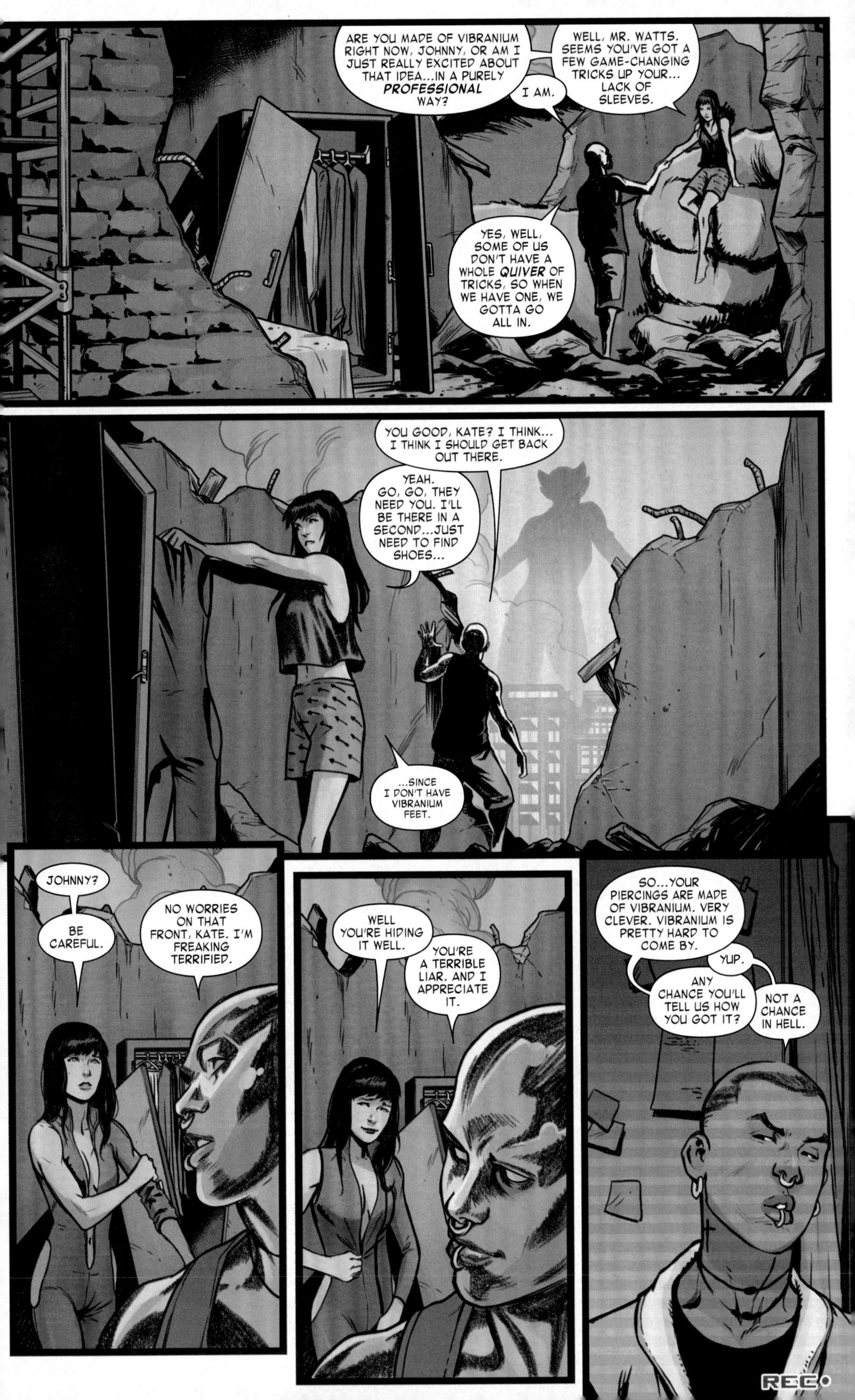
ARE YOU MADE OF VIBRANIUM RIGHT NOW, JOHNNY, OR AM I JUST REALLY EXCITED ABOUT THAT IDEA...IN A PURELY PROFESSIONAL WAY?
I AM.
WELL, MR. WATTS. SEEMS YOU'VE GOT A FEW GAME-CHANGING TRICKS UP YOUR... LACK OF SLEEVES.
YES, WELL, SOME OF US DON'T HAVE A WHOLE QUIVER OF TRICKS, SO WHEN WE HAVE ONE, WE GOTTA GO ALL IN.
YOU GOOD, KATE? I THINK... I THINK I SHOULD GET BACK OUT THERE.
YEAH. GO, GO, THEY NEED YOU. I'LL BE THERE IN A SECOND...JUST NEED TO FIND SHOES...
...SINCE I DON'T HAVE VIBRANIUM FEET.
JOHNNY?
BE CAREFUL.
NO WORRIES ON THAT FRONT, KATE. I'M FREAKING TERRIFIED.
WELL YOU'RE HIDING IT WELL.
YOU'RE A TERRIBLE LIAR. AND I APPRECIATE IT.
SO...YOUR PIERCINGS ARE MADE OF VIBRANIUM. VERY CLEVER. VIBRANIUM IS PRETTY HARD TO COME BY.
YUP.
ANY CHANCE YOU'LL TELL US HOW YOU GOT IT?
NOT A CHANCE IN HELL.
REC

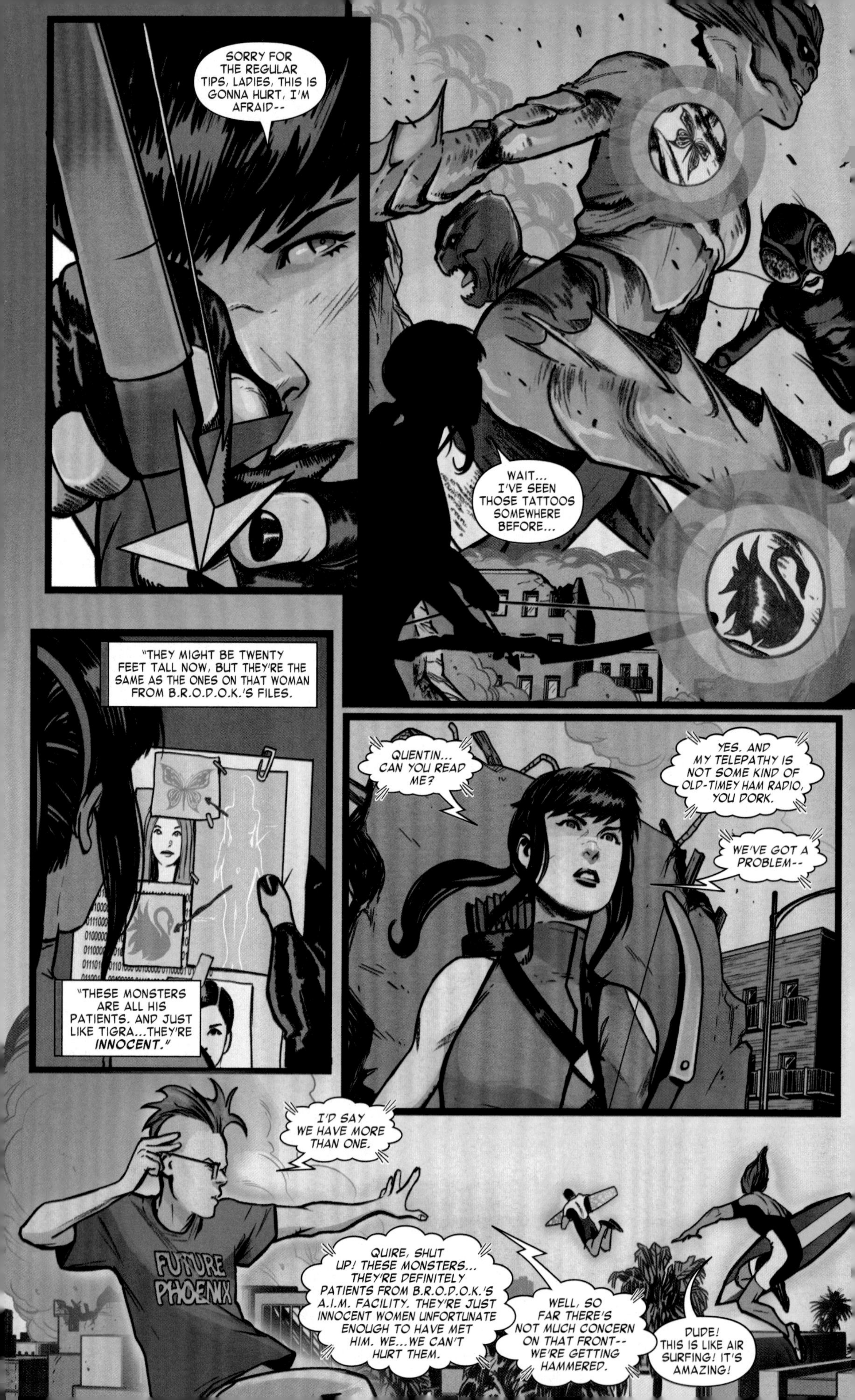
SORRY FOR THE REGULAR TIPS, LADIES, THIS IS GONNA HURT, I'M AFRAID--
WAIT... I'VE SEEN THOSE TATTOOS SOMEWHERE BEFORE...
"THEY MIGHT BE TWENTY FEET TALL NOW, BUT THEY'RE THE SAME AS THE ONES ON THAT WOMAN FROM B.R.O.D.O.K.'S FILES.
"THESE MONSTERS ARE ALL HIS PATIENTS. AND JUST LIKE TIGRA...THEY'RE *INNOCENT.*"
QUENTIN... CAN YOU READ ME?
YES. AND MY TELEPATHY IS NOT SOME KIND OF OLD-TIMEY HAM RADIO, YOU DORK.
WE'VE GOT A PROBLEM--
I'D SAY WE HAVE MORE THAN ONE.
FUTURE PHOENIX
QUIRE, SHUT UP! THESE MONSTERS... THEY'RE DEFINITELY PATIENTS FROM B.R.O.D.O.K.'S A.I.M. FACILITY. THEY'RE JUST INNOCENT WOMEN UNFORTUNATE ENOUGH TO HAVE MET HIM. WE...WE CAN'T HURT THEM.
WELL, SO FAR THERE'S NOT MUCH CONCERN ON THAT FRONT-- WE'RE GETTING HAMMERED.
DUDE! THIS IS LIKE AIR SURFING! IT'S AMAZING!

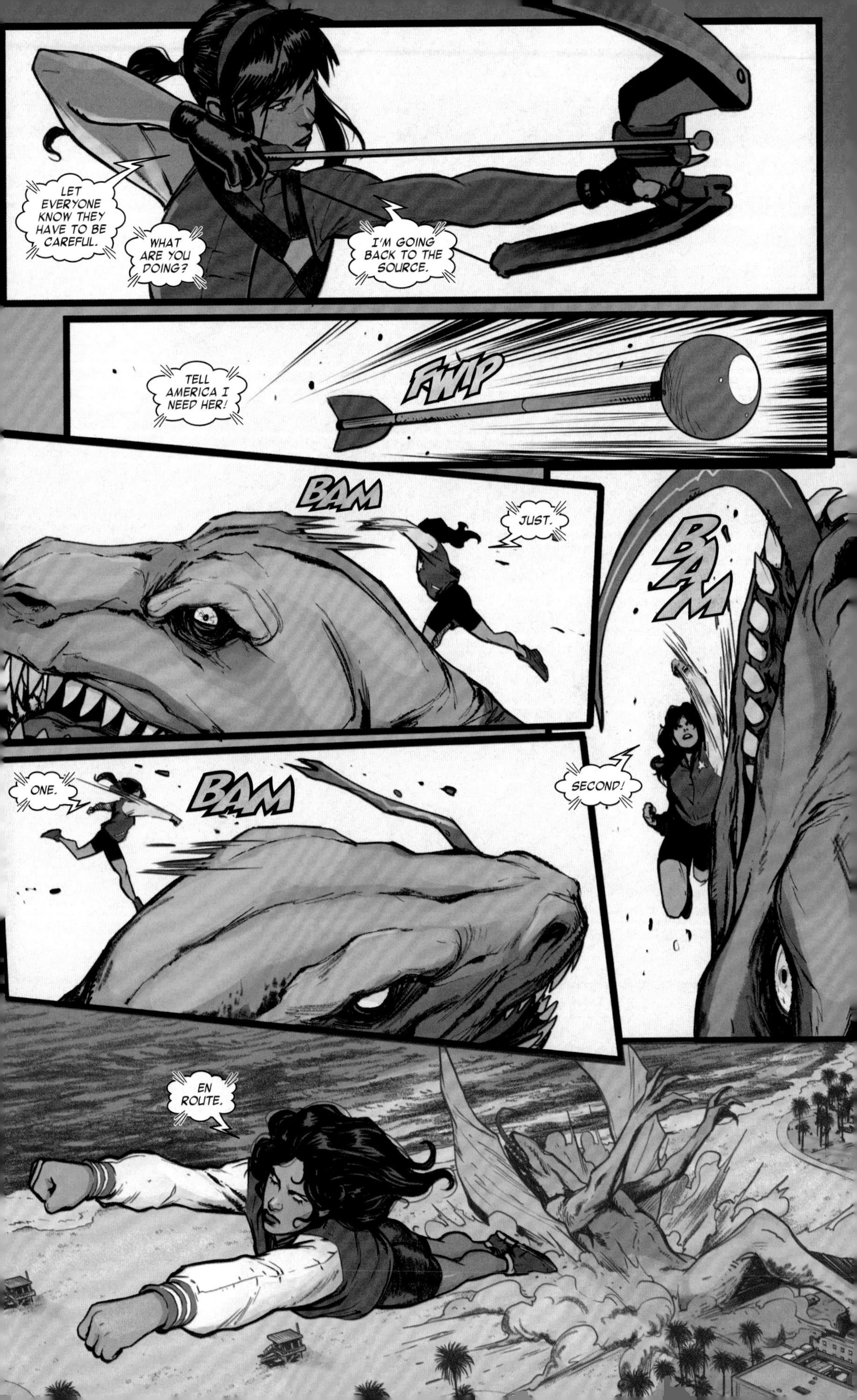
LET EVERYONE KNOW THEY HAVE TO BE CAREFUL.
WHAT ARE YOU DOING?
I'M GOING BACK TO THE SOURCE.
TELL AMERICA I NEED HER!
FWIP
BAM
JUST.
BAM
ONE.
BAM
SECOND!
EN ROUTE.

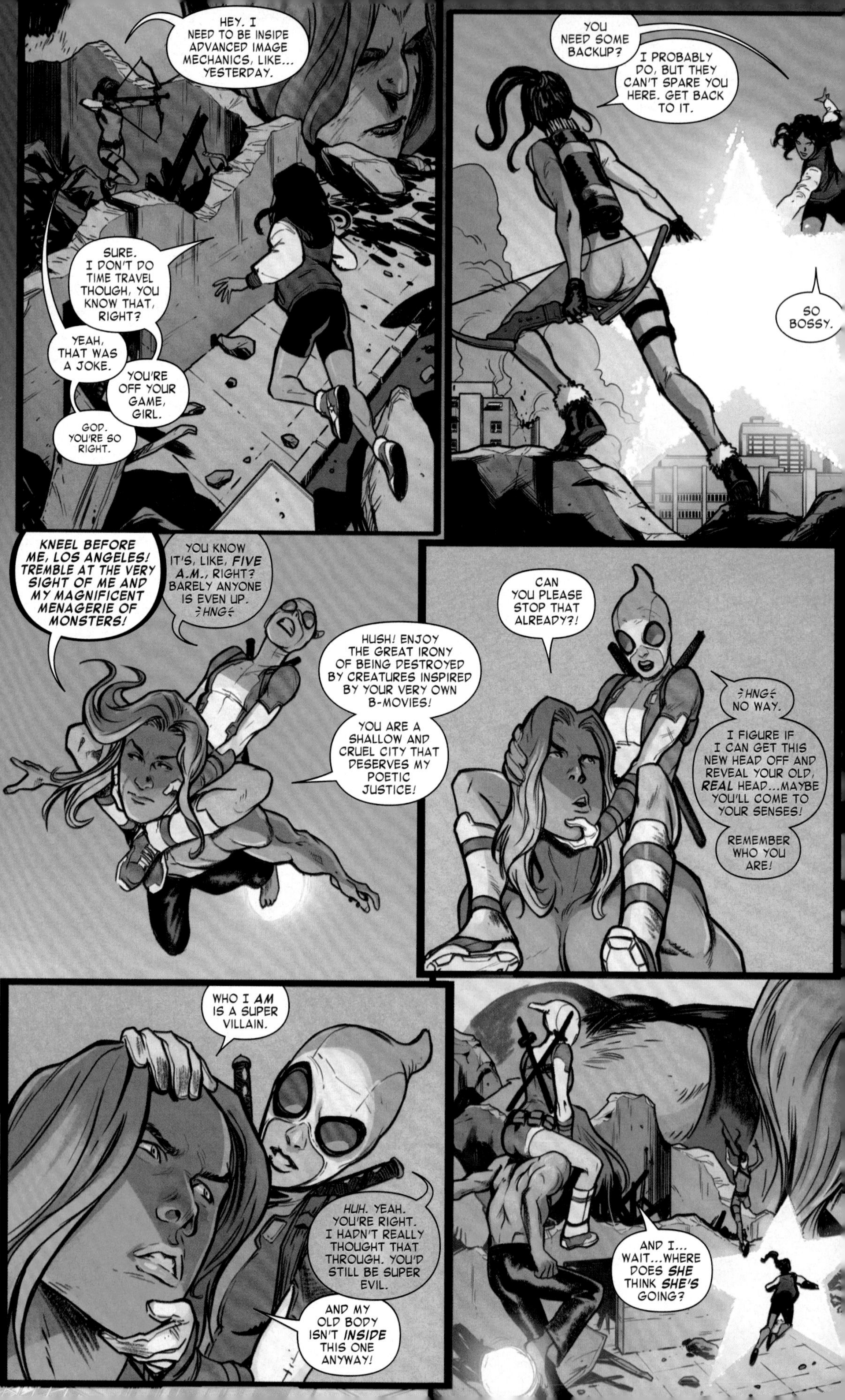
HEY. I NEED TO BE INSIDE ADVANCED IMAGE MECHANICS, LIKE... YESTERDAY.
SURE. I DON'T DO TIME TRAVEL THOUGH, YOU KNOW THAT, RIGHT?
YEAH, THAT WAS A JOKE.
YOU'RE OFF YOUR GAME, GIRL.
GOD. YOU'RE SO RIGHT.
YOU NEED SOME BACKUP?
I PROBABLY DO, BUT THEY CAN'T SPARE YOU HERE. GET BACK TO IT.
SO BOSSY.
KNEEL BEFORE ME, LOS ANGELES! TREMBLE AT THE VERY SIGHT OF ME AND MY MAGNIFICENT MENAGERIE OF MONSTERS!
YOU KNOW IT'S, LIKE, FIVE A.M., RIGHT? BARELY ANYONE IS EVEN UP. HNG
HUSH! ENJOY THE GREAT IRONY OF BEING DESTROYED BY CREATURES INSPIRED BY YOUR VERY OWN B-MOVIES!
YOU ARE A SHALLOW AND CRUEL CITY THAT DESERVES MY POETIC JUSTICE!
CAN YOU PLEASE STOP THAT ALREADY?!
HNG NO WAY.
I FIGURE IF I CAN GET THIS NEW HEAD OFF AND REVEAL YOUR OLD, REAL HEAD...MAYBE YOU'LL COME TO YOUR SENSES!
REMEMBER WHO YOU ARE!
WHO I AM IS A SUPER VILLAIN.
HUH. YEAH. YOU'RE RIGHT. I HADN'T REALLY THOUGHT THAT THROUGH. YOU'D STILL BE SUPER EVIL.
AND MY OLD BODY ISN'T INSIDE THIS ONE ANYWAY!
AND I... WAIT...WHERE DOES SHE THINK SHE'S GOING?

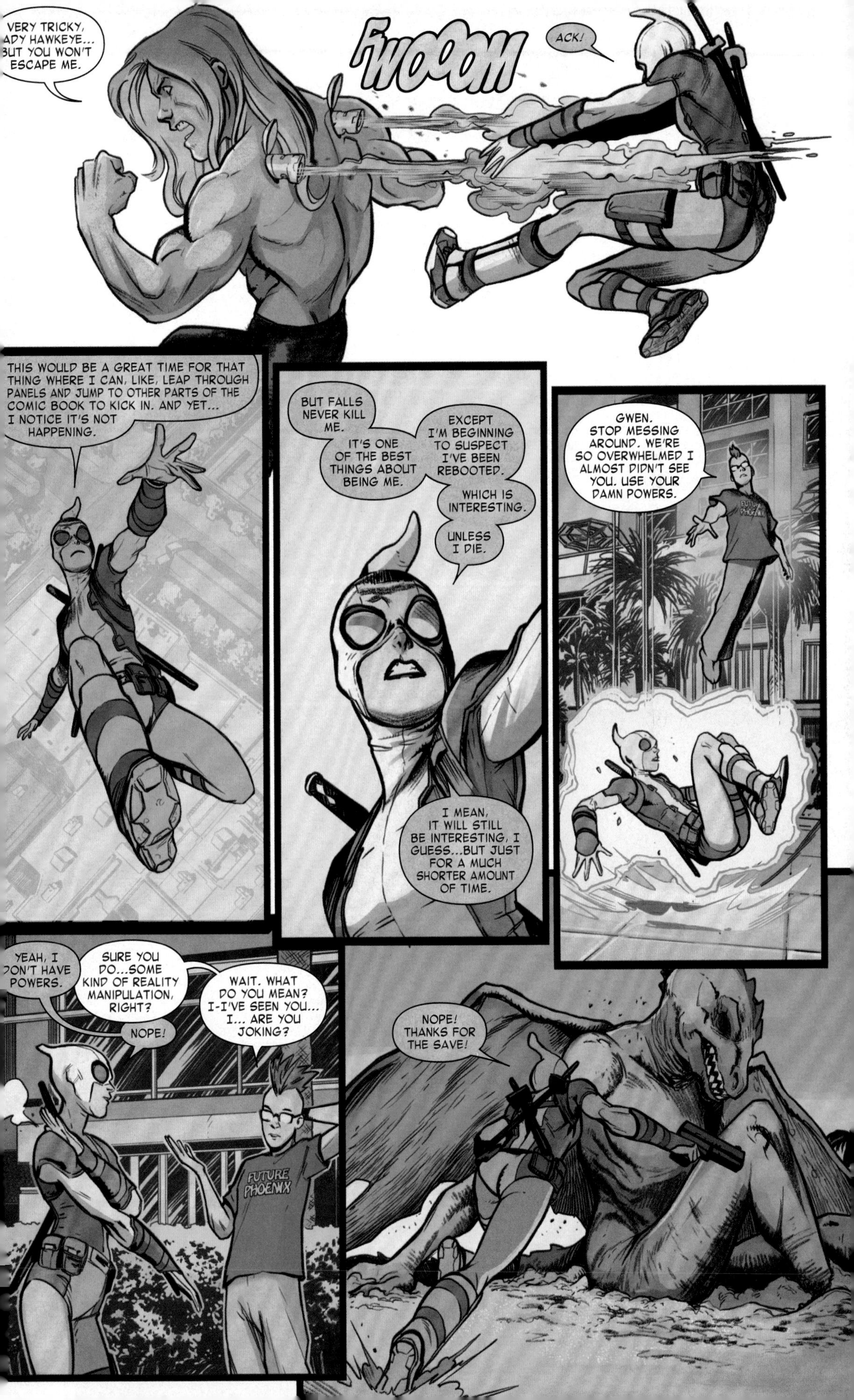
VERY TRICKY, ADY HAWKEYE... BUT YOU WON'T ESCAPE ME.
FWOOOM
ACK!
THIS WOULD BE A GREAT TIME FOR THAT THING WHERE I CAN, LIKE, LEAP THROUGH PANELS AND JUMP TO OTHER PARTS OF THE COMIC BOOK TO KICK IN. AND YET... I NOTICE IT'S NOT HAPPENING.
BUT FALLS NEVER KILL ME.
IT'S ONE OF THE BEST THINGS ABOUT BEING ME.
EXCEPT I'M BEGINNING TO SUSPECT I'VE BEEN REBOOTED.
WHICH IS INTERESTING.
UNLESS I DIE.
I MEAN, IT WILL STILL BE INTERESTING, I GUESS...BUT JUST FOR A MUCH SHORTER AMOUNT OF TIME.
GWEN. STOP MESSING AROUND. WE'RE SO OVERWHELMED I ALMOST DIDN'T SEE YOU. USE YOUR DAMN POWERS.
FUTURE PHOENIX
YEAH, I DON'T HAVE POWERS.
SURE YOU DO...SOME KIND OF REALITY MANIPULATION, RIGHT?
NOPE!
WAIT. WHAT DO YOU MEAN? I-I'VE SEEN YOU... I... ARE YOU JOKING?
FUTURE PHOENIX
NOPE! THANKS FOR THE SAVE!

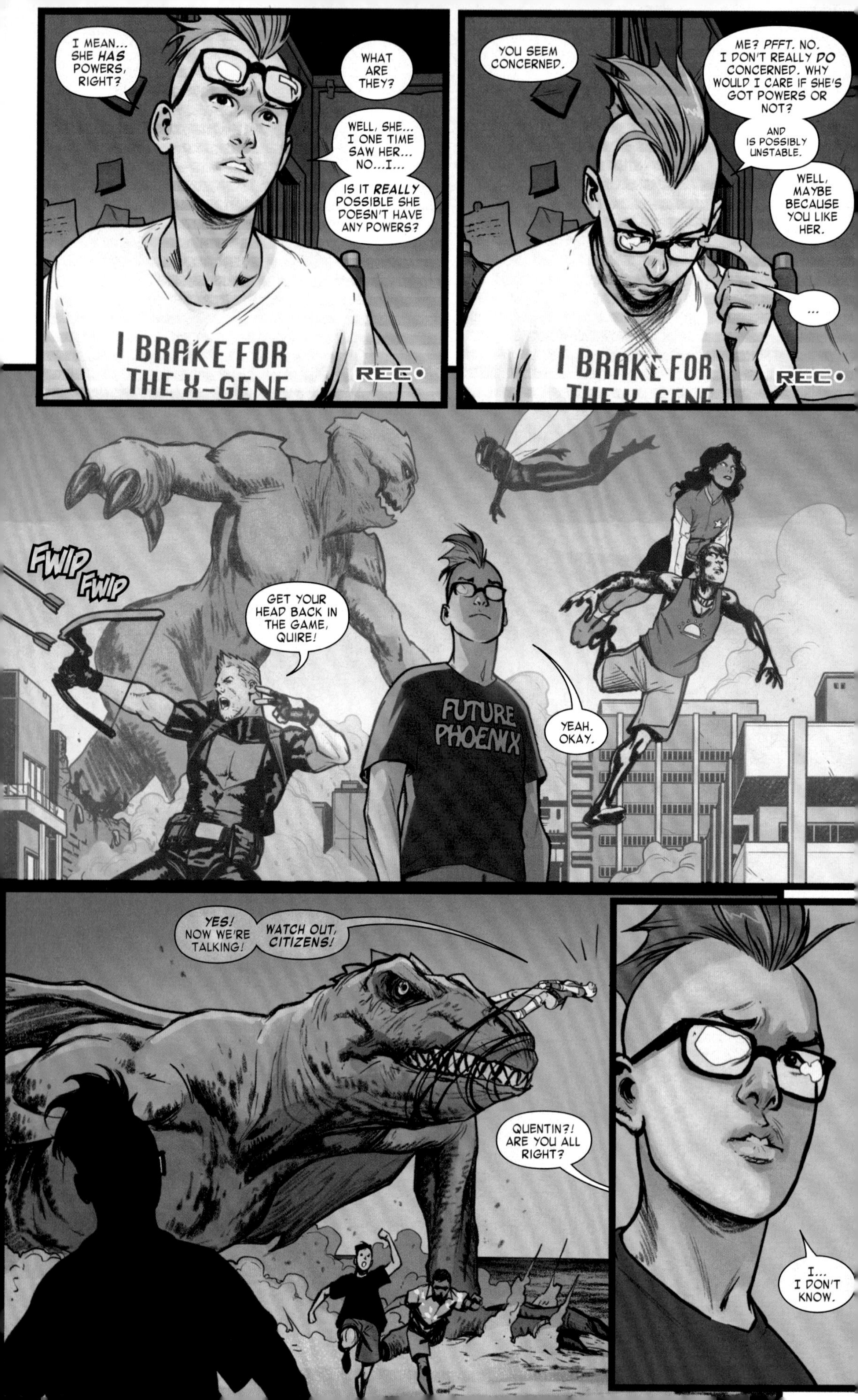
I MEAN... SHE *HAS* POWERS, RIGHT?
WHAT ARE THEY?
WELL, SHE... I ONE TIME SAW HER... NO...I...
IS IT *REALLY* POSSIBLE SHE DOESN'T HAVE ANY POWERS?
I BRAKE FOR THE X-GENE
REC
YOU SEEM CONCERNED.
ME? *PFFT.* NO. I DON'T REALLY *DO* CONCERNED. WHY WOULD I CARE IF SHE'S GOT POWERS OR NOT?
AND IS POSSIBLY UNSTABLE.
WELL, MAYBE BECAUSE YOU LIKE HER.
...
I BRAKE FOR THE X-GENE
REC
FWIP FWIP
GET YOUR HEAD BACK IN THE GAME, QUIRE!
FUTURE PHOENIX
YEAH. OKAY.
YES! NOW WE'RE TALKING!
WATCH OUT, *CITIZENS!*
QUENTIN?! ARE YOU ALL RIGHT?
I... I DON'T KNOW.

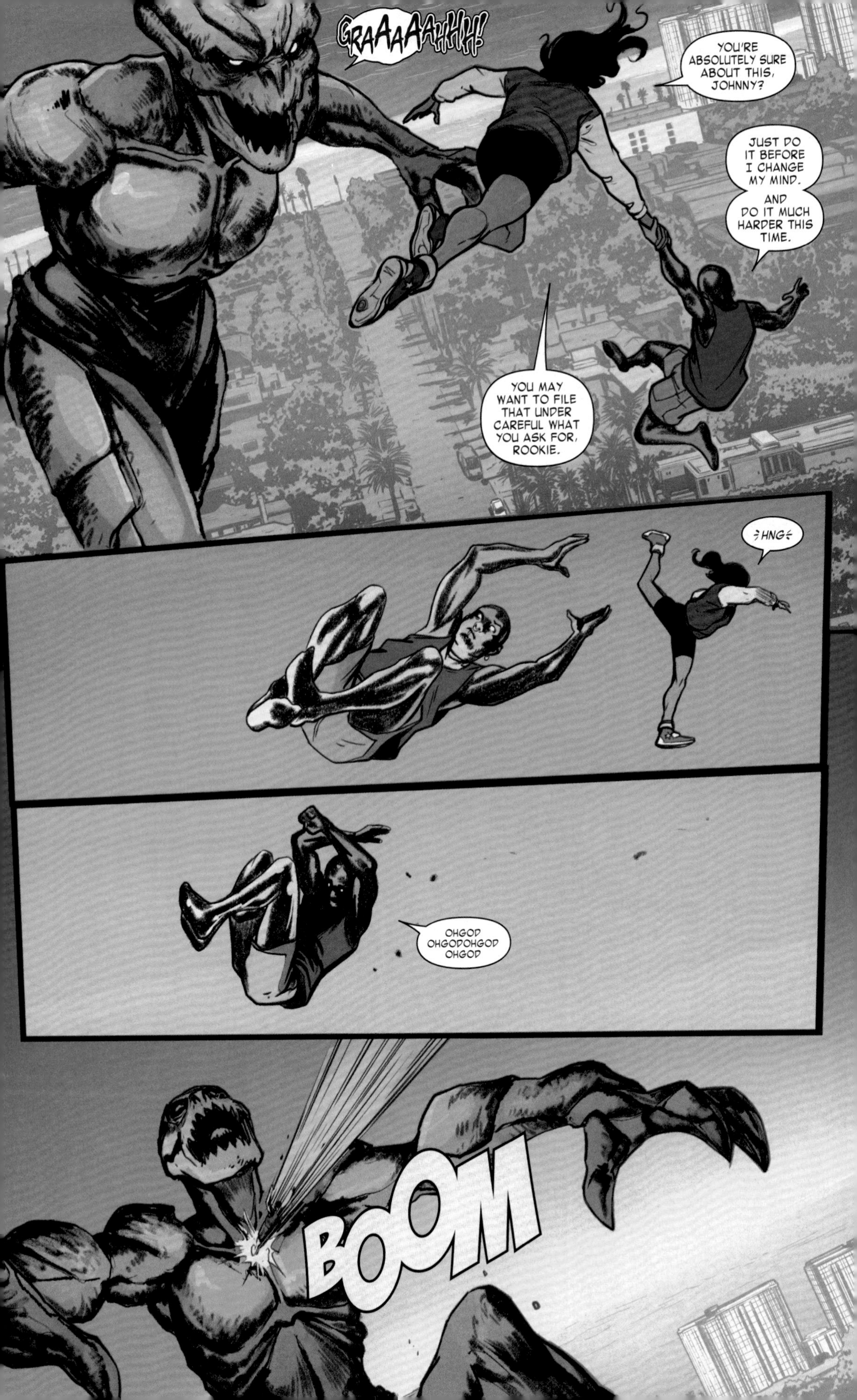
GRAAAAAHHH!
YOU'RE ABSOLUTELY SURE ABOUT THIS, JOHNNY?
JUST DO IT BEFORE I CHANGE MY MIND.
AND DO IT MUCH HARDER THIS TIME.
YOU MAY WANT TO FILE THAT UNDER CAREFUL WHAT YOU ASK FOR, ROOKIE.
HNG
OHGOD OHGODOHGOD OHGOD
BOOM

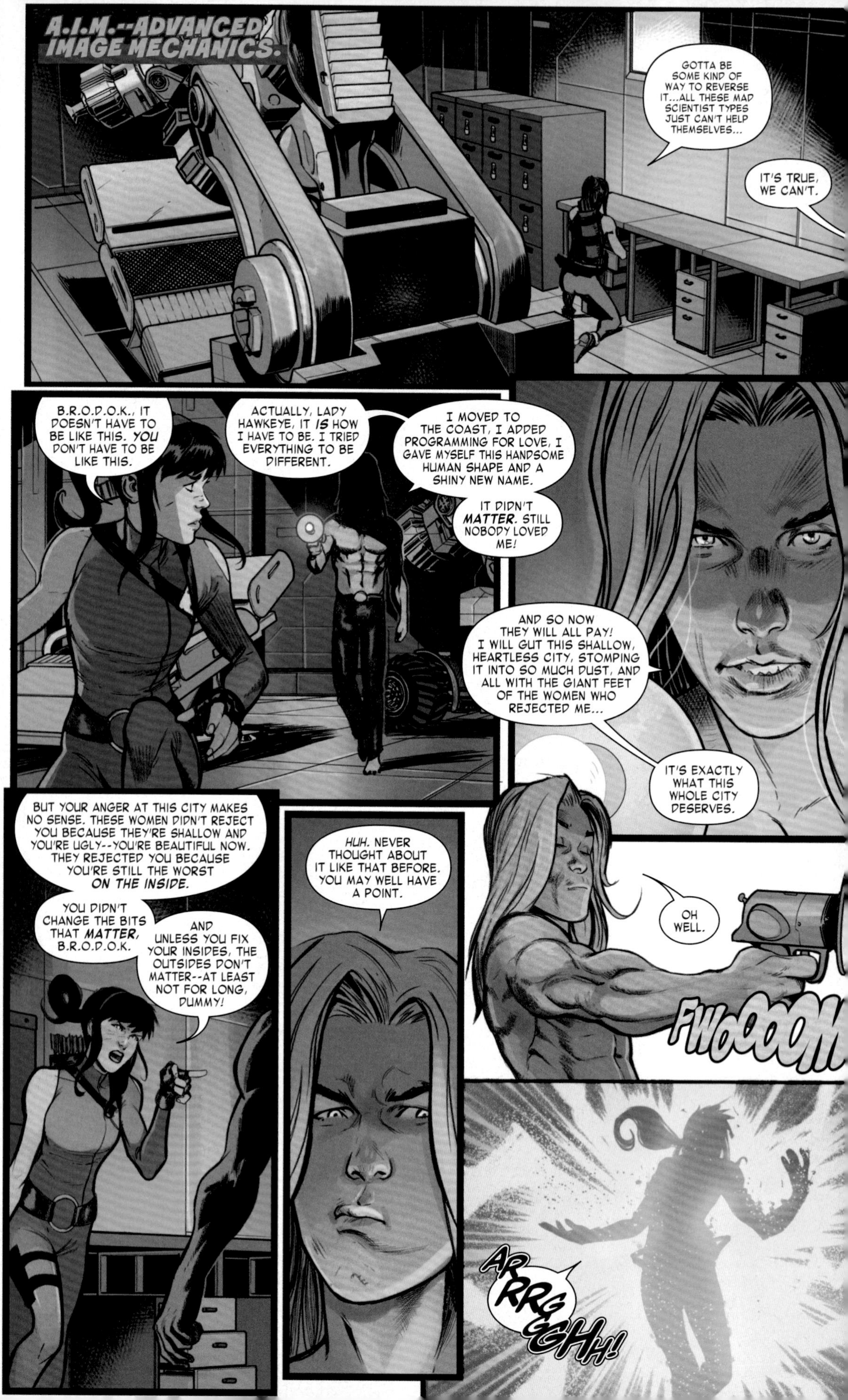
A.I.M.--ADVANCED IMAGE MECHANICS.
GOTTA BE SOME KIND OF WAY TO REVERSE IT...ALL THESE MAD SCIENTIST TYPES JUST CAN'T HELP THEMSELVES...
IT'S TRUE, WE CAN'T.
B.R.O.D.O.K., IT DOESN'T HAVE TO BE LIKE THIS. YOU DON'T HAVE TO BE LIKE THIS.
ACTUALLY, LADY HAWKEYE, IT IS HOW I HAVE TO BE. I TRIED EVERYTHING TO BE DIFFERENT.
I MOVED TO THE COAST, I ADDED PROGRAMMING FOR LOVE, I GAVE MYSELF THIS HANDSOME HUMAN SHAPE AND A SHINY NEW NAME.
IT DIDN'T MATTER. STILL NOBODY LOVED ME!
AND SO NOW THEY WILL ALL PAY! I WILL GUT THIS SHALLOW, HEARTLESS CITY, STOMPING IT INTO SO MUCH DUST, AND ALL WITH THE GIANT FEET OF THE WOMEN WHO REJECTED ME...
IT'S EXACTLY WHAT THIS WHOLE CITY DESERVES.
BUT YOUR ANGER AT THIS CITY MAKES NO SENSE. THESE WOMEN DIDN'T REJECT YOU BECAUSE THEY'RE SHALLOW AND YOU'RE UGLY--YOU'RE BEAUTIFUL NOW. THEY REJECTED YOU BECAUSE YOU'RE STILL THE WORST ON THE INSIDE.
YOU DIDN'T CHANGE THE BITS THAT MATTER, B.R.O.D.O.K.
AND UNLESS YOU FIX YOUR INSIDES, THE OUTSIDES DON'T MATTER--AT LEAST NOT FOR LONG, DUMMY!
HUH. NEVER THOUGHT ABOUT IT LIKE THAT BEFORE. YOU MAY WELL HAVE A POINT.
OH WELL.
FWOOOOM
ARRRGGGHH!

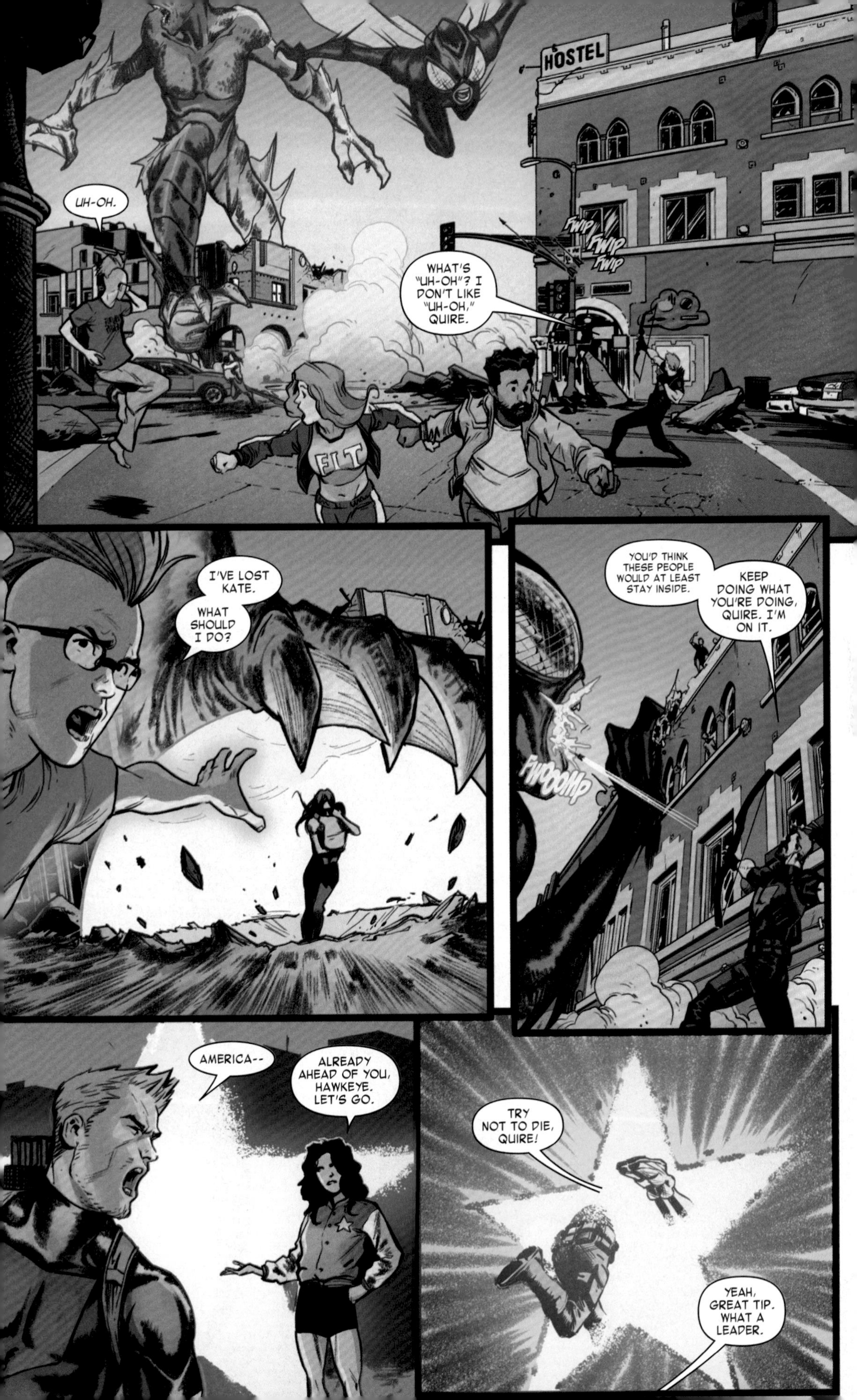
HOSTEL
UH-OH.
WHAT'S "UH-OH"? I DON'T LIKE "UH-OH," QUIRE.
FWIP FWIP FWIP
I'VE LOST KATE.
WHAT SHOULD I DO?
YOU'D THINK THESE PEOPLE WOULD AT LEAST STAY INSIDE.
KEEP DOING WHAT YOU'RE DOING, QUIRE. I'M ON IT.
FWOOOMP
AMERICA--
ALREADY AHEAD OF YOU, HAWKEYE. LET'S GO.
TRY NOT TO DIE, QUIRE!
YEAH, GREAT TIP. WHAT A LEADER.

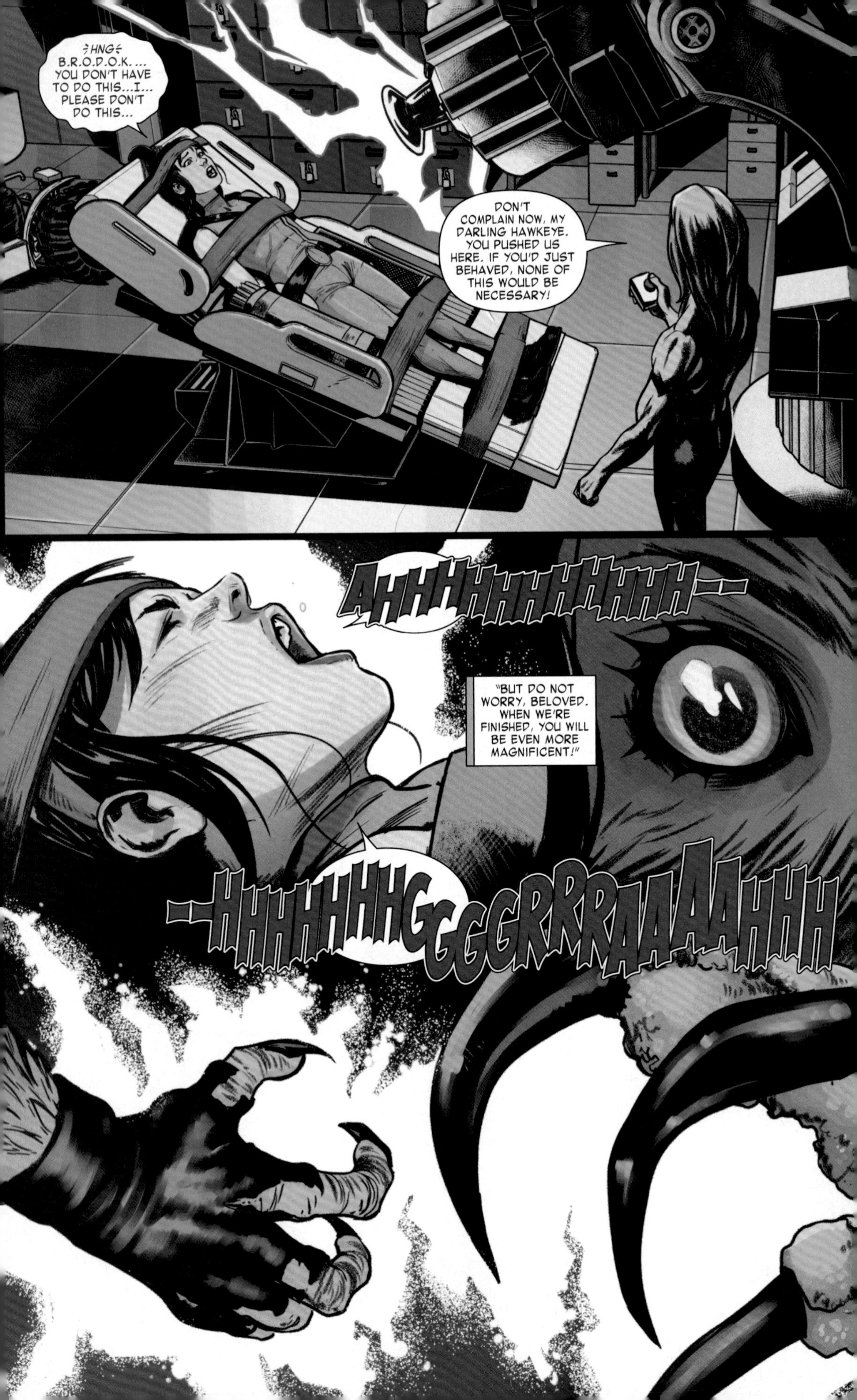
HNG
B.R.O.D.O.K. ... YOU DON'T HAVE TO DO THIS...I... PLEASE DON'T DO THIS...
DON'T COMPLAIN NOW, MY DARLING HAWKEYE. YOU PUSHED US HERE. IF YOU'D JUST BEHAVED, NONE OF THIS WOULD BE NECESSARY!
AHHHHHHHHHH--
"BUT DO NOT WORRY, BELOVED. WHEN WE'RE FINISHED, YOU WILL BE EVEN MORE MAGNIFICENT!"
--HHHHHHGGGRRRAAAAHHH

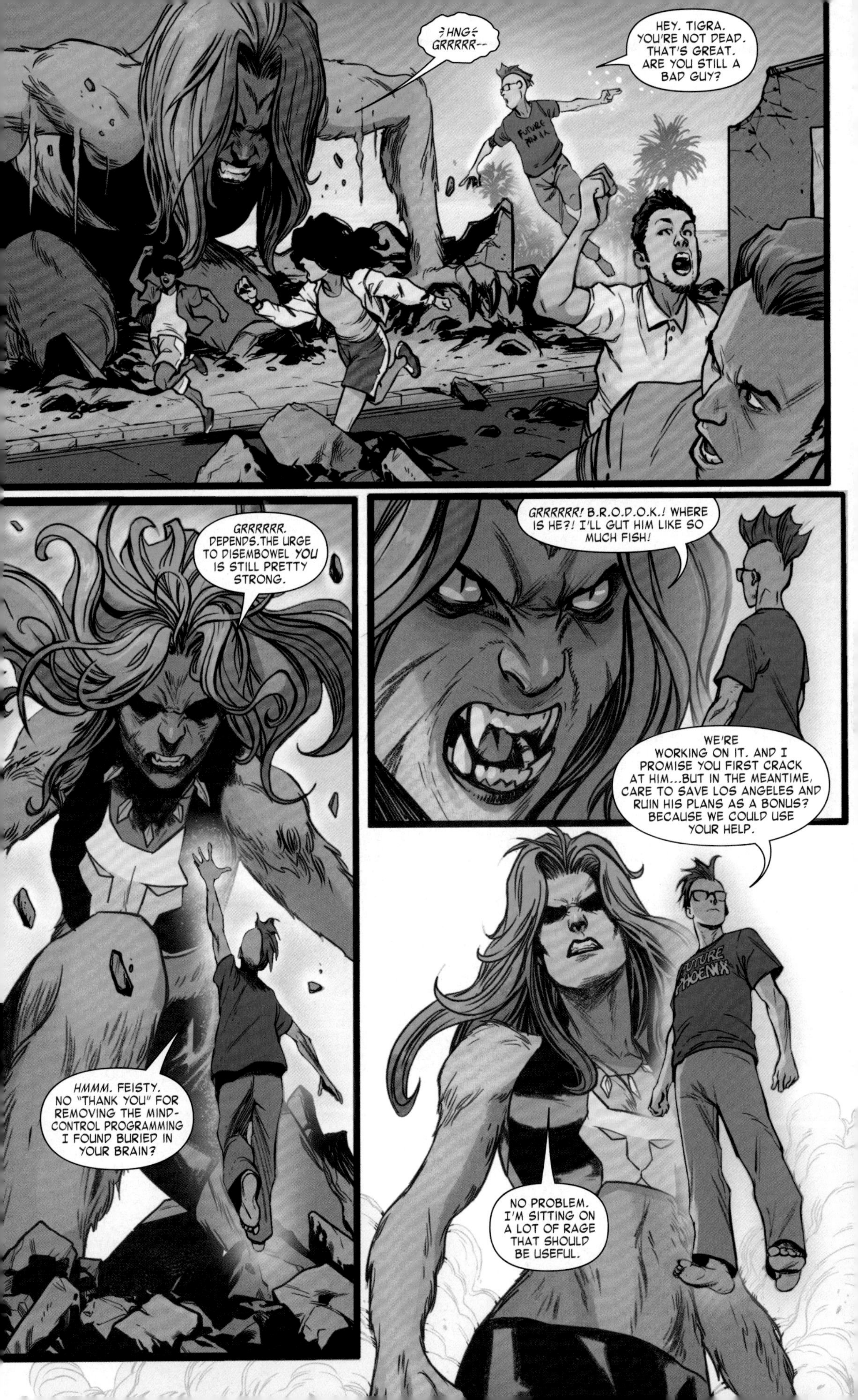
HNG GRRRRR--
HEY. TIGRA. YOU'RE NOT DEAD. THAT'S GREAT. ARE YOU STILL A BAD GUY?
GRRRRRR. DEPENDS. THE URGE TO DISEMBOWEL YOU IS STILL PRETTY STRONG.
HMMM. FEISTY. NO "THANK YOU" FOR REMOVING THE MIND-CONTROL PROGRAMMING I FOUND BURIED IN YOUR BRAIN?
GRRRRRR! B.R.O.D.O.K.! WHERE IS HE?! I'LL GUT HIM LIKE SO MUCH FISH!
WE'RE WORKING ON IT. AND I PROMISE YOU FIRST CRACK AT HIM...BUT IN THE MEANTIME, CARE TO SAVE LOS ANGELES AND RUIN HIS PLANS AS A BONUS? BECAUSE WE COULD USE YOUR HELP.
FUTURE PHOENIX
NO PROBLEM. I'M SITTING ON A LOT OF RAGE THAT SHOULD BE USEFUL.

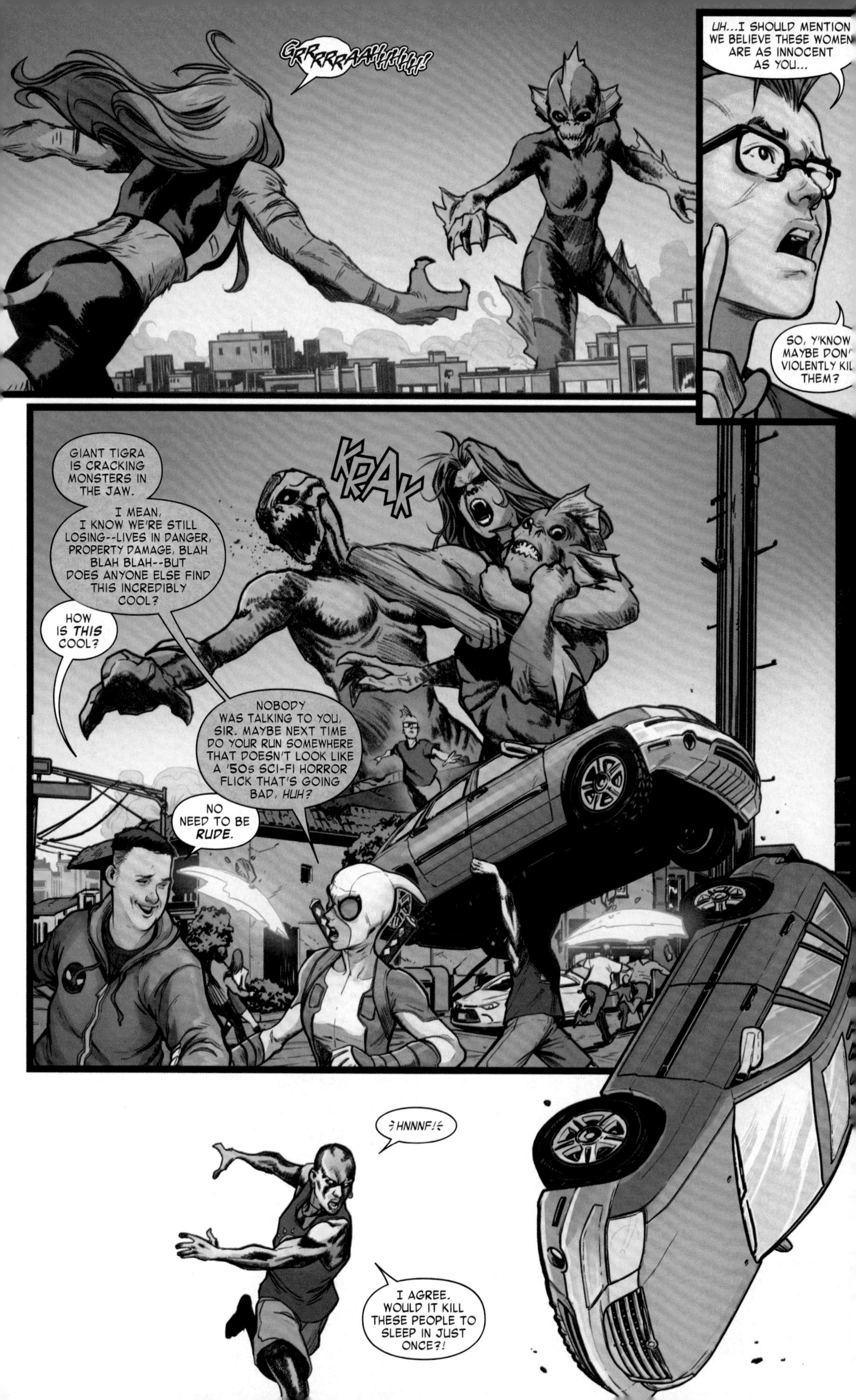
GRRRRRAAHHHHH!
UH...I SHOULD MENTION WE BELIEVE THESE WOMEN ARE AS INNOCENT AS YOU...
SO, Y'KNOW MAYBE DON'T VIOLENTLY KILL THEM?
GIANT TIGRA IS CRACKING MONSTERS IN THE JAW.
I MEAN, I KNOW WE'RE STILL LOSING--LIVES IN DANGER, PROPERTY DAMAGE, BLAH BLAH BLAH--BUT DOES ANYONE ELSE FIND THIS INCREDIBLY COOL?
KRAK
HOW IS THIS COOL?
NOBODY WAS TALKING TO YOU, SIR. MAYBE NEXT TIME DO YOUR RUN SOMEWHERE THAT DOESN'T LOOK LIKE A '50s SCI-FI HORROR FLICK THAT'S GOING BAD, HUH?
NO NEED TO BE RUDE.
HNNNF!
I AGREE. WOULD IT KILL THESE PEOPLE TO SLEEP IN JUST ONCE?!

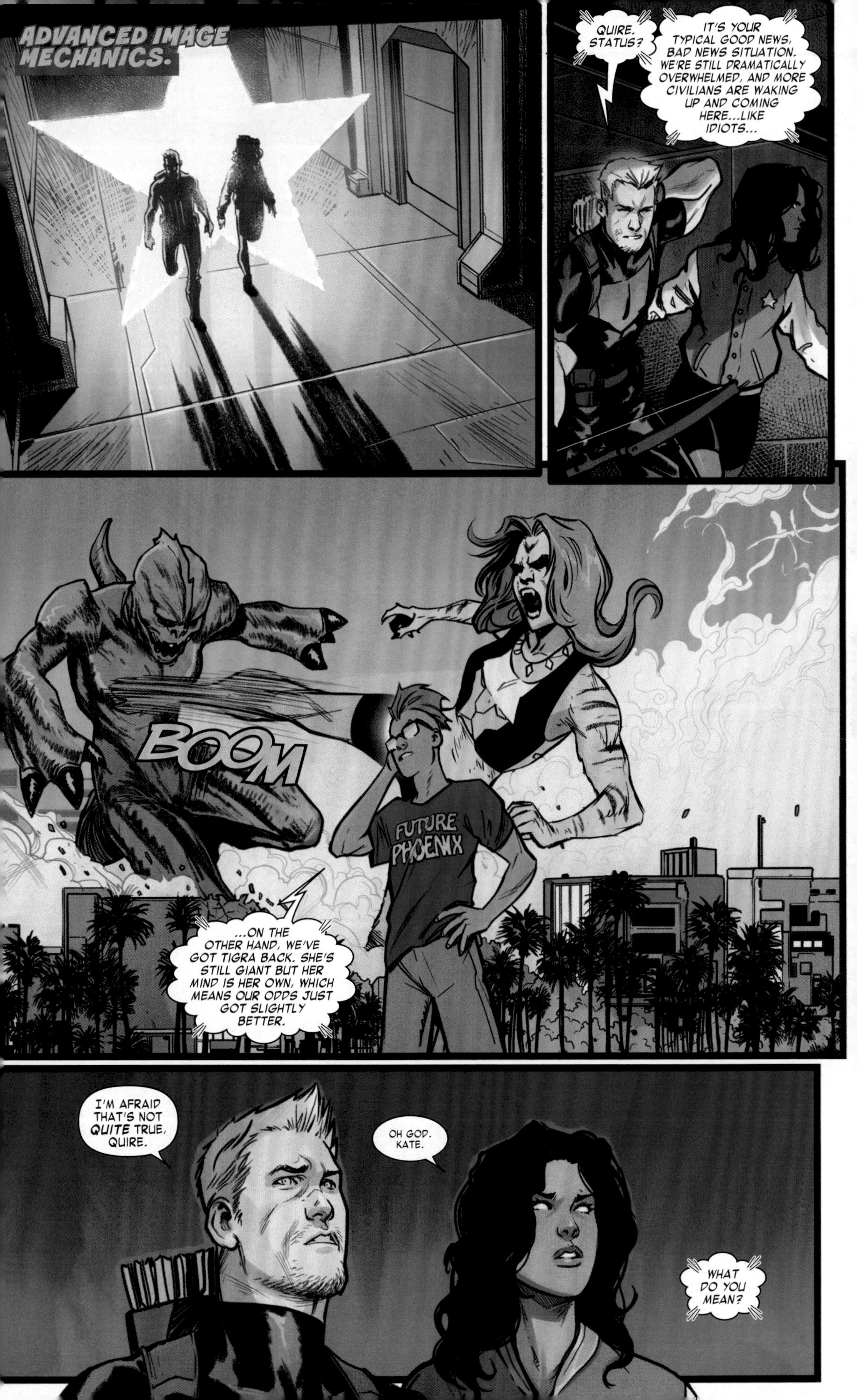
ADVANCED IMAGE MECHANICS.
QUIRE. STATUS?
IT'S YOUR TYPICAL GOOD NEWS, BAD NEWS SITUATION. WE'RE STILL DRAMATICALLY OVERWHELMED, AND MORE CIVILIANS ARE WAKING UP AND COMING HERE...LIKE IDIOTS...
BOOM
FUTURE PHOENIX
...ON THE OTHER HAND, WE'VE GOT TIGRA BACK. SHE'S STILL GIANT BUT HER MIND IS HER OWN, WHICH MEANS OUR ODDS JUST GOT SLIGHTLY BETTER.
I'M AFRAID THAT'S NOT QUITE TRUE, QUIRE.
OH GOD. KATE.
WHAT DO YOU MEAN?

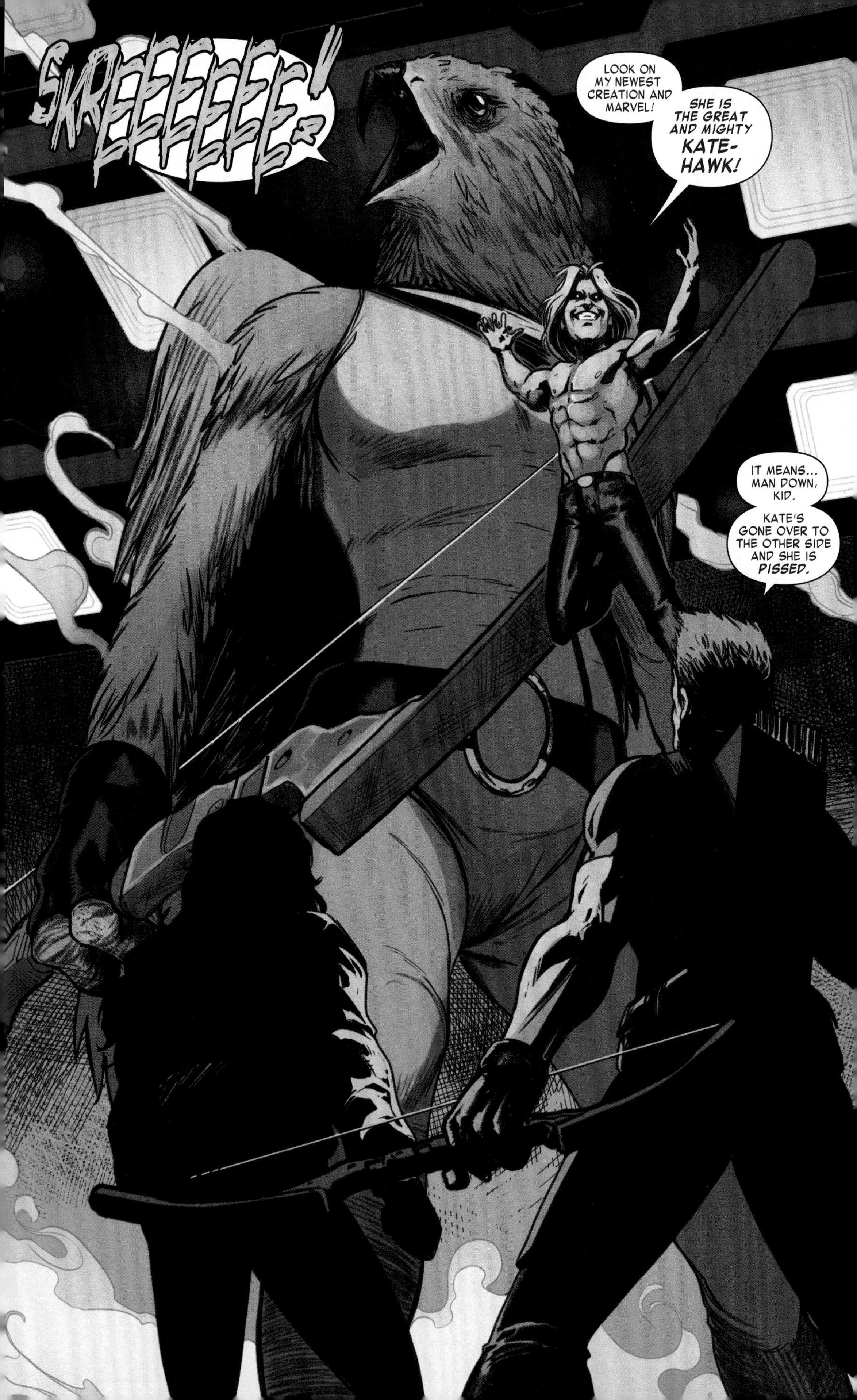
SKREEEEEEEE!
LOOK ON MY NEWEST CREATION AND MARVEL!
SHE IS THE GREAT AND MIGHTY KATE-HAWK!
IT MEANS... MAN DOWN, KID.
KATE'S GONE OVER TO THE OTHER SIDE AND SHE IS PISSED.

#1 VARIANT BY TERRY DODSON & RACHEL DODSON

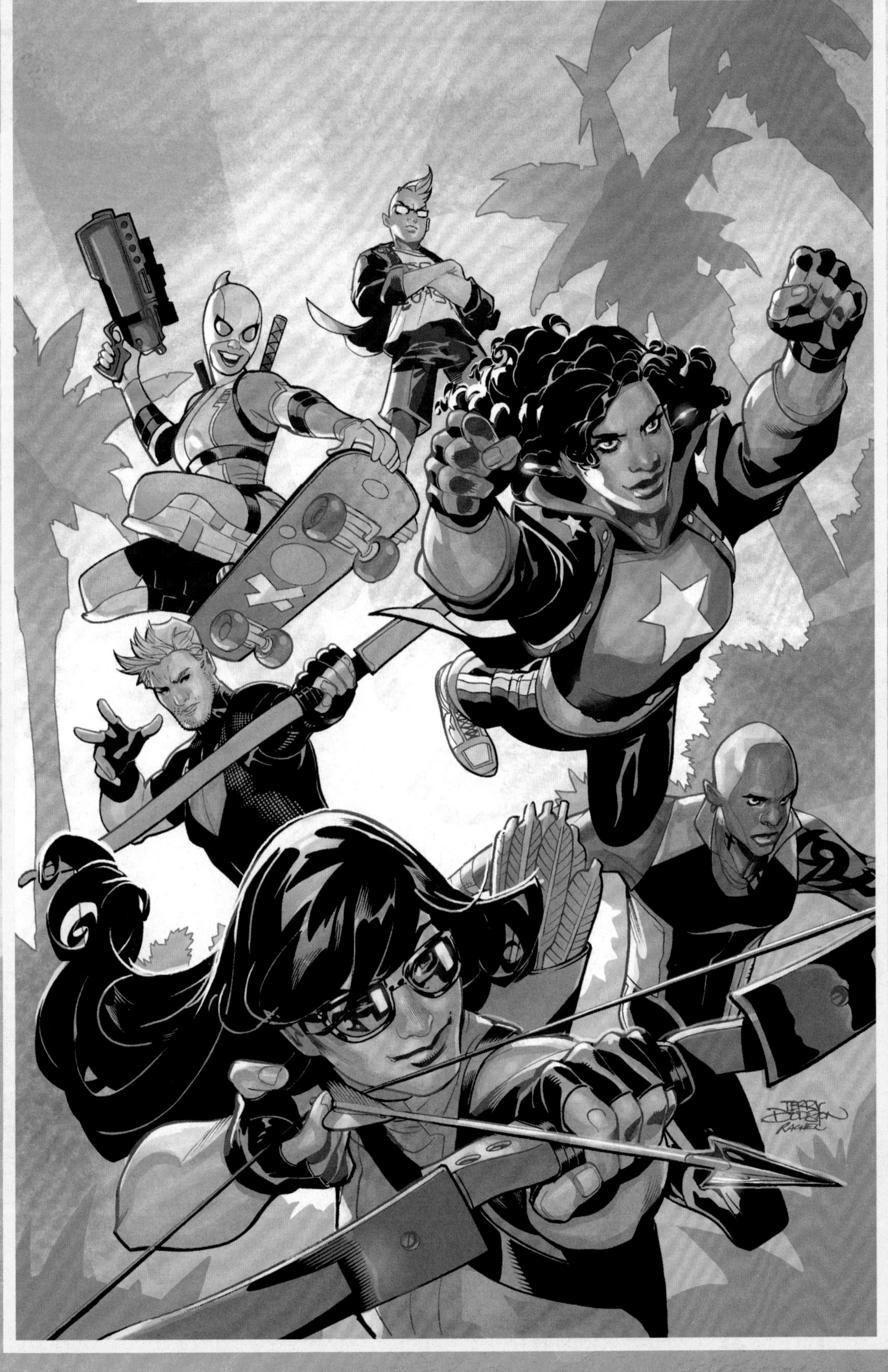
TERRY DODSON
RACHEL

ARE THESE THE NEW

West Coast

AVENGERS?

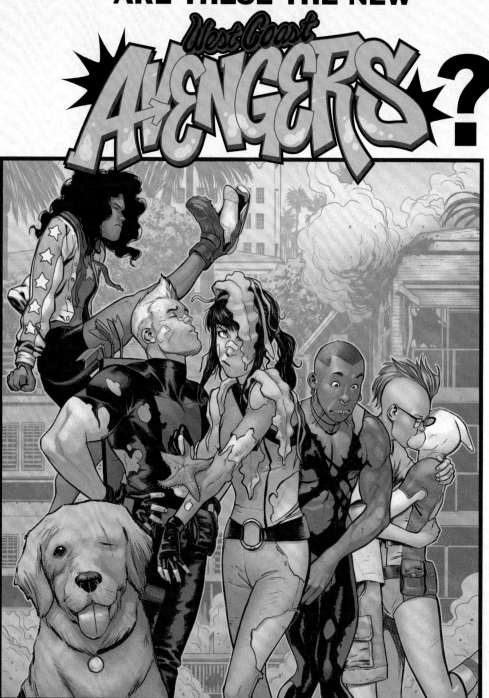

THERE GOES THE NEIGHBORHOOD!

Supers in Santa Monica? Say it ain't so! An untested new team claiming to be Avengers has some Californians wishing that a certain P.I. never moved west!

Witnesses identified former West Coast Avengers founder Hawkeye (Clint Barton) as well as his protégé Hawkeye (Kate Bishop) as the leaders of what, according to one bystander, "Looked like maybe it could be the West Coast Avengers?" Also identified were X-Men dropout Quentin Quire,

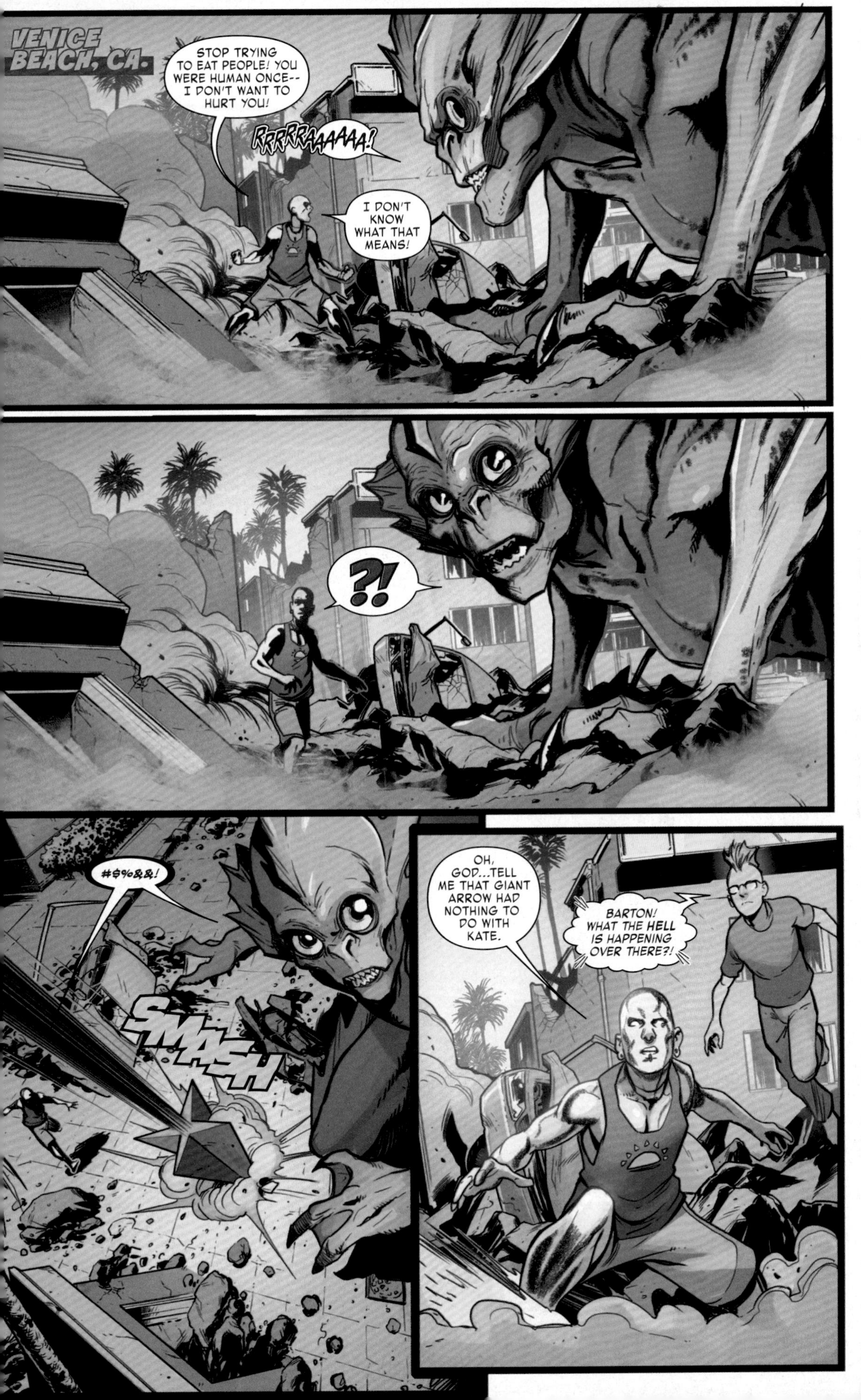
VENICE BEACH, CA.
STOP TRYING TO EAT PEOPLE! YOU WERE HUMAN ONCE-- I DON'T WANT TO HURT YOU!
RRRRRAAAAAA!
I DON'T KNOW WHAT THAT MEANS!
?!
#$%&&!
SMASH
OH, GOD...TELL ME THAT GIANT ARROW HAD NOTHING TO DO WITH KATE.
BARTON! WHAT THE HELL IS HAPPENING OVER THERE?!

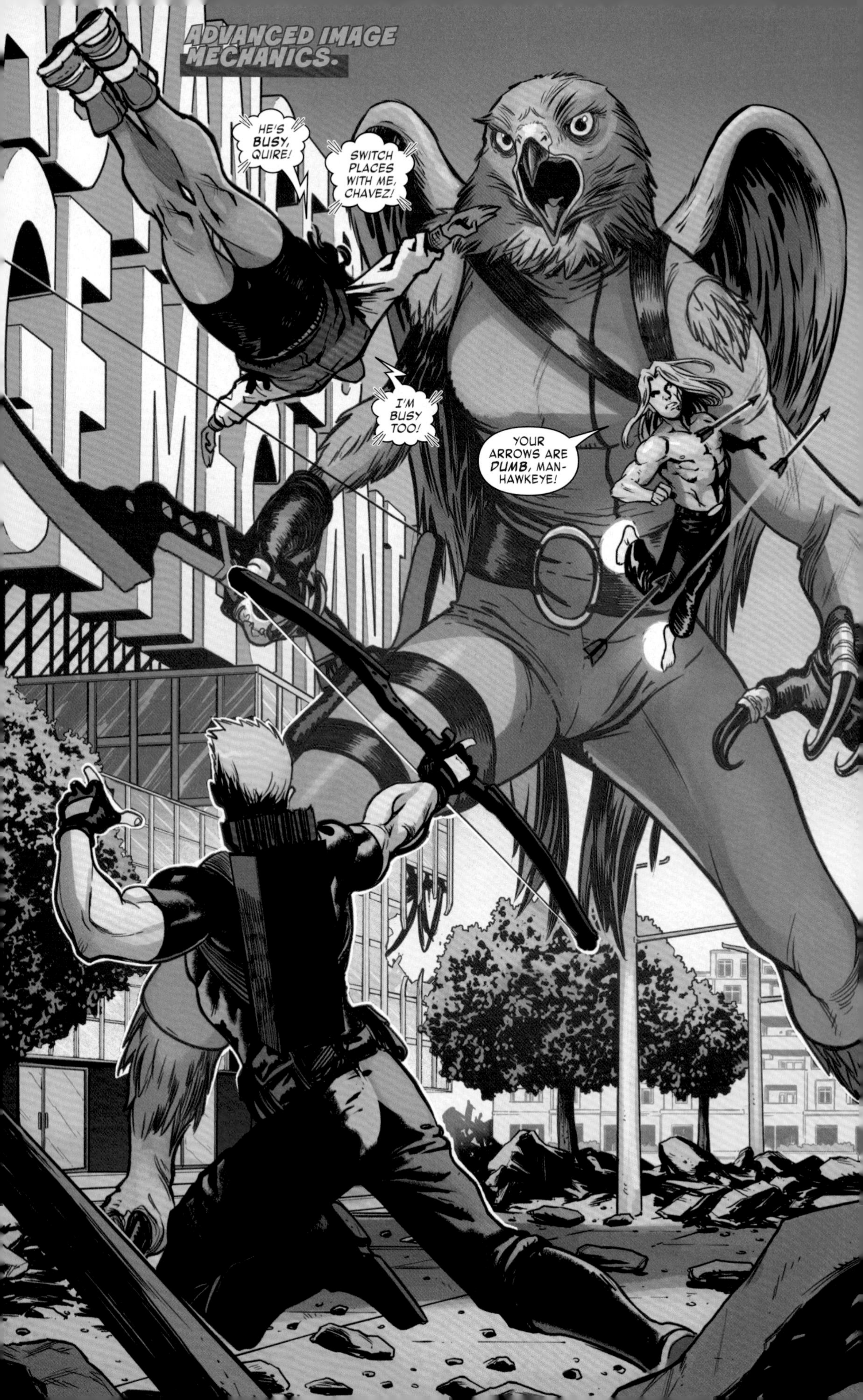
ADVANCED IMAGE MECHANICS.
HE'S BUSY, QUIRE!
SWITCH PLACES WITH ME, CHAVEZ!
I'M BUSY TOO!
YOUR ARROWS ARE DUMB, MAN-HAWKEYE!

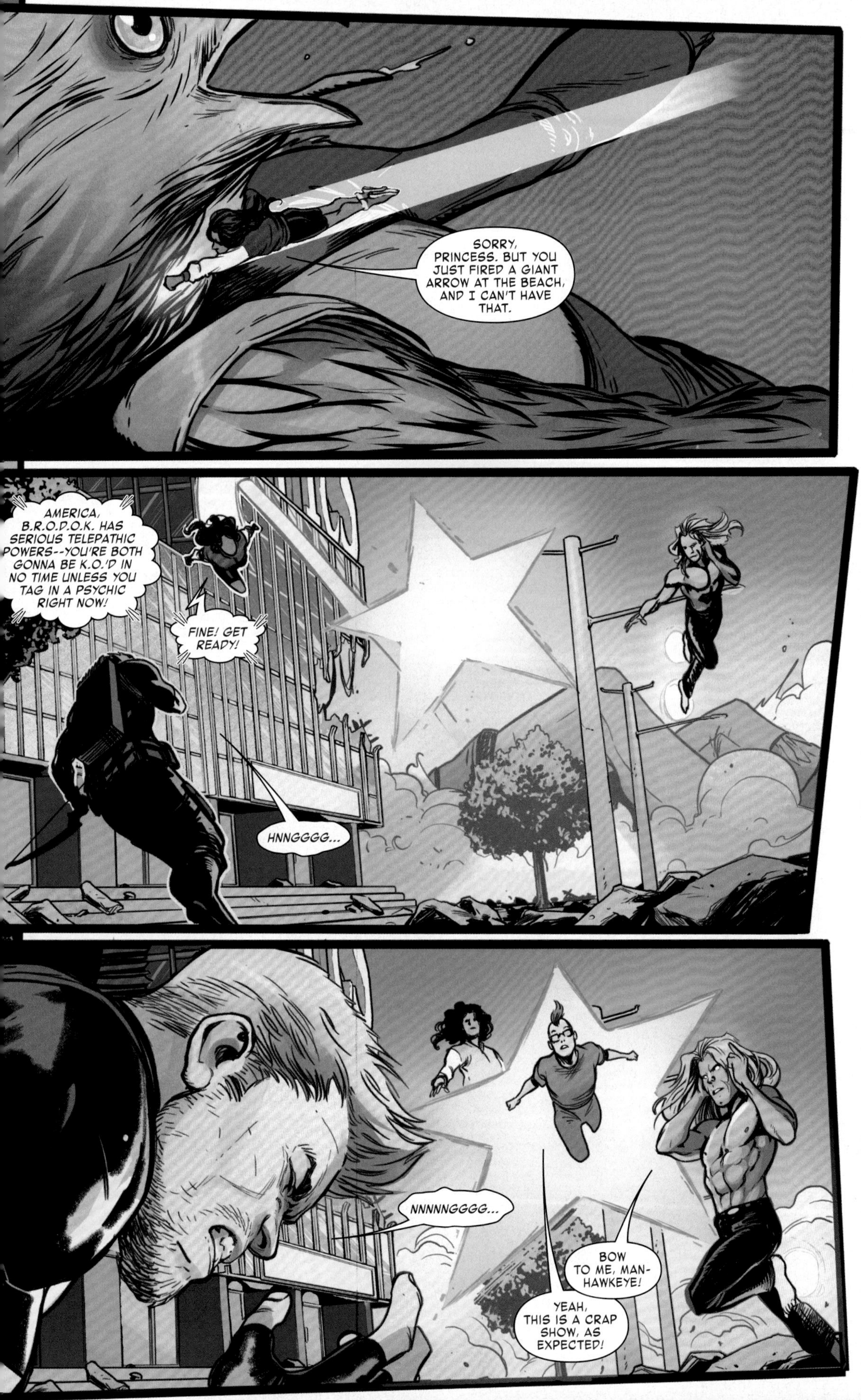
SORRY, PRINCESS. BUT YOU JUST FIRED A GIANT ARROW AT THE BEACH, AND I CAN'T HAVE THAT.
AMERICA, B.R.O.D.O.K. HAS SERIOUS TELEPATHIC POWERS--YOU'RE BOTH GONNA BE K.O.'D IN NO TIME UNLESS YOU TAG IN A PSYCHIC RIGHT NOW!
FINE! GET READY!
HNNGGGG...
NNNNNGGGG...
BOW TO ME, MAN-HAWKEYE!
YEAH, THIS IS A CRAP SHOW, AS EXPECTED!

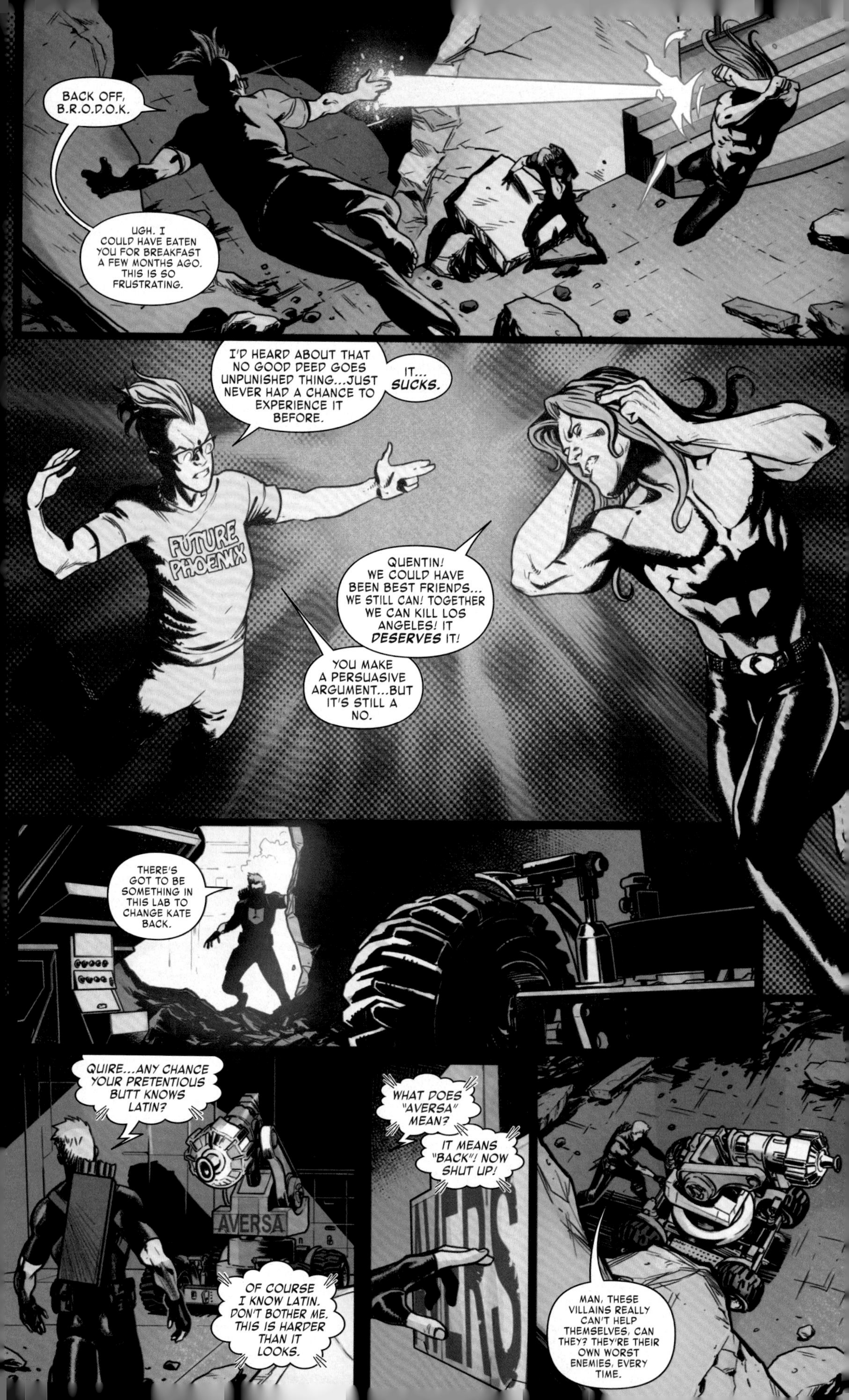
BACK OFF, B.R.O.D.O.K.
UGH. I COULD HAVE EATEN YOU FOR BREAKFAST A FEW MONTHS AGO. THIS IS SO FRUSTRATING.
I'D HEARD ABOUT THAT NO GOOD DEED GOES UNPUNISHED THING...JUST NEVER HAD A CHANCE TO EXPERIENCE IT BEFORE.
IT... SUCKS.
FUTURE PHOENIX
QUENTIN! WE COULD HAVE BEEN BEST FRIENDS... WE STILL CAN! TOGETHER WE CAN KILL LOS ANGELES! IT DESERVES IT!
YOU MAKE A PERSUASIVE ARGUMENT...BUT IT'S STILL A NO.
THERE'S GOT TO BE SOMETHING IN THIS LAB TO CHANGE KATE BACK.
QUIRE...ANY CHANCE YOUR PRETENTIOUS BUTT KNOWS LATIN?
AVERSA
OF COURSE I KNOW LATIN. DON'T BOTHER ME. THIS IS HARDER THAN IT LOOKS.
WHAT DOES "AVERSA" MEAN?
IT MEANS "BACK"! NOW SHUT UP!
MAN, THESE VILLAINS REALLY CAN'T HELP THEMSELVES, CAN THEY? THEY'RE THEIR OWN WORST ENEMIES, EVERY TIME.

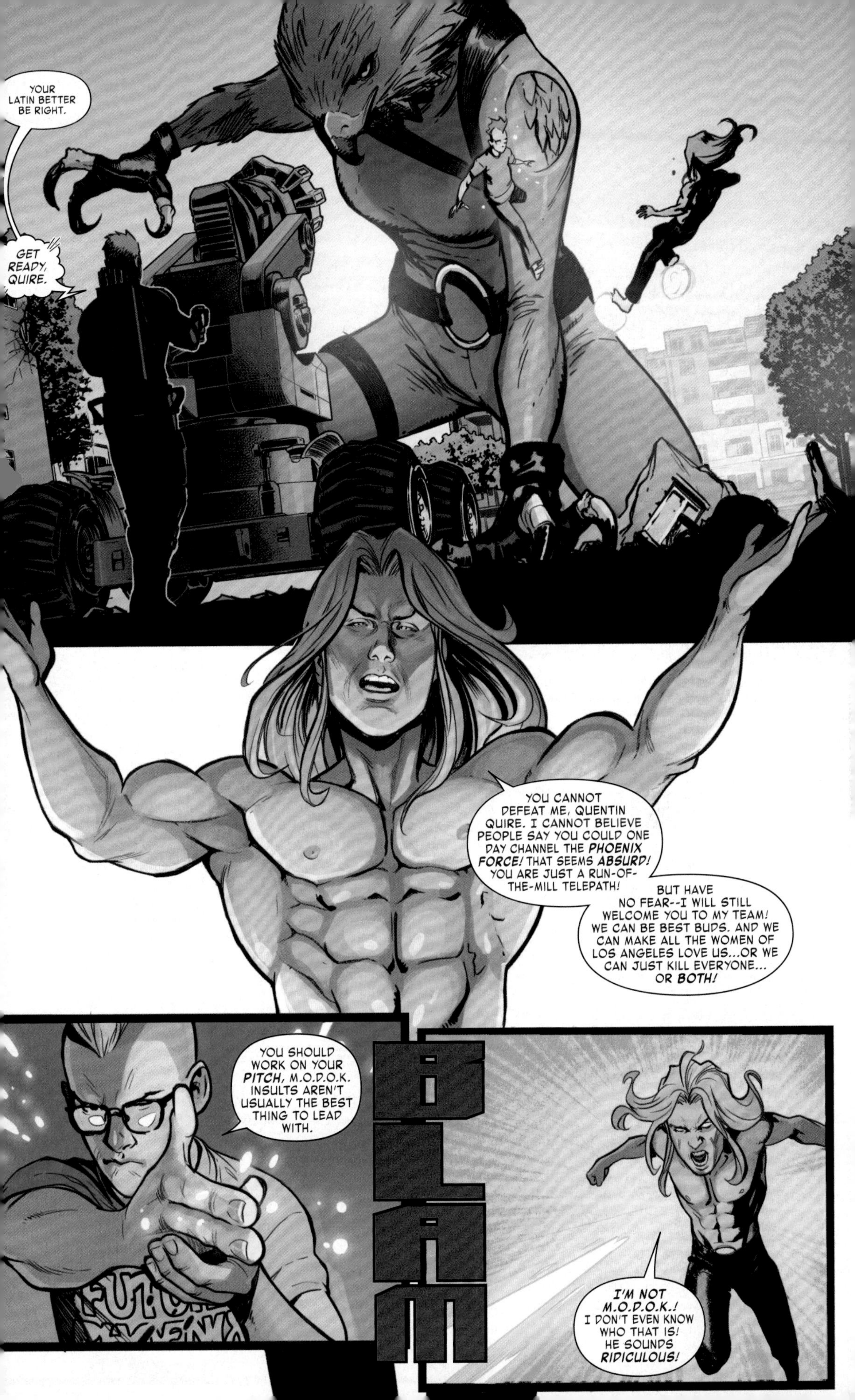

YOUR LATIN BETTER BE RIGHT.
GET READY, QUIRE.
YOU CANNOT DEFEAT ME, QUENTIN QUIRE. I CANNOT BELIEVE PEOPLE SAY YOU COULD ONE DAY CHANNEL THE PHOENIX FORCE! THAT SEEMS ABSURD! YOU ARE JUST A RUN-OF-THE-MILL TELEPATH!
BUT HAVE NO FEAR--I WILL STILL WELCOME YOU TO MY TEAM! WE CAN BE BEST BUDS. AND WE CAN MAKE ALL THE WOMEN OF LOS ANGELES LOVE US...OR WE CAN JUST KILL EVERYONE... OR BOTH!
YOU SHOULD WORK ON YOUR PITCH, M.O.D.O.K. INSULTS AREN'T USUALLY THE BEST THING TO LEAD WITH.
BLAM
I'M NOT M.O.D.O.K.! I DON'T EVEN KNOW WHO THAT IS! HE SOUNDS RIDICULOUS!

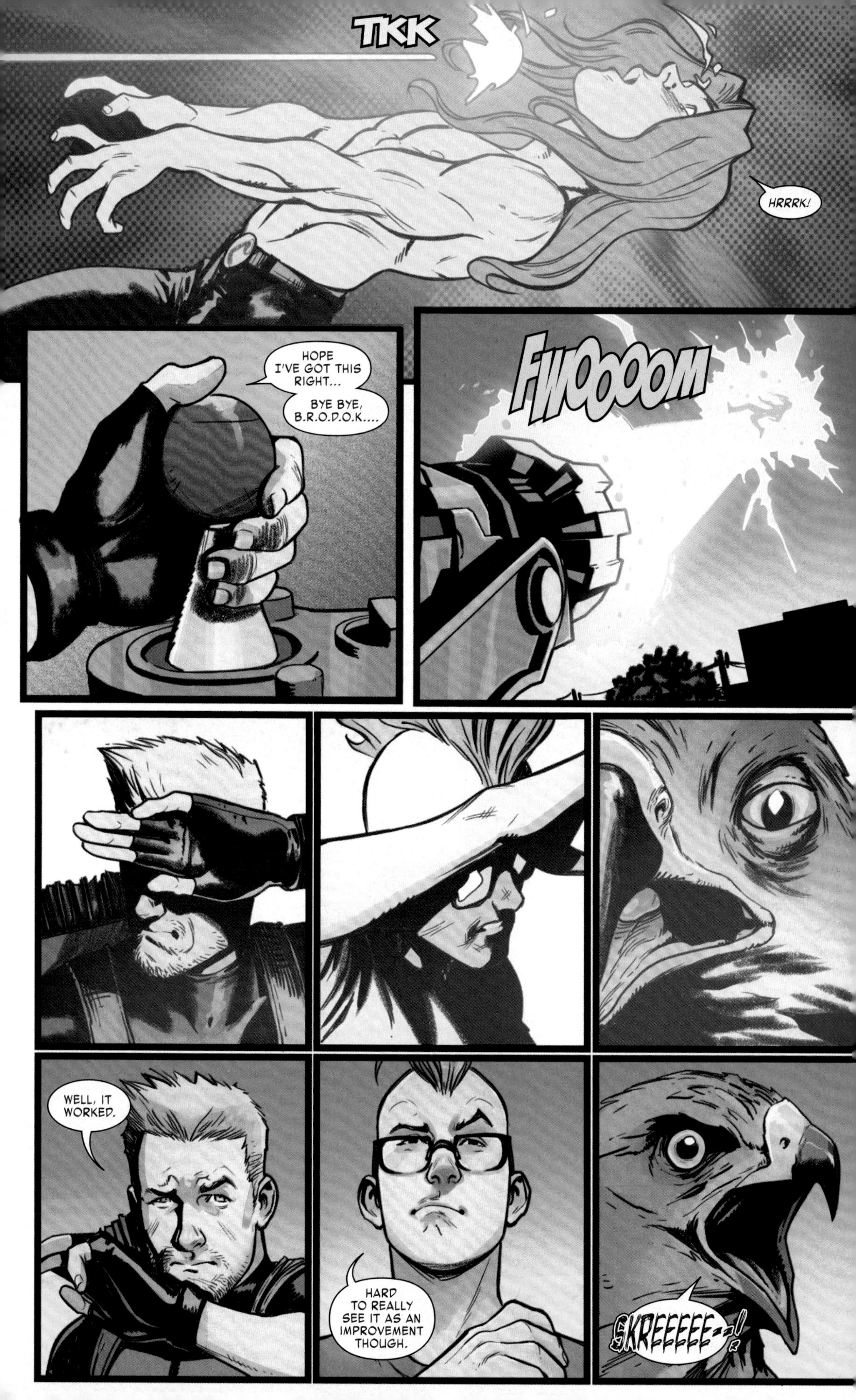
TKK
HRRRK!
HOPE I'VE GOT THIS RIGHT...
BYE BYE, B.R.O.D.O.K....
FWOOOOM
WELL, IT WORKED.
HARD TO REALLY SEE IT AS AN IMPROVEMENT THOUGH.
SKREEEEE--!

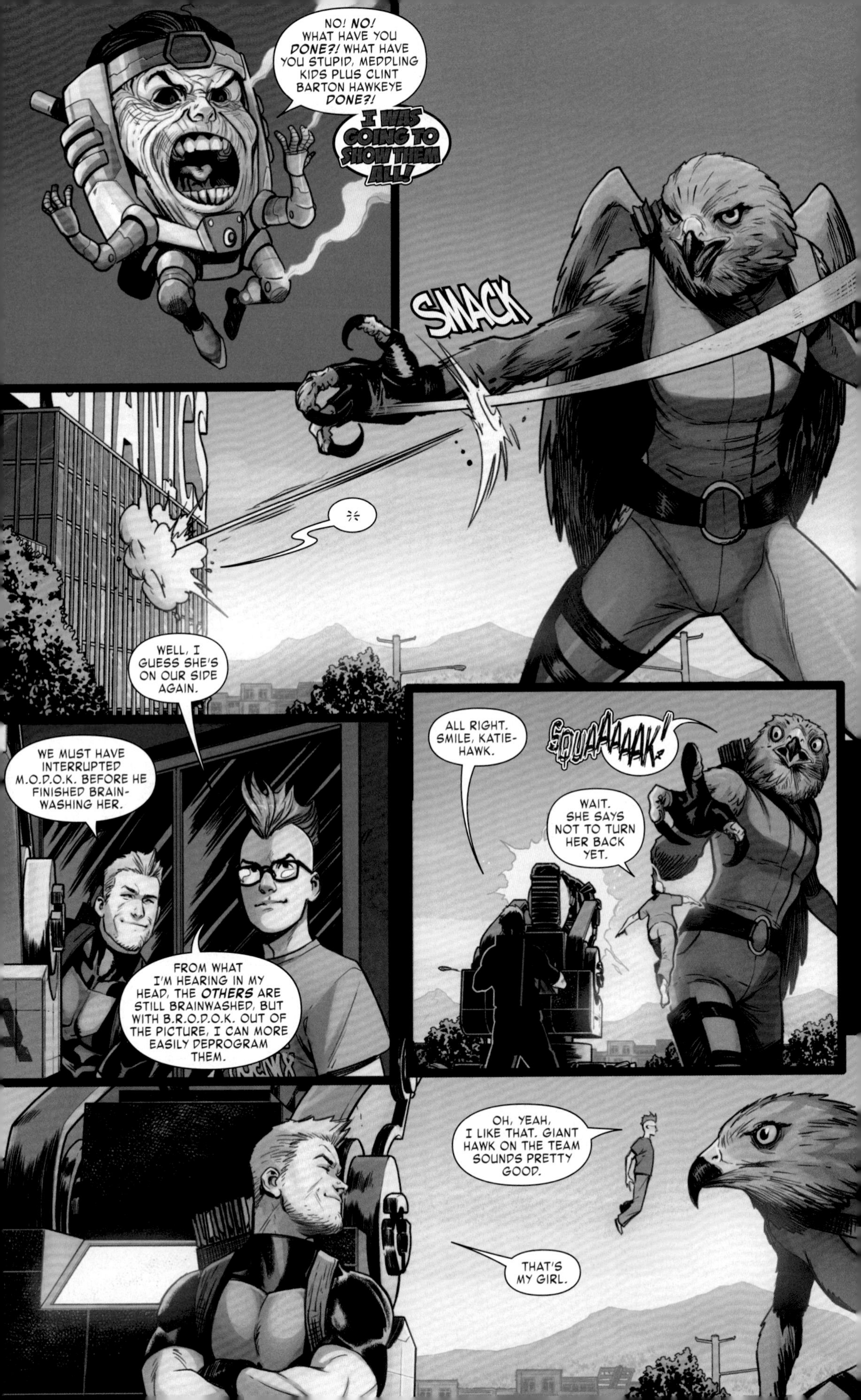

NO! NO! WHAT HAVE YOU DONE?! WHAT HAVE YOU STUPID, MEDDLING KIDS PLUS CLINT BARTON HAWKEYE DONE?!
I WAS GOING TO SHOW THEM ALL!
SMACK
WELL, I GUESS SHE'S ON OUR SIDE AGAIN.
WE MUST HAVE INTERRUPTED M.O.D.O.K. BEFORE HE FINISHED BRAIN-WASHING HER.
FROM WHAT I'M HEARING IN MY HEAD, THE OTHERS ARE STILL BRAINWASHED, BUT WITH B.R.O.D.O.K. OUT OF THE PICTURE, I CAN MORE EASILY DEPROGRAM THEM.
ALL RIGHT. SMILE, KATIE-HAWK.
SQUAAAAAK!
WAIT. SHE SAYS NOT TO TURN HER BACK YET.
OH, YEAH, I LIKE THAT. GIANT HAWK ON THE TEAM SOUNDS PRETTY GOOD.
THAT'S MY GIRL.

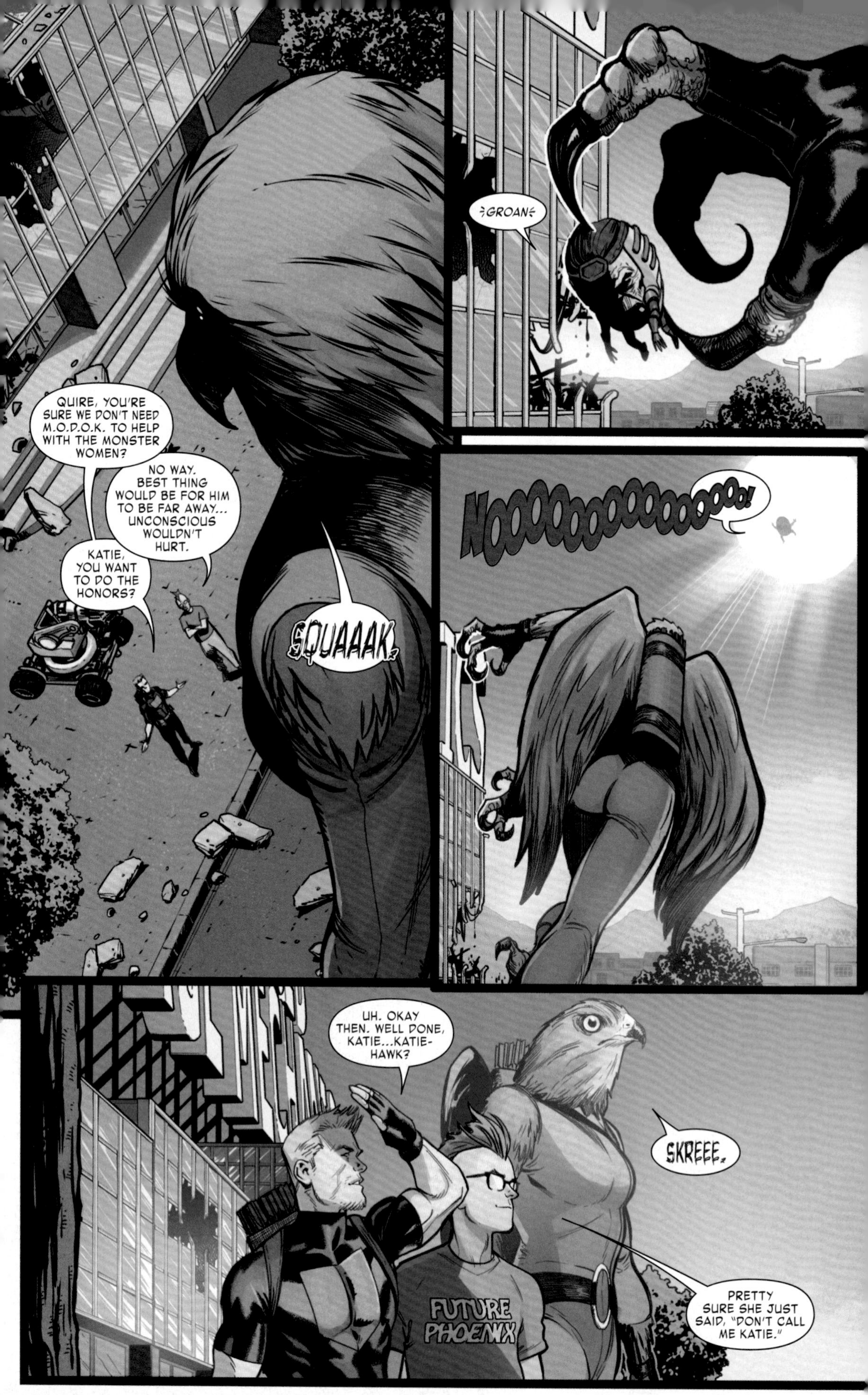
GROAN
QUIRE, YOU'RE SURE WE DON'T NEED M.O.D.O.K. TO HELP WITH THE MONSTER WOMEN?
NO WAY. BEST THING WOULD BE FOR HIM TO BE FAR AWAY... UNCONSCIOUS WOULDN'T HURT.
KATIE, YOU WANT TO DO THE HONORS?
SQUAAAK
NOOOOOOOOOOOOOOOOO!
UH. OKAY THEN. WELL DONE, KATIE...KATIE-HAWK?
SKREEE
FUTURE PHOENIX
PRETTY SURE SHE JUST SAID, "DON'T CALL ME KATIE."

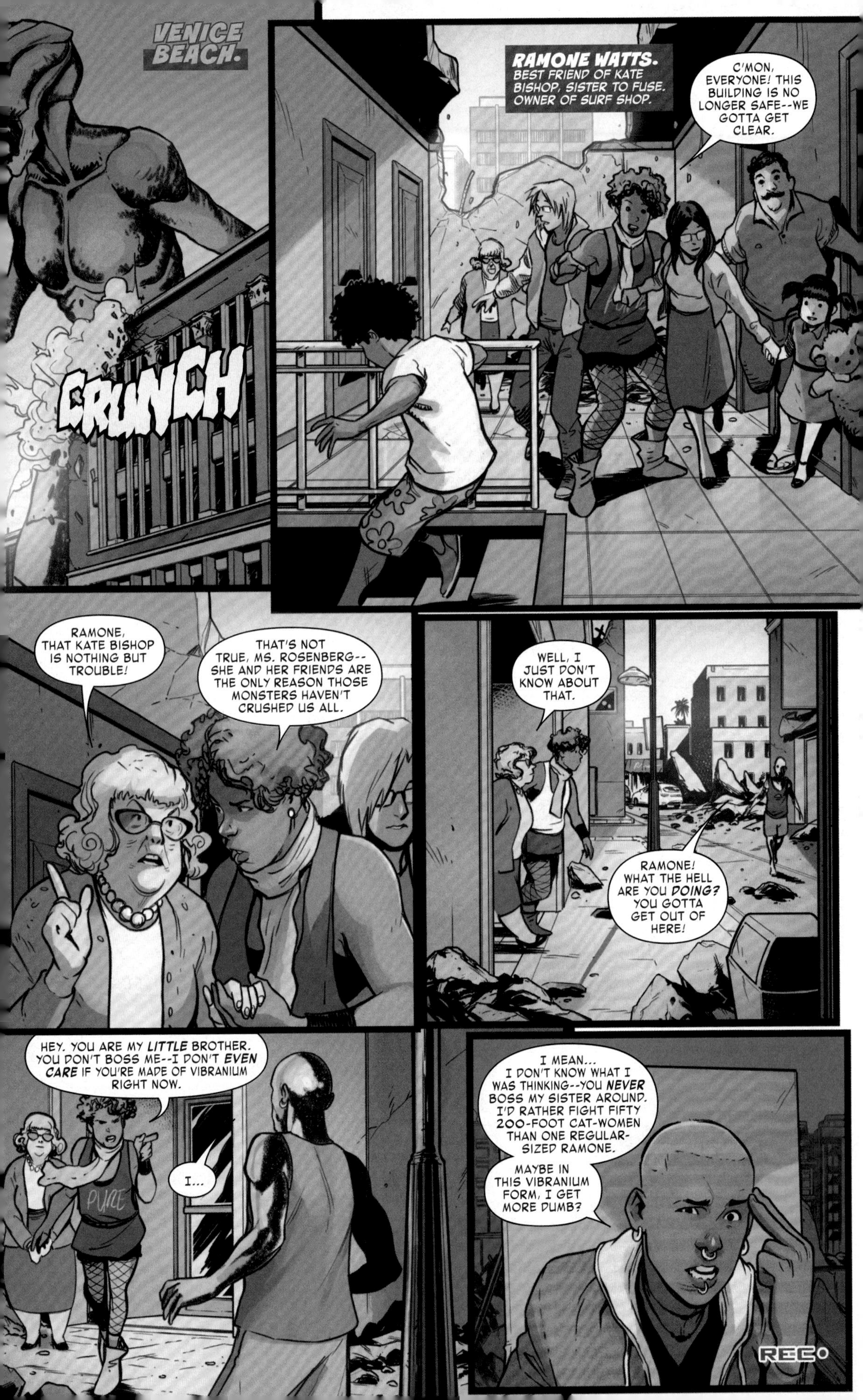
VENICE BEACH.
CRUNCH
RAMONE WATTS. BEST FRIEND OF KATE BISHOP, SISTER TO FUSE. OWNER OF SURF SHOP.
C'MON, EVERYONE! THIS BUILDING IS NO LONGER SAFE--WE GOTTA GET CLEAR.
RAMONE, THAT KATE BISHOP IS NOTHING BUT TROUBLE!
THAT'S NOT TRUE, MS. ROSENBERG--SHE AND HER FRIENDS ARE THE ONLY REASON THOSE MONSTERS HAVEN'T CRUSHED US ALL.
WELL, I JUST DON'T KNOW ABOUT THAT.
RAMONE! WHAT THE HELL ARE YOU DOING? YOU GOTTA GET OUT OF HERE!
HEY. YOU ARE MY LITTLE BROTHER. YOU DON'T BOSS ME--I DON'T EVEN CARE IF YOU'RE MADE OF VIBRANIUM RIGHT NOW.
I...
I MEAN... I DON'T KNOW WHAT I WAS THINKING--YOU NEVER BOSS MY SISTER AROUND. I'D RATHER FIGHT FIFTY 200-FOOT CAT-WOMEN THAN ONE REGULAR-SIZED RAMONE.
MAYBE IN THIS VIBRANIUM FORM, I GET MORE DUMB?
PURE
REC

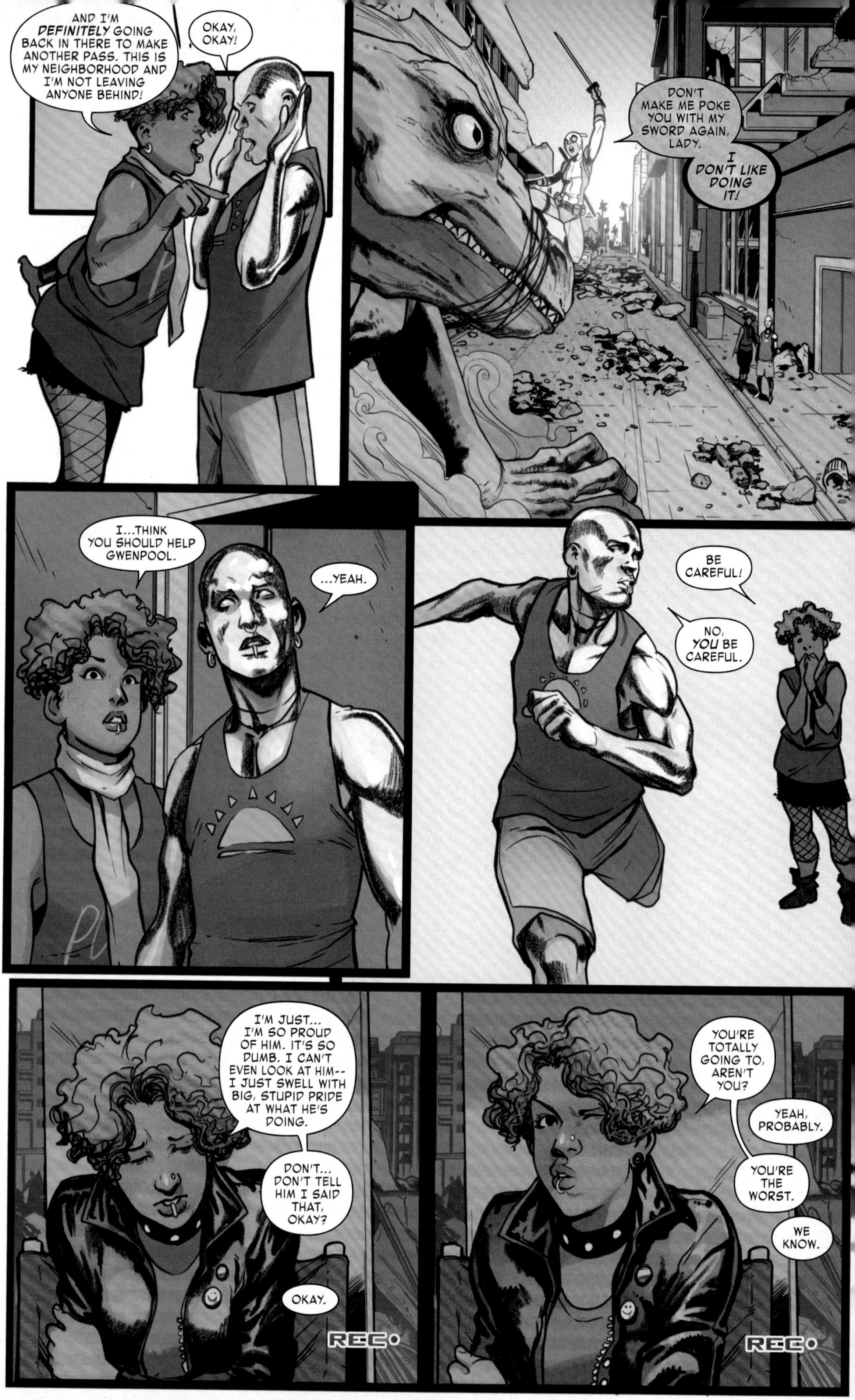
AND I'M DEFINITELY GOING BACK IN THERE TO MAKE ANOTHER PASS. THIS IS MY NEIGHBORHOOD AND I'M NOT LEAVING ANYONE BEHIND!
OKAY, OKAY!
DON'T MAKE ME POKE YOU WITH MY SWORD AGAIN, LADY.
I DON'T LIKE DOING IT!
I...THINK YOU SHOULD HELP GWENPOOL.
...YEAH.
BE CAREFUL!
NO, YOU BE CAREFUL.
I'M JUST... I'M SO PROUD OF HIM. IT'S SO DUMB. I CAN'T EVEN LOOK AT HIM-- I JUST SWELL WITH BIG, STUPID PRIDE AT WHAT HE'S DOING.
DON'T... DON'T TELL HIM I SAID THAT, OKAY?
OKAY.
REC
YOU'RE TOTALLY GOING TO, AREN'T YOU?
YEAH, PROBABLY.
YOU'RE THE WORST.
WE KNOW.
REC

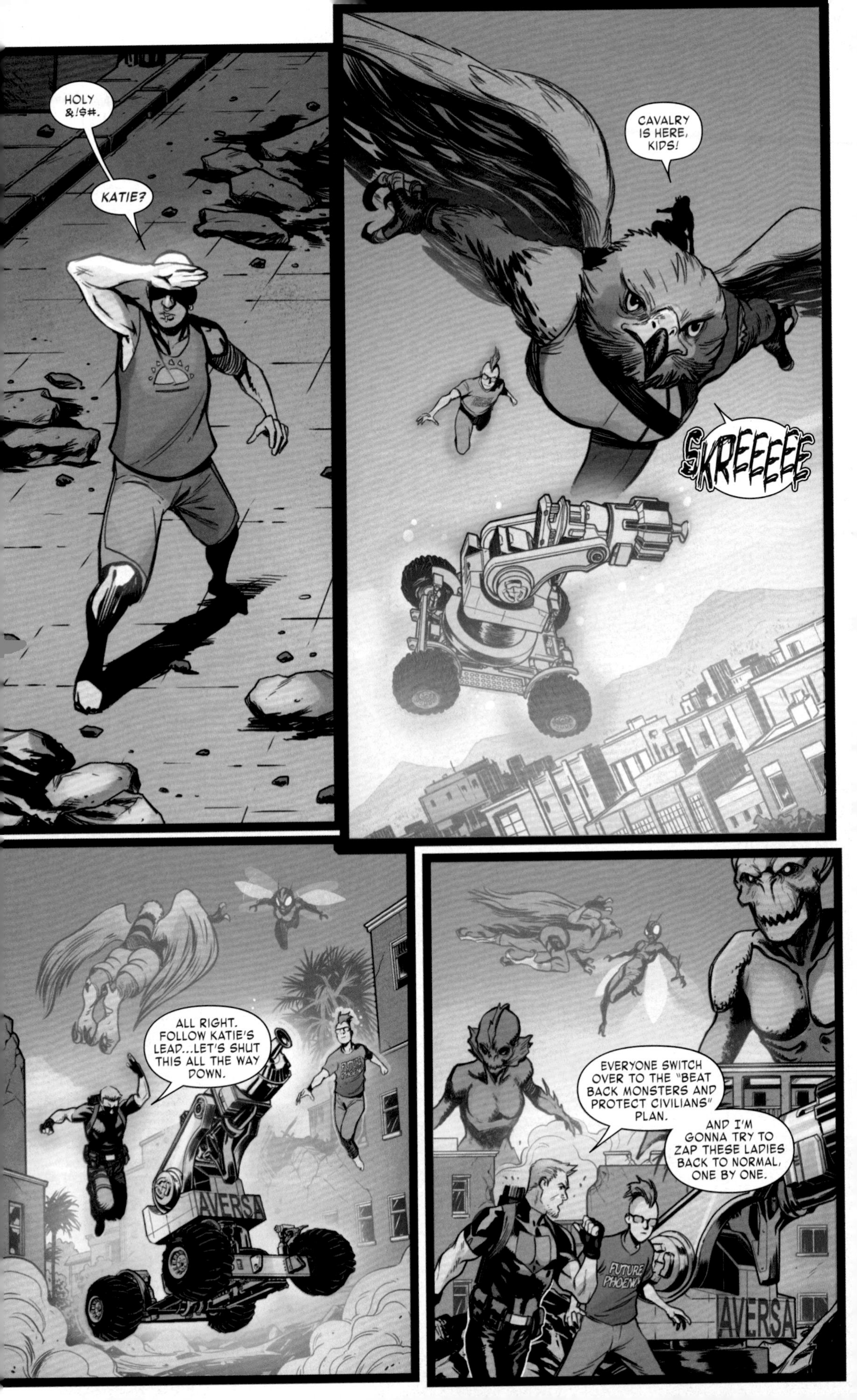
HOLY &!$#.
KATIE?
CAVALRY IS HERE, KIDS!
SKREEEEE
ALL RIGHT. FOLLOW KATIE'S LEAD...LET'S SHUT THIS ALL THE WAY DOWN.
AVERSA
EVERYONE SWITCH OVER TO THE "BEAT BACK MONSTERS AND PROTECT CIVILIANS" PLAN.
AND I'M GONNA TRY TO ZAP THESE LADIES BACK TO NORMAL, ONE BY ONE.
AVERSA

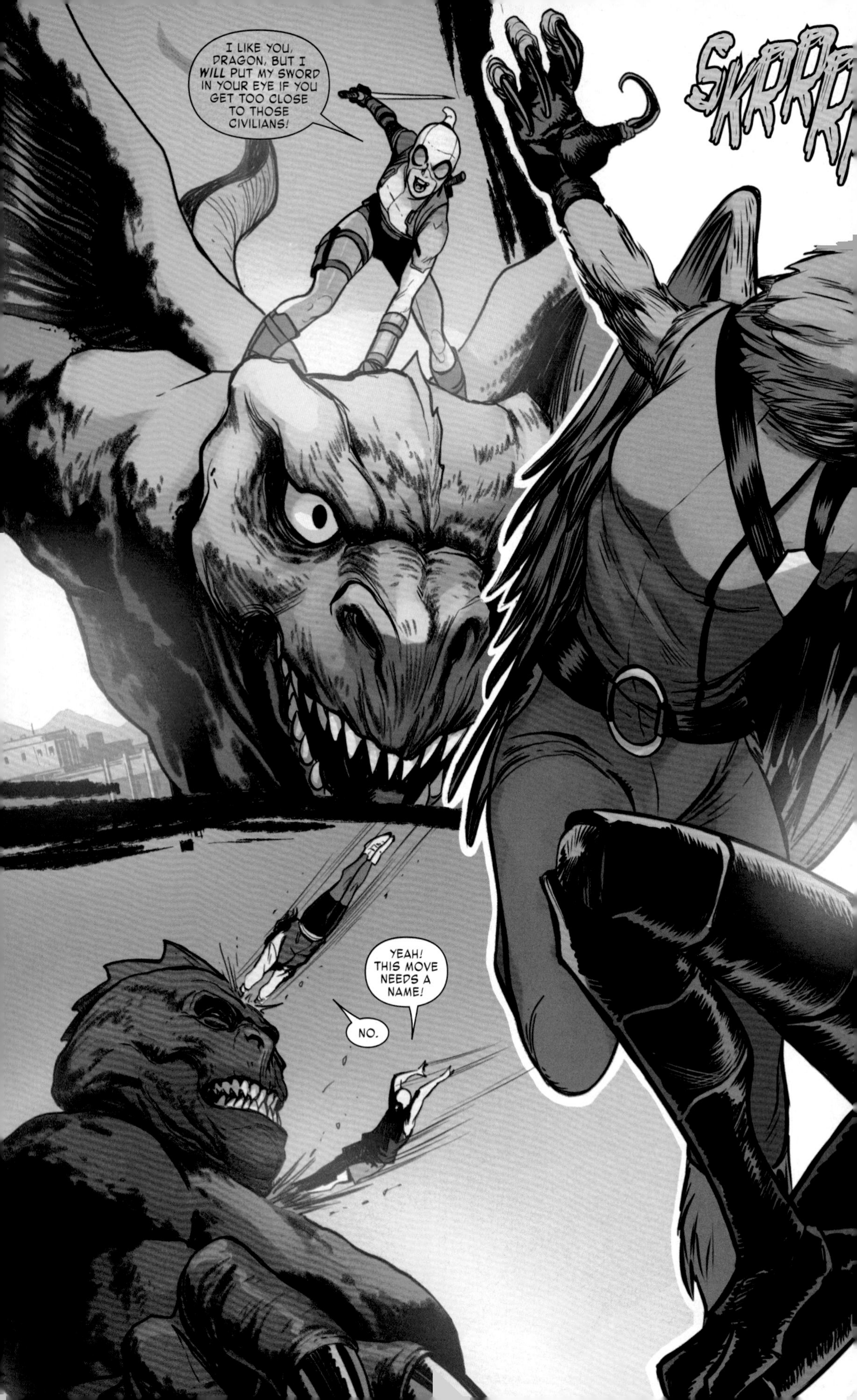
I LIKE YOU, DRAGON, BUT I WILL PUT MY SWORD IN YOUR EYE IF YOU GET TOO CLOSE TO THOSE CIVILIANS!
SKRRR
YEAH! THIS MOVE NEEDS A NAME!
NO.

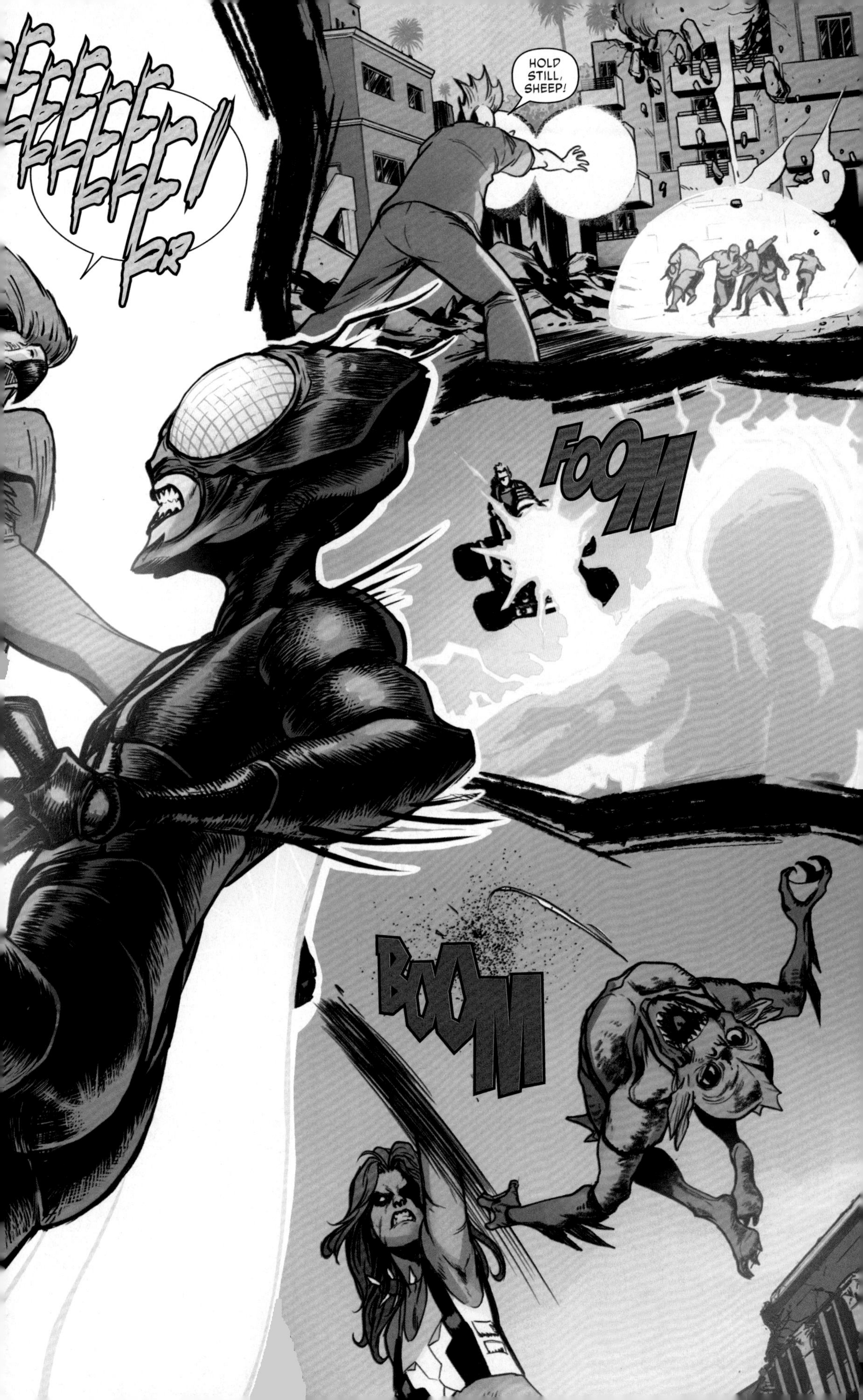
EEEEEEEE!!
HOLD STILL, SHEEP!
FOOM
BOOM

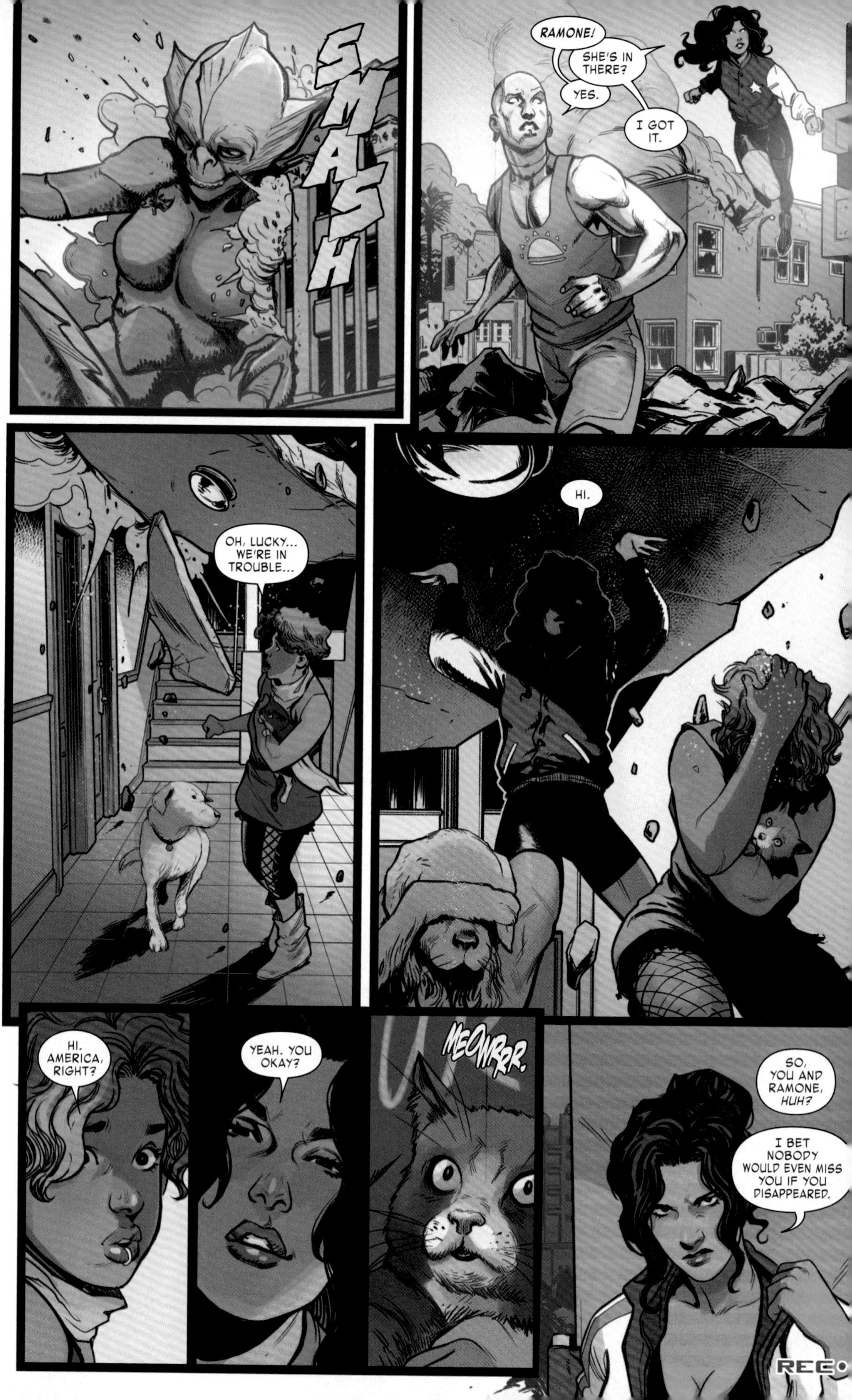
SMASH
RAMONE!
SHE'S IN THERE?
YES.
I GOT IT.
OH, LUCKY... WE'RE IN TROUBLE...
HI.
HI. AMERICA, RIGHT?
YEAH. YOU OKAY?
MEOWRRR.
SO, YOU AND RAMONE, HUH?
I BET NOBODY WOULD EVEN MISS YOU IF YOU DISAPPEARED.

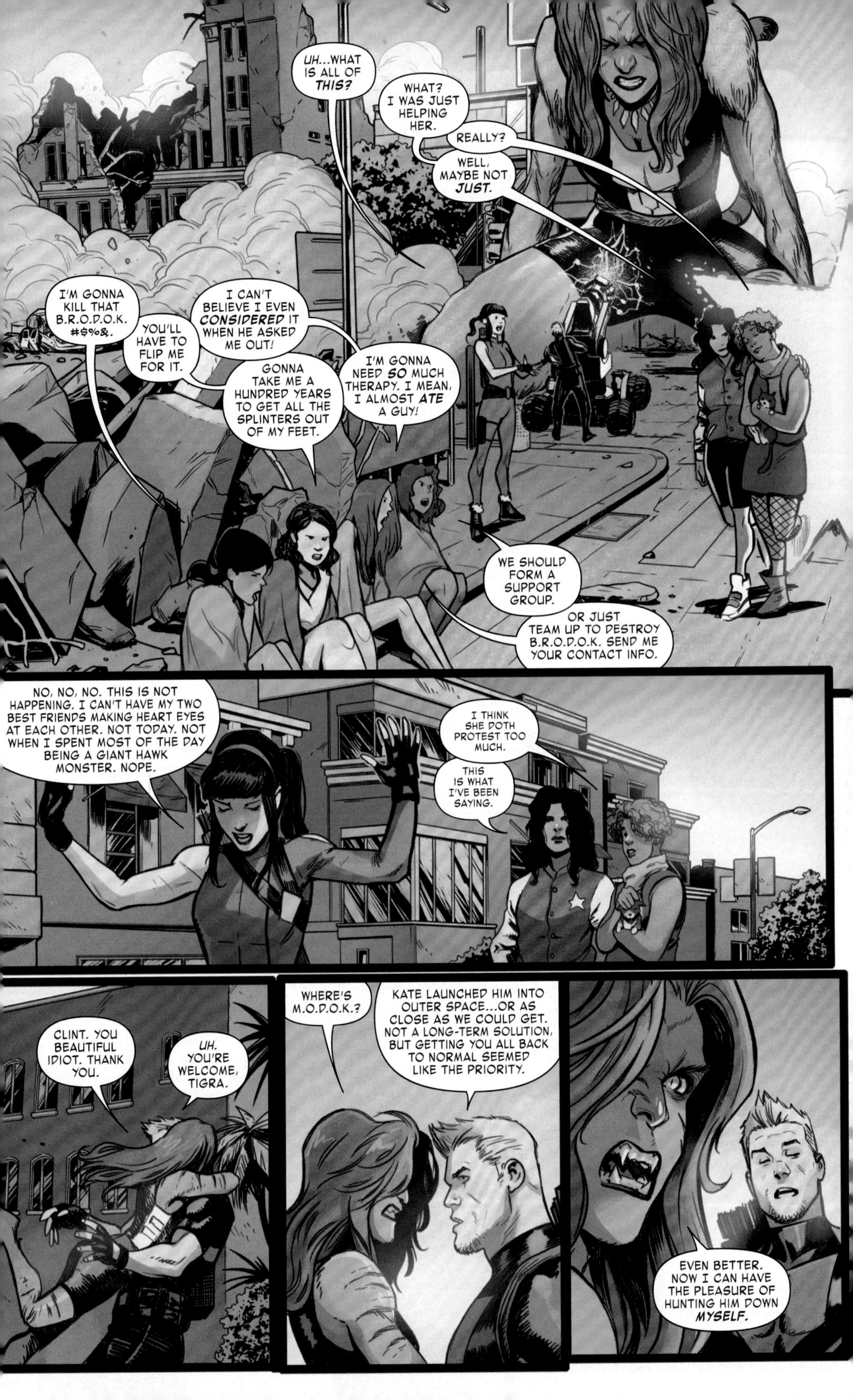
UH...WHAT IS ALL OF THIS?
WHAT? I WAS JUST HELPING HER.
REALLY?
WELL, MAYBE NOT JUST.
I'M GONNA KILL THAT B.R.O.D.O.K. #$%&.
YOU'LL HAVE TO FLIP ME FOR IT.
I CAN'T BELIEVE I EVEN CONSIDERED IT WHEN HE ASKED ME OUT!
GONNA TAKE ME A HUNDRED YEARS TO GET ALL THE SPLINTERS OUT OF MY FEET.
I'M GONNA NEED SO MUCH THERAPY. I MEAN, I ALMOST ATE A GUY!
WE SHOULD FORM A SUPPORT GROUP.
OR JUST TEAM UP TO DESTROY B.R.O.D.O.K. SEND ME YOUR CONTACT INFO.
NO, NO, NO. THIS IS NOT HAPPENING. I CAN'T HAVE MY TWO BEST FRIENDS MAKING HEART EYES AT EACH OTHER. NOT TODAY. NOT WHEN I SPENT MOST OF THE DAY BEING A GIANT HAWK MONSTER. NOPE.
I THINK SHE DOTH PROTEST TOO MUCH.
THIS IS WHAT I'VE BEEN SAYING.
CLINT. YOU BEAUTIFUL IDIOT. THANK YOU.
UH. YOU'RE WELCOME, TIGRA.
WHERE'S M.O.D.O.K.?
KATE LAUNCHED HIM INTO OUTER SPACE...OR AS CLOSE AS WE COULD GET. NOT A LONG-TERM SOLUTION, BUT GETTING YOU ALL BACK TO NORMAL SEEMED LIKE THE PRIORITY.
EVEN BETTER. NOW I CAN HAVE THE PLEASURE OF HUNTING HIM DOWN MYSELF.

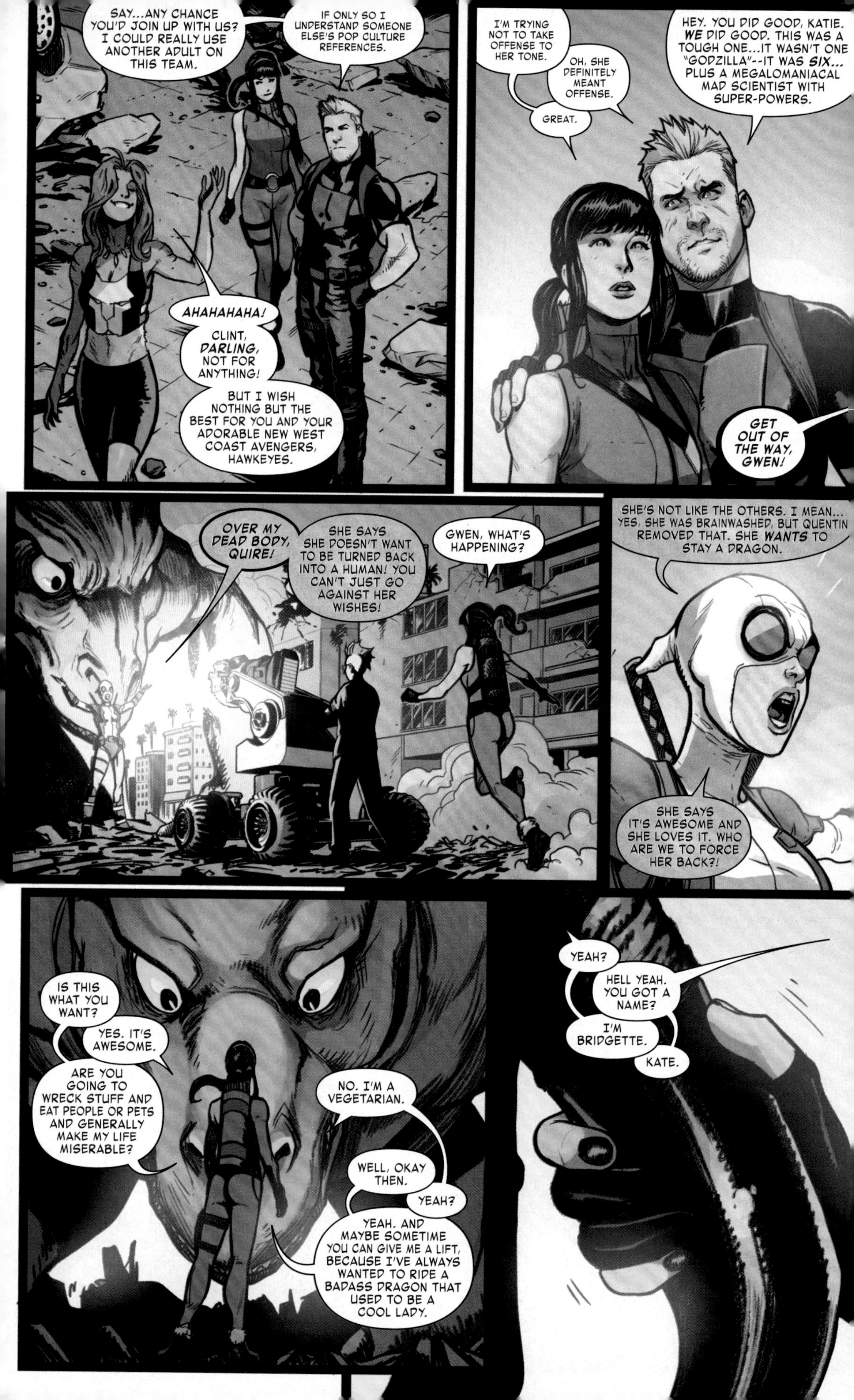
SAY...ANY CHANCE YOU'D JOIN UP WITH US? I COULD REALLY USE ANOTHER ADULT ON THIS TEAM.
IF ONLY SO I UNDERSTAND SOMEONE ELSE'S POP CULTURE REFERENCES.
AHAHAHAHA!
CLINT, DARLING, NOT FOR ANYTHING!
BUT I WISH NOTHING BUT THE BEST FOR YOU AND YOUR ADORABLE NEW WEST COAST AVENGERS, HAWKEYES.
I'M TRYING NOT TO TAKE OFFENSE TO HER TONE.
OH, SHE DEFINITELY MEANT OFFENSE.
GREAT.
HEY. YOU DID GOOD, KATIE. WE DID GOOD. THIS WAS A TOUGH ONE...IT WASN'T ONE "GODZILLA"--IT WAS SIX... PLUS A MEGALOMANIACAL MAD SCIENTIST WITH SUPER-POWERS.
GET OUT OF THE WAY, GWEN!
OVER MY DEAD BODY, QUIRE!
SHE SAYS SHE DOESN'T WANT TO BE TURNED BACK INTO A HUMAN! YOU CAN'T JUST GO AGAINST HER WISHES!
GWEN, WHAT'S HAPPENING?
SHE'S NOT LIKE THE OTHERS. I MEAN... YES, SHE WAS BRAINWASHED, BUT QUENTIN REMOVED THAT. SHE WANTS TO STAY A DRAGON.
SHE SAYS IT'S AWESOME AND SHE LOVES IT. WHO ARE WE TO FORCE HER BACK?!
IS THIS WHAT YOU WANT?
YES. IT'S AWESOME.
ARE YOU GOING TO WRECK STUFF AND EAT PEOPLE OR PETS AND GENERALLY MAKE MY LIFE MISERABLE?
NO. I'M A VEGETARIAN.
WELL, OKAY THEN.
YEAH?
YEAH. AND MAYBE SOMETIME YOU CAN GIVE ME A LIFT, BECAUSE I'VE ALWAYS WANTED TO RIDE A BADASS DRAGON THAT USED TO BE A COOL LADY.
YEAH?
HELL YEAH. YOU GOT A NAME?
I'M BRIDGETTE.
KATE.

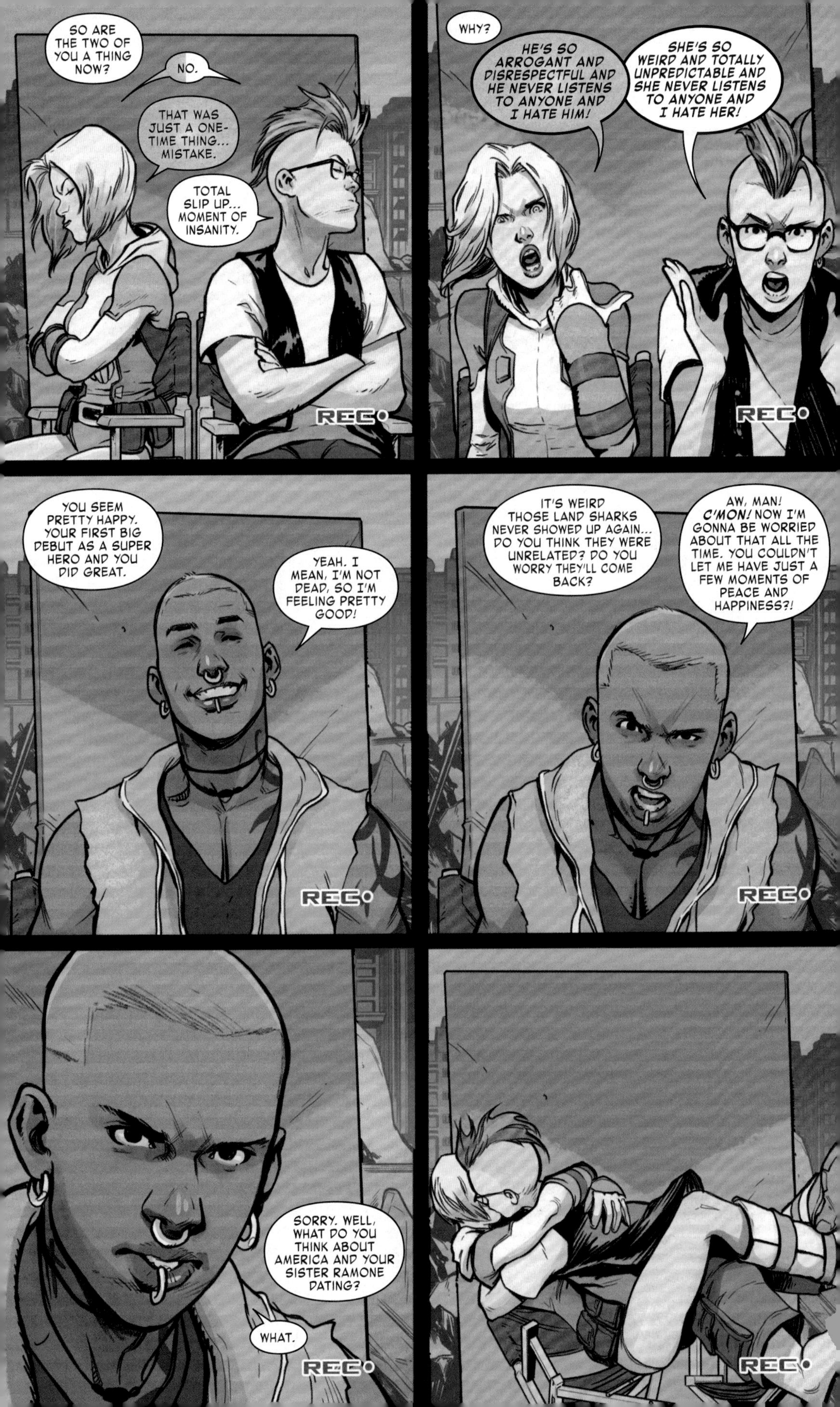
SO ARE THE TWO OF YOU A THING NOW?
NO.
THAT WAS JUST A ONE-TIME THING... MISTAKE.
TOTAL SLIP UP... MOMENT OF INSANITY.
REC
WHY?
HE'S SO ARROGANT AND DISRESPECTFUL AND HE NEVER LISTENS TO ANYONE AND I HATE HIM!
SHE'S SO WEIRD AND TOTALLY UNPREDICTABLE AND SHE NEVER LISTENS TO ANYONE AND I HATE HER!
REC
YOU SEEM PRETTY HAPPY. YOUR FIRST BIG DEBUT AS A SUPER HERO AND YOU DID GREAT.
YEAH. I MEAN, I'M NOT DEAD, SO I'M FEELING PRETTY GOOD!
REC
IT'S WEIRD THOSE LAND SHARKS NEVER SHOWED UP AGAIN... DO YOU THINK THEY WERE UNRELATED? DO YOU WORRY THEY'LL COME BACK?
AW, MAN! C'MON! NOW I'M GONNA BE WORRIED ABOUT THAT ALL THE TIME. YOU COULDN'T LET ME HAVE JUST A FEW MOMENTS OF PEACE AND HAPPINESS?!
REC
SORRY. WELL, WHAT DO YOU THINK ABOUT AMERICA AND YOUR SISTER RAMONE DATING?
WHAT.
REC
REC

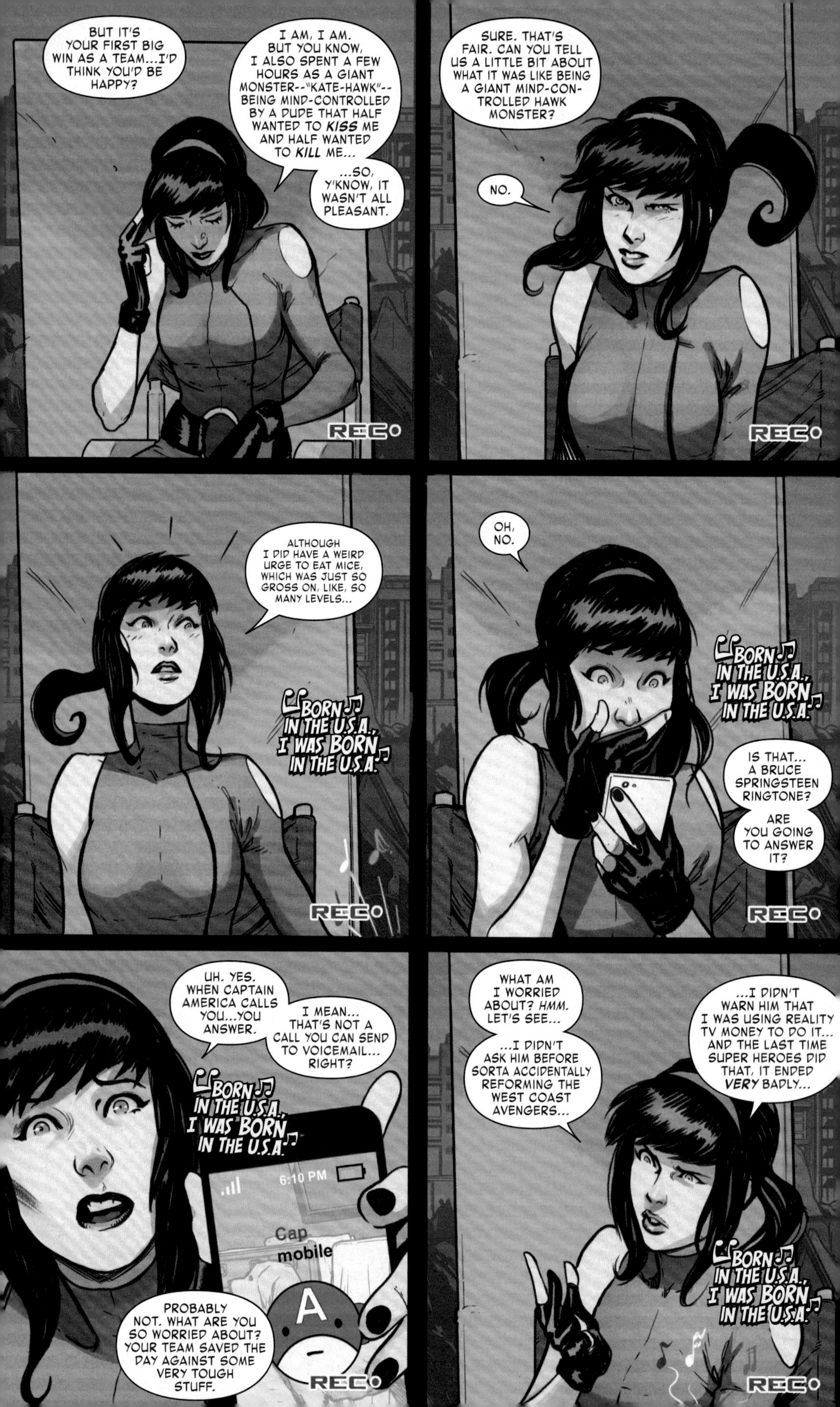

BUT IT'S YOUR FIRST BIG WIN AS A TEAM...I'D THINK YOU'D BE HAPPY?
I AM, I AM. BUT YOU KNOW, I ALSO SPENT A FEW HOURS AS A GIANT MONSTER--"KATE-HAWK"--BEING MIND-CONTROLLED BY A DUDE THAT HALF WANTED TO KISS ME AND HALF WANTED TO KILL ME...
...SO, Y'KNOW, IT WASN'T ALL PLEASANT.
REC
SURE. THAT'S FAIR. CAN YOU TELL US A LITTLE BIT ABOUT WHAT IT WAS LIKE BEING A GIANT MIND-CONTROLLED HAWK MONSTER?
NO.
REC
ALTHOUGH I DID HAVE A WEIRD URGE TO EAT MICE, WHICH WAS JUST SO GROSS ON, LIKE, SO MANY LEVELS...
BORN IN THE U.S.A., I WAS BORN IN THE U.S.A.
REC
OH, NO.
BORN IN THE U.S.A., I WAS BORN IN THE U.S.A.
IS THAT... A BRUCE SPRINGSTEEN RINGTONE?
ARE YOU GOING TO ANSWER IT?
REC
UH. YES. WHEN CAPTAIN AMERICA CALLS YOU...YOU ANSWER.
I MEAN... THAT'S NOT A CALL YOU CAN SEND TO VOICEMAIL... RIGHT?
BORN IN THE U.S.A., I WAS BORN IN THE U.S.A.
6:10 PM
Cap mobile
A
PROBABLY NOT. WHAT ARE YOU SO WORRIED ABOUT? YOUR TEAM SAVED THE DAY AGAINST SOME VERY TOUGH STUFF.
REC
WHAT AM I WORRIED ABOUT? HMM. LET'S SEE...
...I DIDN'T ASK HIM BEFORE SORTA ACCIDENTALLY REFORMING THE WEST COAST AVENGERS...
...I DIDN'T WARN HIM THAT I WAS USING REALITY TV MONEY TO DO IT... AND THE LAST TIME SUPER HEROES DID THAT, IT ENDED VERY BADLY...
BORN IN THE U.S.A., I WAS BORN IN THE U.S.A.
REC

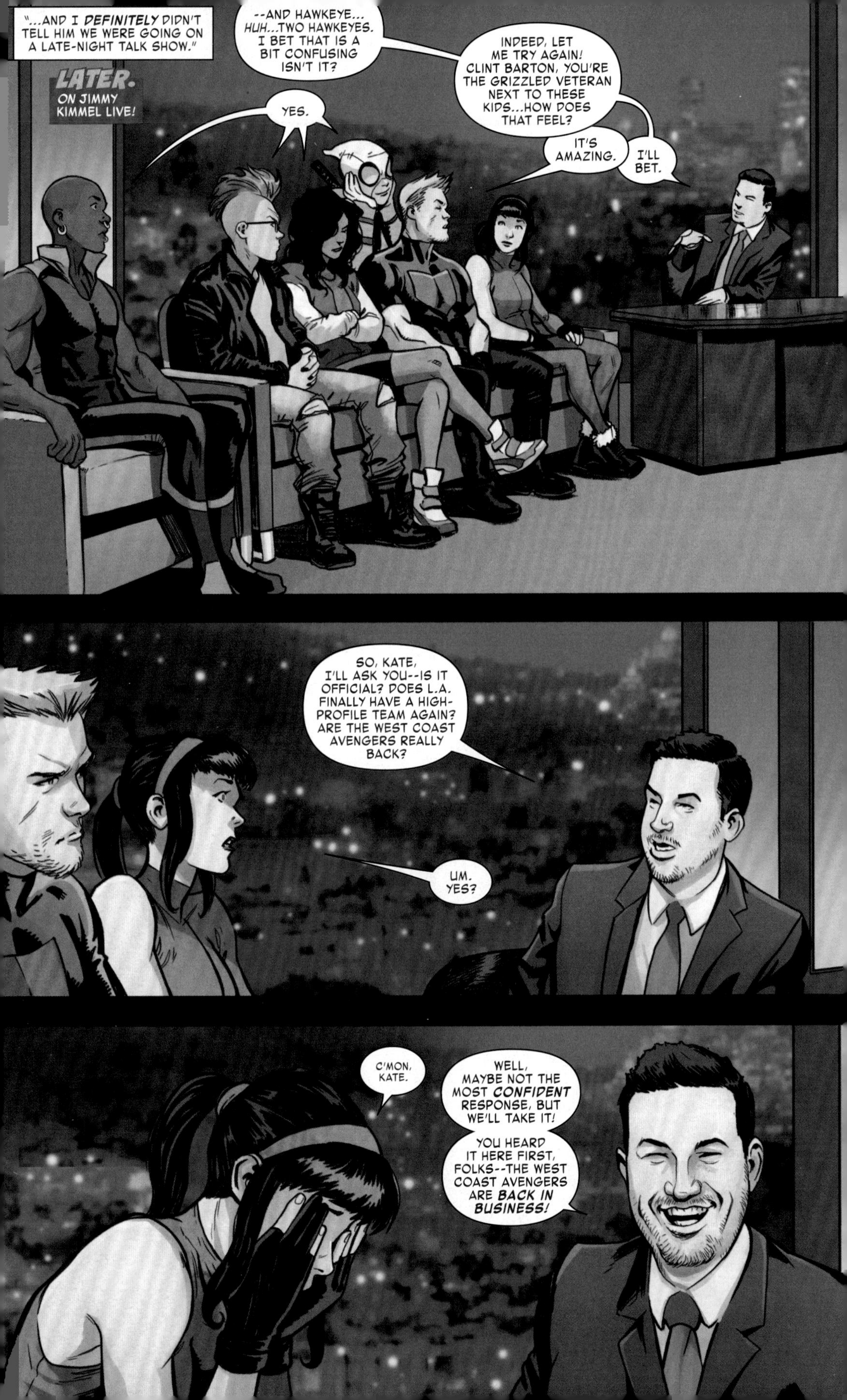
"...AND I DEFINITELY DIDN'T TELL HIM WE WERE GOING ON A LATE-NIGHT TALK SHOW."
LATER. ON JIMMY KIMMEL LIVE!
--AND HAWKEYE... HUH...TWO HAWKEYES. I BET THAT IS A BIT CONFUSING ISN'T IT?
YES.
INDEED, LET ME TRY AGAIN! CLINT BARTON, YOU'RE THE GRIZZLED VETERAN NEXT TO THESE KIDS...HOW DOES THAT FEEL?
IT'S AMAZING.
I'LL BET.
SO, KATE, I'LL ASK YOU--IS IT OFFICIAL? DOES L.A. FINALLY HAVE A HIGH-PROFILE TEAM AGAIN? ARE THE WEST COAST AVENGERS REALLY BACK?
UM. YES?
C'MON, KATE.
WELL, MAYBE NOT THE MOST CONFIDENT RESPONSE, BUT WE'LL TAKE IT!
YOU HEARD IT HERE FIRST, FOLKS--THE WEST COAST AVENGERS ARE BACK IN BUSINESS!

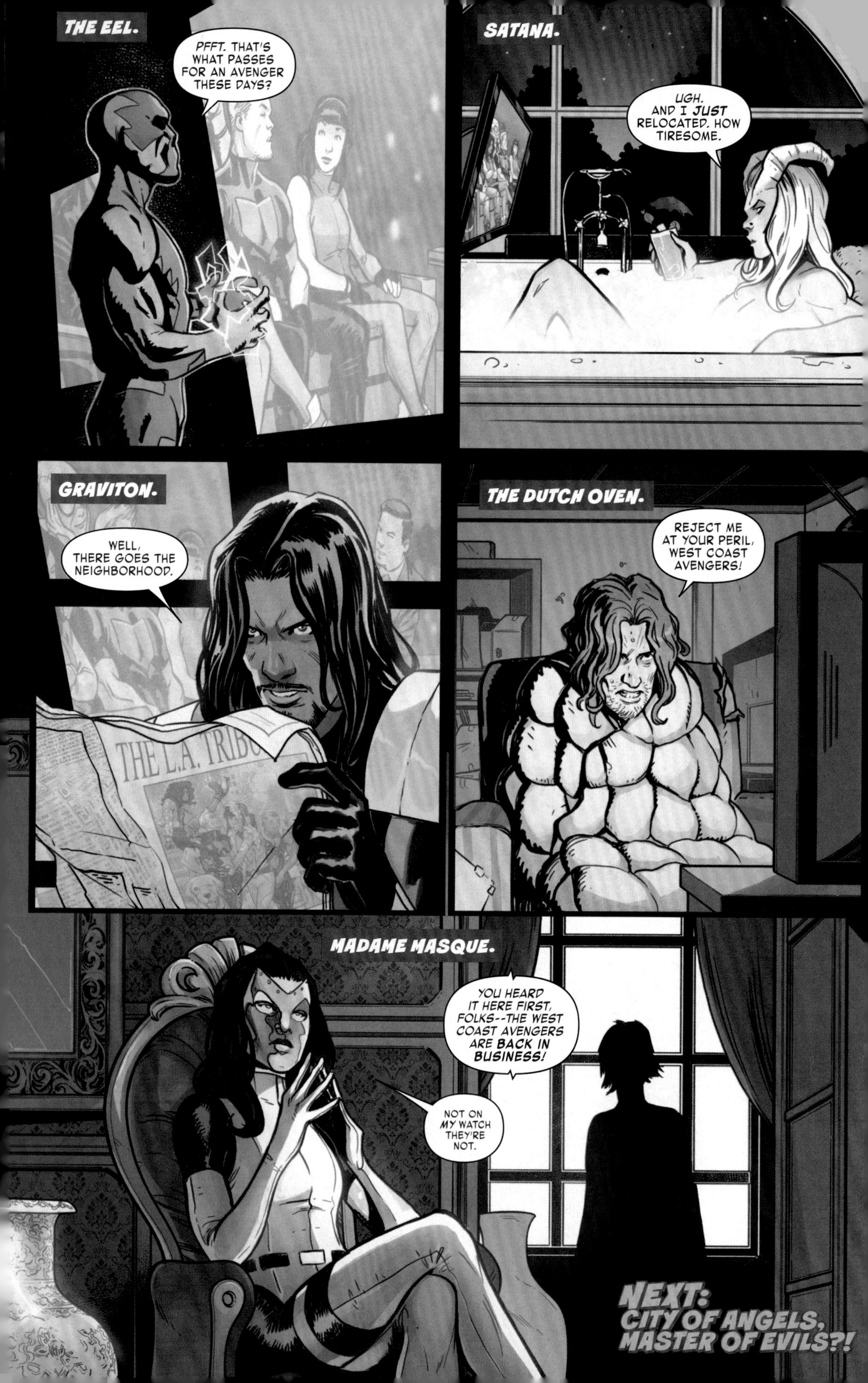

THE EEL.
PFFT. THAT'S WHAT PASSES FOR AN AVENGER THESE DAYS?
SATANA.
UGH. AND I JUST RELOCATED. HOW TIRESOME.
GRAVITON.
WELL, THERE GOES THE NEIGHBORHOOD.
THE L.A. TRIBU
THE DUTCH OVEN.
REJECT ME AT YOUR PERIL, WEST COAST AVENGERS!
MADAME MASQUE.
YOU HEARD IT HERE FIRST, FOLKS--THE WEST COAST AVENGERS ARE BACK IN BUSINESS!
NOT ON MY WATCH THEY'RE NOT.
NEXT: CITY OF ANGELS, MASTER OF EVILS?!

YOUNG AVENGERS PRESENTS #6

IT'S A CLASH OF ARCHERS AS CLINT BARTON RETURNS TO RECLAIM THE TITLE OF HAWKEYE AND HIS BOW FROM KATE BISHOP.

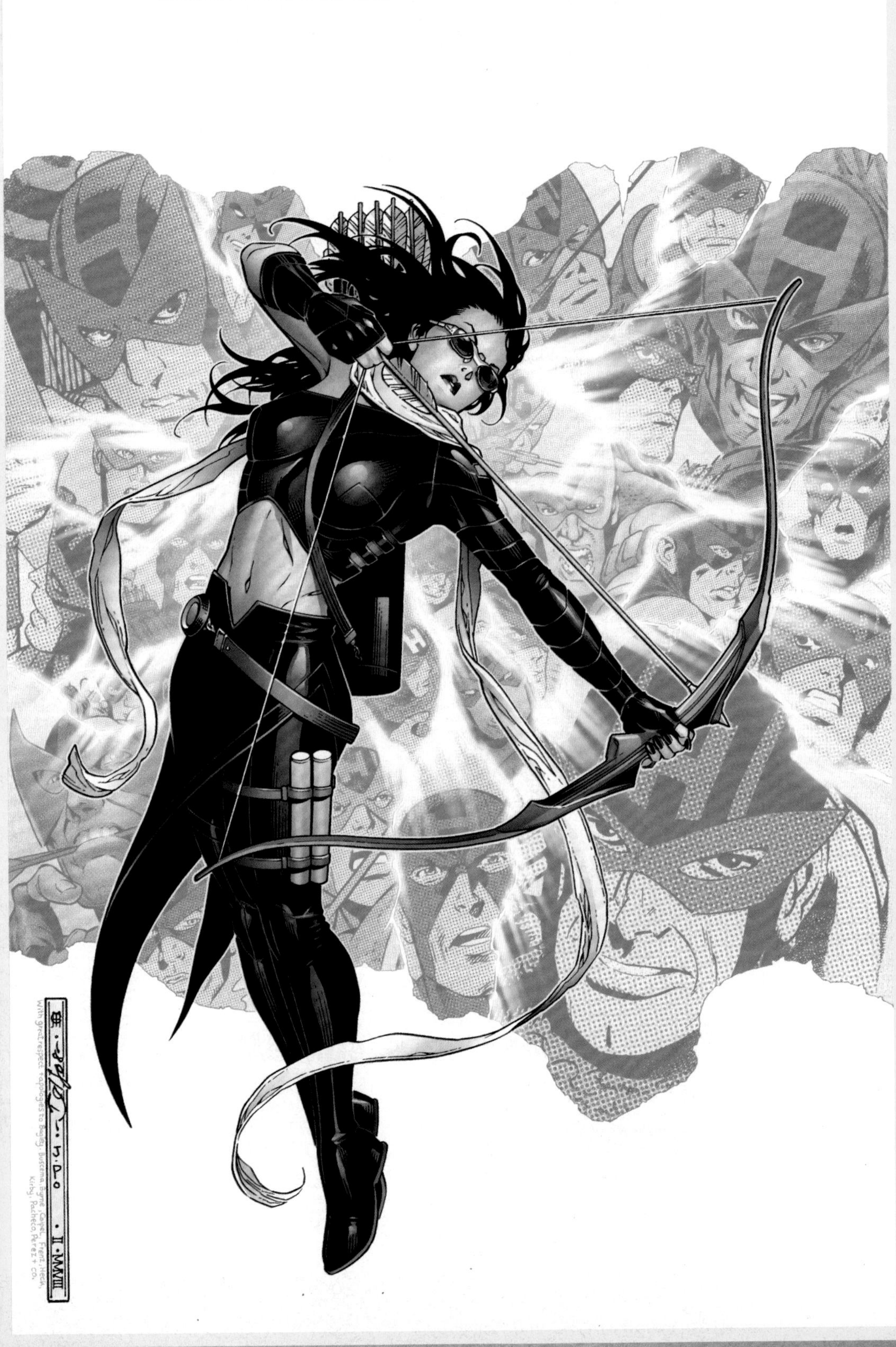

II·MMVIII
With great respect + apologies to Bagley, Buscema, Byrne, Ceipel, Frenz, Heck, Kirby, Pacheco, Perez + co.

United by friendship and bravery, Patriot, Hawkeye, Wiccan, Hulkling, Stature, Speed and the Vision are the Young Avengers, following in the footsteps of Earth's mightiest heroes! While superhuman registration temporarily caused the team to cease operations, they are ready to return to the streets to take on the threats no single super hero can withstand!

YOUNG AVENGERS PRESENTS HAWKEYE

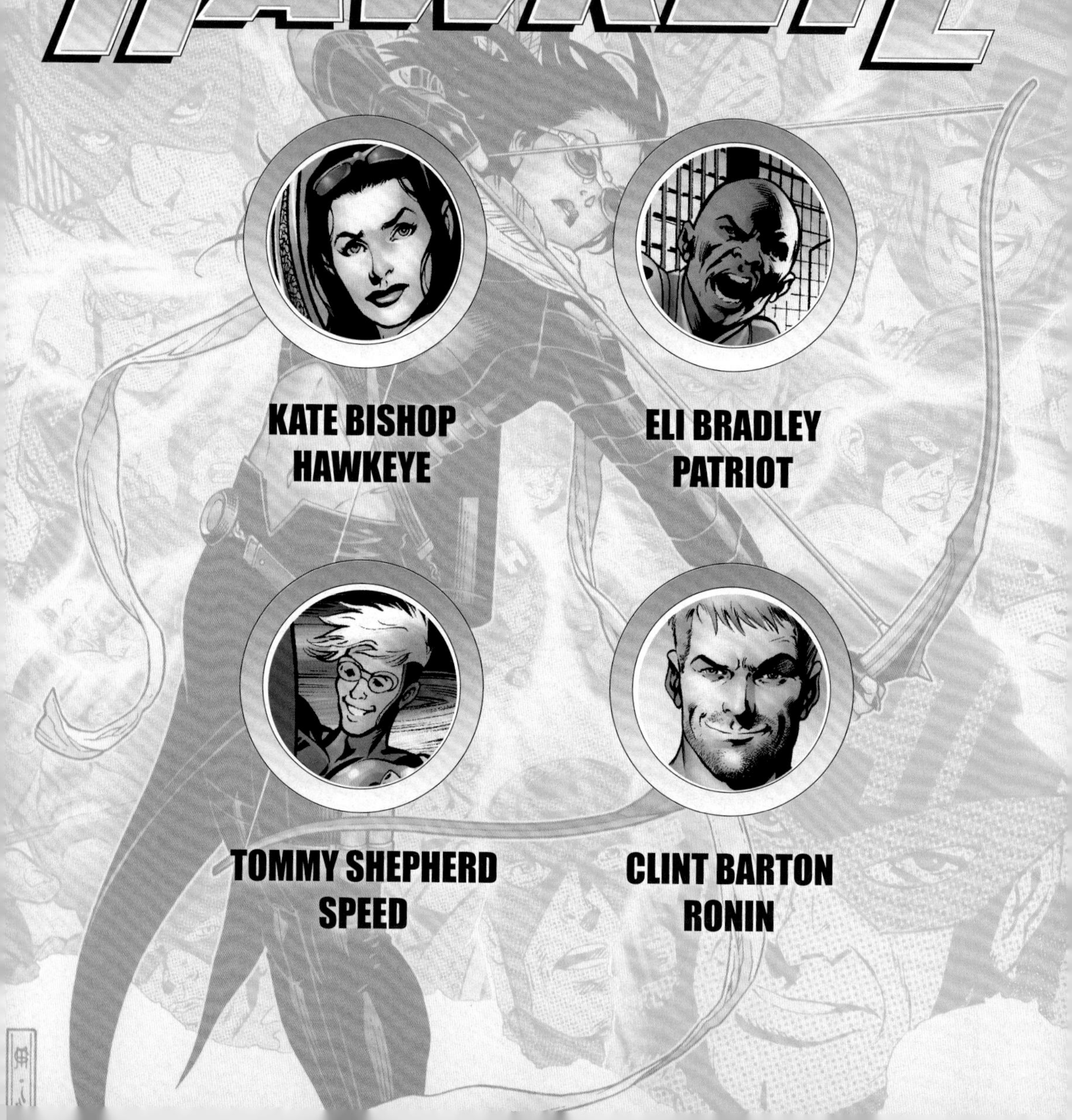
KATE BISHOP
HAWKEYE
ELI BRADLEY
PATRIOT
TOMMY SHEPHERD
SPEED
CLINT BARTON
RONIN

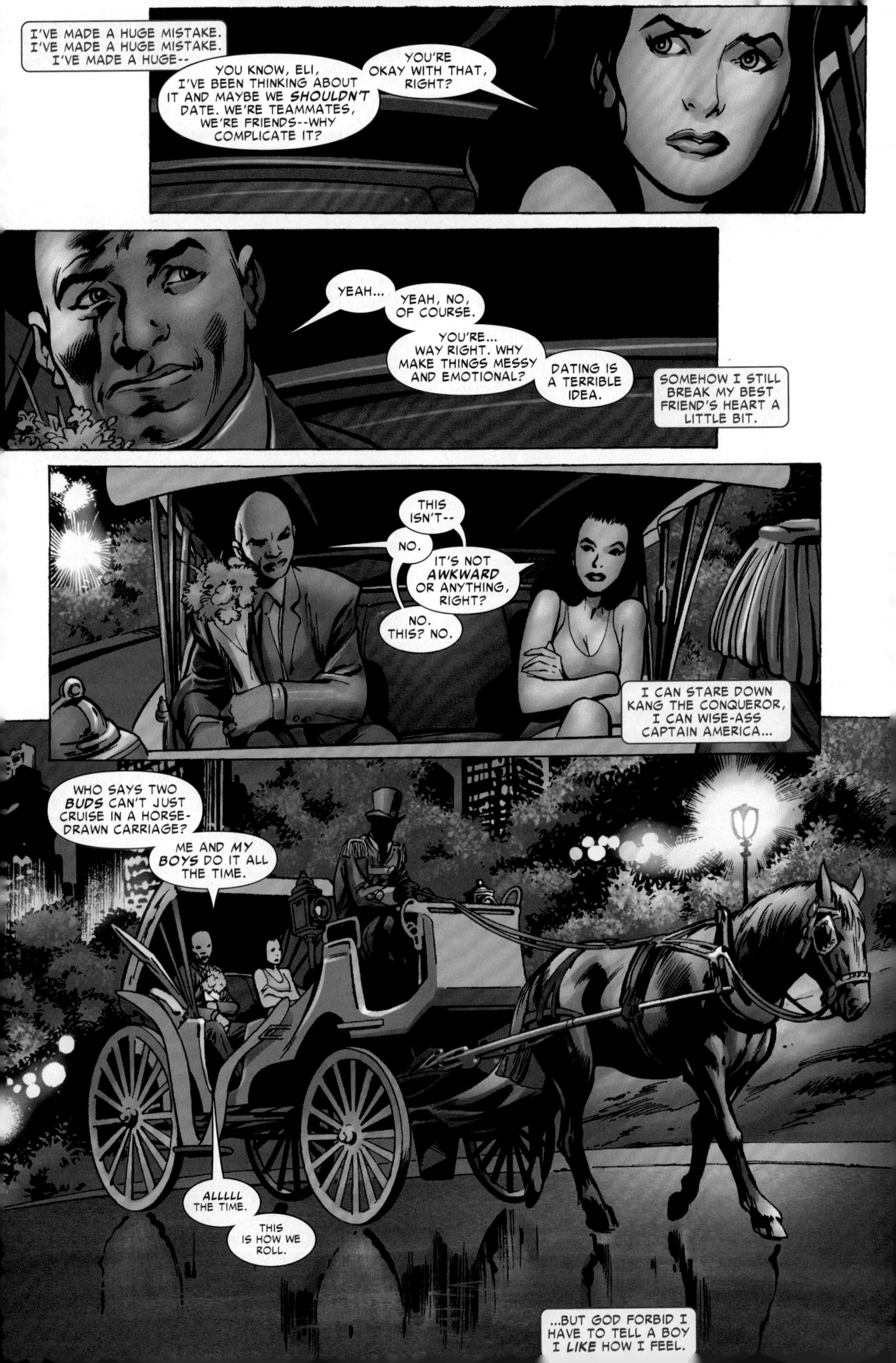
I'VE MADE A HUGE MISTAKE. I'VE MADE A HUGE MISTAKE. I'VE MADE A HUGE--
YOU KNOW, ELI, I'VE BEEN THINKING ABOUT IT AND MAYBE WE SHOULDN'T DATE. WE'RE TEAMMATES, WE'RE FRIENDS--WHY COMPLICATE IT?
YOU'RE OKAY WITH THAT, RIGHT?
YEAH...
YEAH, NO, OF COURSE.
YOU'RE... WAY RIGHT. WHY MAKE THINGS MESSY AND EMOTIONAL?
DATING IS A TERRIBLE IDEA.
SOMEHOW I STILL BREAK MY BEST FRIEND'S HEART A LITTLE BIT.
THIS ISN'T--
NO.
IT'S NOT AWKWARD OR ANYTHING, RIGHT?
NO. THIS? NO.
I CAN STARE DOWN KANG THE CONQUEROR, I CAN WISE-ASS CAPTAIN AMERICA...
WHO SAYS TWO BUDS CAN'T JUST CRUISE IN A HORSE-DRAWN CARRIAGE?
ME AND MY BOYS DO IT ALL THE TIME.
ALLLLL THE TIME.
THIS IS HOW WE ROLL.
...BUT GOD FORBID I HAVE TO TELL A BOY I LIKE HOW I FEEL.

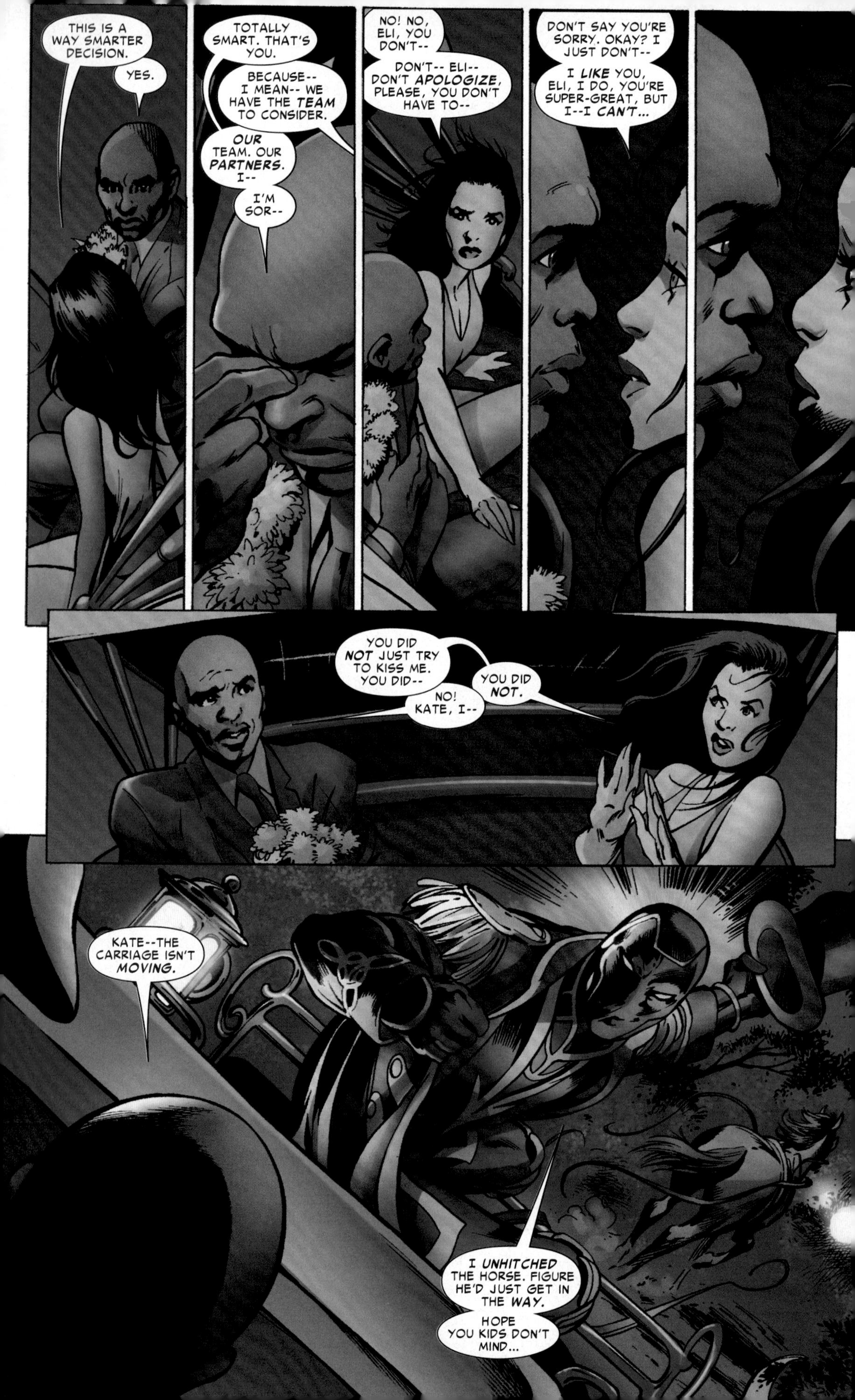
THIS IS A WAY SMARTER DECISION.
YES.
TOTALLY SMART. THAT'S YOU.
BECAUSE-- I MEAN-- WE HAVE THE TEAM TO CONSIDER.
OUR TEAM. OUR PARTNERS. I--
I'M SOR--
NO! NO, ELI, YOU DON'T--
DON'T-- ELI-- DON'T APOLOGIZE, PLEASE, YOU DON'T HAVE TO--
DON'T SAY YOU'RE SORRY. OKAY? I JUST DON'T--
I LIKE YOU, ELI, I DO, YOU'RE SUPER-GREAT, BUT I--I CAN'T...
YOU DID NOT JUST TRY TO KISS ME. YOU DID--
NO! KATE, I--
YOU DID NOT.
KATE--THE CARRIAGE ISN'T MOVING.
I UNHITCHED THE HORSE. FIGURE HE'D JUST GET IN THE WAY.
HOPE YOU KIDS DON'T MIND...

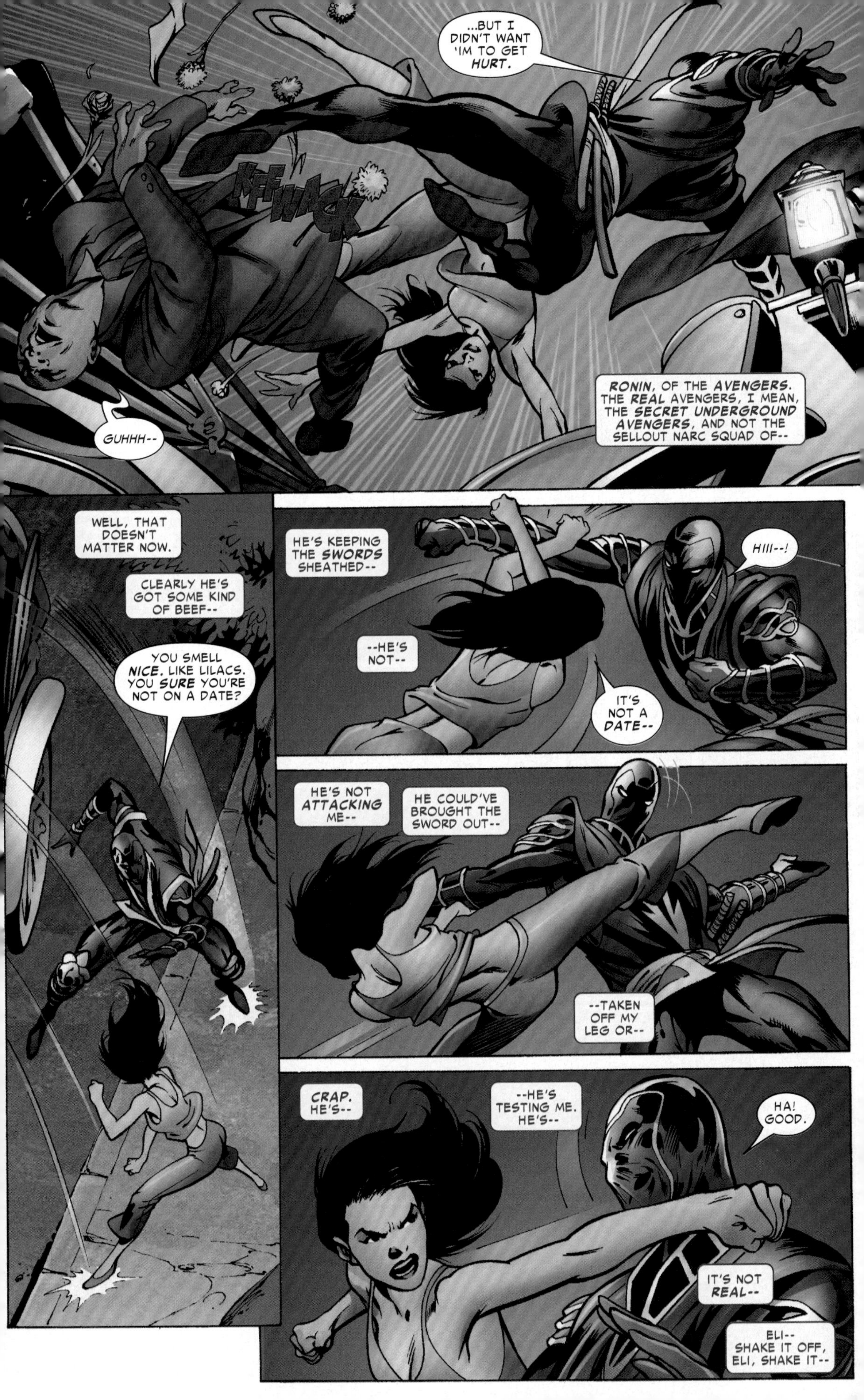
...BUT I DIDN'T WANT 'IM TO GET HURT.
KFFWACK
GUHHH--
RONIN, OF THE AVENGERS. THE REAL AVENGERS, I MEAN, THE SECRET UNDERGROUND AVENGERS, AND NOT THE SELLOUT NARC SQUAD OF--
WELL, THAT DOESN'T MATTER NOW.
CLEARLY HE'S GOT SOME KIND OF BEEF--
YOU SMELL NICE. LIKE LILACS. YOU SURE YOU'RE NOT ON A DATE?
HE'S KEEPING THE SWORDS SHEATHED--
HIII--!
--HE'S NOT--
IT'S NOT A DATE--
HE'S NOT ATTACKING ME--
HE COULD'VE BROUGHT THE SWORD OUT--
--TAKEN OFF MY LEG OR--
CRAP. HE'S--
--HE'S TESTING ME. HE'S--
HA! GOOD.
IT'S NOT REAL--
ELI-- SHAKE IT OFF, ELI, SHAKE IT--

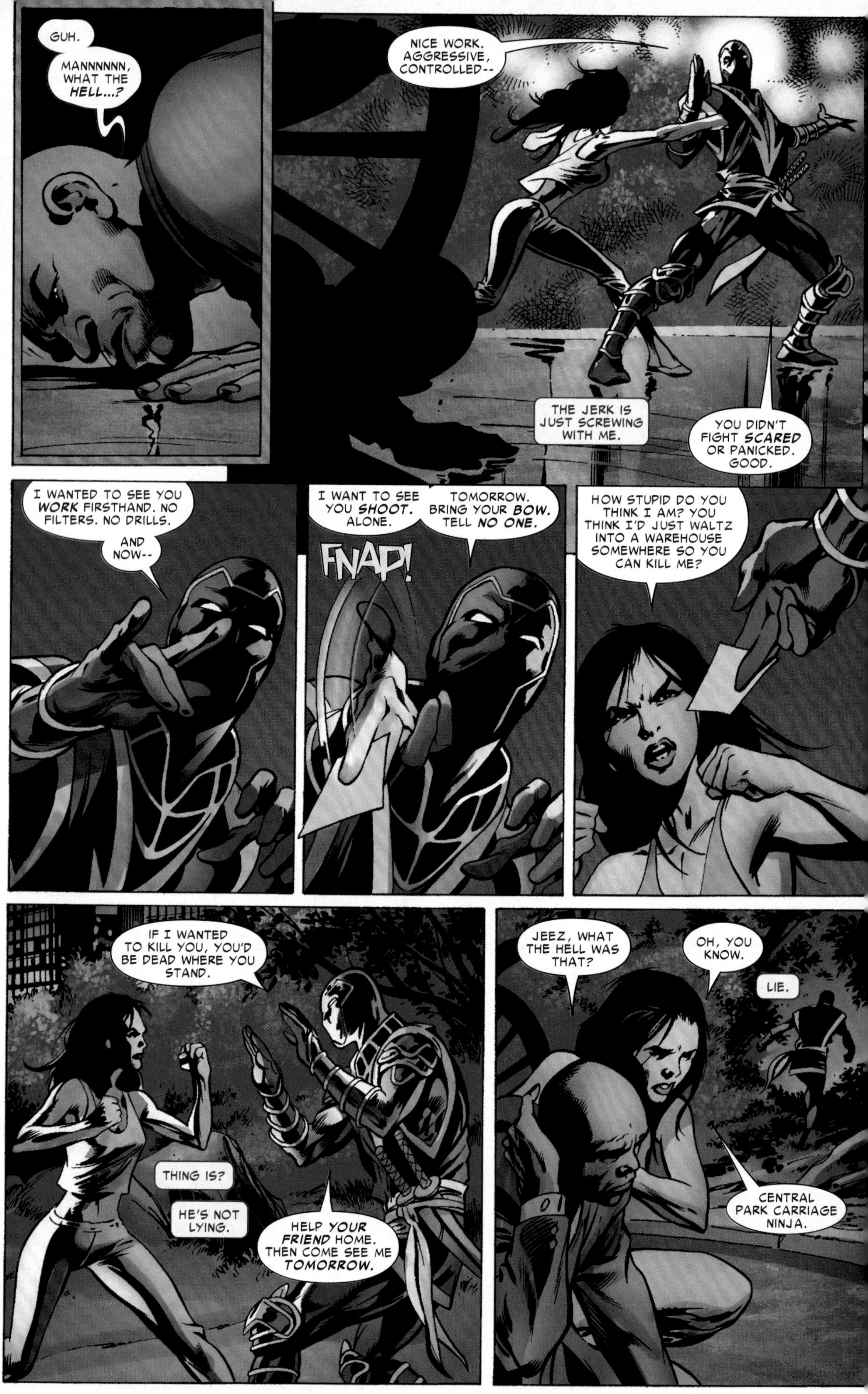
GUH.
MANNNNNN, WHAT THE HELL...?
NICE WORK. AGGRESSIVE, CONTROLLED--
THE JERK IS JUST SCREWING WITH ME.
YOU DIDN'T FIGHT SCARED OR PANICKED. GOOD.
I WANTED TO SEE YOU WORK FIRSTHAND. NO FILTERS. NO DRILLS.
AND NOW--
I WANT TO SEE YOU SHOOT. ALONE.
TOMORROW. BRING YOUR BOW. TELL NO ONE.
FNAP!
HOW STUPID DO YOU THINK I AM? YOU THINK I'D JUST WALTZ INTO A WAREHOUSE SOMEWHERE SO YOU CAN KILL ME?
IF I WANTED TO KILL YOU, YOU'D BE DEAD WHERE YOU STAND.
THING IS?
HE'S NOT LYING.
HELP YOUR FRIEND HOME. THEN COME SEE ME TOMORROW.
JEEZ, WHAT THE HELL WAS THAT?
OH, YOU KNOW.
LIE.
CENTRAL PARK CARRIAGE NINJA.

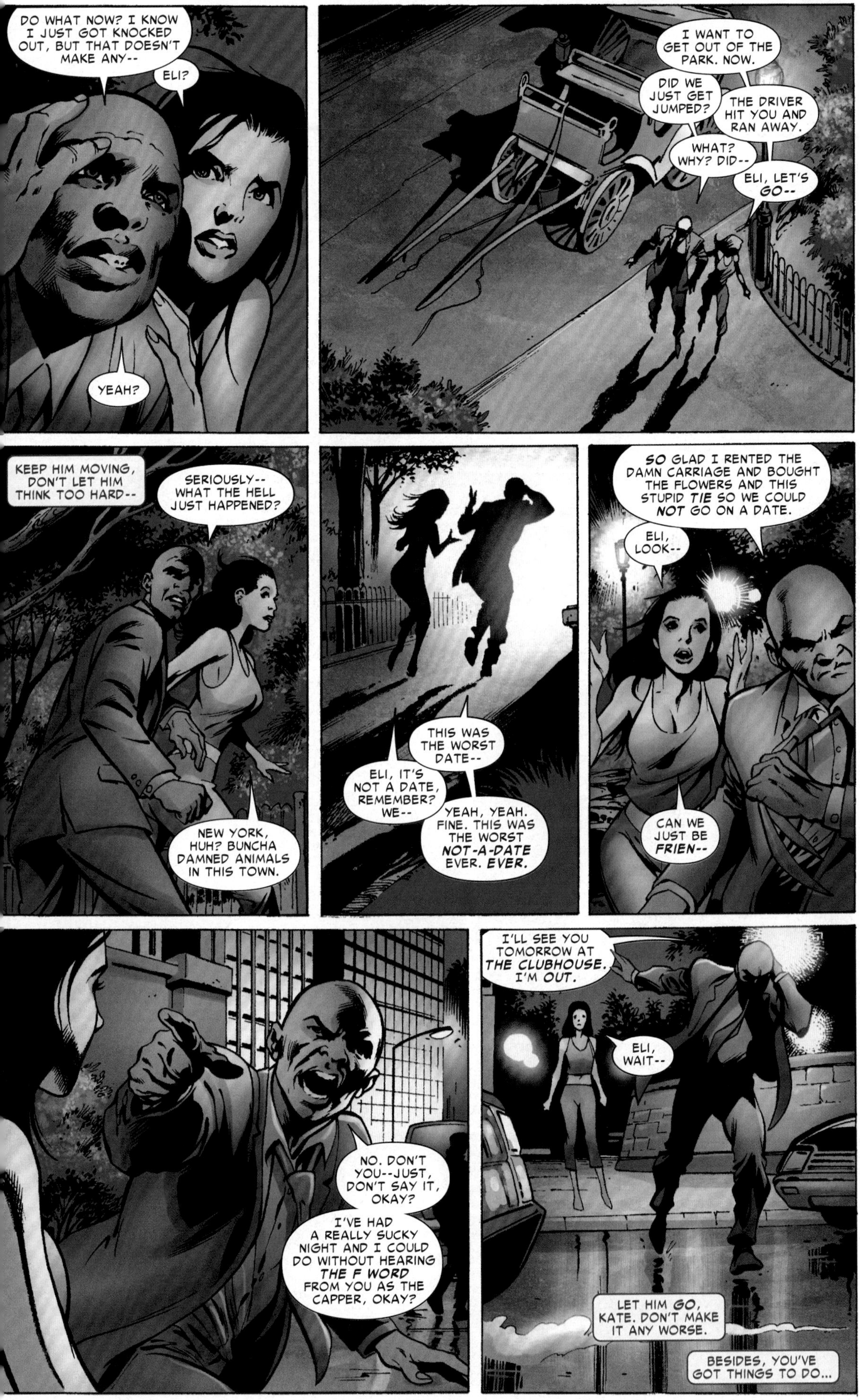
DO WHAT NOW? I KNOW I JUST GOT KNOCKED OUT, BUT THAT DOESN'T MAKE ANY--
ELI?
YEAH?
I WANT TO GET OUT OF THE PARK. NOW.
DID WE JUST GET JUMPED?
THE DRIVER HIT YOU AND RAN AWAY.
WHAT? WHY? DID--
ELI, LET'S GO--
KEEP HIM MOVING, DON'T LET HIM THINK TOO HARD--
SERIOUSLY-- WHAT THE HELL JUST HAPPENED?
NEW YORK, HUH? BUNCHA DAMNED ANIMALS IN THIS TOWN.
THIS WAS THE WORST DATE--
ELI, IT'S NOT A DATE, REMEMBER? WE--
YEAH, YEAH. FINE. THIS WAS THE WORST NOT-A-DATE EVER. EVER.
SO GLAD I RENTED THE DAMN CARRIAGE AND BOUGHT THE FLOWERS AND THIS STUPID TIE SO WE COULD NOT GO ON A DATE.
ELI, LOOK--
CAN WE JUST BE FRIEN--
NO. DON'T YOU--JUST, DON'T SAY IT, OKAY?
I'VE HAD A REALLY SUCKY NIGHT AND I COULD DO WITHOUT HEARING THE F WORD FROM YOU AS THE CAPPER, OKAY?
I'LL SEE YOU TOMORROW AT THE CLUBHOUSE. I'M OUT.
ELI, WAIT--
LET HIM GO, KATE. DON'T MAKE IT ANY WORSE.
BESIDES, YOU'VE GOT THINGS TO DO...

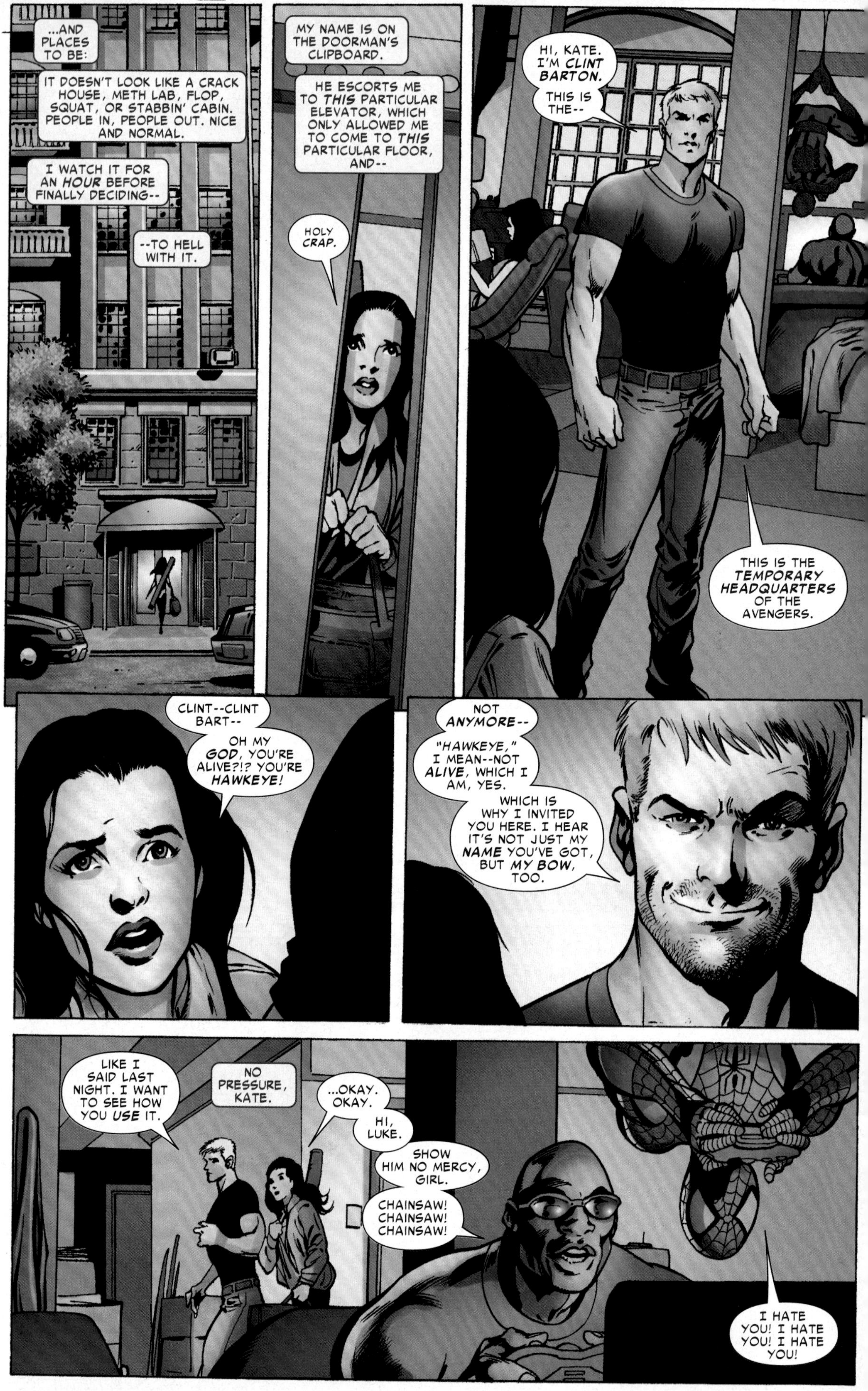

...AND PLACES TO BE:
IT DOESN'T LOOK LIKE A CRACK HOUSE, METH LAB, FLOP, SQUAT, OR STABBIN' CABIN. PEOPLE IN, PEOPLE OUT. NICE AND NORMAL.
I WATCH IT FOR AN HOUR BEFORE FINALLY DECIDING--
--TO HELL WITH IT.
MY NAME IS ON THE DOORMAN'S CLIPBOARD.
HE ESCORTS ME TO THIS PARTICULAR ELEVATOR, WHICH ONLY ALLOWED ME TO COME TO THIS PARTICULAR FLOOR, AND--
HOLY CRAP.
HI, KATE. I'M CLINT BARTON.
THIS IS THE--
THIS IS THE TEMPORARY HEADQUARTERS OF THE AVENGERS.
CLINT--CLINT BART--
OH MY GOD, YOU'RE ALIVE?!? YOU'RE HAWKEYE!
NOT ANYMORE--
"HAWKEYE," I MEAN--NOT ALIVE, WHICH I AM, YES.
WHICH IS WHY I INVITED YOU HERE. I HEAR IT'S NOT JUST MY NAME YOU'VE GOT, BUT MY BOW, TOO.
LIKE I SAID LAST NIGHT. I WANT TO SEE HOW YOU USE IT.
NO PRESSURE, KATE.
...OKAY. OKAY.
HI, LUKE.
SHOW HIM NO MERCY, GIRL.
CHAINSAW! CHAINSAW! CHAINSAW!
I HATE YOU! I HATE YOU! I HATE YOU!

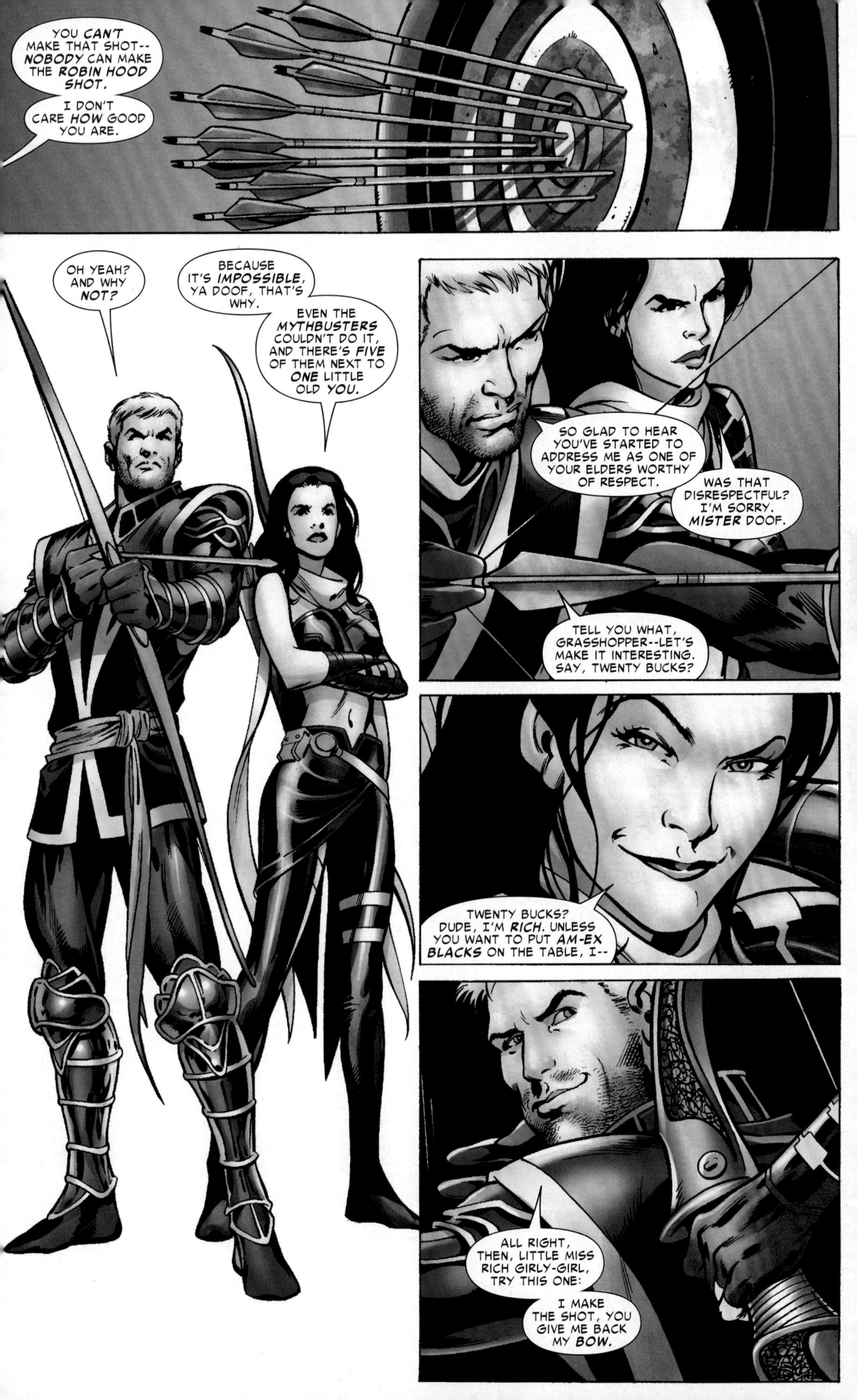
YOU CAN'T MAKE THAT SHOT-- NOBODY CAN MAKE THE ROBIN HOOD SHOT.
I DON'T CARE HOW GOOD YOU ARE.
OH YEAH? AND WHY NOT?
BECAUSE IT'S IMPOSSIBLE, YA DOOF, THAT'S WHY.
EVEN THE MYTHBUSTERS COULDN'T DO IT, AND THERE'S FIVE OF THEM NEXT TO ONE LITTLE OLD YOU.
SO GLAD TO HEAR YOU'VE STARTED TO ADDRESS ME AS ONE OF YOUR ELDERS WORTHY OF RESPECT.
WAS THAT DISRESPECTFUL? I'M SORRY. MISTER DOOF.
TELL YOU WHAT, GRASSHOPPER--LET'S MAKE IT INTERESTING. SAY, TWENTY BUCKS?
TWENTY BUCKS? DUDE, I'M RICH. UNLESS YOU WANT TO PUT AM-EX BLACKS ON THE TABLE, I--
ALL RIGHT, THEN, LITTLE MISS RICH GIRLY-GIRL, TRY THIS ONE:
I MAKE THE SHOT, YOU GIVE ME BACK MY BOW.

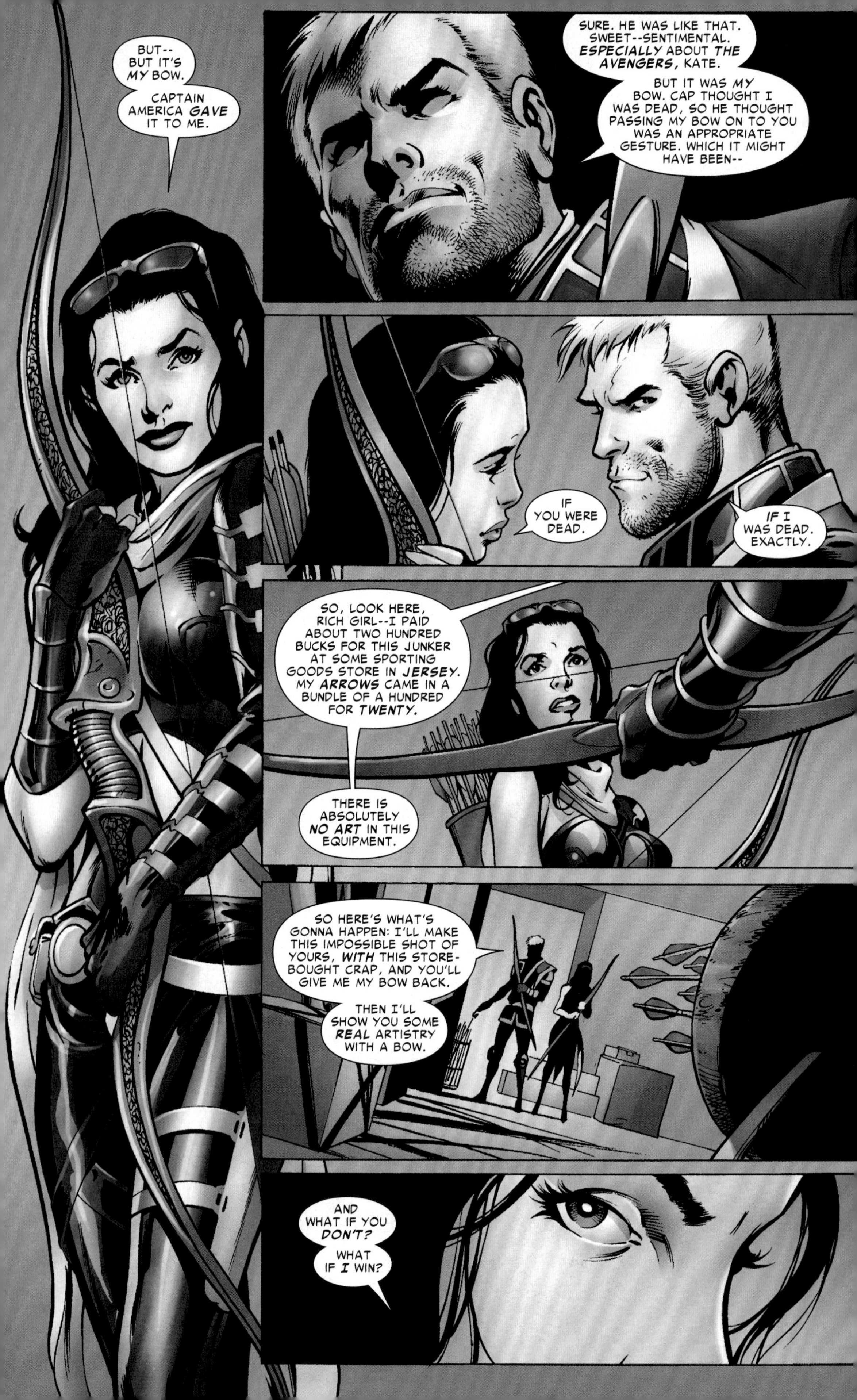
BUT-- BUT IT'S MY BOW.
CAPTAIN AMERICA GAVE IT TO ME.
SURE. HE WAS LIKE THAT. SWEET--SENTIMENTAL. ESPECIALLY ABOUT THE AVENGERS, KATE.
BUT IT WAS MY BOW. CAP THOUGHT I WAS DEAD, SO HE THOUGHT PASSING MY BOW ON TO YOU WAS AN APPROPRIATE GESTURE. WHICH IT MIGHT HAVE BEEN--
IF YOU WERE DEAD.
IF I WAS DEAD. EXACTLY.
SO, LOOK HERE, RICH GIRL--I PAID ABOUT TWO HUNDRED BUCKS FOR THIS JUNKER AT SOME SPORTING GOODS STORE IN JERSEY. MY ARROWS CAME IN A BUNDLE OF A HUNDRED FOR TWENTY.
THERE IS ABSOLUTELY NO ART IN THIS EQUIPMENT.
SO HERE'S WHAT'S GONNA HAPPEN: I'LL MAKE THIS IMPOSSIBLE SHOT OF YOURS, WITH THIS STORE-BOUGHT CRAP, AND YOU'LL GIVE ME MY BOW BACK.
THEN I'LL SHOW YOU SOME REAL ARTISTRY WITH A BOW.
AND WHAT IF YOU DON'T?
WHAT IF I WIN?

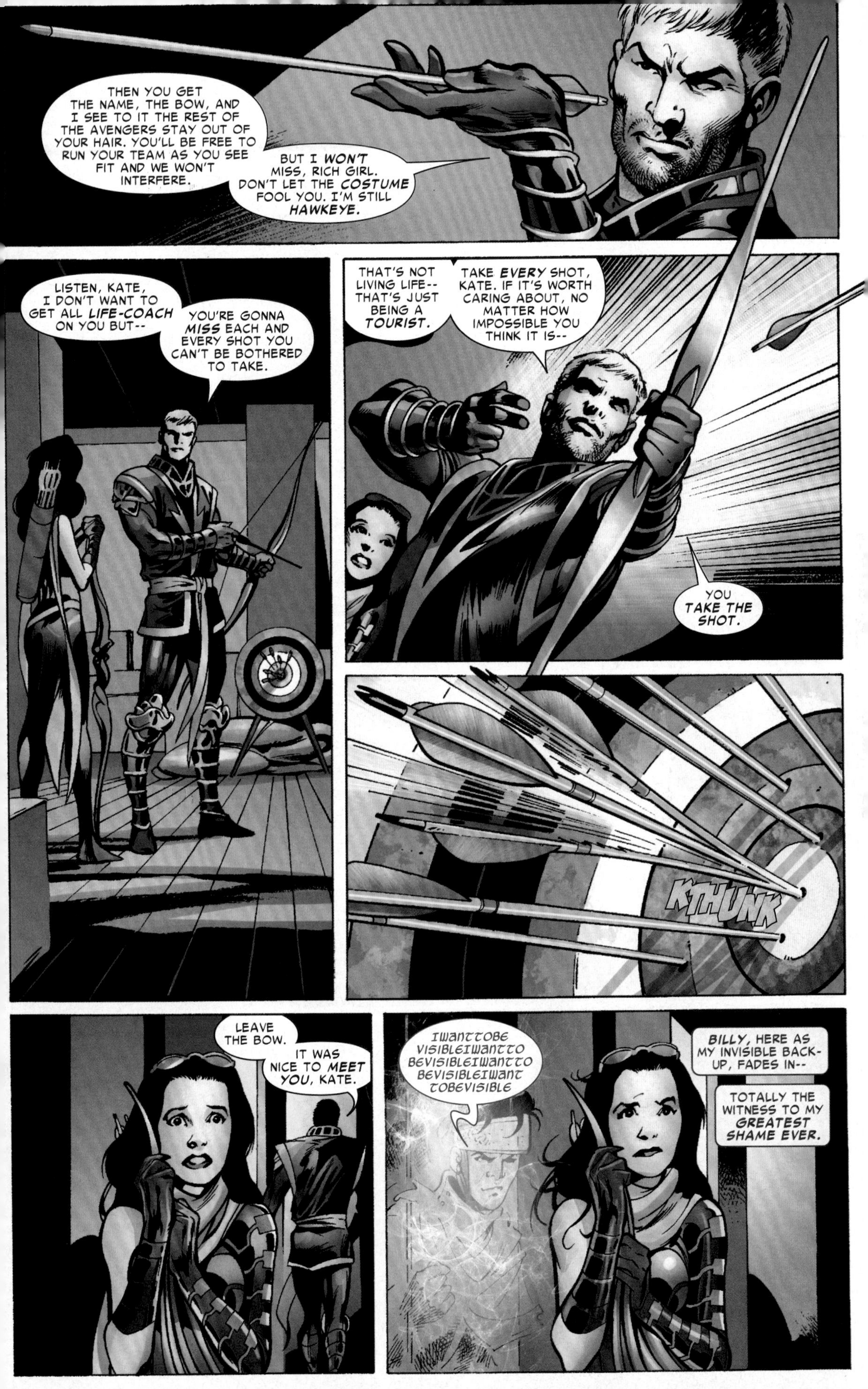
THEN YOU GET THE NAME, THE BOW, AND I SEE TO IT THE REST OF THE AVENGERS STAY OUT OF YOUR HAIR. YOU'LL BE FREE TO RUN YOUR TEAM AS YOU SEE FIT AND WE WON'T INTERFERE.
BUT I WON'T MISS, RICH GIRL. DON'T LET THE COSTUME FOOL YOU. I'M STILL HAWKEYE.
LISTEN, KATE, I DON'T WANT TO GET ALL LIFE-COACH ON YOU BUT--
YOU'RE GONNA MISS EACH AND EVERY SHOT YOU CAN'T BE BOTHERED TO TAKE.
THAT'S NOT LIVING LIFE-- THAT'S JUST BEING A TOURIST.
TAKE EVERY SHOT, KATE. IF IT'S WORTH CARING ABOUT, NO MATTER HOW IMPOSSIBLE YOU THINK IT IS--
YOU TAKE THE SHOT.
KTHUNK
LEAVE THE BOW.
IT WAS NICE TO MEET YOU, KATE.
IWANTTOBE VISIBLEIWANTTO BEVISIBLEIWANTTO BEVISIBLEIWANT TOBEVISIBLE
BILLY, HERE AS MY INVISIBLE BACK-UP, FADES IN--
TOTALLY THE WITNESS TO MY GREATEST SHAME EVER.

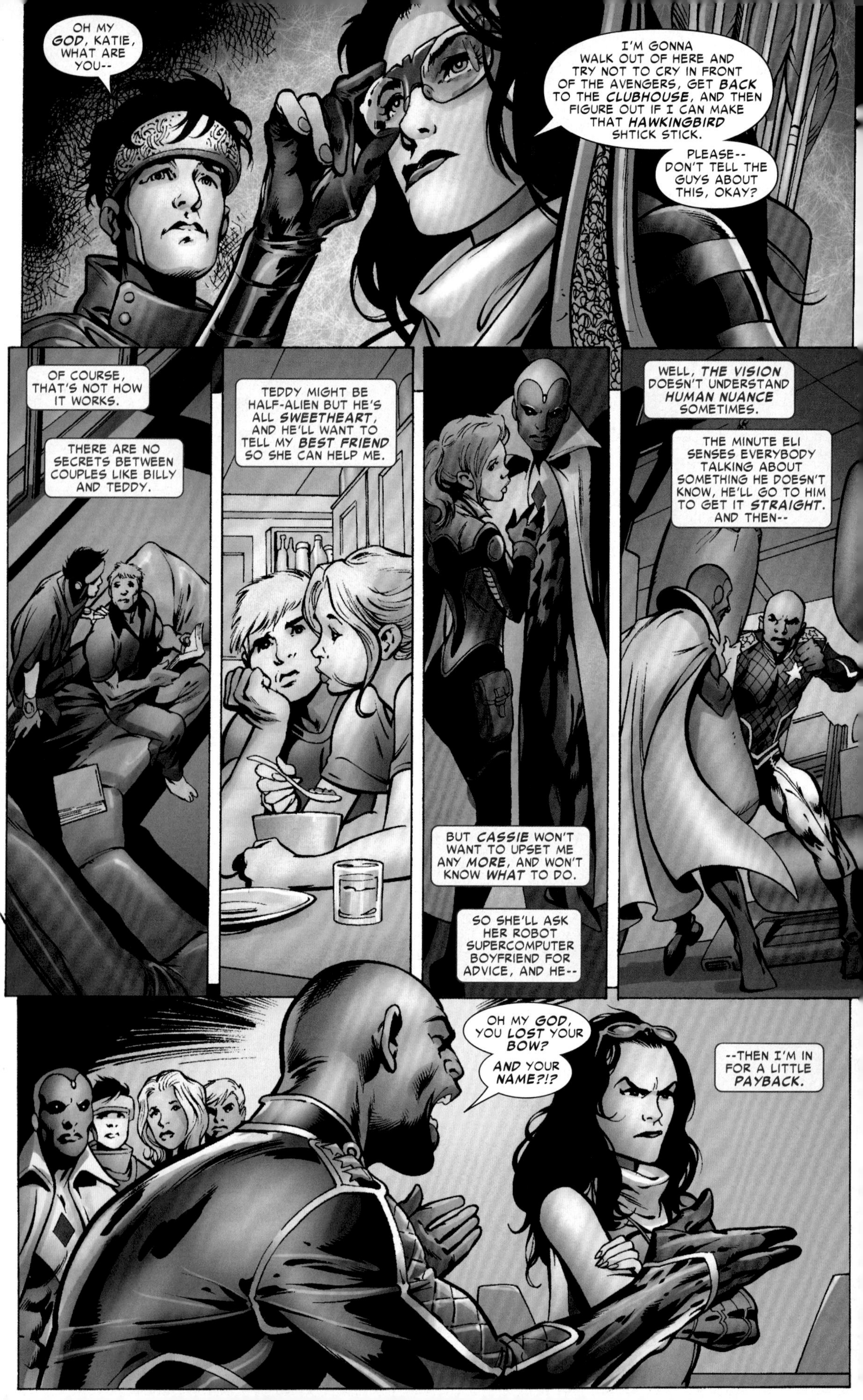
OH MY GOD, KATIE, WHAT ARE YOU--
I'M GONNA WALK OUT OF HERE AND TRY NOT TO CRY IN FRONT OF THE AVENGERS, GET BACK TO THE CLUBHOUSE, AND THEN FIGURE OUT IF I CAN MAKE THAT HAWKINGBIRD SHTICK STICK.
PLEASE-- DON'T TELL THE GUYS ABOUT THIS, OKAY?
OF COURSE, THAT'S NOT HOW IT WORKS.
THERE ARE NO SECRETS BETWEEN COUPLES LIKE BILLY AND TEDDY.
TEDDY MIGHT BE HALF-ALIEN BUT HE'S ALL SWEETHEART, AND HE'LL WANT TO TELL MY BEST FRIEND SO SHE CAN HELP ME.
BUT CASSIE WON'T WANT TO UPSET ME ANY MORE, AND WON'T KNOW WHAT TO DO.
SO SHE'LL ASK HER ROBOT SUPERCOMPUTER BOYFRIEND FOR ADVICE, AND HE--
WELL, THE VISION DOESN'T UNDERSTAND HUMAN NUANCE SOMETIMES.
THE MINUTE ELI SENSES EVERYBODY TALKING ABOUT SOMETHING HE DOESN'T KNOW, HE'LL GO TO HIM TO GET IT STRAIGHT. AND THEN--
OH MY GOD, YOU LOST YOUR BOW?
AND YOUR NAME?!?
--THEN I'M IN FOR A LITTLE PAYBACK.

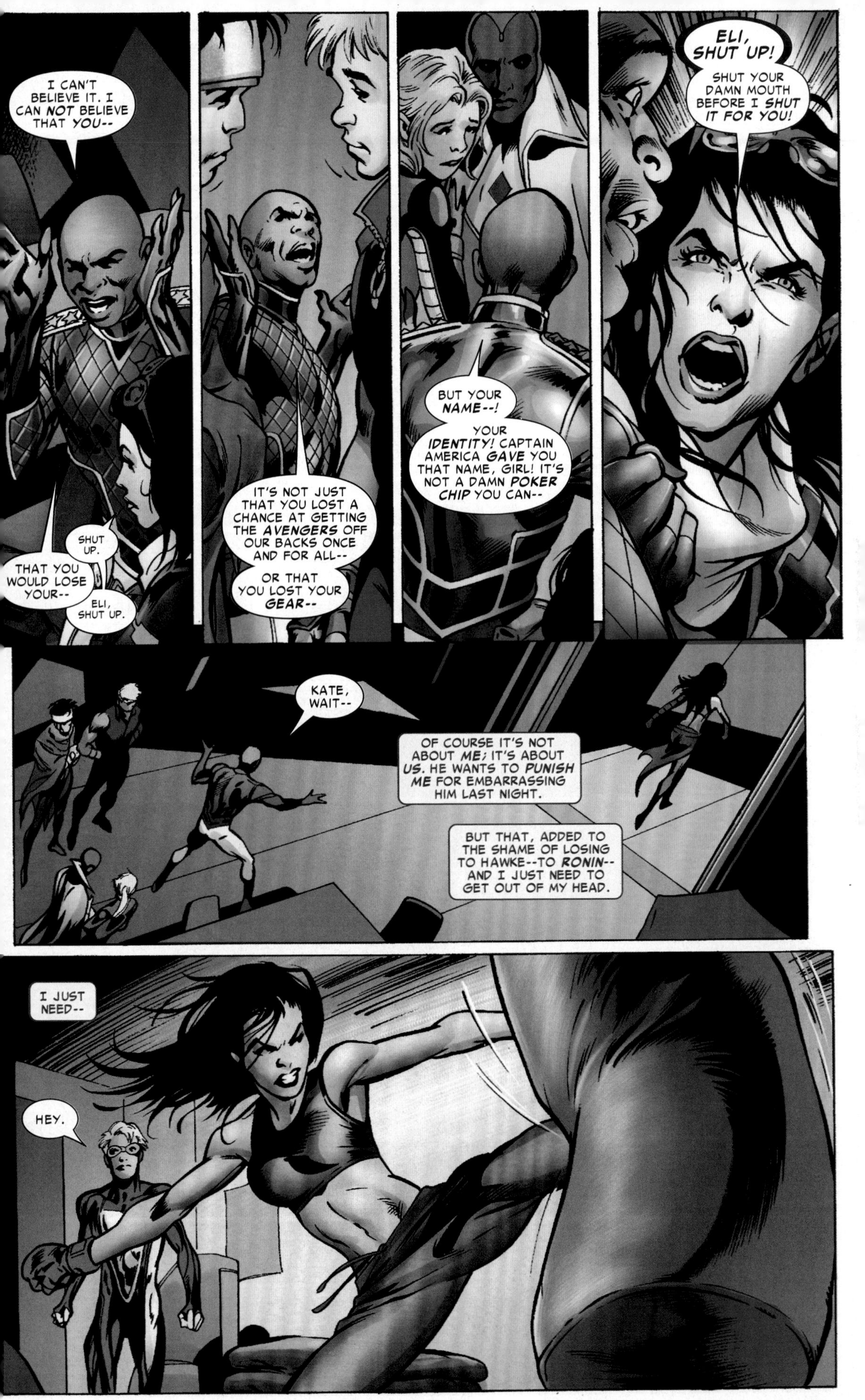

I CAN'T BELIEVE IT. I CAN NOT BELIEVE THAT YOU--
SHUT UP.
THAT YOU WOULD LOSE YOUR--
ELI, SHUT UP.
IT'S NOT JUST THAT YOU LOST A CHANCE AT GETTING THE AVENGERS OFF OUR BACKS ONCE AND FOR ALL--
OR THAT YOU LOST YOUR GEAR--
BUT YOUR NAME--!
YOUR IDENTITY! CAPTAIN AMERICA GAVE YOU THAT NAME, GIRL! IT'S NOT A DAMN POKER CHIP YOU CAN--
ELI, SHUT UP!
SHUT YOUR DAMN MOUTH BEFORE I SHUT IT FOR YOU!
KATE, WAIT--
OF COURSE IT'S NOT ABOUT ME; IT'S ABOUT US. HE WANTS TO PUNISH ME FOR EMBARRASSING HIM LAST NIGHT.
BUT THAT, ADDED TO THE SHAME OF LOSING TO HAWKE--TO RONIN--AND I JUST NEED TO GET OUT OF MY HEAD.
I JUST NEED--
HEY.

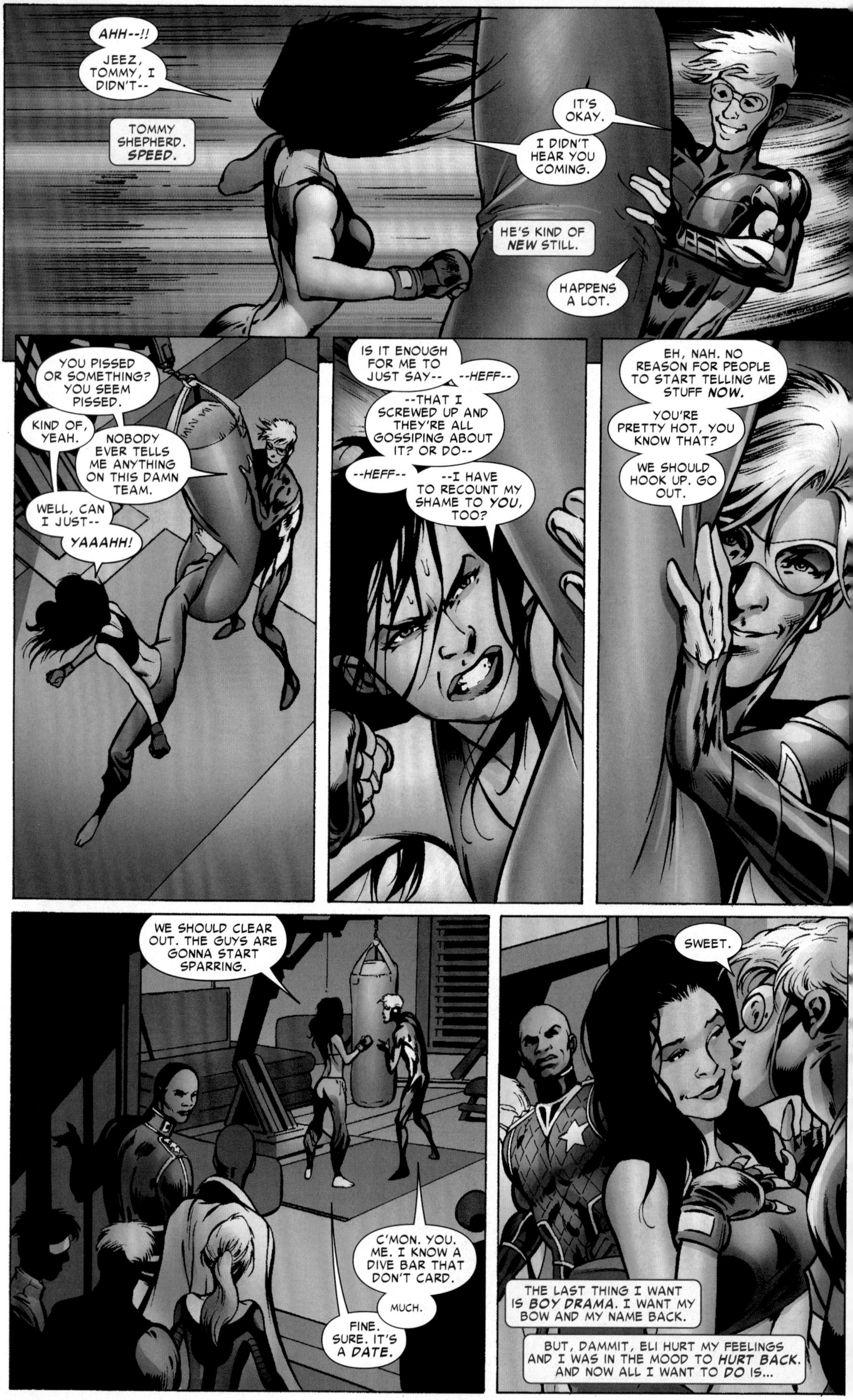
AHH--!!
JEEZ, TOMMY, I DIDN'T--
TOMMY SHEPHERD. SPEED.
IT'S OKAY.
I DIDN'T HEAR YOU COMING.
HE'S KIND OF NEW STILL.
HAPPENS A LOT.
YOU PISSED OR SOMETHING? YOU SEEM PISSED.
KIND OF, YEAH.
NOBODY EVER TELLS ME ANYTHING ON THIS DAMN TEAM.
WELL, CAN I JUST--
YAAAHH!
IS IT ENOUGH FOR ME TO JUST SAY--
--HEFF--
--THAT I SCREWED UP AND THEY'RE ALL GOSSIPING ABOUT IT? OR DO--
--HEFF--
--I HAVE TO RECOUNT MY SHAME TO YOU, TOO?
EH, NAH. NO REASON FOR PEOPLE TO START TELLING ME STUFF NOW.
YOU'RE PRETTY HOT, YOU KNOW THAT?
WE SHOULD HOOK UP. GO OUT.
WE SHOULD CLEAR OUT. THE GUYS ARE GONNA START SPARRING.
C'MON. YOU. ME. I KNOW A DIVE BAR THAT DON'T CARD.
MUCH.
FINE. SURE. IT'S A DATE.
SWEET.
THE LAST THING I WANT IS BOY DRAMA. I WANT MY BOW AND MY NAME BACK.
BUT, DAMMIT, ELI HURT MY FEELINGS AND I WAS IN THE MOOD TO HURT BACK. AND NOW ALL I WANT TO DO IS...

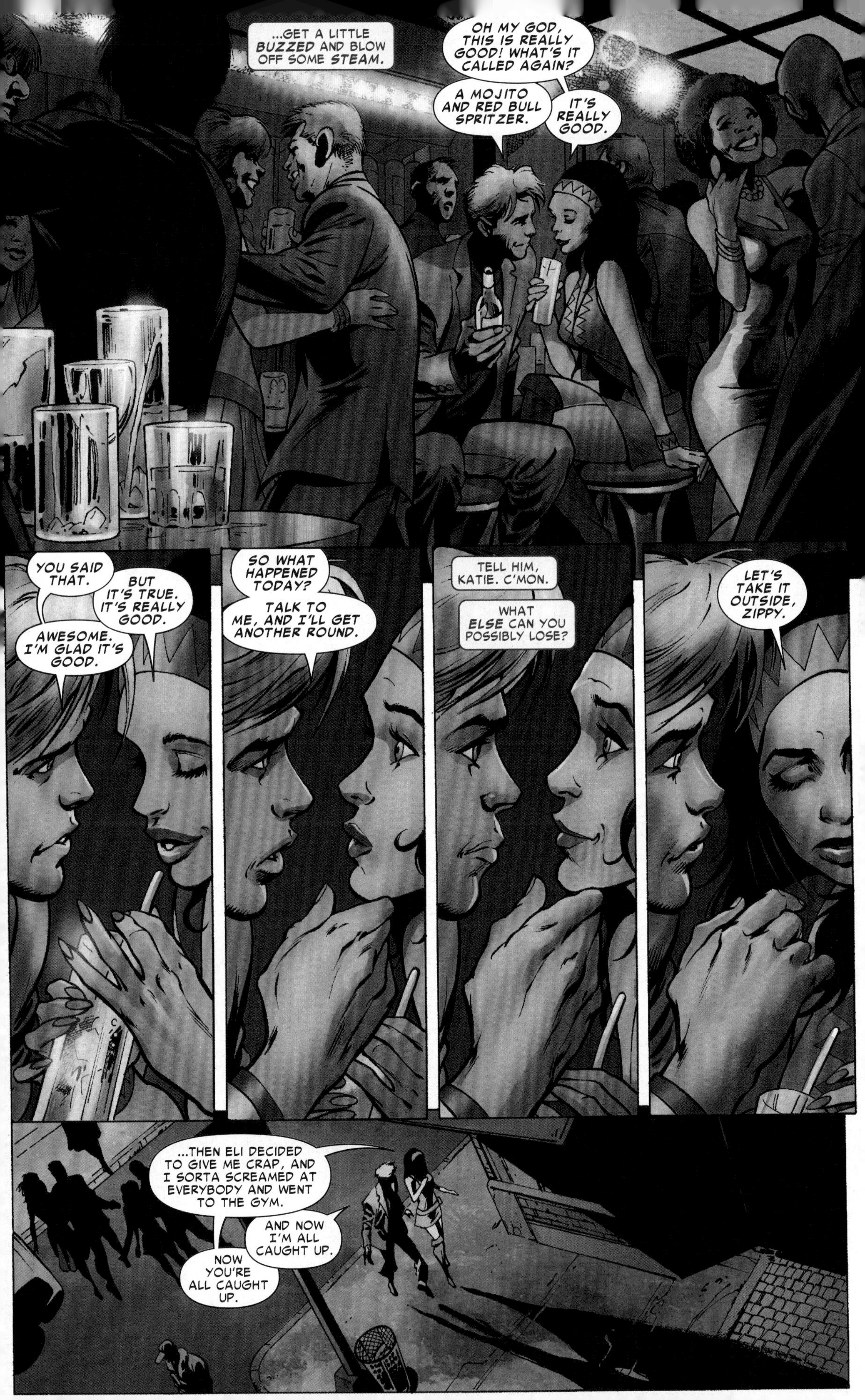
...GET A LITTLE BUZZED AND BLOW OFF SOME STEAM.
OH MY GOD, THIS IS REALLY GOOD! WHAT'S IT CALLED AGAIN?
A MOJITO AND RED BULL SPRITZER.
IT'S REALLY GOOD.
YOU SAID THAT.
BUT IT'S TRUE. IT'S REALLY GOOD.
AWESOME. I'M GLAD IT'S GOOD.
SO WHAT HAPPENED TODAY?
TALK TO ME, AND I'LL GET ANOTHER ROUND.
TELL HIM, KATIE. C'MON.
WHAT ELSE CAN YOU POSSIBLY LOSE?
LET'S TAKE IT OUTSIDE, ZIPPY.
...THEN ELI DECIDED TO GIVE ME CRAP, AND I SORTA SCREAMED AT EVERYBODY AND WENT TO THE GYM.
AND NOW I'M ALL CAUGHT UP.
NOW YOU'RE ALL CAUGHT UP.

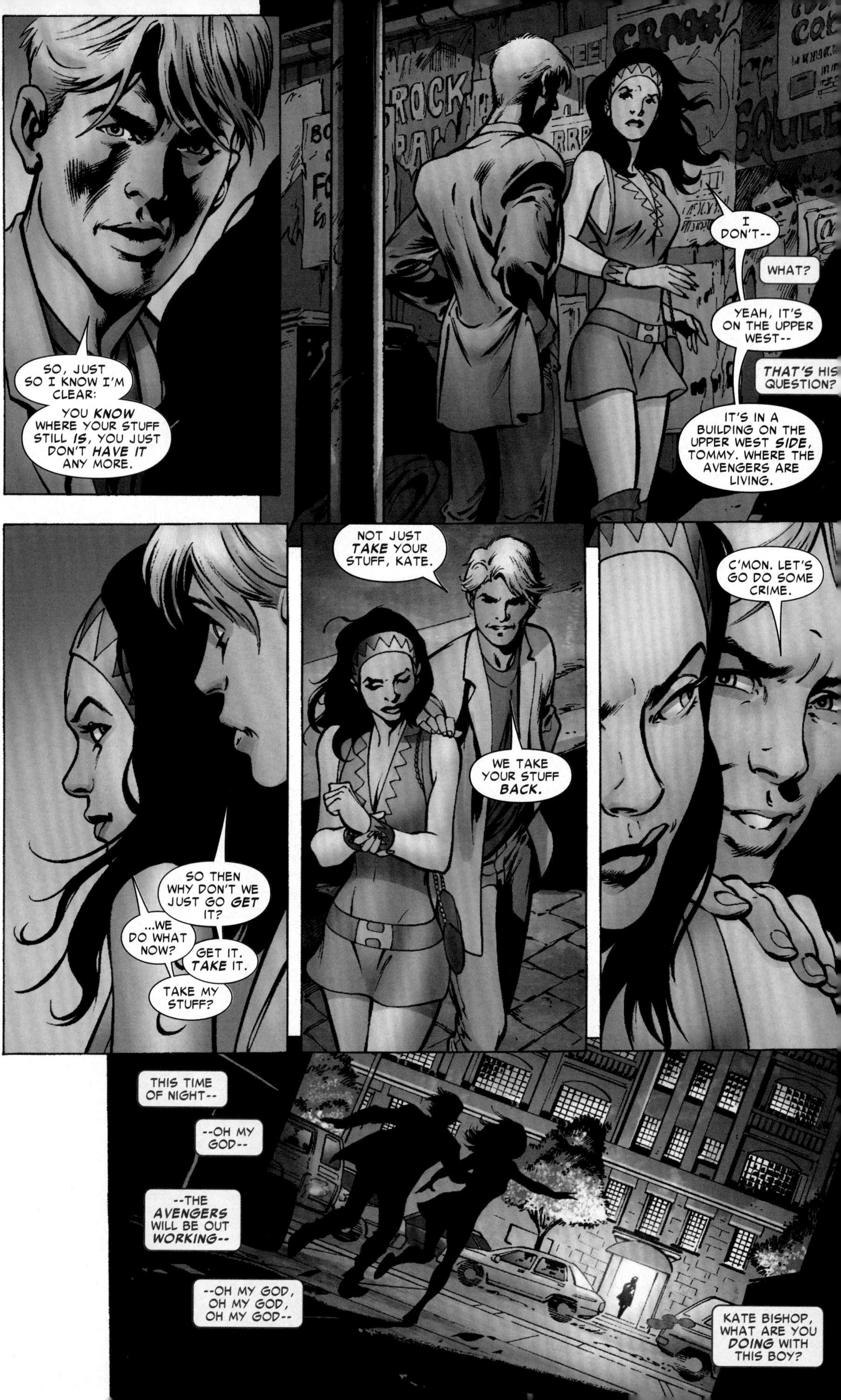

SO, JUST SO I KNOW I'M CLEAR:
YOU KNOW WHERE YOUR STUFF STILL IS, YOU JUST DON'T HAVE IT ANY MORE.
I DON'T--
WHAT?
YEAH, IT'S ON THE UPPER WEST--
THAT'S HIS QUESTION?
IT'S IN A BUILDING ON THE UPPER WEST SIDE, TOMMY. WHERE THE AVENGERS ARE LIVING.
SO THEN WHY DON'T WE JUST GO GET IT?
...WE DO WHAT NOW?
GET IT. TAKE IT.
TAKE MY STUFF?
NOT JUST TAKE YOUR STUFF, KATE.
WE TAKE YOUR STUFF BACK.
C'MON. LET'S GO DO SOME CRIME.
THIS TIME OF NIGHT--
--OH MY GOD--
--THE AVENGERS WILL BE OUT WORKING--
--OH MY GOD, OH MY GOD, OH MY GOD--
KATE BISHOP, WHAT ARE YOU DOING WITH THIS BOY?

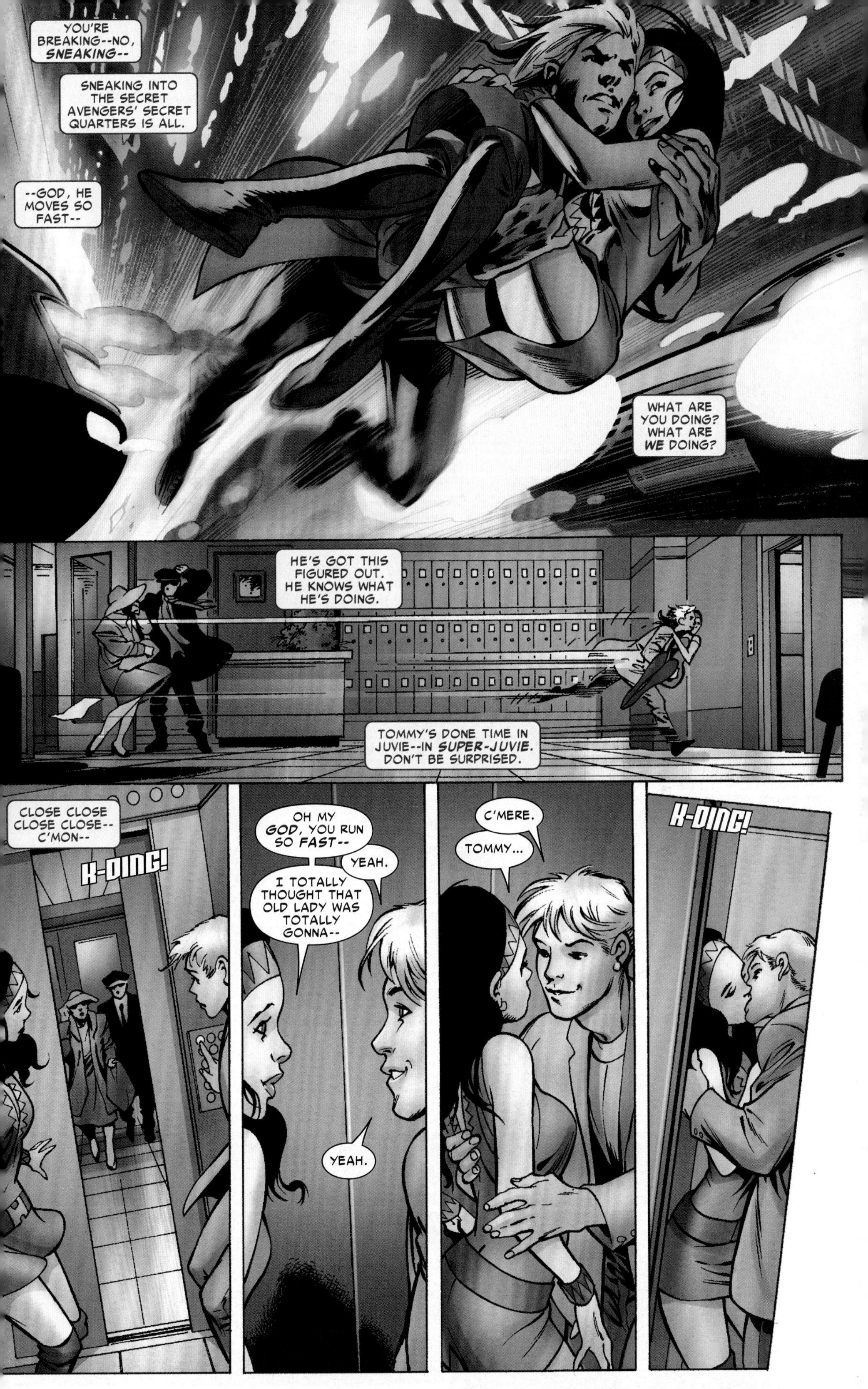
YOU'RE BREAKING--NO, SNEAKING--
SNEAKING INTO THE SECRET AVENGERS' SECRET QUARTERS IS ALL.
--GOD, HE MOVES SO FAST--
WHAT ARE YOU DOING? WHAT ARE WE DOING?
HE'S GOT THIS FIGURED OUT. HE KNOWS WHAT HE'S DOING.
TOMMY'S DONE TIME IN JUVIE--IN SUPER-JUVIE. DON'T BE SURPRISED.
CLOSE CLOSE CLOSE CLOSE--C'MON--
K-DING!
OH MY GOD, YOU RUN SO FAST--
YEAH.
I TOTALLY THOUGHT THAT OLD LADY WAS TOTALLY GONNA--
YEAH.
C'MERE.
TOMMY...
K-DING!

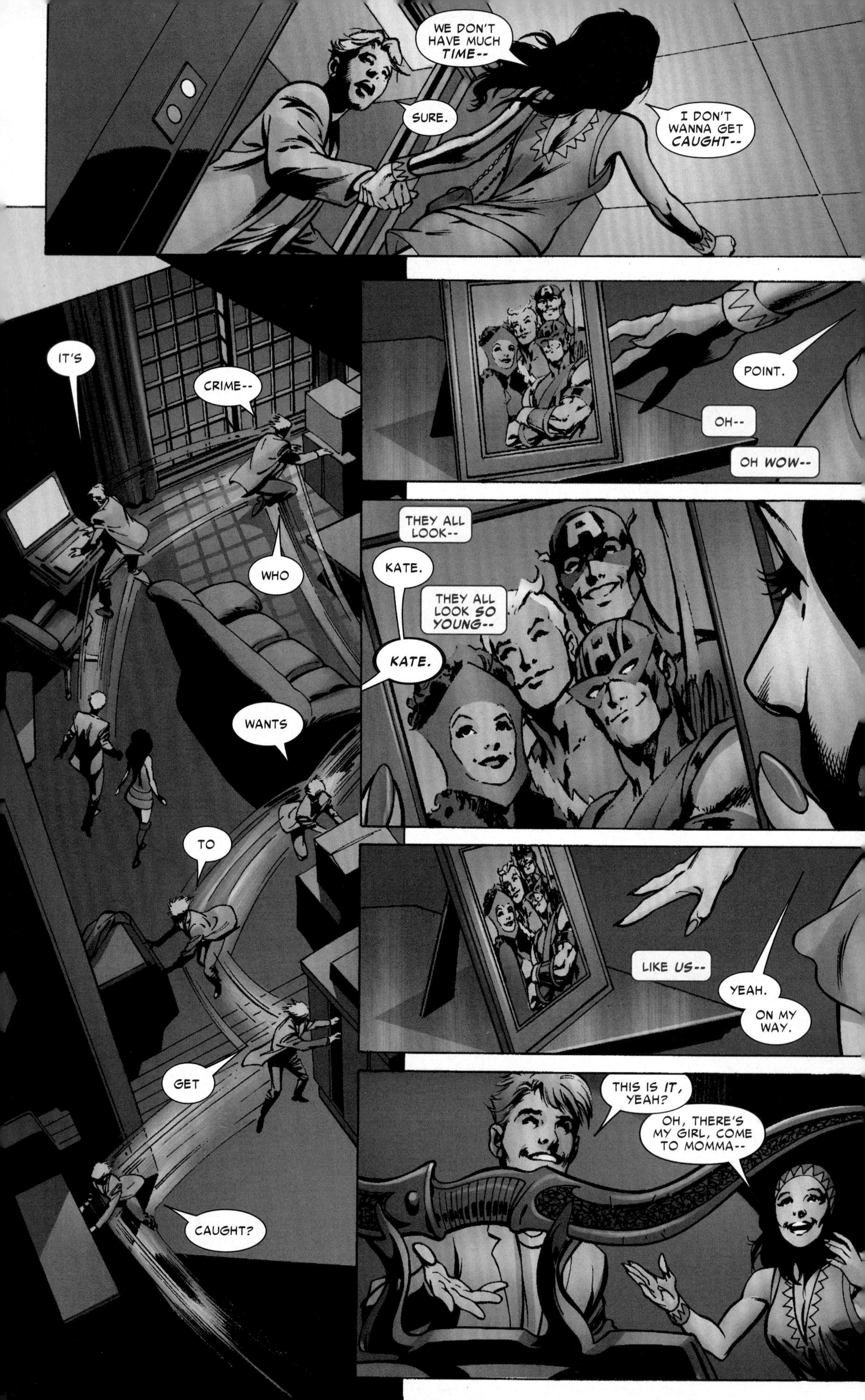
WE DON'T HAVE MUCH TIME--
SURE.
I DON'T WANNA GET CAUGHT--
IT'S
CRIME--
WHO
WANTS
TO
GET
CAUGHT?
POINT.
OH--
OH WOW--
THEY ALL LOOK--
KATE.
THEY ALL LOOK SO YOUNG--
KATE.
LIKE US--
YEAH.
ON MY WAY.
THIS IS IT, YEAH?
OH, THERE'S MY GIRL, COME TO MOMMA--

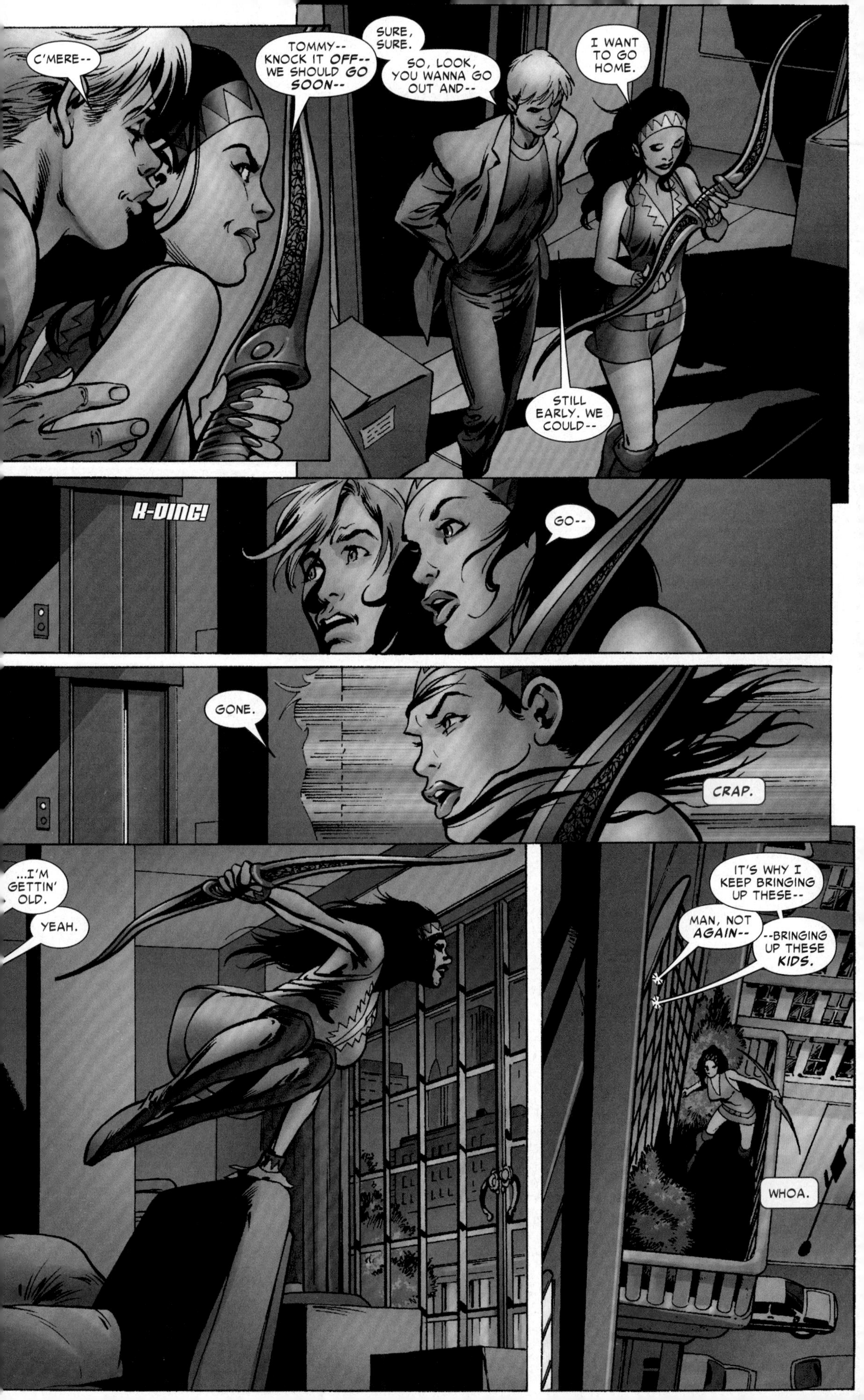
C'MERE--
TOMMY-- KNOCK IT *OFF*-- WE SHOULD *GO SOON*--
SURE, SURE.
SO, LOOK, YOU WANNA GO OUT AND--
I WANT TO GO HOME.
STILL EARLY. WE COULD--
K-DING!
GO--
GONE.
CRAP.
...I'M GETTIN' OLD.
YEAH.
IT'S WHY I KEEP BRINGING UP THESE--
MAN, NOT *AGAIN*--
--BRINGING UP THESE *KIDS*.
WHOA.

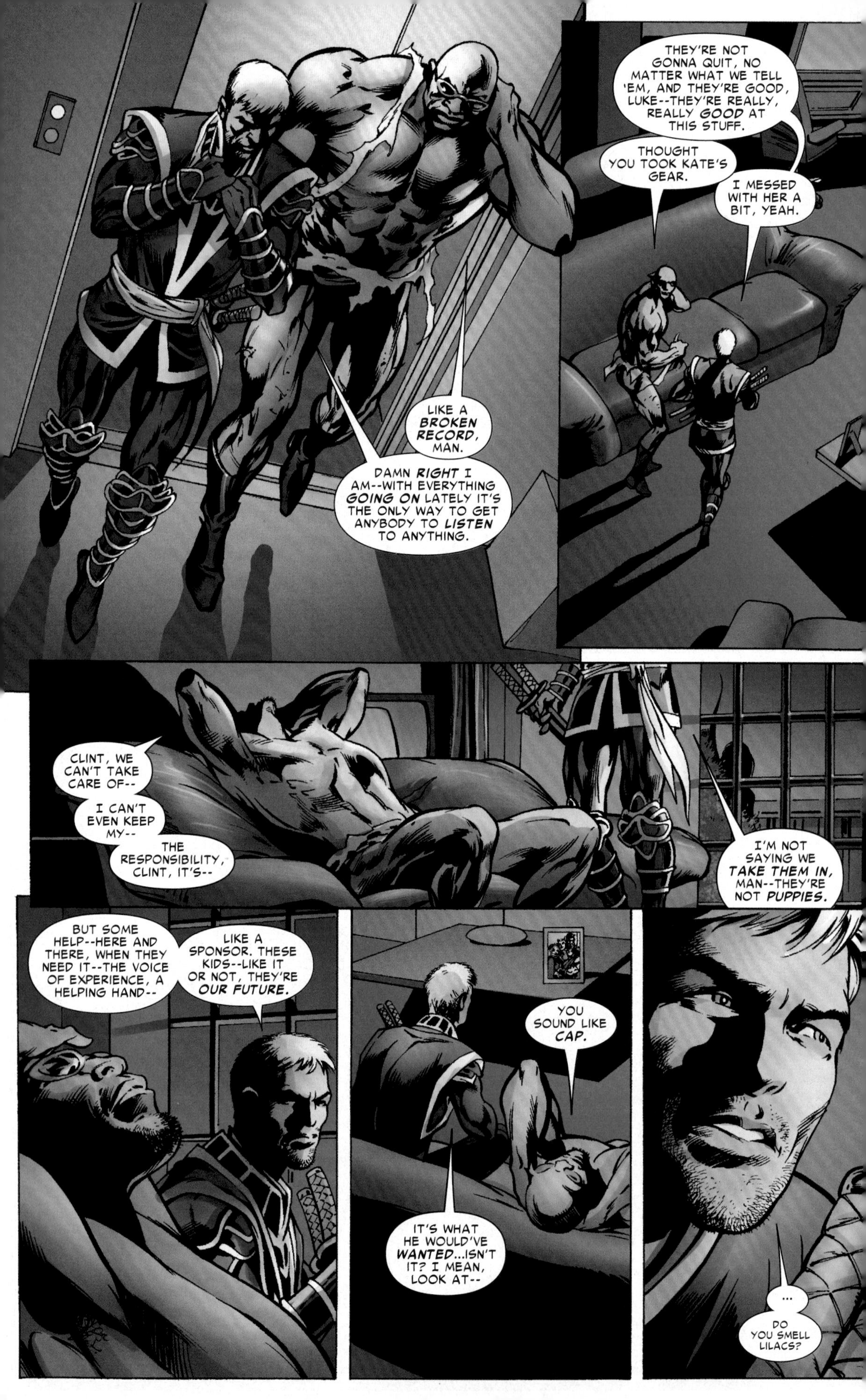
THEY'RE NOT GONNA QUIT, NO MATTER WHAT WE TELL 'EM, AND THEY'RE GOOD, LUKE--THEY'RE REALLY, REALLY GOOD AT THIS STUFF.
THOUGHT YOU TOOK KATE'S GEAR.
I MESSED WITH HER A BIT, YEAH.
LIKE A BROKEN RECORD, MAN.
DAMN RIGHT I AM--WITH EVERYTHING GOING ON LATELY IT'S THE ONLY WAY TO GET ANYBODY TO LISTEN TO ANYTHING.
CLINT, WE CAN'T TAKE CARE OF--
I CAN'T EVEN KEEP MY--
THE RESPONSIBILITY, CLINT, IT'S--
I'M NOT SAYING WE TAKE THEM IN, MAN--THEY'RE NOT PUPPIES.
BUT SOME HELP--HERE AND THERE, WHEN THEY NEED IT--THE VOICE OF EXPERIENCE, A HELPING HAND--
LIKE A SPONSOR. THESE KIDS--LIKE IT OR NOT, THEY'RE OUR FUTURE.
YOU SOUND LIKE CAP.
IT'S WHAT HE WOULD'VE WANTED...ISN'T IT? I MEAN, LOOK AT--
...
DO YOU SMELL LILACS?

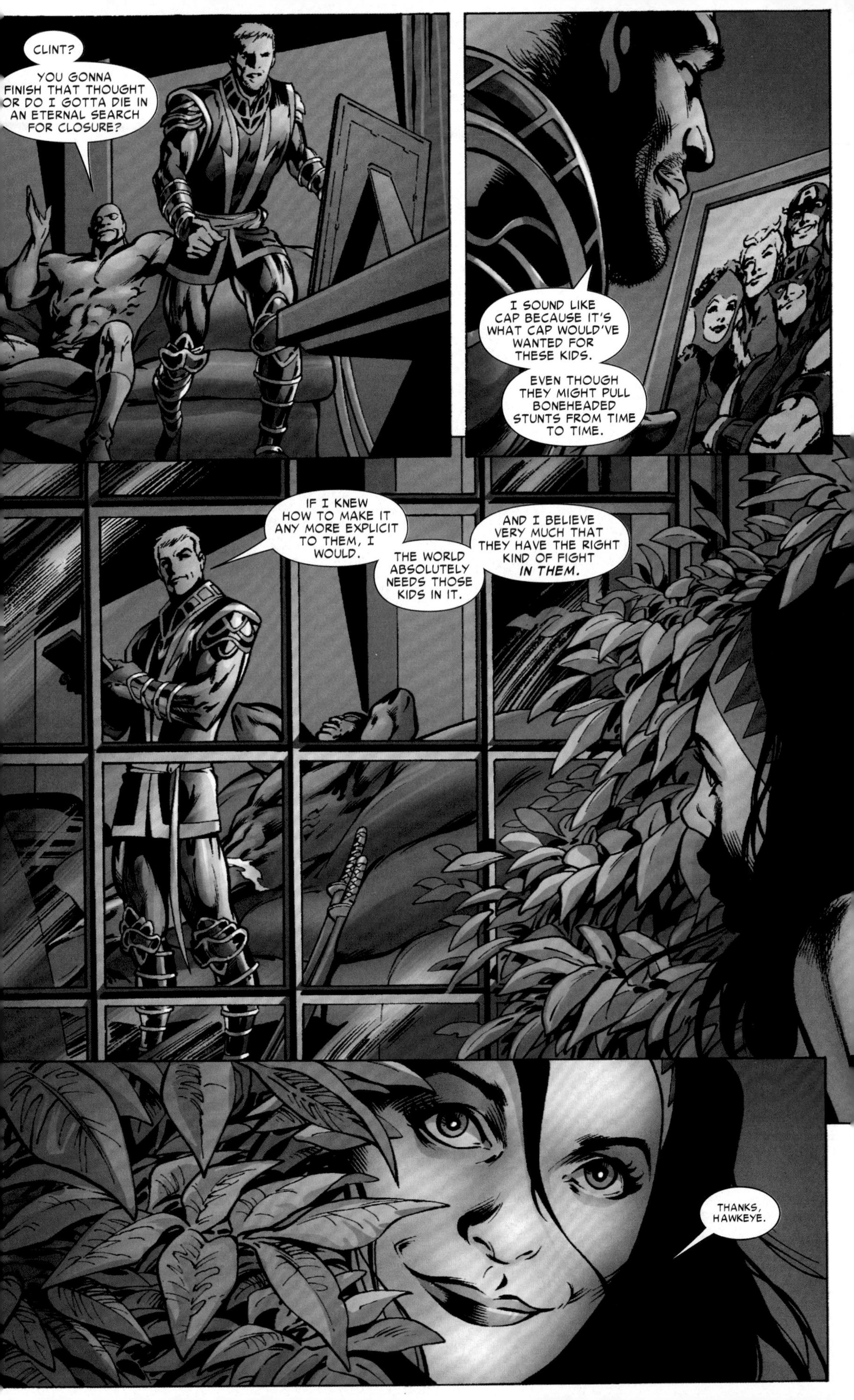
CLINT?
YOU GONNA FINISH THAT THOUGHT OR DO I GOTTA DIE IN AN ETERNAL SEARCH FOR CLOSURE?
I SOUND LIKE CAP BECAUSE IT'S WHAT CAP WOULD'VE WANTED FOR THESE KIDS.
EVEN THOUGH THEY MIGHT PULL BONEHEADED STUNTS FROM TIME TO TIME.
IF I KNEW HOW TO MAKE IT ANY MORE EXPLICIT TO THEM, I WOULD.
THE WORLD ABSOLUTELY NEEDS THOSE KIDS IN IT.
AND I BELIEVE VERY MUCH THAT THEY HAVE THE RIGHT KIND OF FIGHT *IN THEM.*
THANKS, HAWKEYE.

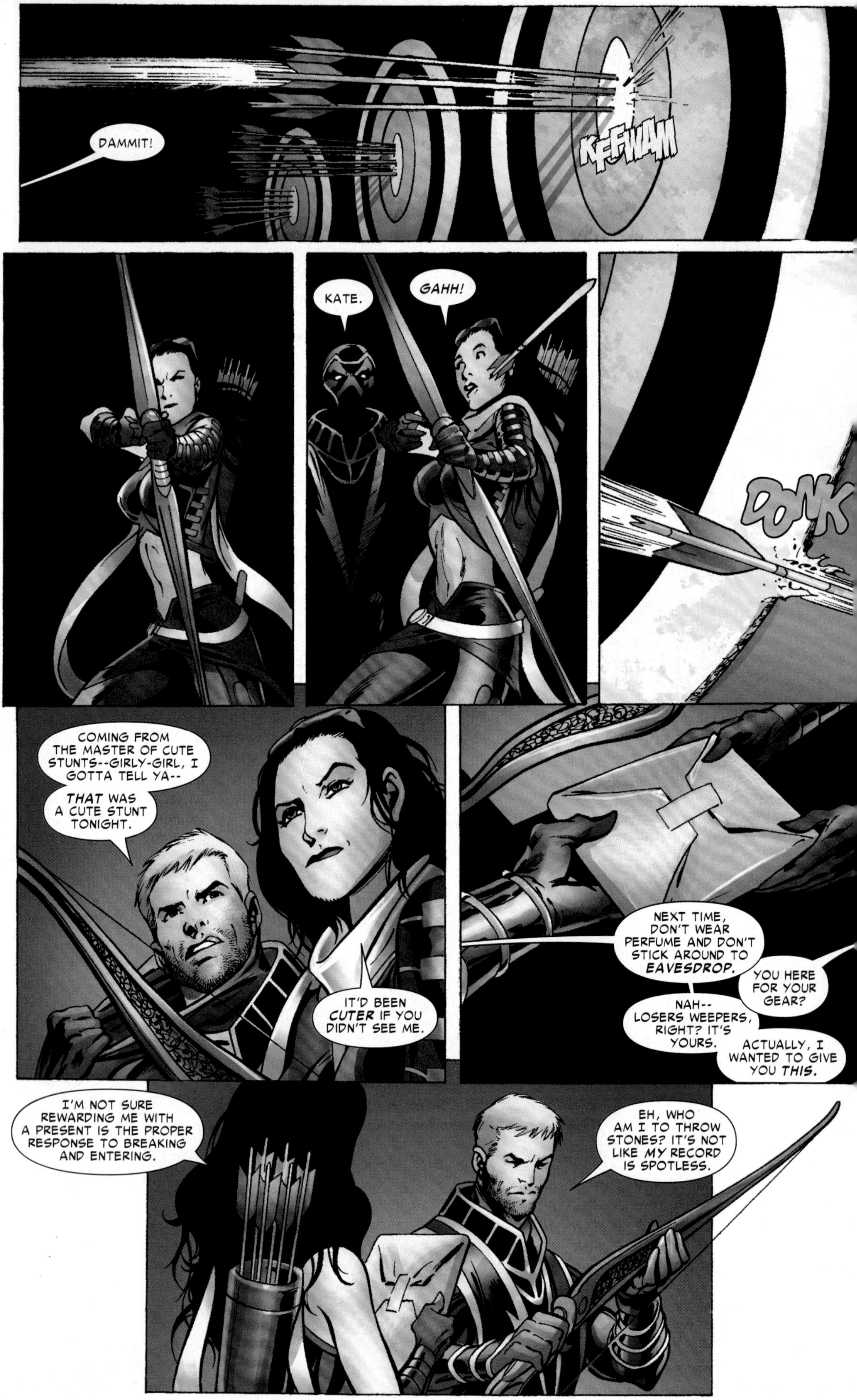
DAMMIT!
KFFWAM
KATE.
GAHH!
DONK
COMING FROM THE MASTER OF CUTE STUNTS--GIRLY-GIRL, I GOTTA TELL YA--
THAT WAS A CUTE STUNT TONIGHT.
IT'D BEEN CUTER IF YOU DIDN'T SEE ME.
NEXT TIME, DON'T WEAR PERFUME AND DON'T STICK AROUND TO EAVESDROP.
YOU HERE FOR YOUR GEAR?
NAH-- LOSERS WEEPERS, RIGHT? IT'S YOURS.
ACTUALLY, I WANTED TO GIVE YOU THIS.
I'M NOT SURE REWARDING ME WITH A PRESENT IS THE PROPER RESPONSE TO BREAKING AND ENTERING.
EH, WHO AM I TO THROW STONES? IT'S NOT LIKE MY RECORD IS SPOTLESS.

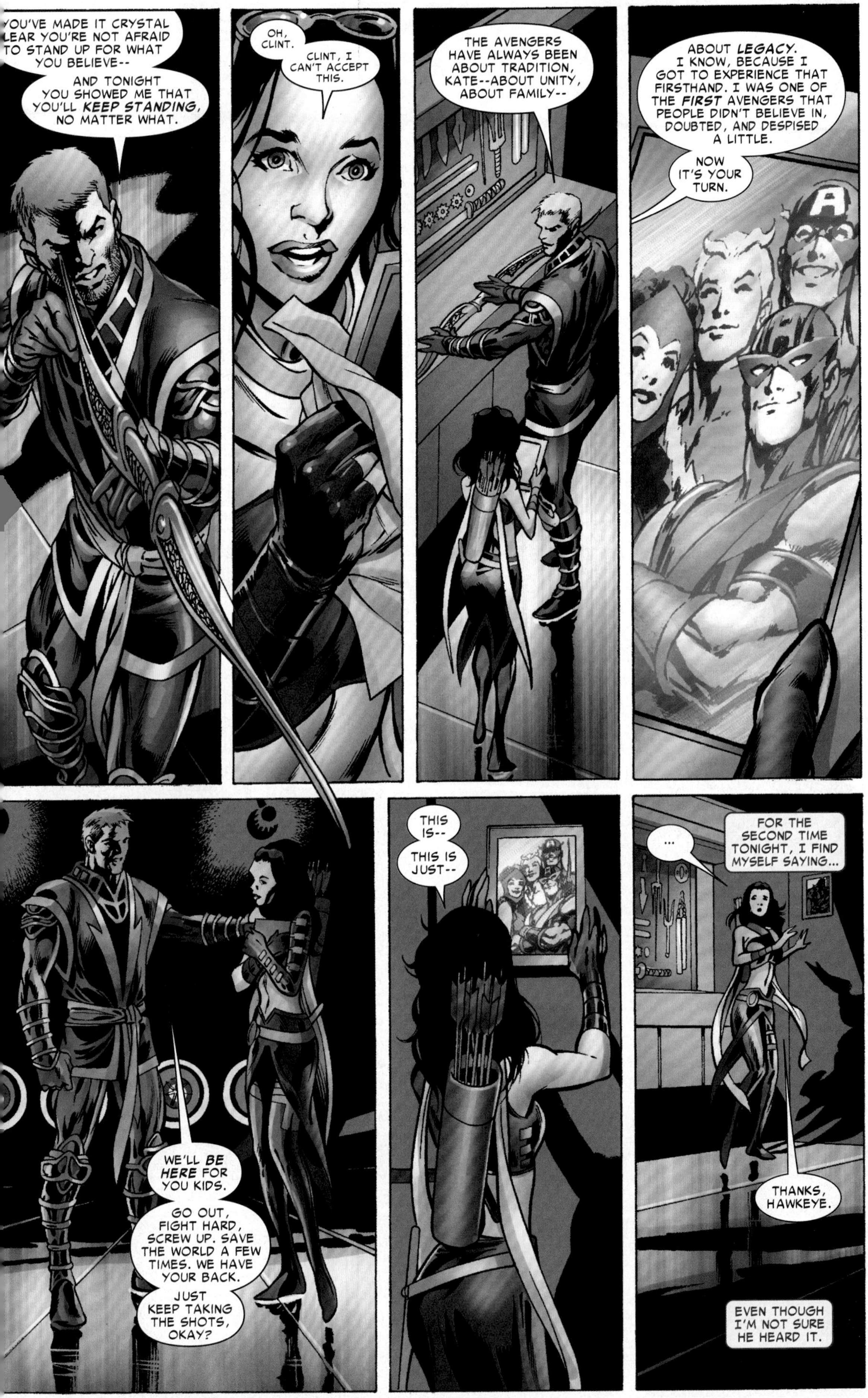

YOU'VE MADE IT CRYSTAL LEAR YOU'RE NOT AFRAID TO STAND UP FOR WHAT YOU BELIEVE--
AND TONIGHT YOU SHOWED ME THAT YOU'LL KEEP STANDING, NO MATTER WHAT.
OH, CLINT.
CLINT, I CAN'T ACCEPT THIS.
THE AVENGERS HAVE ALWAYS BEEN ABOUT TRADITION, KATE--ABOUT UNITY, ABOUT FAMILY--
ABOUT LEGACY. I KNOW, BECAUSE I GOT TO EXPERIENCE THAT FIRSTHAND. I WAS ONE OF THE FIRST AVENGERS THAT PEOPLE DIDN'T BELIEVE IN, DOUBTED, AND DESPISED A LITTLE.
NOW IT'S YOUR TURN.
WE'LL BE HERE FOR YOU KIDS.
GO OUT, FIGHT HARD, SCREW UP. SAVE THE WORLD A FEW TIMES. WE HAVE YOUR BACK.
JUST KEEP TAKING THE SHOTS, OKAY?
THIS IS--
THIS IS JUST--
...
FOR THE SECOND TIME TONIGHT, I FIND MYSELF SAYING...
THANKS, HAWKEYE.
EVEN THOUGH I'M NOT SURE HE HEARD IT.

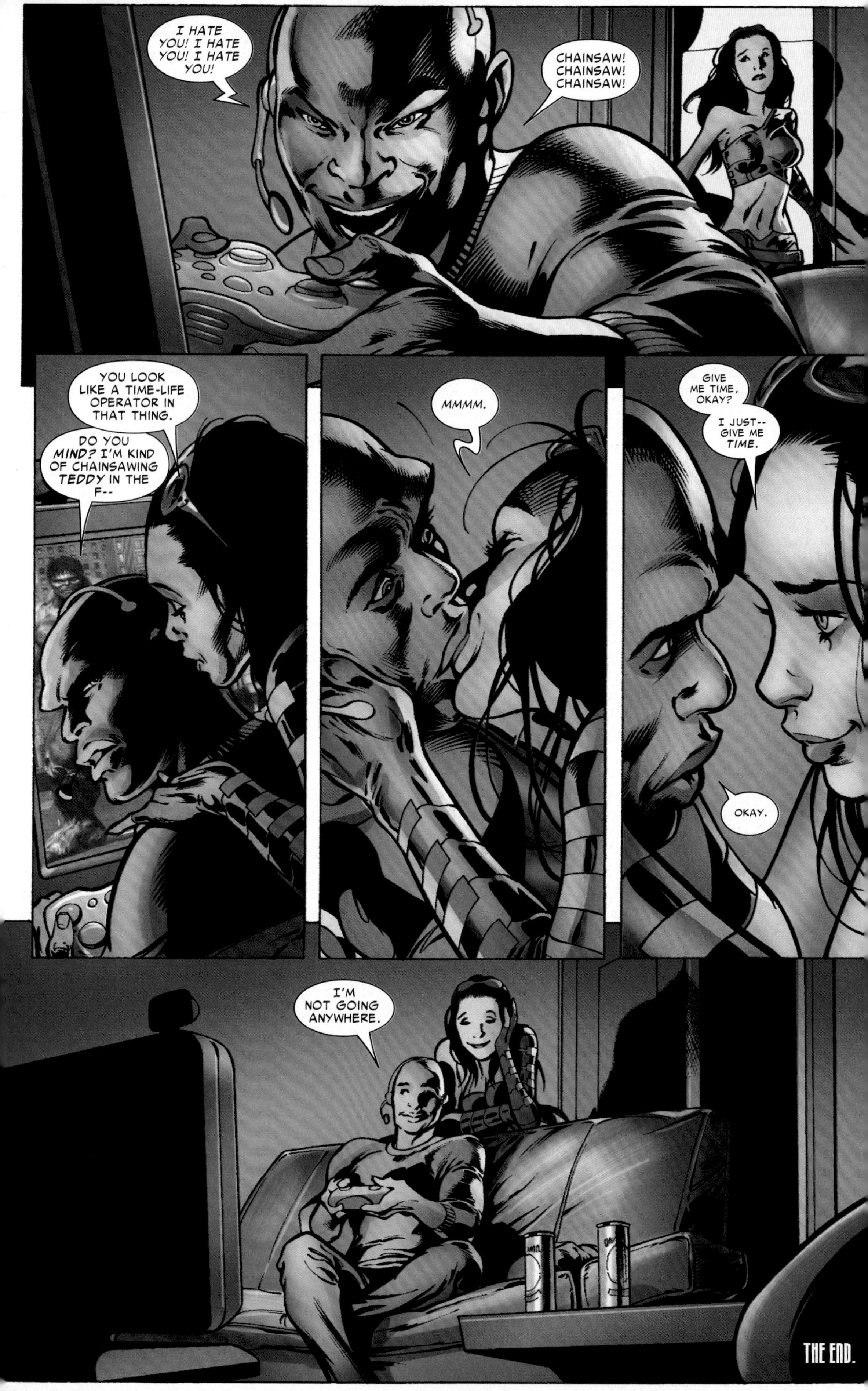
I HATE YOU! I HATE YOU! I HATE YOU!
CHAINSAW! CHAINSAW! CHAINSAW!
YOU LOOK LIKE A TIME-LIFE OPERATOR IN THAT THING.
DO YOU MIND? I'M KIND OF CHAINSAWING TEDDY IN THE F--
MMMM.
GIVE ME TIME, OKAY?
I JUST-- GIVE ME TIME.
OKAY.
I'M NOT GOING ANYWHERE.
THE END.

THE UNBELIEVABLE GWENPOOL #1

GWENDOLYN POOLE FOUND HERSELF FLUNG FROM OUR WORLD INTO THE MARVEL UNIVERSE. ARMED WITH HER VAST COMIC-BOOK KNOWLEDGE, SHE DECIDED TO BECOME THE MERC FOR HIRE GWENPOOL!

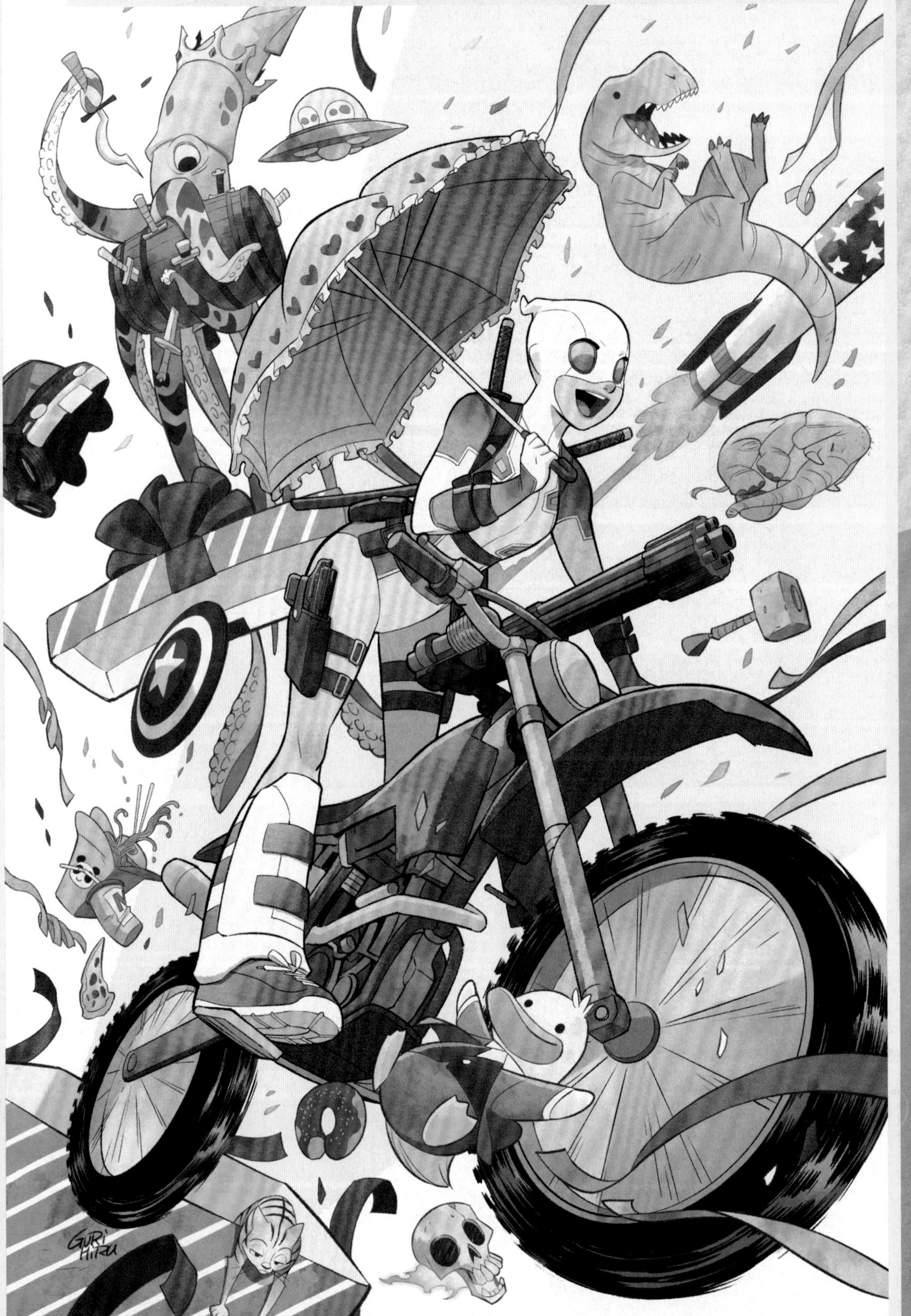

GURI HIRU

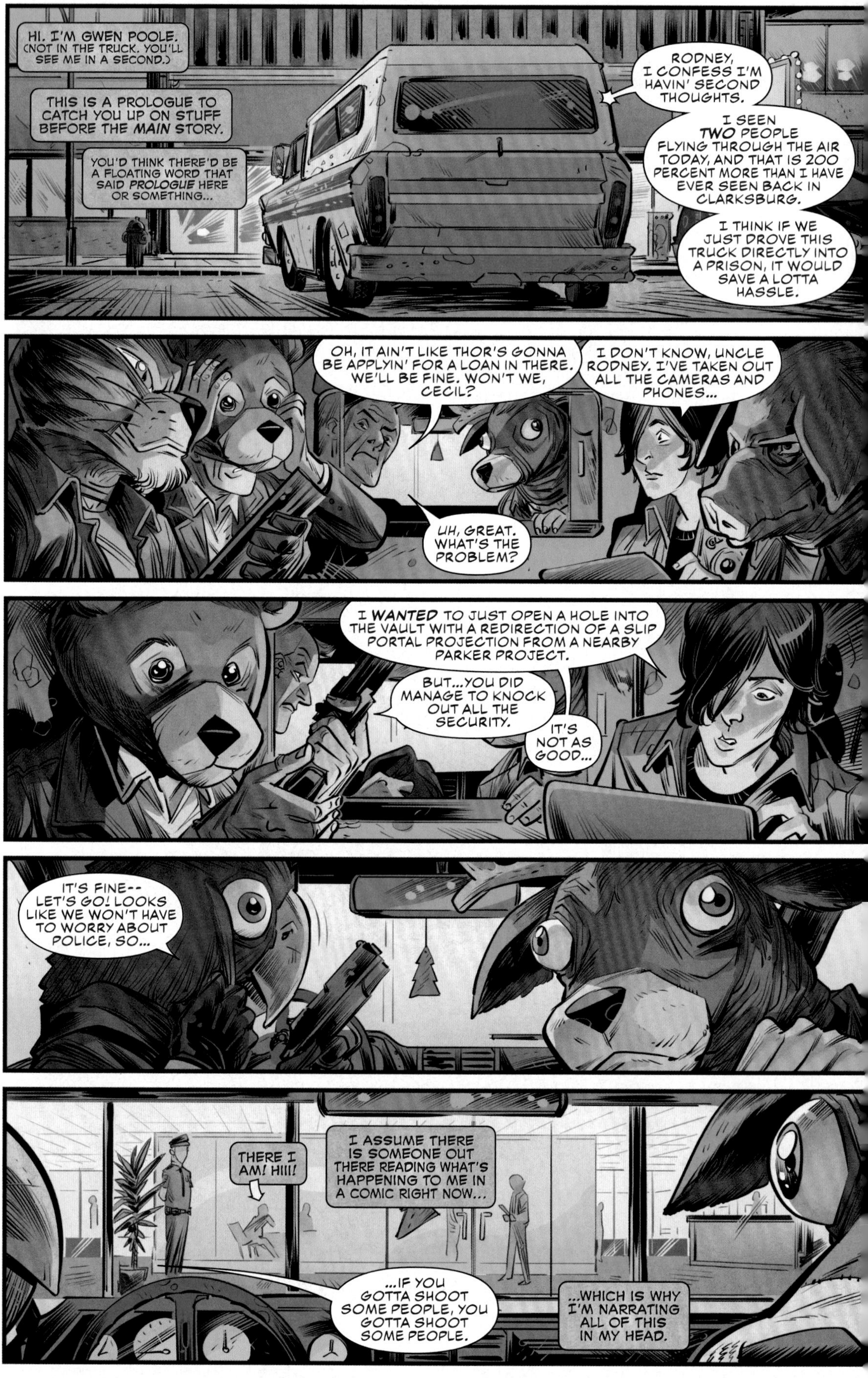
HI. I'M GWEN POOLE. (NOT IN THE TRUCK. YOU'LL SEE ME IN A SECOND.)
THIS IS A PROLOGUE TO CATCH YOU UP ON STUFF BEFORE THE MAIN STORY.
YOU'D THINK THERE'D BE A FLOATING WORD THAT SAID PROLOGUE HERE OR SOMETHING...
RODNEY, I CONFESS I'M HAVIN' SECOND THOUGHTS.
I SEEN TWO PEOPLE FLYING THROUGH THE AIR TODAY, AND THAT IS 200 PERCENT MORE THAN I HAVE EVER SEEN BACK IN CLARKSBURG.
I THINK IF WE JUST DROVE THIS TRUCK DIRECTLY INTO A PRISON, IT WOULD SAVE A LOTTA HASSLE.
OH, IT AIN'T LIKE THOR'S GONNA BE APPLYIN' FOR A LOAN IN THERE. WE'LL BE FINE. WON'T WE, CECIL?
I DON'T KNOW, UNCLE RODNEY. I'VE TAKEN OUT ALL THE CAMERAS AND PHONES...
UH, GREAT. WHAT'S THE PROBLEM?
I WANTED TO JUST OPEN A HOLE INTO THE VAULT WITH A REDIRECTION OF A SLIP PORTAL PROJECTION FROM A NEARBY PARKER PROJECT.
BUT...YOU DID MANAGE TO KNOCK OUT ALL THE SECURITY.
IT'S NOT AS GOOD...
IT'S FINE--LET'S GO! LOOKS LIKE WE WON'T HAVE TO WORRY ABOUT POLICE, SO...
THERE I AM! HIII!
I ASSUME THERE IS SOMEONE OUT THERE READING WHAT'S HAPPENING TO ME IN A COMIC RIGHT NOW...
...IF YOU GOTTA SHOOT SOME PEOPLE, YOU GOTTA SHOOT SOME PEOPLE.
...WHICH IS WHY I'M NARRATING ALL OF THIS IN MY HEAD.

I BET YOU'RE CURIOUS WHAT MY DEAL IS. BUT I'M AFRAID YOU'RE NOT GETTING MY ORIGIN TODAY.

I MEAN, HOW MANY TIMES DO WE *NEED* NEW ORIGINS?

YOU'D LIKE TO OPEN A CHECKING ACCOUNT WITH TWO DUFFLE BAGS FILLED WITH CASH?

JUST THE ONE!

BUT THERE'S *TWO*--

DON'T WORRY ABOUT THE SECOND BAG!

I'VE SEEN UNCLE BEN DIE MORE TIMES THAN I'VE EATEN *ARUGULA.*

OKAY, SO WE JUST NEED A PHOTO I.D. AND YOUR SOCIAL SECURITY NUMBER.

I DON'T HAVE THAT. I'M FROM ANOTHER UNIVERSE.

OH! UH... I MIGHT HAVE TO TALK TO SOMEONE--

AAAAAA!

WE'RE ROBBING THIS BANK! YOU'VE SEEN ENOUGH MOVIES TO KNOW THE INSTRUCTIONS HERE!

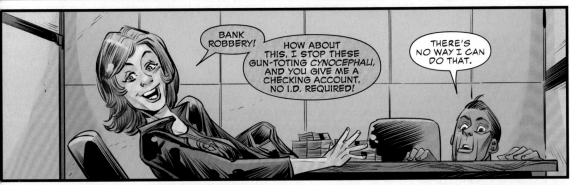

BANK ROBBERY!

HOW ABOUT THIS, I STOP THESE GUN-TOTING *CYNOCEPHALI,* AND YOU GIVE ME A CHECKING ACCOUNT, NO I.D. REQUIRED!

THERE'S NO WAY I CAN DO THAT.

I WILL SAY THIS-- I'M NEW IN TOWN AND I'M *VERY* READY TO PARTICIPATE!

AW, WELL THAT'S OKAY. I'LL STILL DO IT.

I'M A *SUPER* HERO.

DON'T TELL.

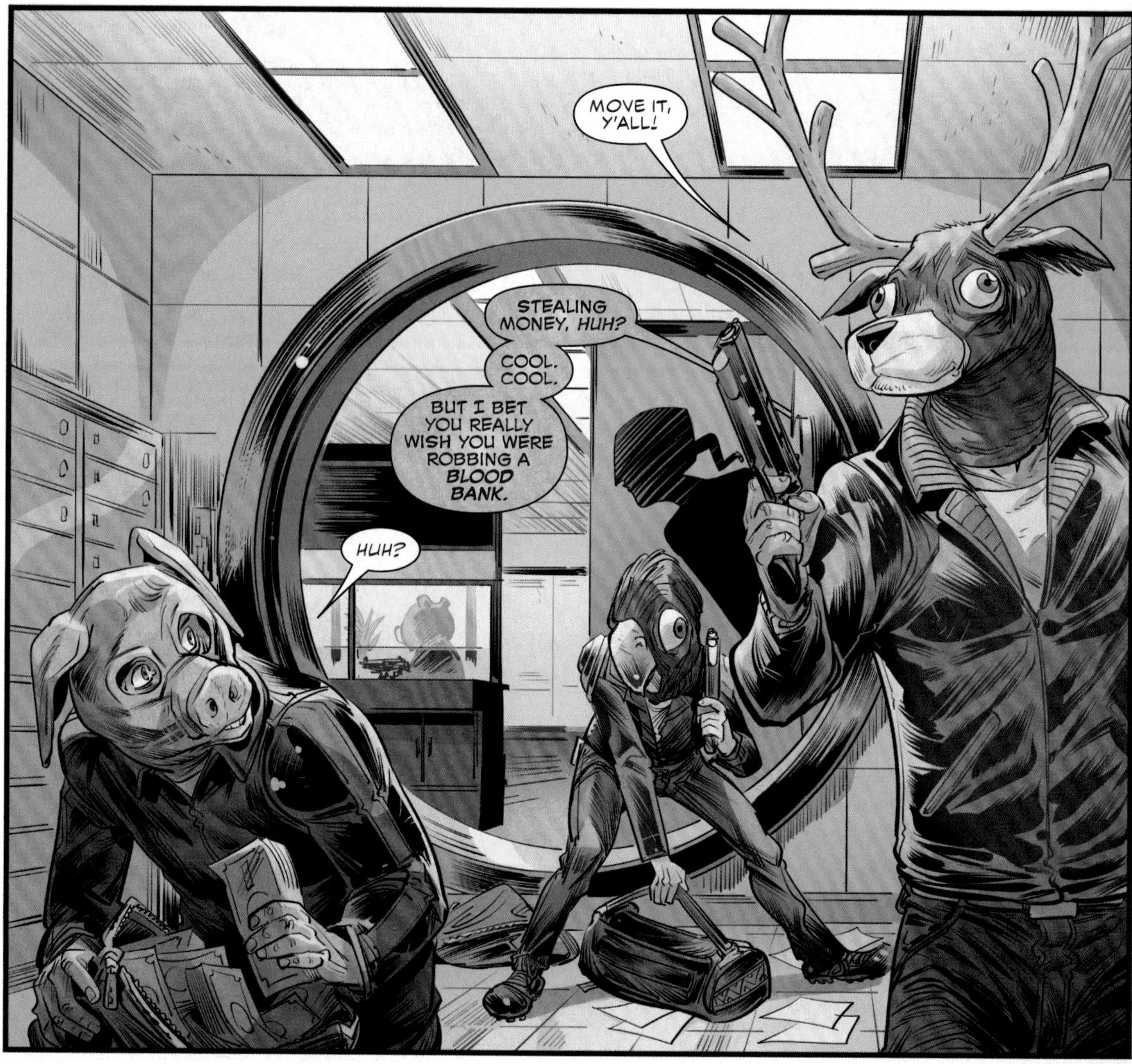
MOVE IT, Y'ALL!
STEALING MONEY, HUH?
COOL. COOL.
BUT I BET YOU REALLY WISH YOU WERE ROBBING A BLOOD BANK.
HUH?

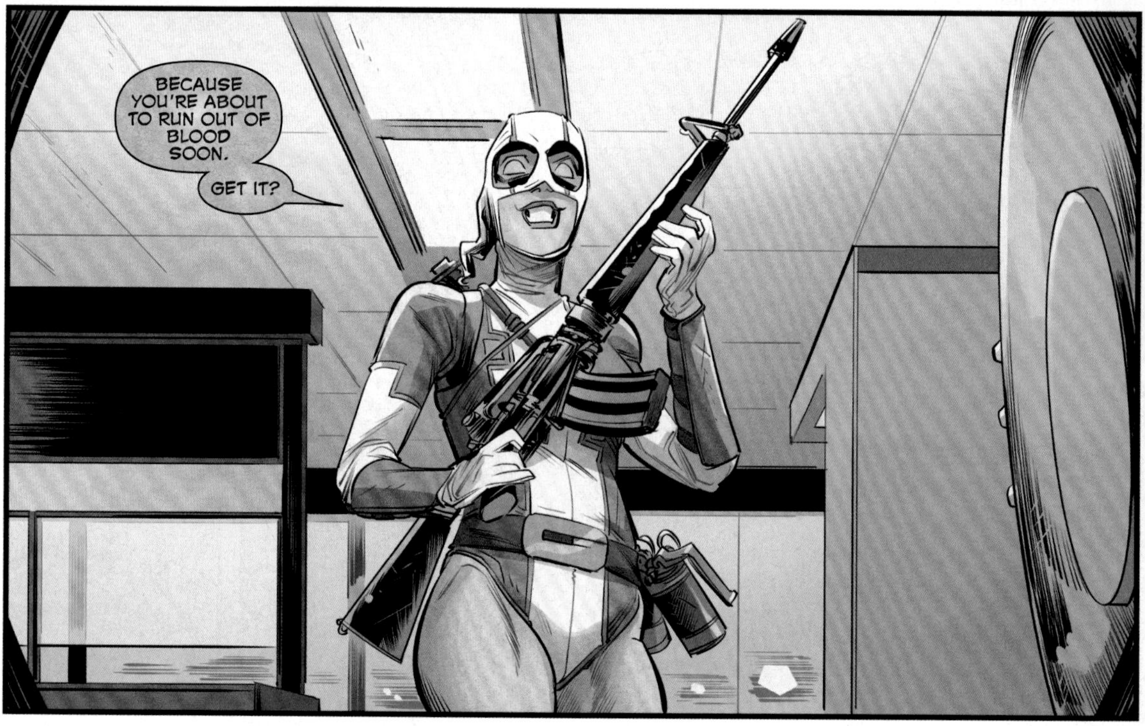
BECAUSE YOU'RE ABOUT TO RUN OUT OF BLOOD SOON.
GET IT?

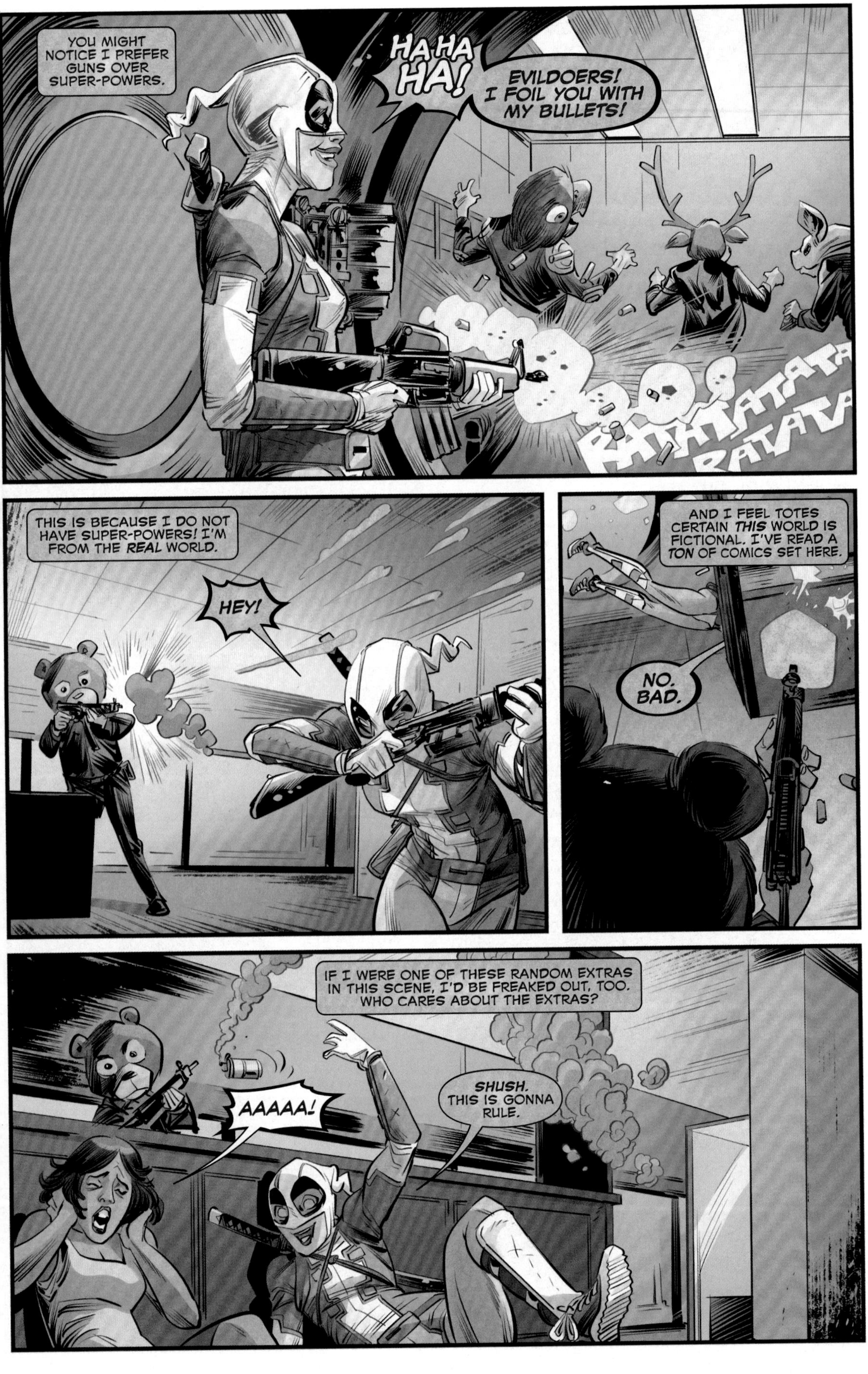
YOU MIGHT NOTICE I PREFER GUNS OVER SUPER-POWERS.
HA HA HA!
EVILDOERS! I FOIL YOU WITH MY BULLETS!
RATATATATA RATATA
THIS IS BECAUSE I DO NOT HAVE SUPER-POWERS! I'M FROM THE REAL WORLD.
HEY!
AND I FEEL TOTES CERTAIN THIS WORLD IS FICTIONAL. I'VE READ A TON OF COMICS SET HERE.
NO. BAD.
IF I WERE ONE OF THESE RANDOM EXTRAS IN THIS SCENE, I'D BE FREAKED OUT, TOO. WHO CARES ABOUT THE EXTRAS?
AAAAA!
SHUSH. THIS IS GONNA RULE.

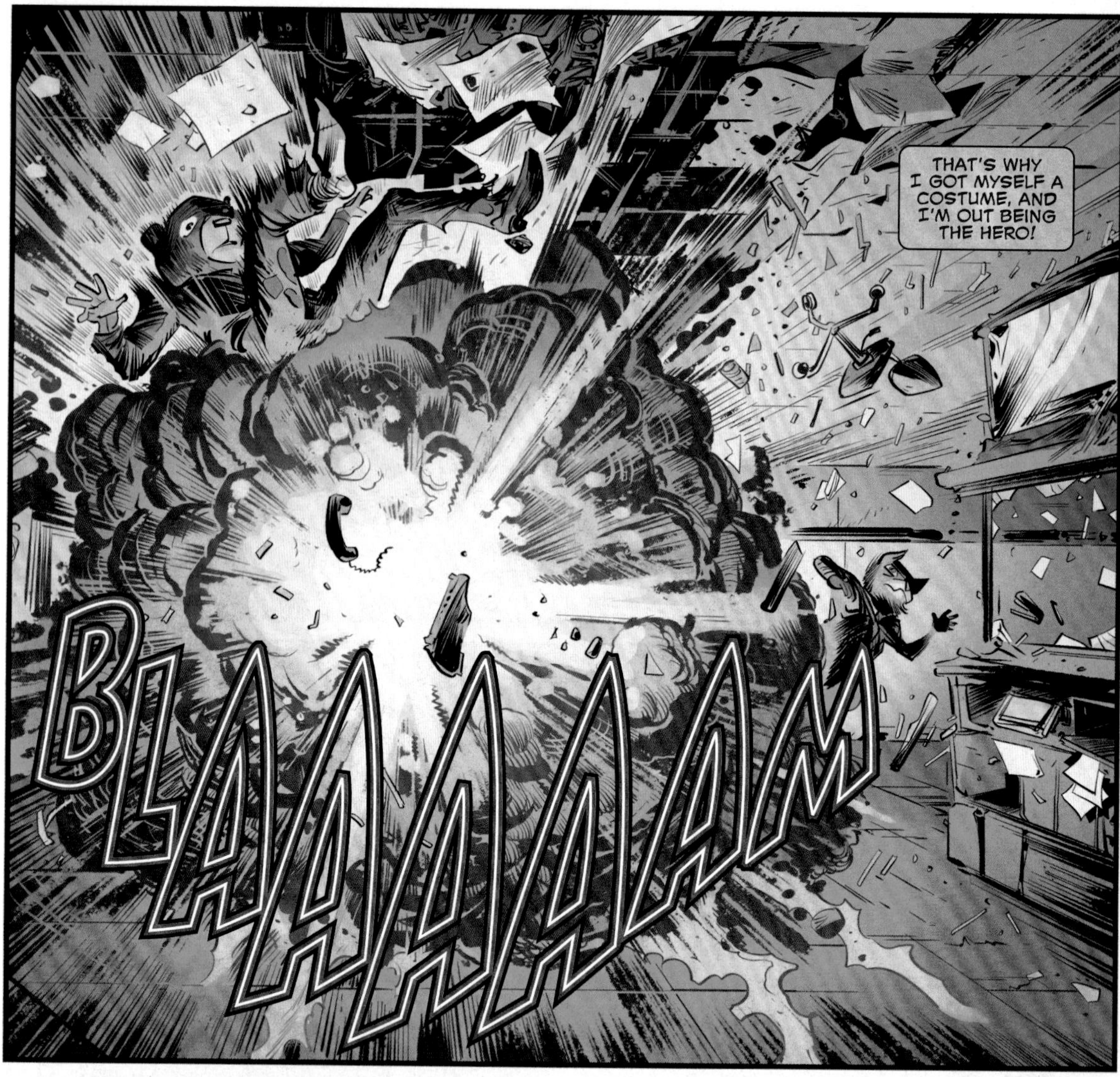
THAT'S WHY I GOT MYSELF A COSTUME, AND I'M OUT BEING THE HERO!
BLAAAAAAM

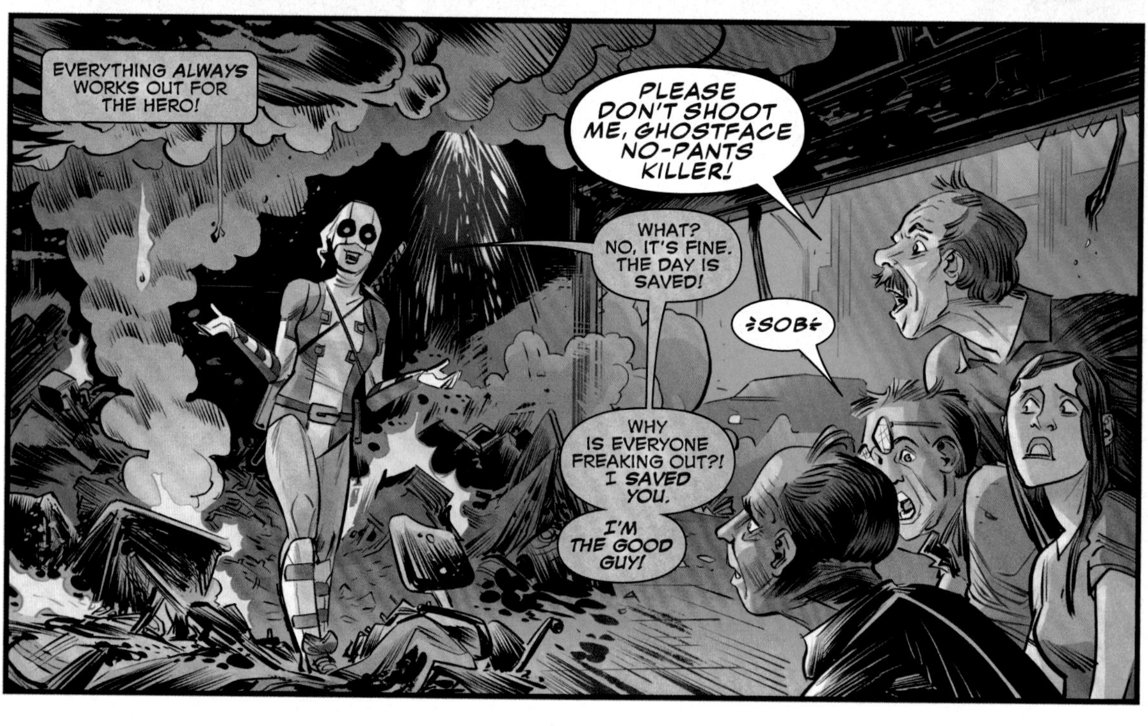
EVERYTHING ALWAYS WORKS OUT FOR THE HERO!
PLEASE DON'T SHOOT ME, GHOSTFACE NO-PANTS KILLER!
WHAT? NO, IT'S FINE. THE DAY IS SAVED!
SOB
WHY IS EVERYONE FREAKING OUT?! I SAVED YOU.
I'M THE GOOD GUY!

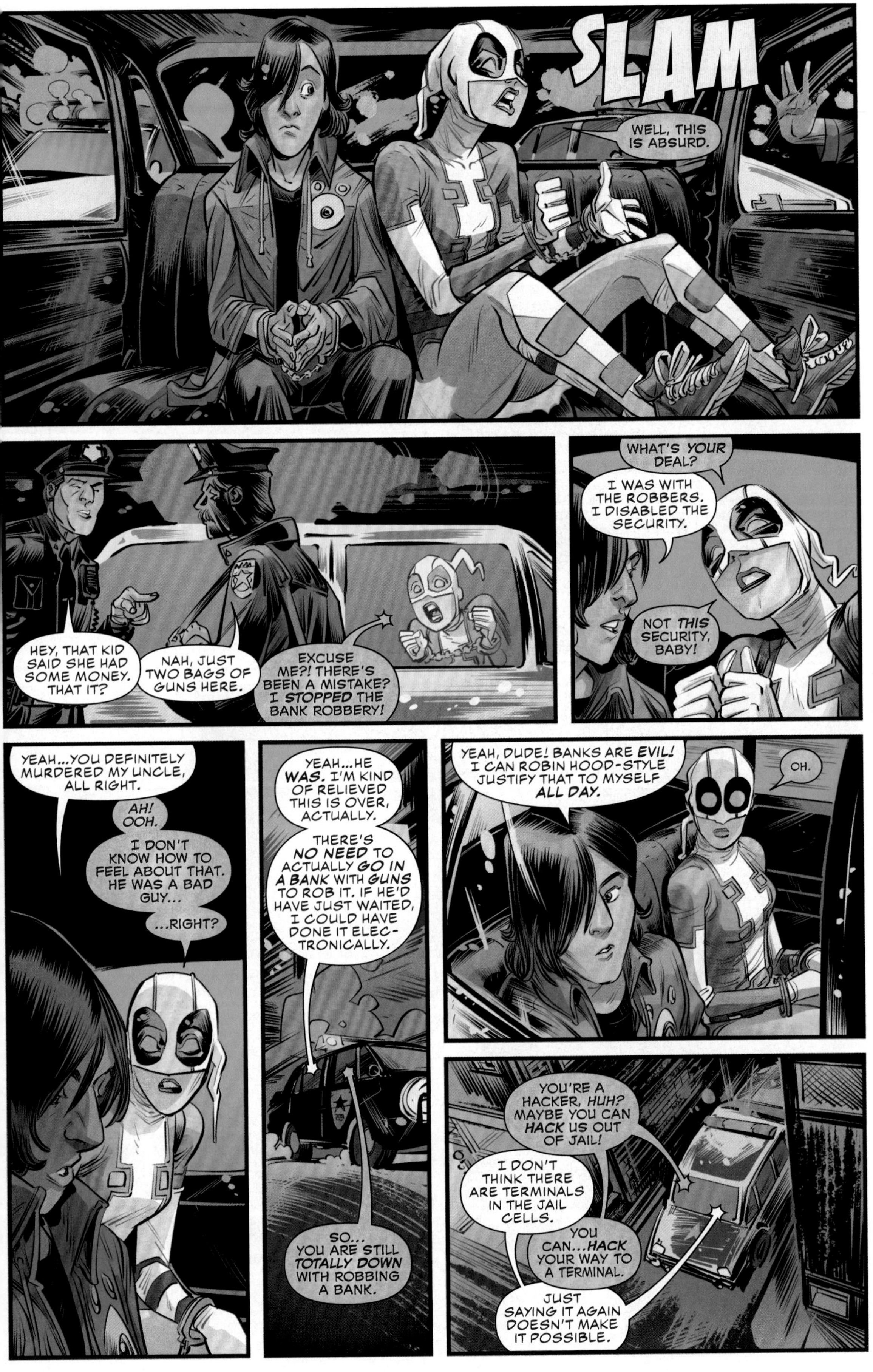
SLAM
WELL, THIS IS ABSURD.
HEY, THAT KID SAID SHE HAD SOME MONEY. THAT IT?
NAH, JUST TWO BAGS OF GUNS HERE.
EXCUSE ME?! THERE'S BEEN A MISTAKE? I STOPPED THE BANK ROBBERY!
WHAT'S YOUR DEAL?
I WAS WITH THE ROBBERS. I DISABLED THE SECURITY.
NOT THIS SECURITY, BABY!
YEAH...YOU DEFINITELY MURDERED MY UNCLE, ALL RIGHT.
AH! OOH.
I DON'T KNOW HOW TO FEEL ABOUT THAT. HE WAS A BAD GUY...
...RIGHT?
YEAH...HE WAS. I'M KIND OF RELIEVED THIS IS OVER, ACTUALLY.
THERE'S NO NEED TO ACTUALLY GO IN A BANK WITH GUNS TO ROB IT. IF HE'D HAVE JUST WAITED, I COULD HAVE DONE IT ELEC-TRONICALLY.
SO... YOU ARE STILL TOTALLY DOWN WITH ROBBING A BANK.
YEAH, DUDE! BANKS ARE EVIL! I CAN ROBIN HOOD-STYLE JUSTIFY THAT TO MYSELF ALL DAY.
OH.
YOU'RE A HACKER, HUH? MAYBE YOU CAN HACK US OUT OF JAIL!
I DON'T THINK THERE ARE TERMINALS IN THE JAIL CELLS.
YOU CAN...HACK YOUR WAY TO A TERMINAL.
JUST SAYING IT AGAIN DOESN'T MAKE IT POSSIBLE.

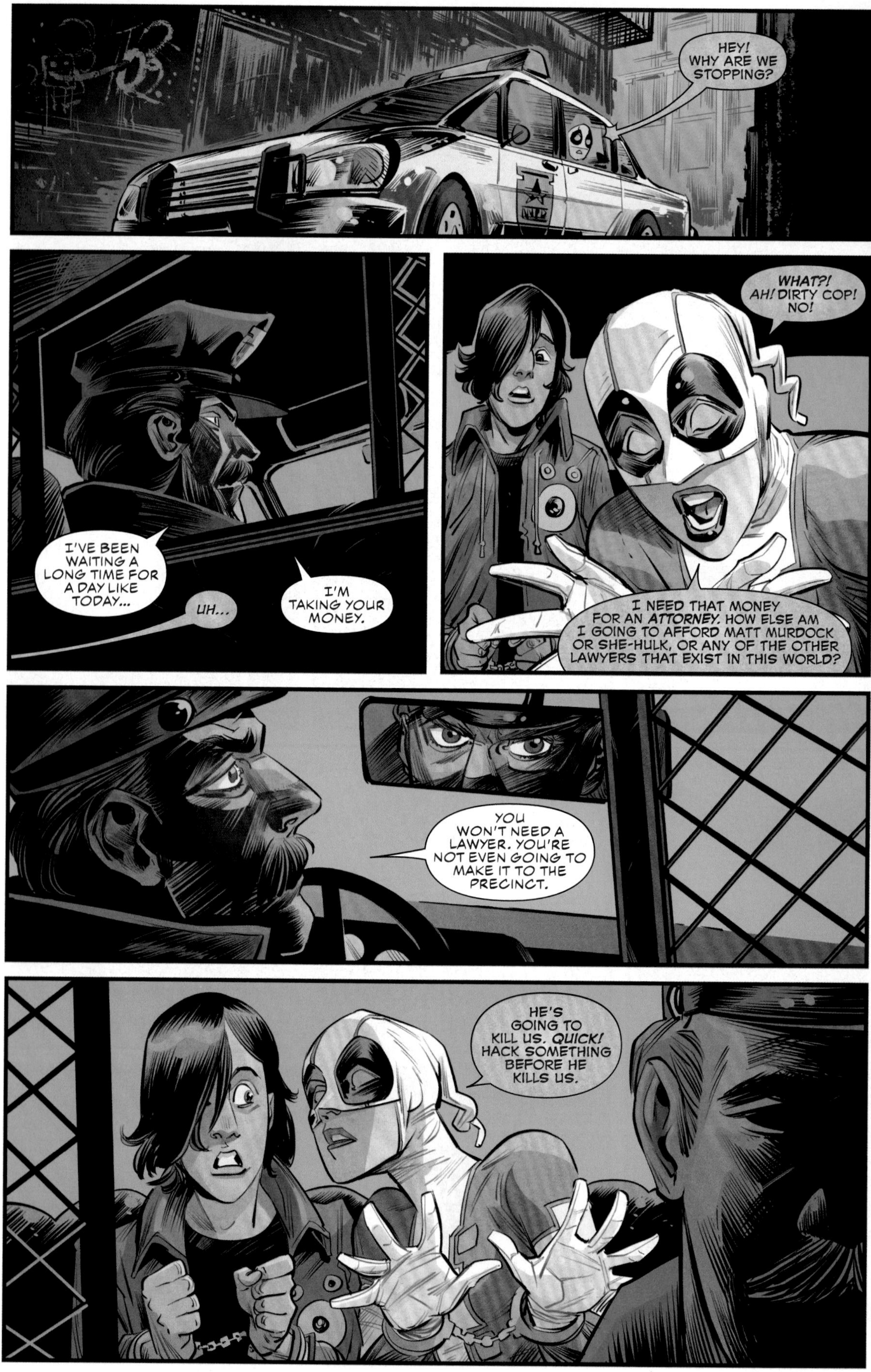

HEY! WHY ARE WE STOPPING?
I'VE BEEN WAITING A LONG TIME FOR A DAY LIKE TODAY...
UH...
I'M TAKING YOUR MONEY.
WHAT?! AH! DIRTY COP! NO!
I NEED THAT MONEY FOR AN ATTORNEY. HOW ELSE AM I GOING TO AFFORD MATT MURDOCK OR SHE-HULK, OR ANY OF THE OTHER LAWYERS THAT EXIST IN THIS WORLD?
YOU WON'T NEED A LAWYER. YOU'RE NOT EVEN GOING TO MAKE IT TO THE PRECINCT.
HE'S GOING TO KILL US. QUICK! HACK SOMETHING BEFORE HE KILLS US.

YOU THINK--*NO!* I'M NOT GOING TO KILL YOU! I'M LETTING YOU GO.

OKAAAAAY... WHY?

BECAUSE I'M *DONE.*

BECAUSE TODAY WAS AN *EASY* DAY.

I COULD ACTUALLY APPREHEND YOU TWO. AND *YOU*, MAYBE YOUR HEART WAS IN THE RIGHT PLACE... KIND OF.

I WOULD *ABSOLUTELY* DO IT AGAIN. I *LOVED* IT.

SHUSH. JUST LISTEN. WHEN SOMEONE LIKE THE *ABSORBING MAN* ROBS A BANK, HE HURTS PEOPLE, AND HE *MEANS* TO HURT PEOPLE. AND I GOTTA BE THERE, AND I CAN'T JUST WAIT FOR SPIDER-MAN TO SHOW UP.

ONE TIME, I BELIEVE A PORTAL TO THE ACTUAL-FOR-REAL *HELL* OPENED UP IN UNION SQUARE. OR IT MIGHT NOT HAVE BEEN--THE OFFICIAL WORD NEVER MAKES IT DOWN TO PEOPLE LIKE ME.

BUT I STILL HAD TO GO AND SHOOT AT STRANGE APPARITIONS WHOSE FACES WOULD CHANGE INTO MY MOTHER'S.

THAT SOUNDS AWESOME.

IT'S NOT.

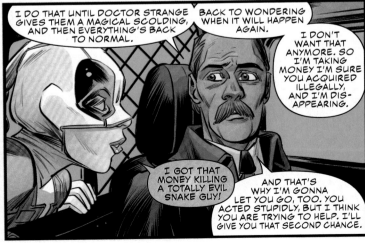
I DO THAT UNTIL DOCTOR STRANGE GIVES THEM A MAGICAL SCOLDING, AND THEN EVERYTHING'S BACK TO NORMAL.

BACK TO WONDERING WHEN IT WILL HAPPEN AGAIN.

I DON'T WANT THAT ANYMORE. SO I'M TAKING MONEY I'M SURE YOU ACQUIRED ILLEGALLY, AND I'M DIS-APPEARING.

I GOT THAT MONEY KILLING A TOTALLY EVIL SNAKE GUY!

AND THAT'S WHY I'M GONNA LET YOU GO, TOO. YOU ACTED STUPIDLY, BUT I THINK YOU ARE TRYING TO HELP. I'LL GIVE YOU THAT SECOND CHANCE.

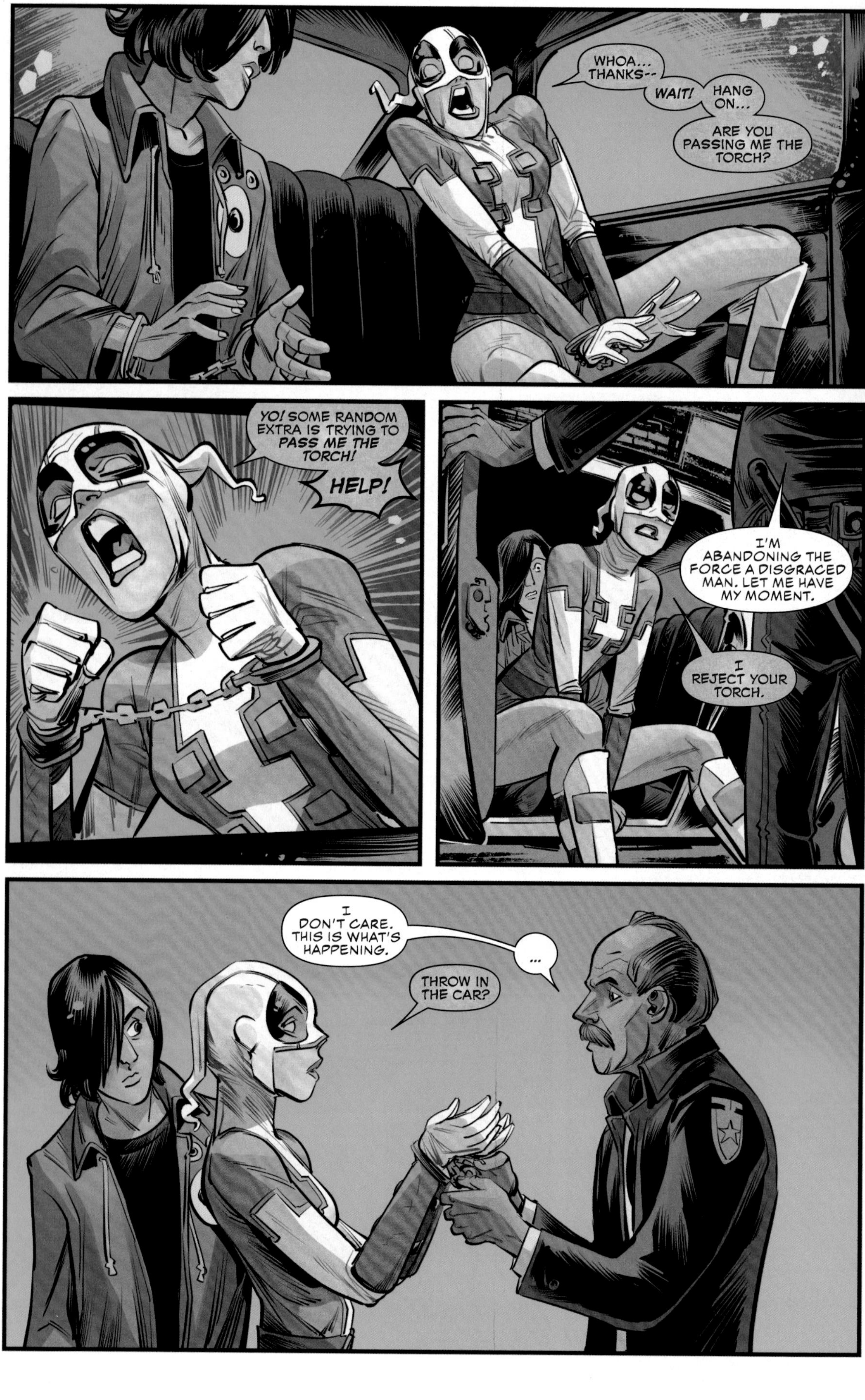
WHOA... THANKS--
WAIT!
HANG ON...
ARE YOU PASSING ME THE TORCH?
YO! SOME RANDOM EXTRA IS TRYING TO PASS ME THE TORCH!
HELP!
I'M ABANDONING THE FORCE A DISGRACED MAN. LET ME HAVE MY MOMENT.
I REJECT YOUR TORCH.
I DON'T CARE. THIS IS WHAT'S HAPPENING.
...
THROW IN THE CAR?

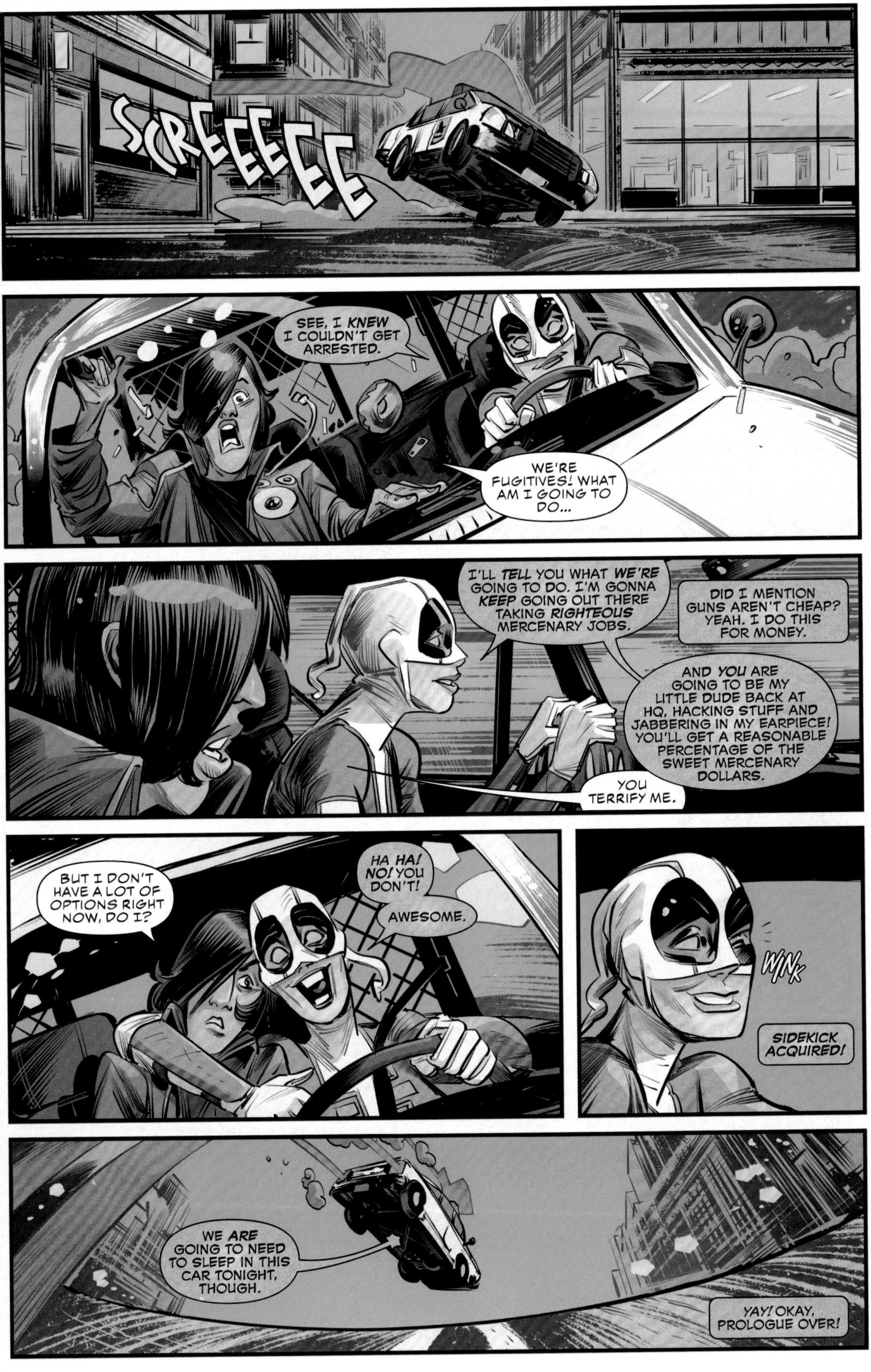
SCREEEEEEE
SEE, I KNEW I COULDN'T GET ARRESTED.
WE'RE FUGITIVES! WHAT AM I GOING TO DO...
I'LL TELL YOU WHAT WE'RE GOING TO DO. I'M GONNA KEEP GOING OUT THERE TAKING RIGHTEOUS MERCENARY JOBS.
DID I MENTION GUNS AREN'T CHEAP? YEAH. I DO THIS FOR MONEY.
AND YOU ARE GOING TO BE MY LITTLE DUDE BACK AT HQ, HACKING STUFF AND JABBERING IN MY EARPIECE! YOU'LL GET A REASONABLE PERCENTAGE OF THE SWEET MERCENARY DOLLARS.
YOU TERRIFY ME.
BUT I DON'T HAVE A LOT OF OPTIONS RIGHT NOW, DO I?
HA HA! NO! YOU DON'T!
AWESOME.
WINK
SIDEKICK ACQUIRED!
WE ARE GOING TO NEED TO SLEEP IN THIS CAR TONIGHT, THOUGH.
YAY! OKAY, PROLOGUE OVER!

THE UNBELIEVABLE GWENPOOL

HEY, TRUE BELIEVERS! GWENPOOL HERE. (OR SHOULD I SAY "GWEN POOLE"?) YOU KNOW, THE TOTALLY RAD SUPER HERO WHO JUMPED FROM OUR NORMAL, ALBEIT *BORING* UNIVERSE INTO THE ACTION-PACKED, EXCITING MARVEL UNIVERSE-- HA!

YOU MAY HAVE SEEN ME VENTURING AROUND THE MARVEL U WITH *HOWARD THE DUCK*, BUT NOW, IT'S *MY* TIME TO SHINE. AND IN MY VERY OWN BOOK THAT YOU SO KINDLY GOT YOUR HANDS ON, NO LESS!

I'M NEW TO THIS WORLD, BUT I'M READY TO KICK. SOME. *BUTT!*

CHRISTOPHER HASTINGS
WRITER

GURIHIRU
MAIN STORY ARTIST

DANILO BEYRUTH
PROLOGUE ARTIST

TAMRA BONVILLAIN
PROLOGUE COLORIST

VC'S CLAYTON COWLES
LETTERER & PRODUCTION

GURIHIRU
COVER ARTIST

JOHN TYLER CHRISTOPHER; SKOTTIE YOUNG; STACEY LEE; FRANCISCO HERRERA & FERNANDA RIZO; CAMERON STEWART
VARIANT COVER ARTISTS

HEATHER ANTOS
ASST. EDITOR

JORDAN D. WHITE
EDITOR

AXEL ALONSO
EDITOR IN CHIEF

JOE QUESADA
CHIEF CREATIVE OFFICER

DAN BUCKLEY
PUBLISHER

ALAN FINE
EXEC. PRODUCER

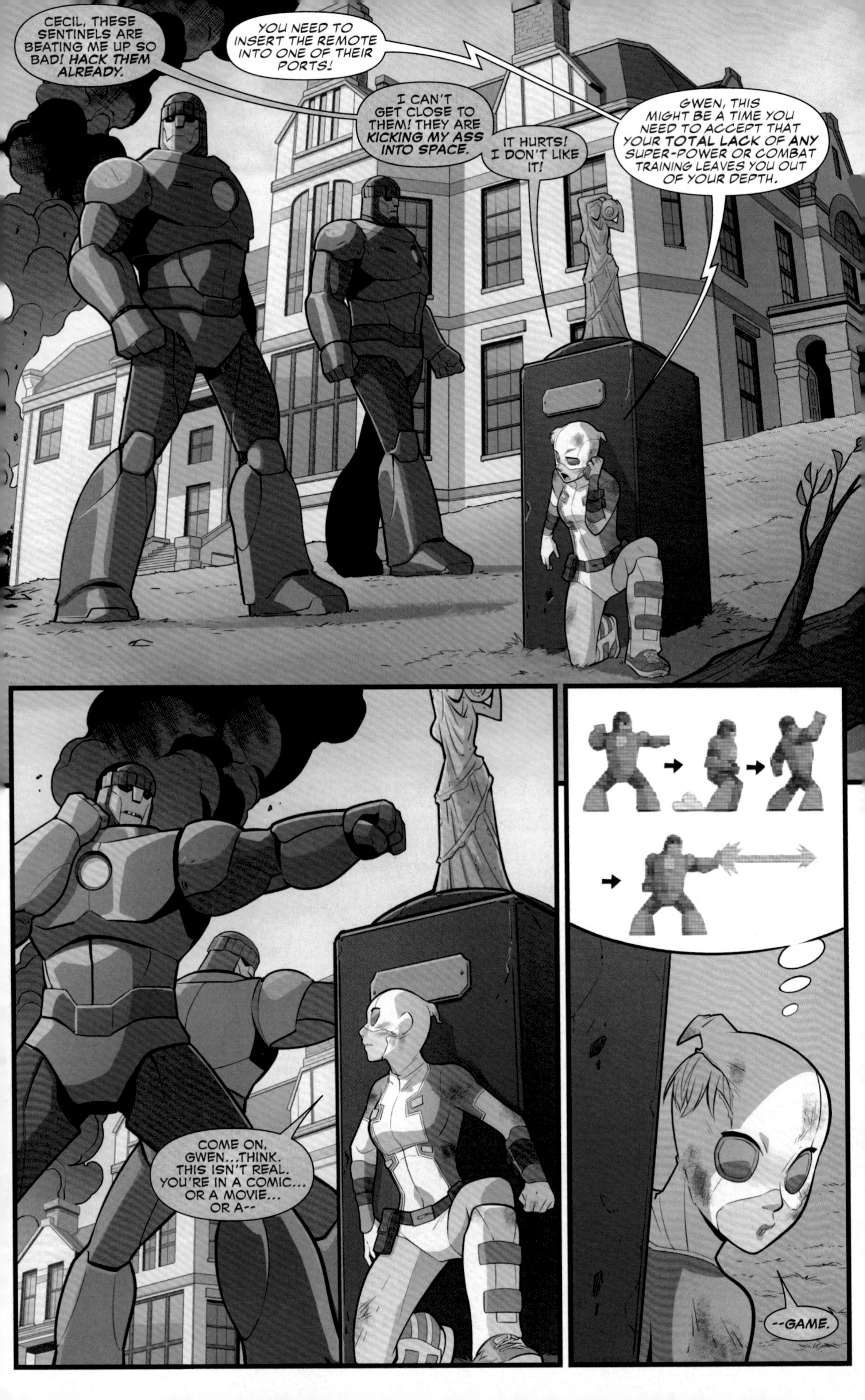
CECIL, THESE SENTINELS ARE BEATING ME UP SO BAD! HACK THEM ALREADY.
YOU NEED TO INSERT THE REMOTE INTO ONE OF THEIR PORTS!
I CAN'T GET CLOSE TO THEM! THEY ARE KICKING MY ASS INTO SPACE.
IT HURTS! I DON'T LIKE IT!
GWEN, THIS MIGHT BE A TIME YOU NEED TO ACCEPT THAT YOUR TOTAL LACK OF ANY SUPER-POWER OR COMBAT TRAINING LEAVES YOU OUT OF YOUR DEPTH.
COME ON, GWEN...THINK. THIS ISN'T REAL. YOU'RE IN A COMIC... OR A MOVIE... OR A--
--GAME.

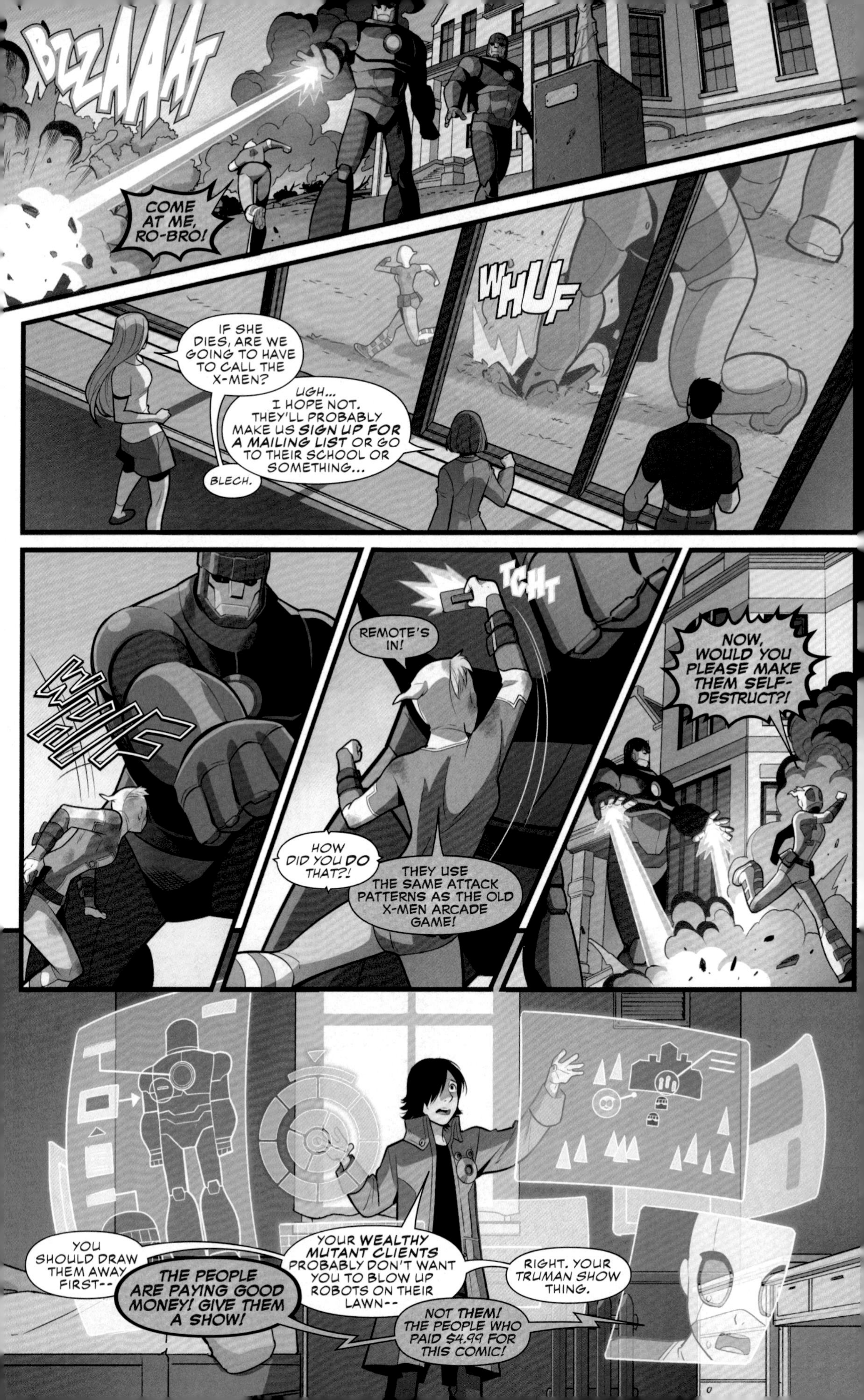
BZZAAAAT
COME AT ME, RO-BRO!
WHUF
IF SHE DIES, ARE WE GOING TO HAVE TO CALL THE X-MEN?
UGH... I HOPE NOT. THEY'LL PROBABLY MAKE US **SIGN UP FOR A MAILING LIST** OR GO TO THEIR SCHOOL OR SOMETHING...
BLECH.
TCHT
REMOTE'S IN!
HOW DID YOU **DO** THAT?!
THEY USE THE SAME ATTACK PATTERNS AS THE OLD X-MEN ARCADE GAME!
NOW, WOULD YOU PLEASE MAKE THEM SELF-DESTRUCT?!
YOU SHOULD DRAW THEM AWAY FIRST--
YOUR **WEALTHY MUTANT CLIENTS** PROBABLY DON'T WANT YOU TO BLOW UP ROBOTS ON THEIR LAWN--
THE PEOPLE ARE PAYING GOOD MONEY! GIVE THEM A SHOW!
RIGHT. YOUR *TRUMAN SHOW* THING.
NOT THEM! THE PEOPLE WHO PAID $4.99 FOR THIS COMIC!

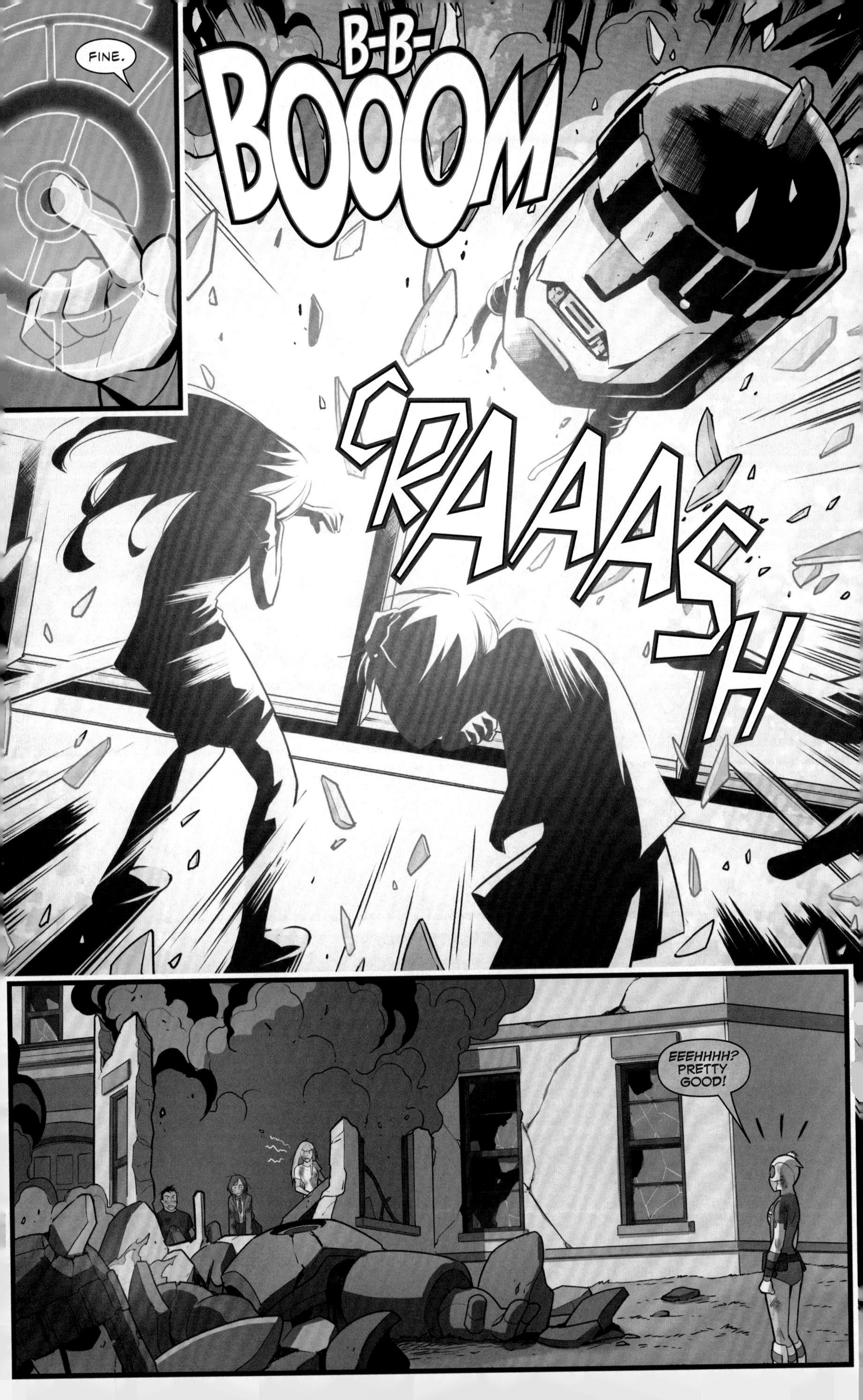
FINE.
B-B-BOOOM
CRAAAS-H
EEEHHHH? PRETTY GOOD!

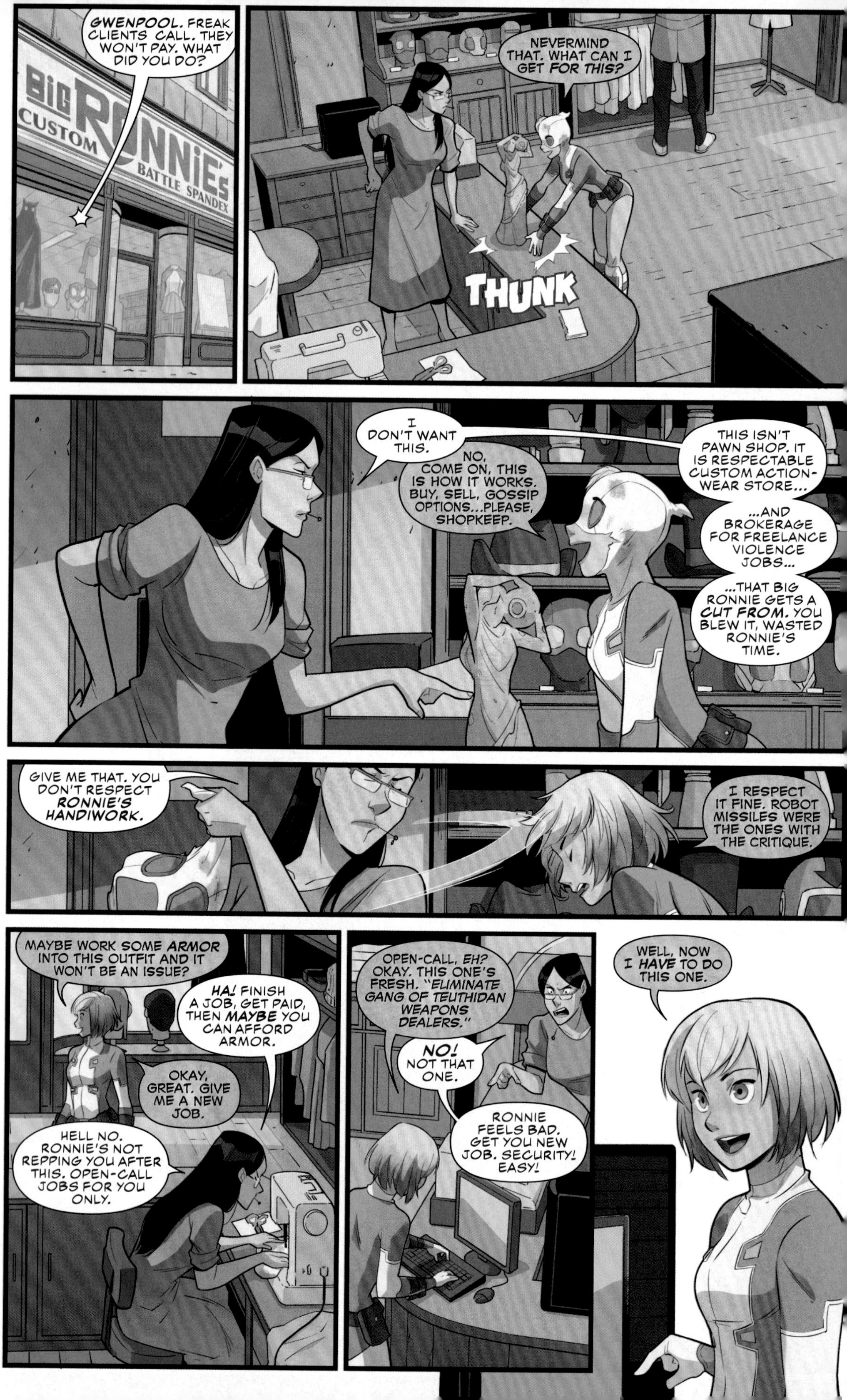
GWENPOOL. FREAK CLIENTS CALL. THEY WON'T PAY. WHAT DID YOU DO?
BIG RONNIE'S CUSTOM BATTLE SPANDEX
NEVERMIND THAT. WHAT CAN I GET FOR THIS?
THUNK
I DON'T WANT THIS.
NO, COME ON, THIS IS HOW IT WORKS. BUY, SELL, GOSSIP OPTIONS...PLEASE, SHOPKEEP.
THIS ISN'T PAWN SHOP. IT IS RESPECTABLE CUSTOM ACTION-WEAR STORE...
...AND BROKERAGE FOR FREELANCE VIOLENCE JOBS...
...THAT BIG RONNIE GETS A CUT FROM. YOU BLEW IT, WASTED RONNIE'S TIME.
GIVE ME THAT. YOU DON'T RESPECT RONNIE'S HANDIWORK.
I RESPECT IT FINE. ROBOT MISSILES WERE THE ONES WITH THE CRITIQUE.
MAYBE WORK SOME ARMOR INTO THIS OUTFIT AND IT WON'T BE AN ISSUE?
HA! FINISH A JOB, GET PAID, THEN MAYBE YOU CAN AFFORD ARMOR.
OKAY, GREAT. GIVE ME A NEW JOB.
HELL NO. RONNIE'S NOT REPPING YOU AFTER THIS. OPEN-CALL JOBS FOR YOU ONLY.
OPEN-CALL, EH? OKAY. THIS ONE'S FRESH. "ELIMINATE GANG OF TEUTHIDAN WEAPONS DEALERS."
NO! NOT THAT ONE.
RONNIE FEELS BAD. GET YOU NEW JOB. SECURITY! EASY!
WELL, NOW I HAVE TO DO THIS ONE.

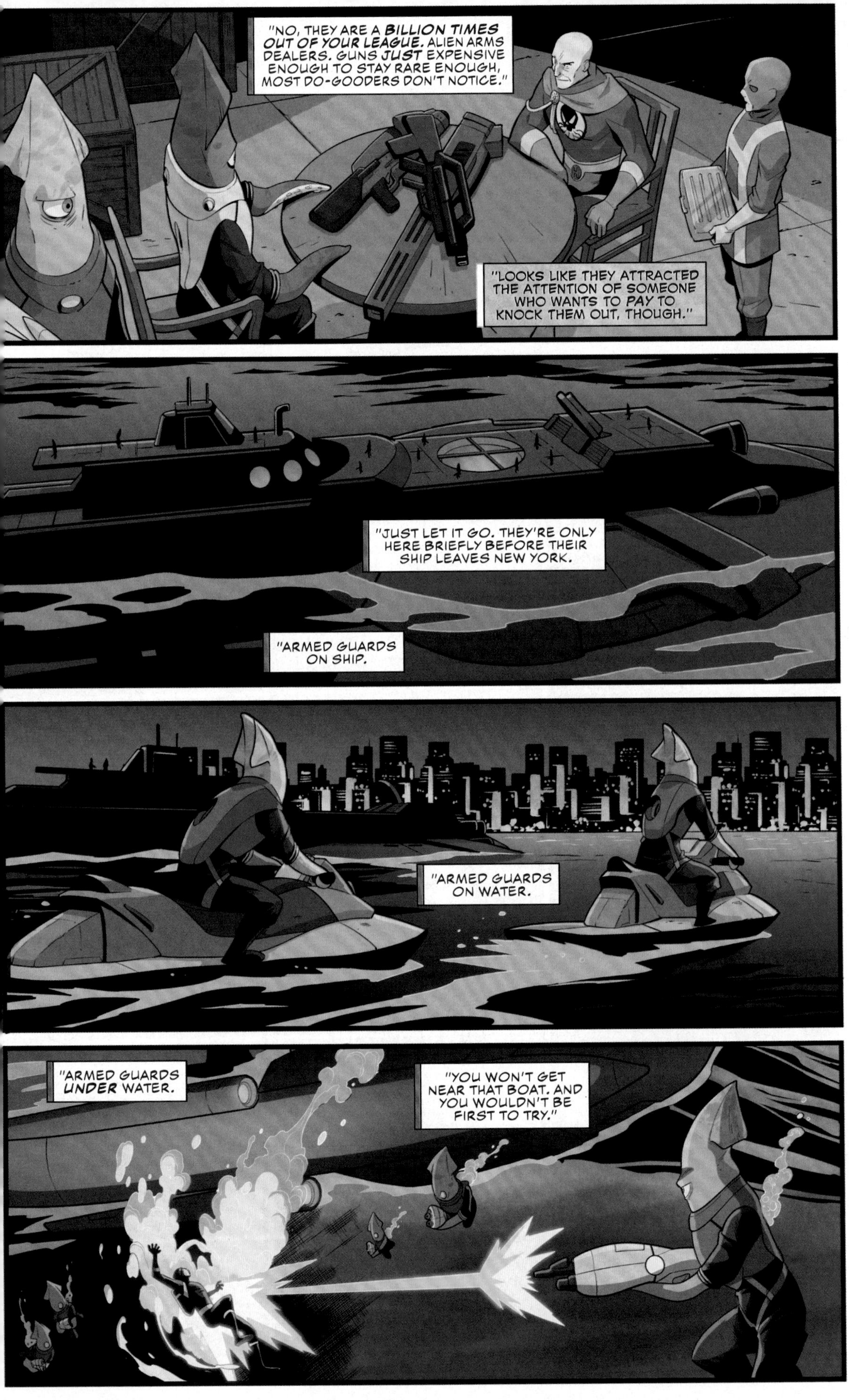
"NO, THEY ARE A BILLION TIMES OUT OF YOUR LEAGUE. ALIEN ARMS DEALERS. GUNS JUST EXPENSIVE ENOUGH TO STAY RARE ENOUGH, MOST DO-GOODERS DON'T NOTICE."
"LOOKS LIKE THEY ATTRACTED THE ATTENTION OF SOMEONE WHO WANTS TO PAY TO KNOCK THEM OUT, THOUGH."
"JUST LET IT GO. THEY'RE ONLY HERE BRIEFLY BEFORE THEIR SHIP LEAVES NEW YORK.
"ARMED GUARDS ON SHIP.
"ARMED GUARDS ON WATER.
"ARMED GUARDS UNDER WATER.
"YOU WON'T GET NEAR THAT BOAT. AND YOU WOULDN'T BE FIRST TO TRY."

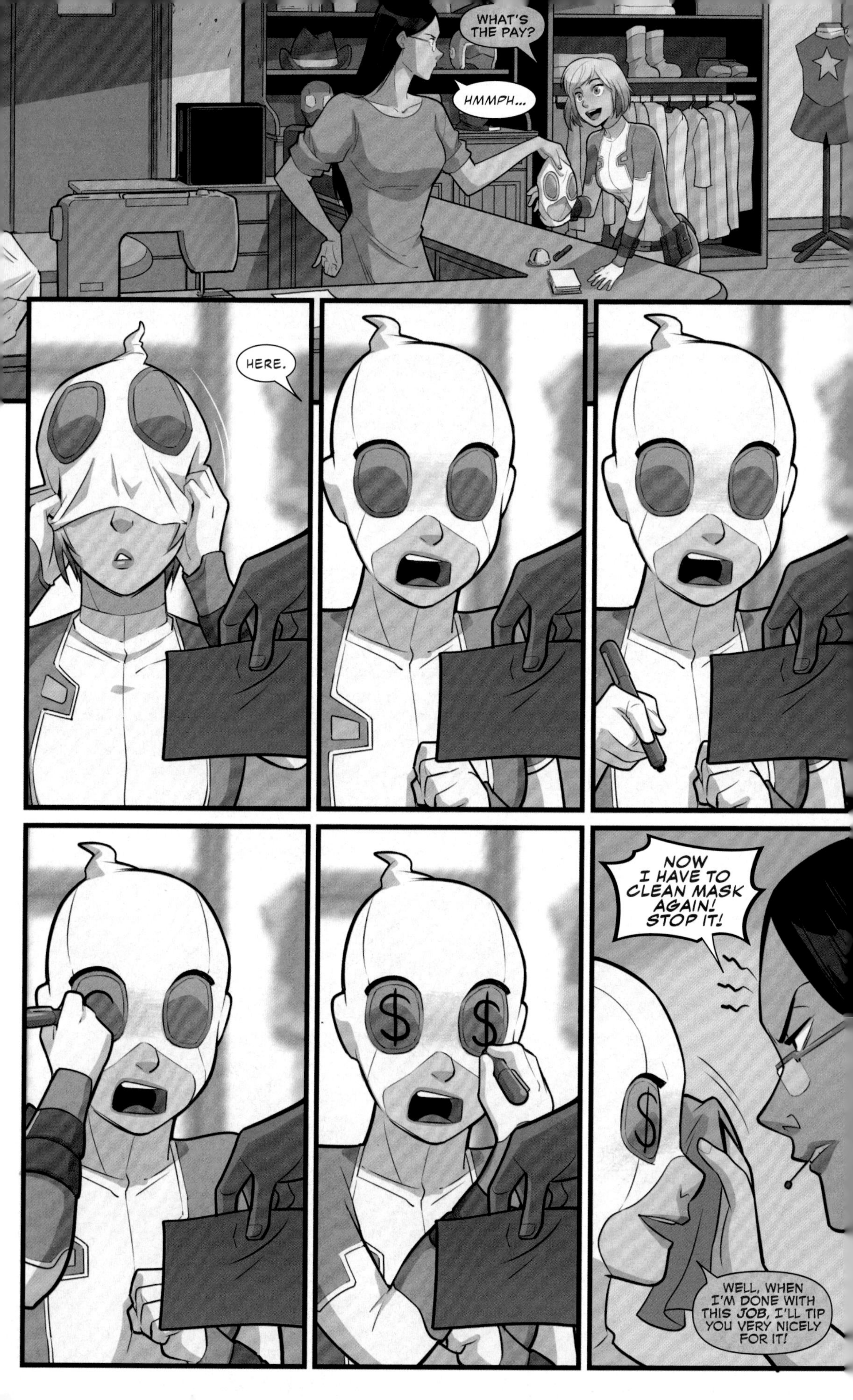
WHAT'S THE PAY?
HMMPH...
HERE.
NOW I HAVE TO CLEAN MASK AGAIN! STOP IT!
WELL, WHEN I'M DONE WITH THIS JOB, I'LL TIP YOU VERY NICELY FOR IT!

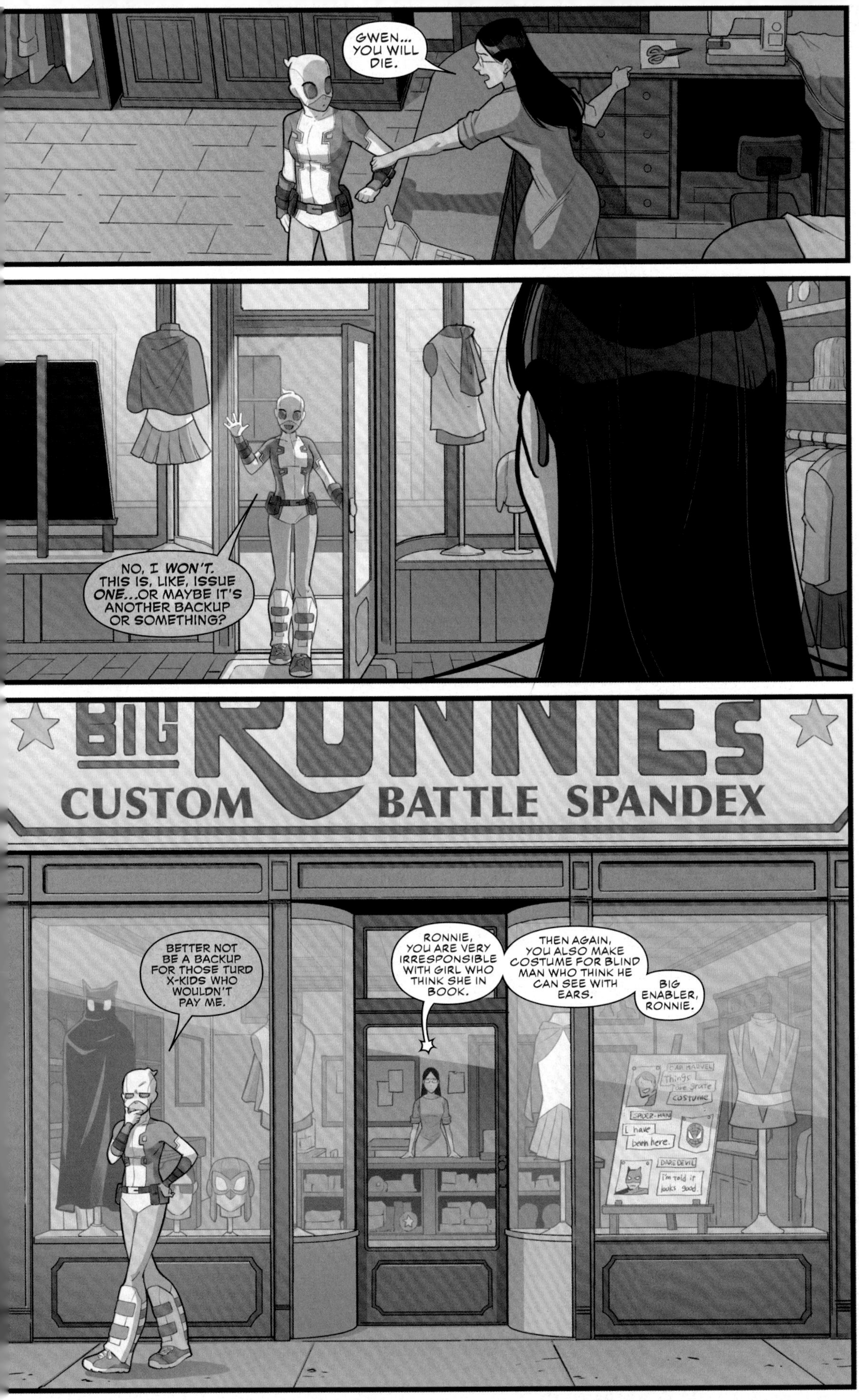
GWEN... YOU WILL DIE.
NO, I *WON'T.* THIS IS, LIKE, ISSUE *ONE*...OR MAYBE IT'S ANOTHER BACKUP OR SOMETHING?
BIG RONNIES
CUSTOM BATTLE SPANDEX
BETTER NOT BE A BACKUP FOR THOSE TURD X-KIDS WHO WOULDN'T PAY ME.
RONNIE, YOU ARE VERY IRRESPONSIBLE WITH GIRL WHO THINK SHE IN BOOK.
THEN AGAIN, YOU ALSO MAKE COSTUME FOR BLIND MAN WHO THINK HE CAN SEE WITH EARS.
BIG ENABLER, RONNIE.
SPIDER-MAN
I have been here.
DAREDEVIL
I'm told it looks good.
Things are grate
costume

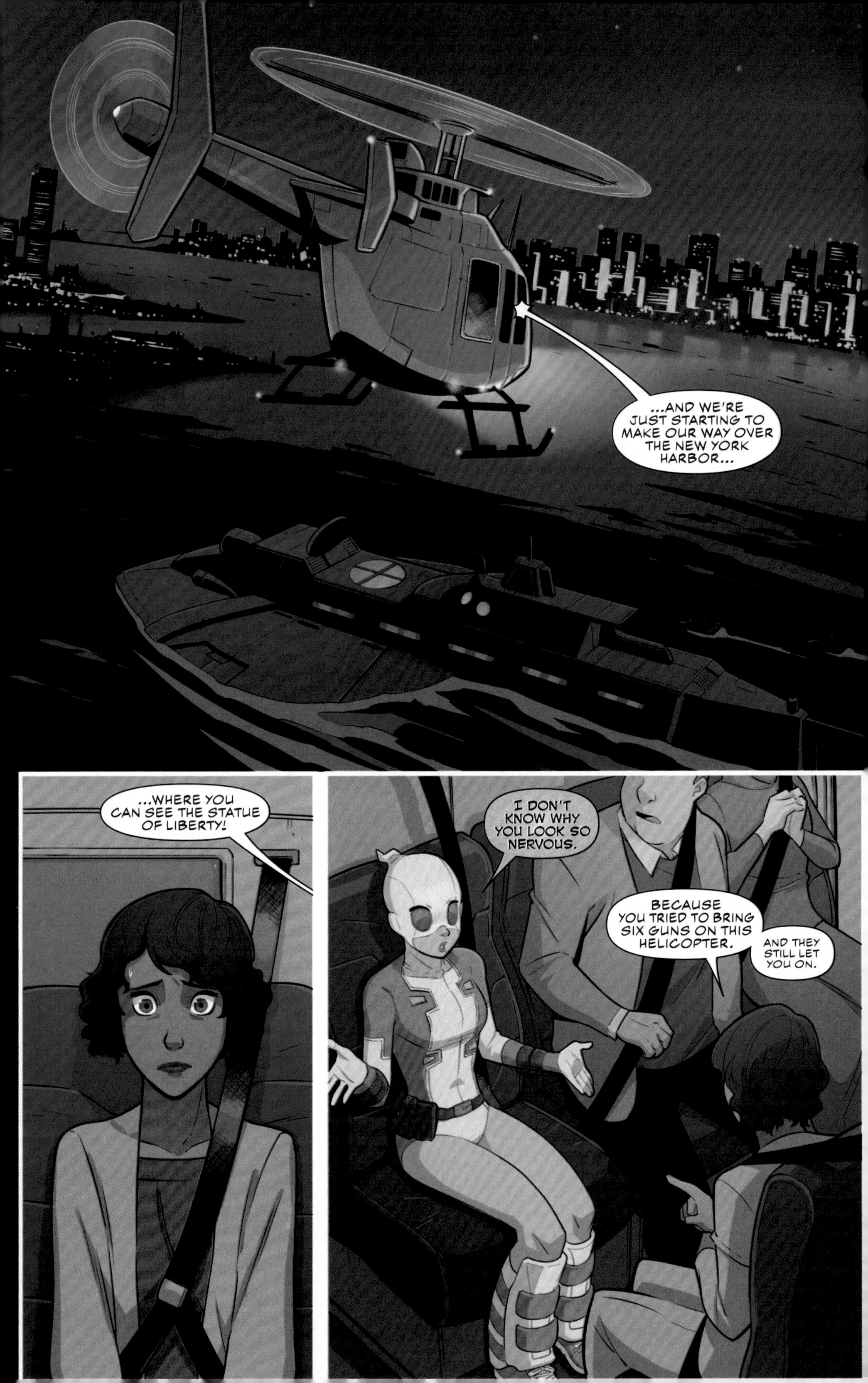
...AND WE'RE JUST STARTING TO MAKE OUR WAY OVER THE NEW YORK HARBOR...
...WHERE YOU CAN SEE THE STATUE OF LIBERTY!
I DON'T KNOW WHY YOU LOOK SO NERVOUS.
BECAUSE YOU TRIED TO BRING SIX GUNS ON THIS HELICOPTER.
AND THEY STILL LET YOU ON.

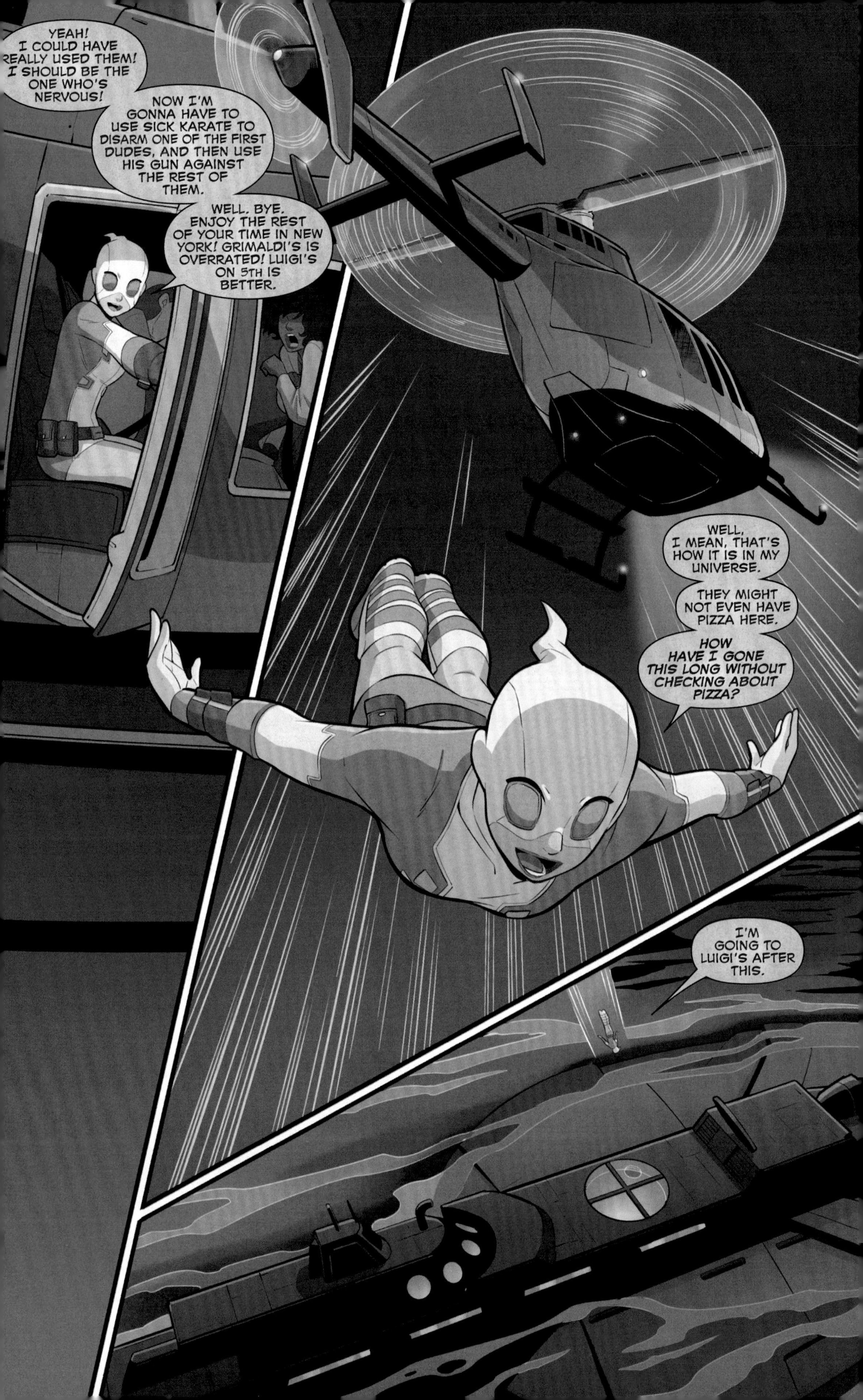

YEAH! I COULD HAVE REALLY USED THEM! I SHOULD BE THE ONE WHO'S NERVOUS!
NOW I'M GONNA HAVE TO USE SICK KARATE TO DISARM ONE OF THE FIRST DUDES, AND THEN USE HIS GUN AGAINST THE REST OF THEM.
WELL, BYE. ENJOY THE REST OF YOUR TIME IN NEW YORK! GRIMALDI'S IS OVERRATED! LUIGI'S ON 5TH IS BETTER.
WELL, I MEAN, THAT'S HOW IT IS IN MY UNIVERSE.
THEY MIGHT NOT EVEN HAVE PIZZA HERE.
HOW HAVE I GONE THIS LONG WITHOUT CHECKING ABOUT PIZZA?
I'M GOING TO LUIGI'S AFTER THIS.

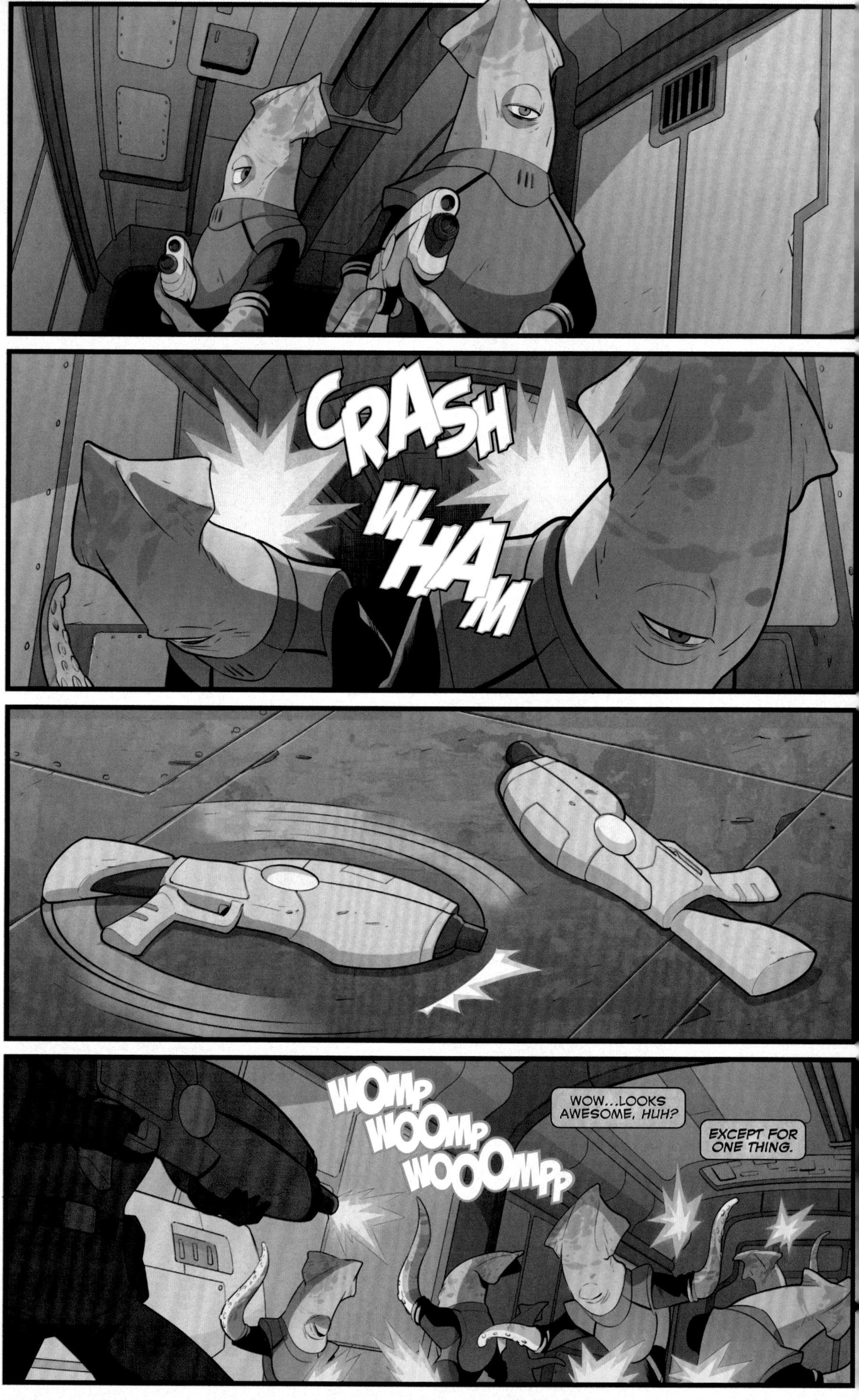
CRASH
WHAM
WOMP
WOOMP
WOOOMPP
WOW...LOOKS AWESOME, HUH?
EXCEPT FOR ONE THING.

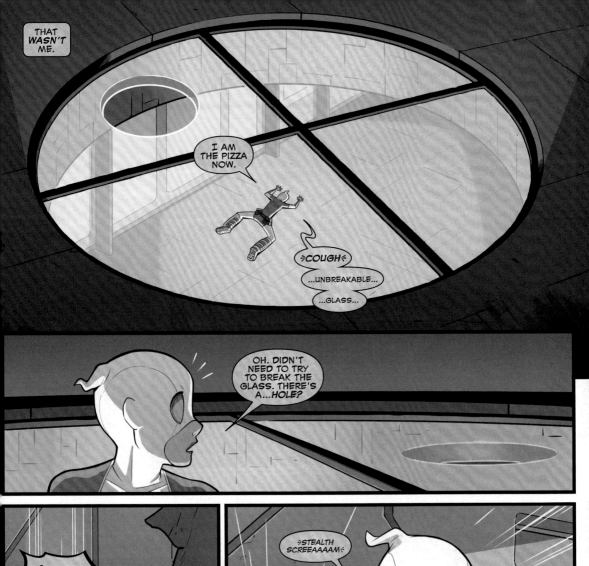

THAT WASN'T ME.

I AM THE PIZZA NOW.

⇏COUGH⇍

...UNBREAKABLE...

...GLASS...

OH. DIDN'T NEED TO TRY TO BREAK THE GLASS. THERE'S A...HOLE?

AAH!

QUIET, GWEN!

⇏GULP⇍

⇏STEALTH SCREEAAAAM⇍

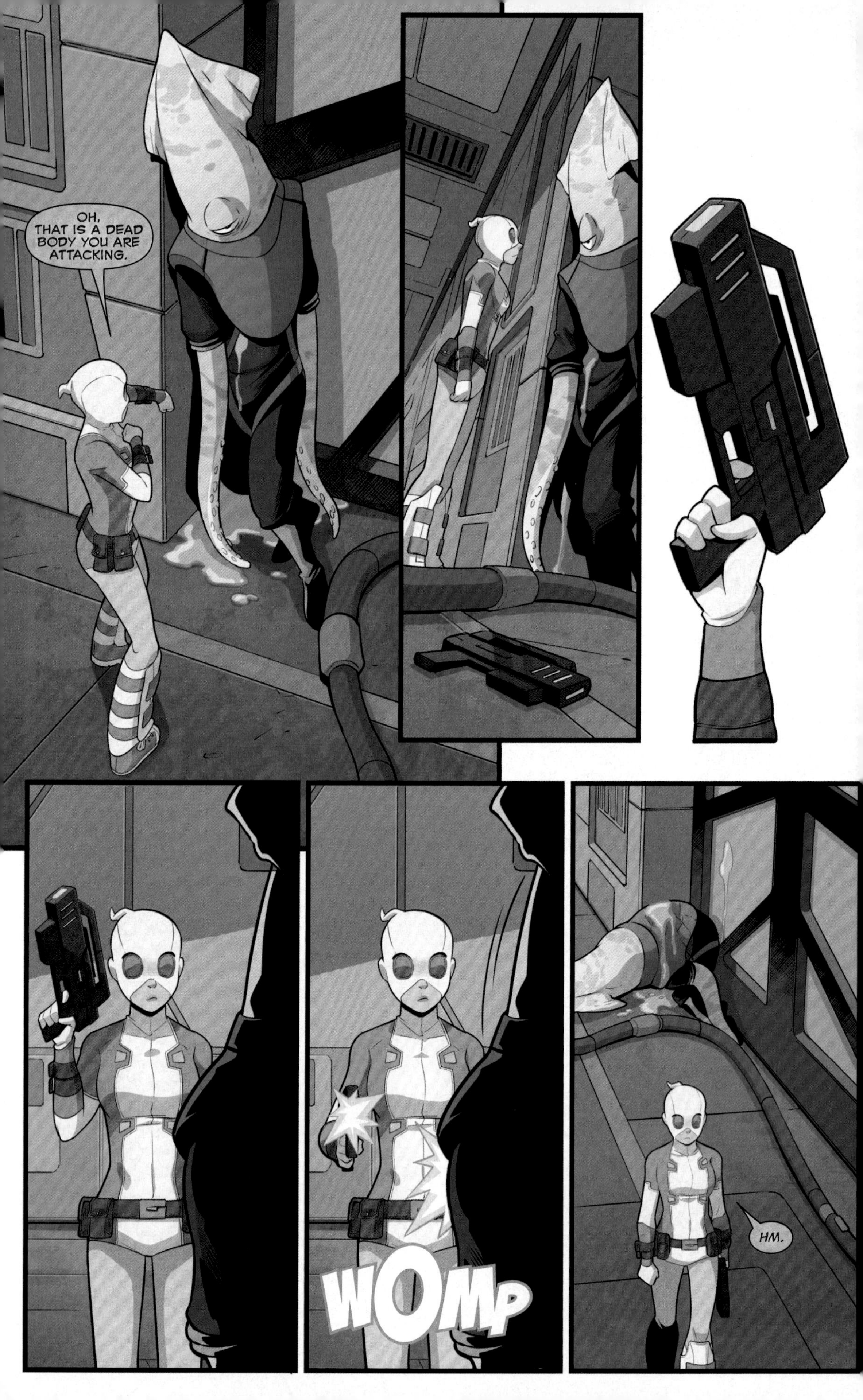
OH, THAT IS A DEAD BODY YOU ARE ATTACKING.
WOMP
HM.

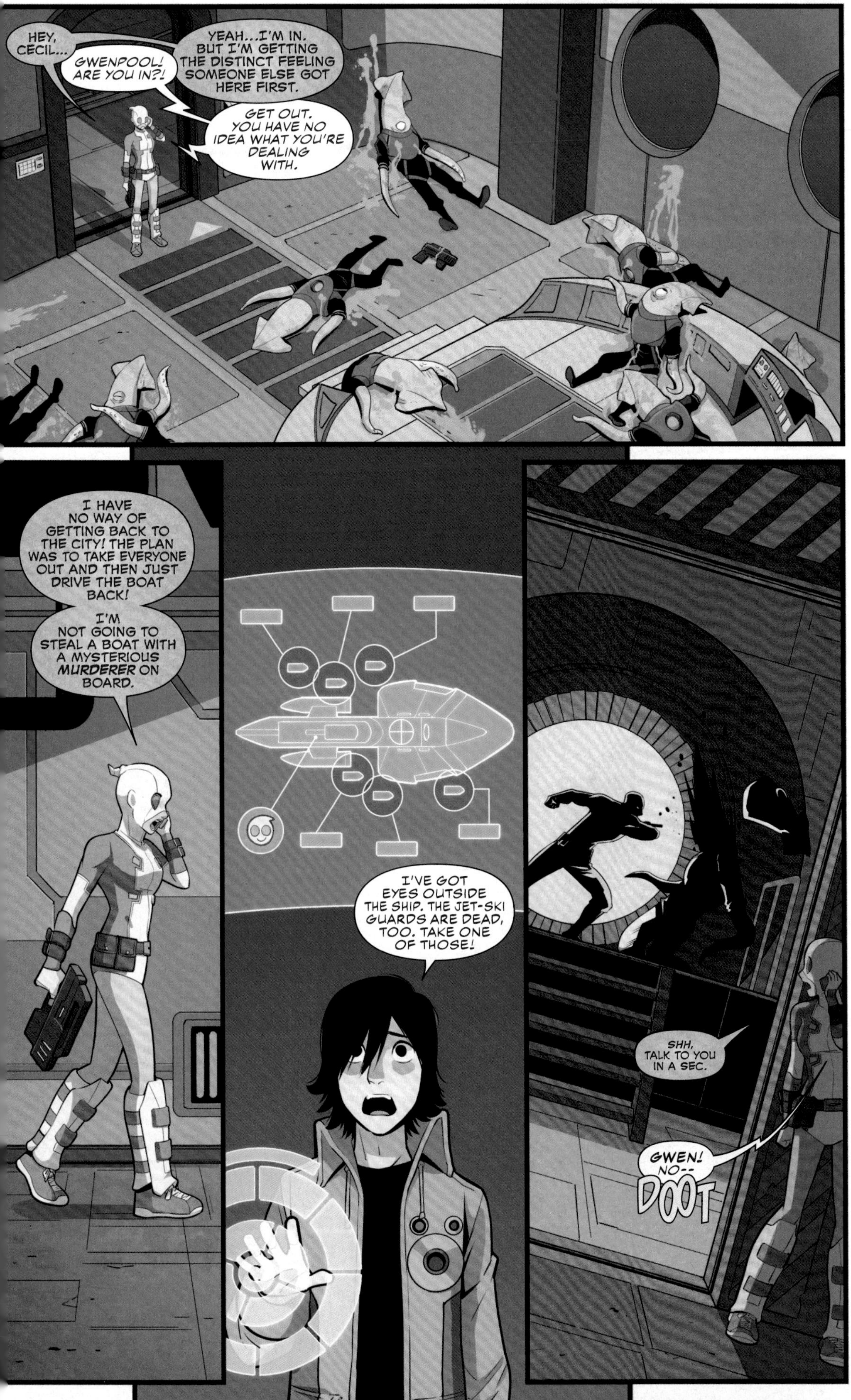

HEY, CECIL...
GWENPOOL! ARE YOU IN?!
YEAH...I'M IN. BUT I'M GETTING THE DISTINCT FEELING SOMEONE ELSE GOT HERE FIRST.
GET OUT. YOU HAVE NO IDEA WHAT YOU'RE DEALING WITH.
I HAVE NO WAY OF GETTING BACK TO THE CITY! THE PLAN WAS TO TAKE EVERYONE OUT AND THEN JUST DRIVE THE BOAT BACK!
I'M NOT GOING TO STEAL A BOAT WITH A MYSTERIOUS MURDERER ON BOARD.
I'VE GOT EYES OUTSIDE THE SHIP. THE JET-SKI GUARDS ARE DEAD, TOO. TAKE ONE OF THOSE!
SHH, TALK TO YOU IN A SEC.
GWEN! NO--
DOOT

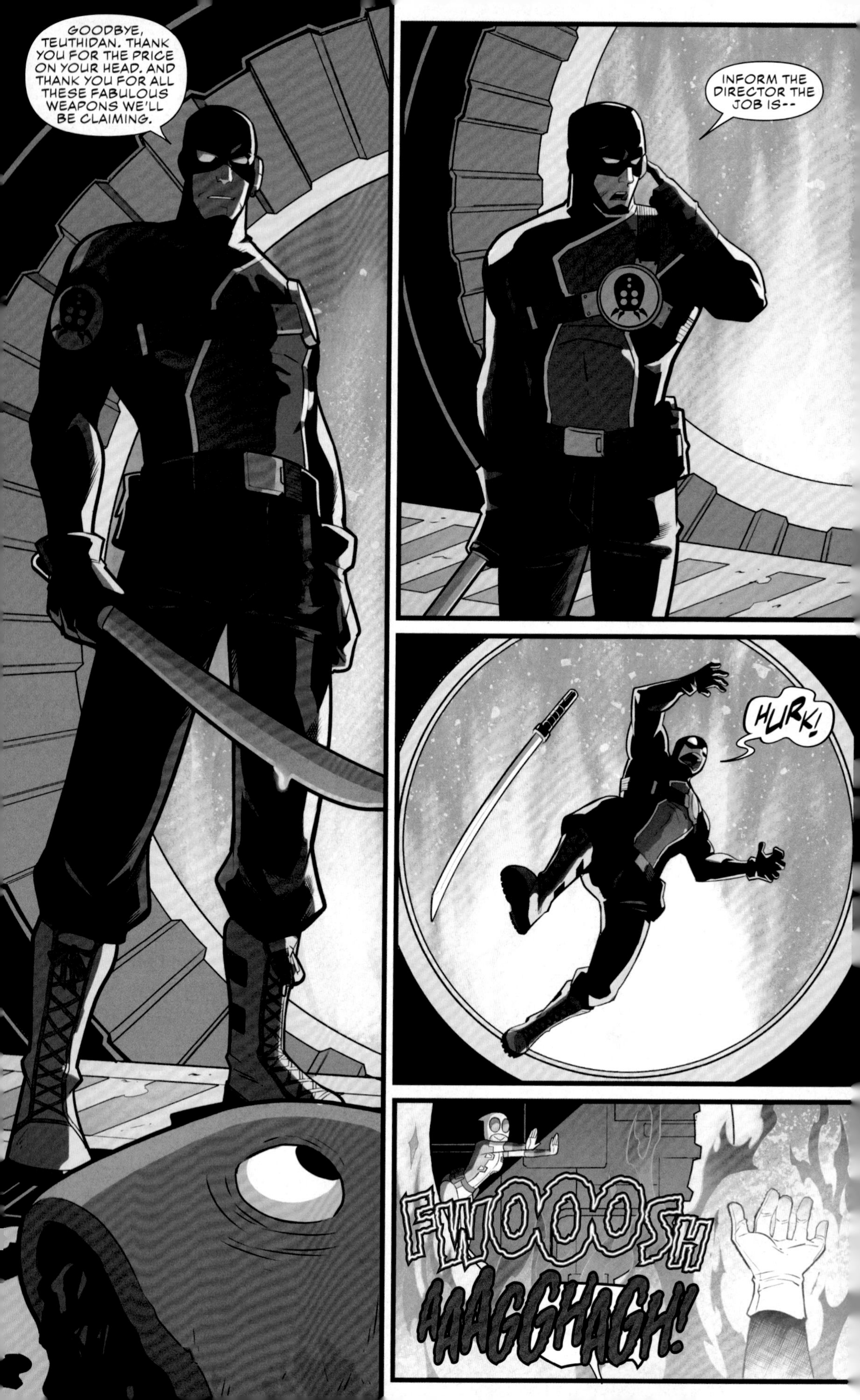
GOODBYE, TEUTHIDAN. THANK YOU FOR THE PRICE ON YOUR HEAD. AND THANK YOU FOR ALL THESE FABULOUS WEAPONS WE'LL BE CLAIMING.
INFORM THE DIRECTOR THE JOB IS--
HURK!
FWOOOSH
AAAGGHAGH!

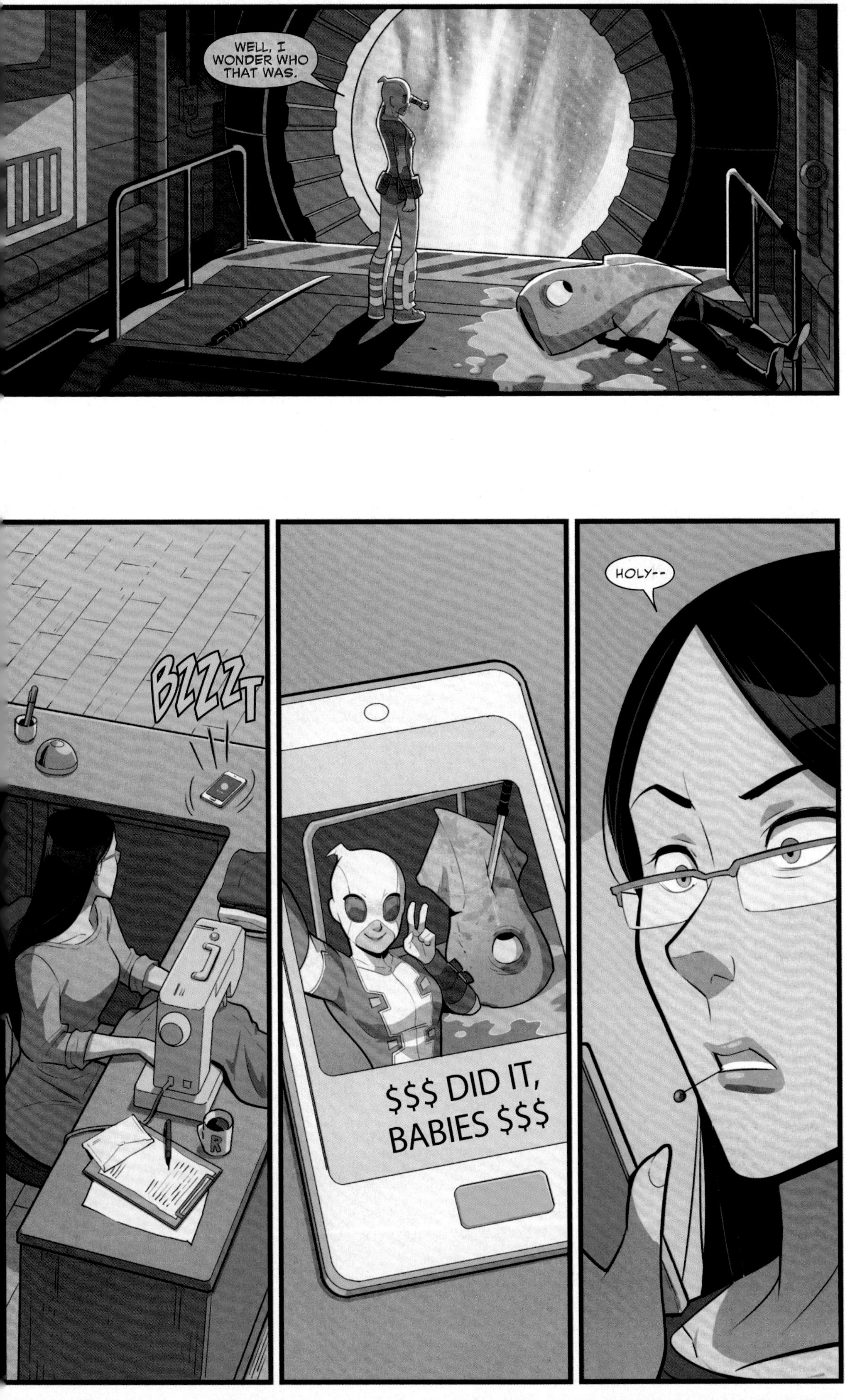
WELL, I WONDER WHO THAT WAS.
BZZZT
$$$ DID IT, BABIES $$$
HOLY--

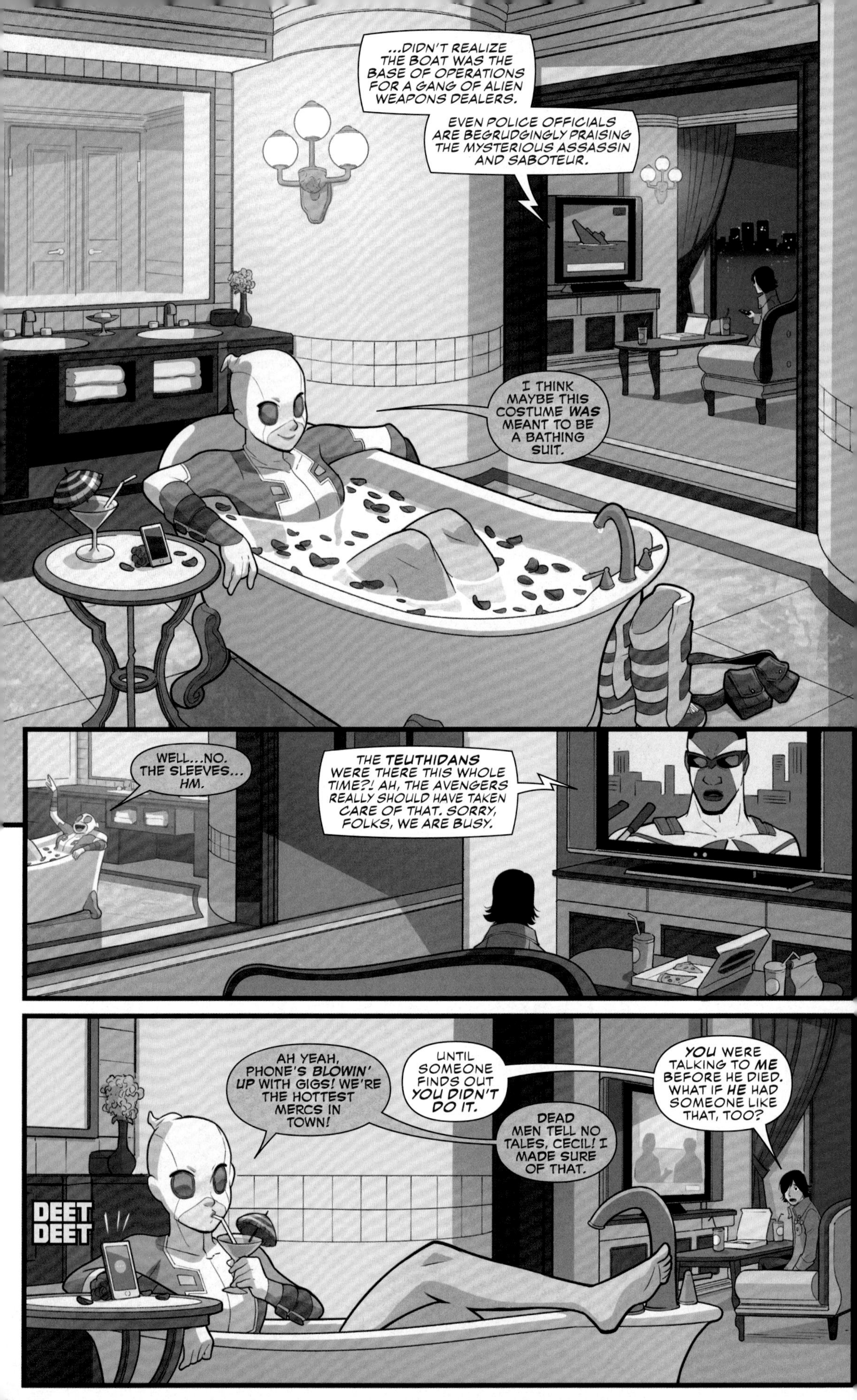
...DIDN'T REALIZE THE BOAT WAS THE BASE OF OPERATIONS FOR A GANG OF ALIEN WEAPONS DEALERS.
EVEN POLICE OFFICIALS ARE BEGRUDGINGLY PRAISING THE MYSTERIOUS ASSASSIN AND SABOTEUR.
I THINK MAYBE THIS COSTUME WAS MEANT TO BE A BATHING SUIT.
WELL...NO. THE SLEEVES... HM.
THE TEUTHIDANS WERE THERE THIS WHOLE TIME?! AH, THE AVENGERS REALLY SHOULD HAVE TAKEN CARE OF THAT. SORRY, FOLKS, WE ARE BUSY.
DEET DEET
AH YEAH, PHONE'S BLOWIN' UP WITH GIGS! WE'RE THE HOTTEST MERCS IN TOWN!
UNTIL SOMEONE FINDS OUT YOU DIDN'T DO IT.
DEAD MEN TELL NO TALES, CECIL! I MADE SURE OF THAT.
YOU WERE TALKING TO ME BEFORE HE DIED. WHAT IF HE HAD SOMEONE LIKE THAT, TOO?

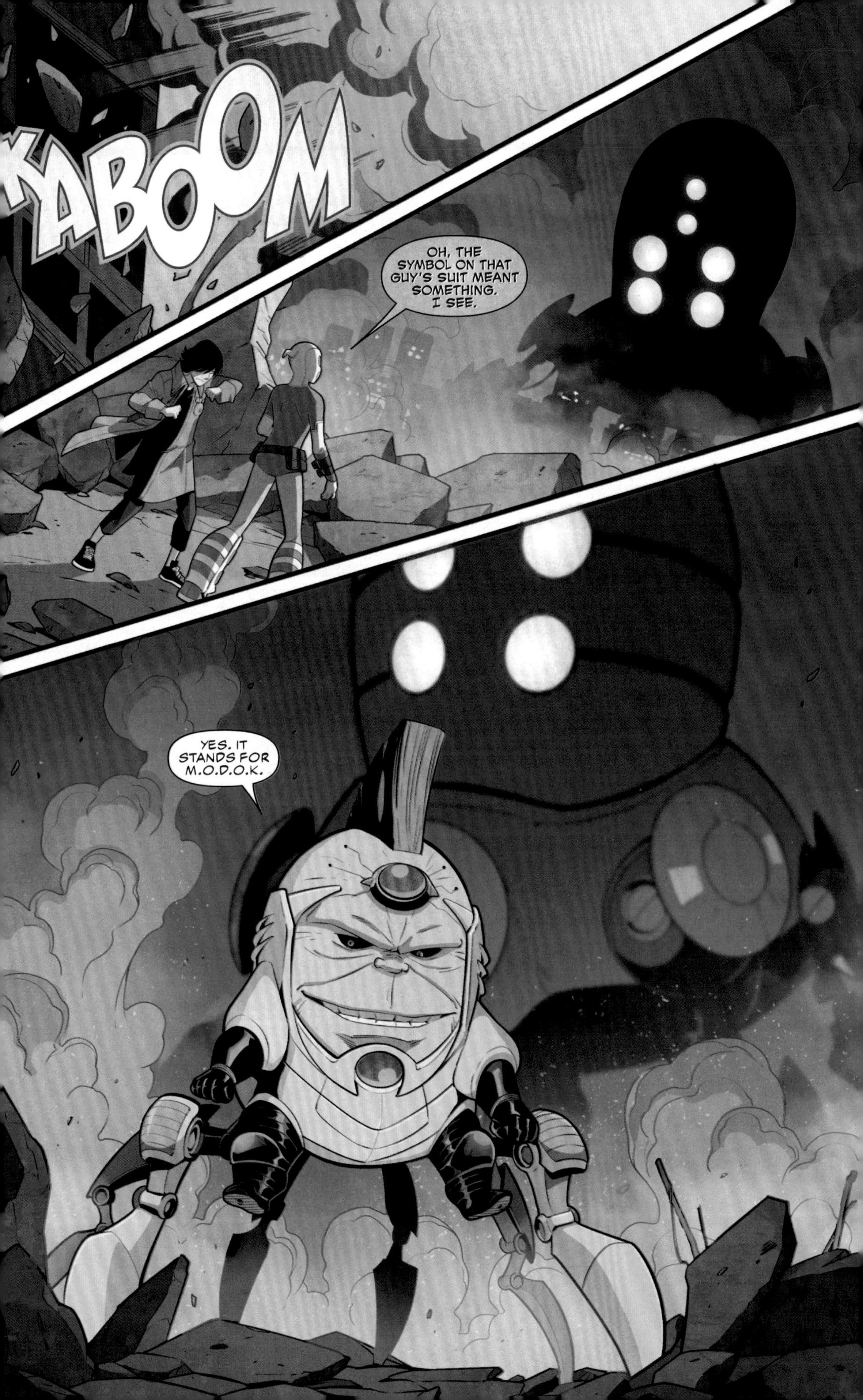
KABOOM
OH, THE SYMBOL ON THAT GUY'S SUIT MEANT SOMETHING. I SEE.
YES. IT STANDS FOR M.O.D.O.K.

SO YOU ARE GWENPOOL. YOU ARE THE BEST.

YEAH, BABY, YOU KNOW IT.

GWEN! WHAT ARE YOU--

YOU HAVE DESTROYED MY BEST.

SO NOW YOU ARE MY BEST.

HUH?

YOU WORK FOR ME NOW. COOPERATE, OR THERE WILL BE CONSEQUENCES.

BWAAAA HA HA HÁ HA!

ARE YOU SERIOUS?

M.O.D.O.K. IS THREATENING ME?!

SERIOUSLY?

M.O.D.O.K.?

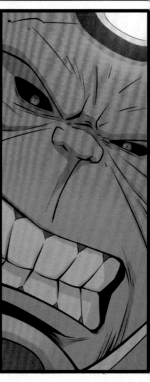

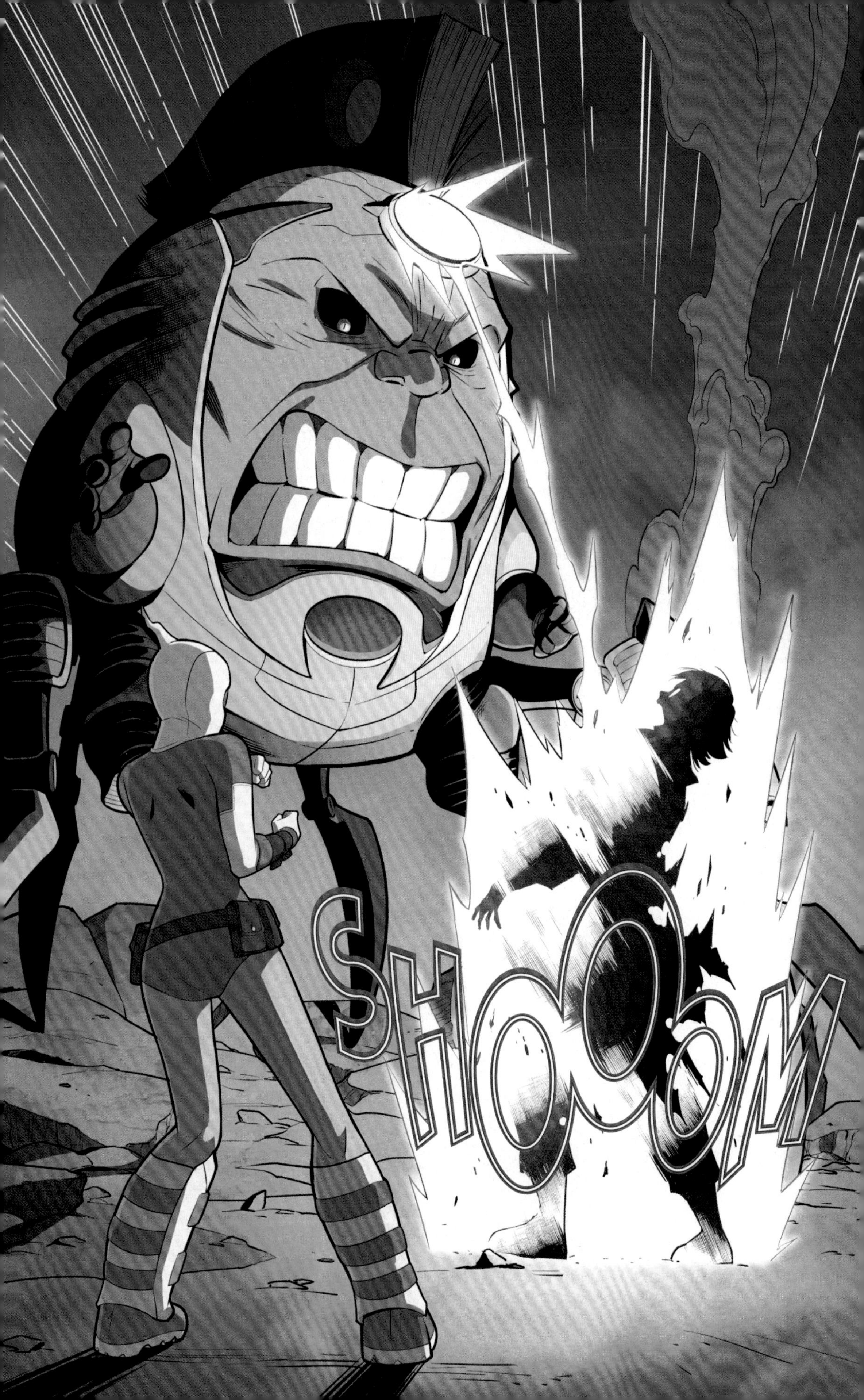
SHOOOM

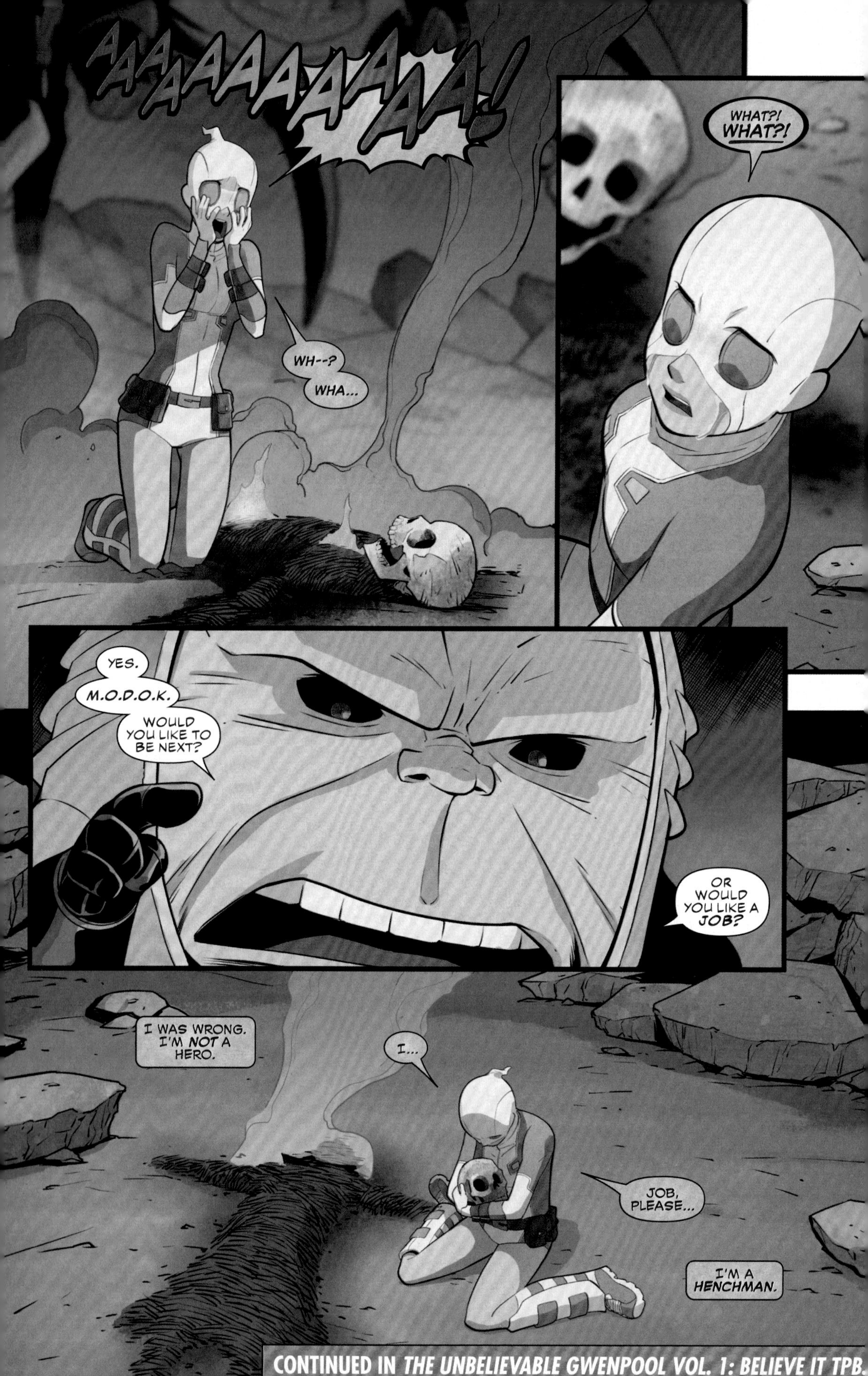

AAAAAAAAAAAA!
WH--?
WHA...
WHAT?! WHAT?!
YES.
M.O.D.O.K.
WOULD YOU LIKE TO BE NEXT?
OR WOULD YOU LIKE A JOB?
I WAS WRONG. I'M NOT A HERO.
I...
JOB, PLEASE...
I'M A HENCHMAN.

CONTINUED IN *THE UNBELIEVABLE GWENPOOL VOL. 1: BELIEVE IT TPB.*

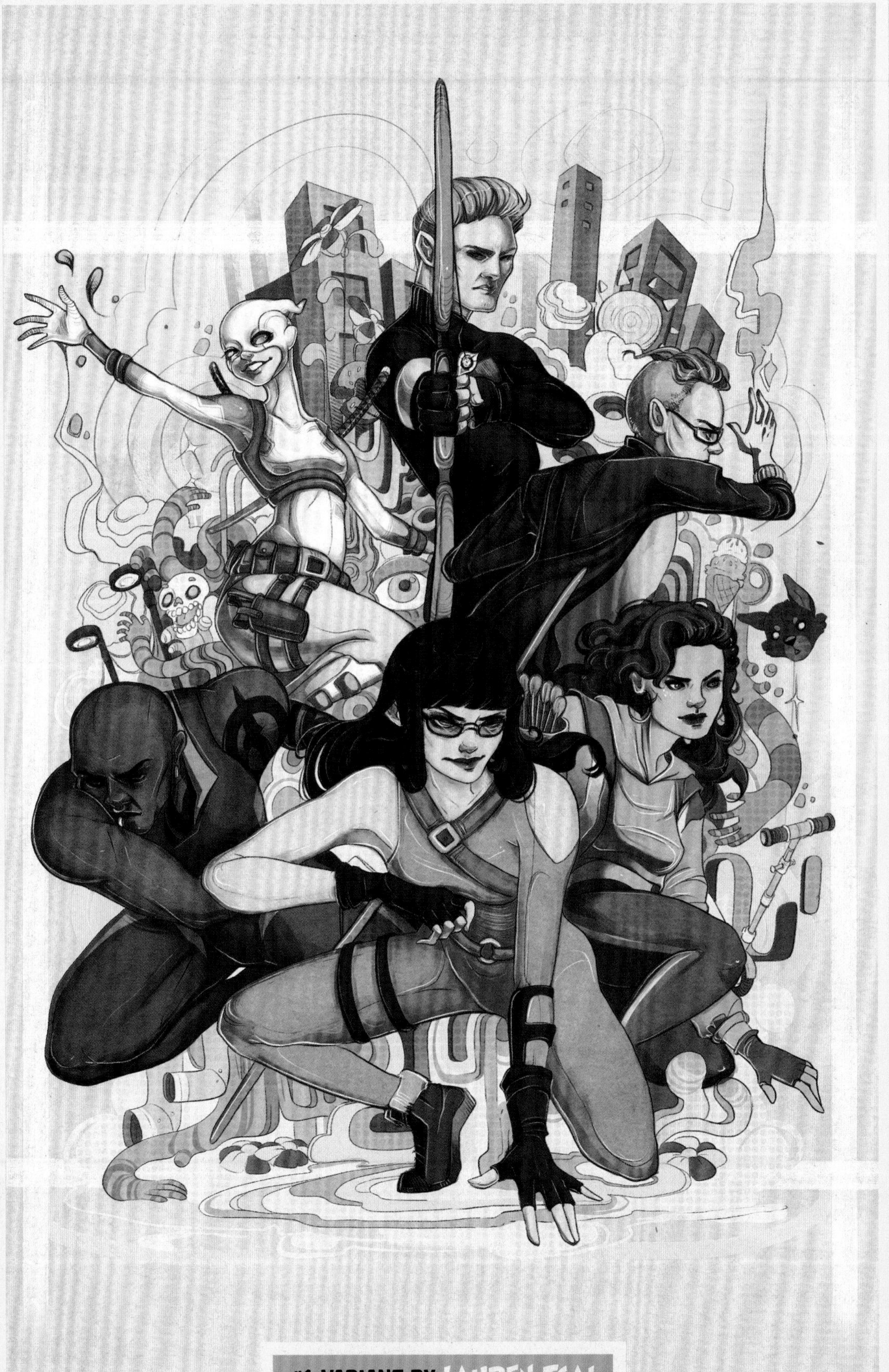

#1 VARIANT BY LAUREN TSAI

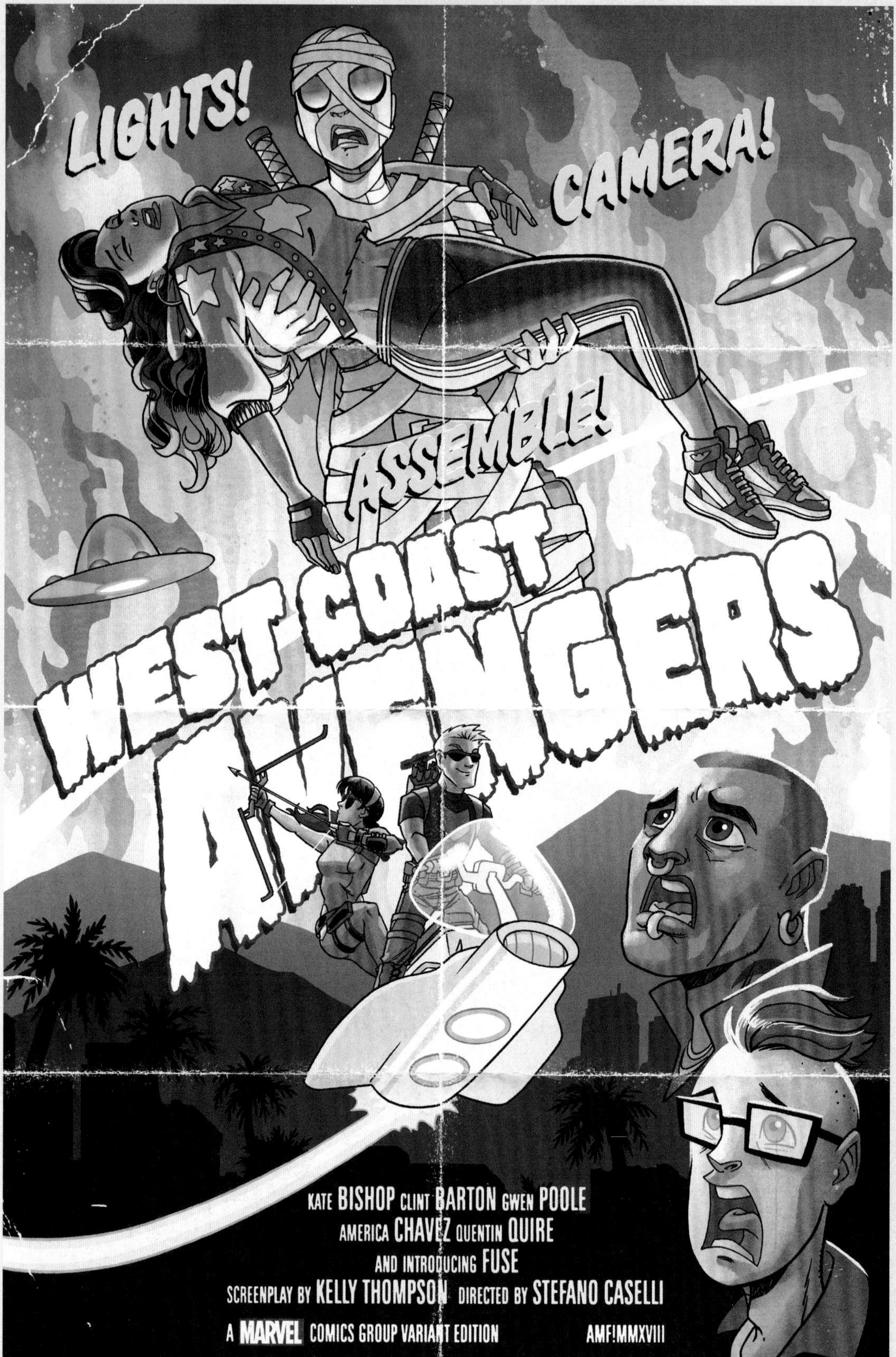
LIGHTS!
CAMERA!
ASSEMBLE!
WEST COAST AVENGERS
KATE BISHOP CLINT BARTON GWEN POOLE
AMERICA CHAVEZ QUENTIN QUIRE
AND INTRODUCING FUSE
SCREENPLAY BY KELLY THOMPSON DIRECTED BY STEFANO CASELLI
A MARVEL COMICS GROUP VARIANT EDITION
AMF!MMXVIII

#2 VARIANT BY TONY FLEECS